Communications
in Computer and Information Science 513

More information about this series at http://www.springer.com/series/7899

Hamido Fujita · Ali Selamat (Eds.)

Intelligent Software Methodologies, Tools and Techniques

13th International Conference, SoMeT 2014
Langkawi, Malaysia, September 22–24, 2014
Revised Selected Papers

 Springer

Editors
Hamido Fujita
Iwate Prefectural University
Takizawa
Japan

Ali Selamat
Universiti Teknologi Malaysia
Johor Baharu
Malaysia

ISSN 1865-0929   ISSN 1865-0937 (electronic)
Communications in Computer and Information Science
ISBN 978-3-319-17529-4   ISBN 978-3-319-17530-0 (eBook)
DOI 10.1007/978-3-319-17530-0

Library of Congress Control Number: 2015937957

Springer Cham Heidelberg New York Dordrecht London
© Springer International Publishing Switzerland 2015

Printed on acid-free paper

Springer International Publishing AG Switzerland is part of Springer Science+Business Media
(www.springer.com)

Preface

Software has a big impact in providing emerging challenge on different and wide range of disciplines. It is overlapped with many research areas, and recently intelligent techniques and methodologies are evolving in how we look to software as important factor in system development and emerging new technologies related, for example to, mobile software systems and big data-related innovations. Conventional software technologies in spite of their high cost were not providing sufficient or reliable services for our evolving demanding needs. Research has participated in providing new better outlook on such technologies and highlighted better awareness in providing new direction using better tools that are more intelligent and adaptable to user needs.

In the early 2000 there was much interest in having software to be involved in an inherent manner in our daily life, in business and economy, thanks to the Internet and other mobile emerging technologies that participated in making users intellectually connected and ubiquitous in integrated virtual environment. Legacy conversion and emerging business models were among these needs. In the early 2000 the SOMET (New Trends in Intelligent Software Methodology Tools, and Techniques) conference series[1] have started to provide researchers and practitioners an up-to-date platform of joint meetings for looking to solution alternatives that could provide better solution to such emerging market needs. The SOMET's platform has provided practical development experience among academia and industries in joint discussions and published conference proceedings and special issues in highly impact journals.

We have in this appealing book the opportunity to publish an extended version of the SOMET proceedings in Springer series: Communications in Computer and Information Science, based on Reviewing Committee which has selected from among 79 published articles these enlisted 27 papers thoroughly revised or enlarged articles.

The book is a collection of best reviewed revised articles selected from the 13th International Conference on New Trends in Intelligent Software Methodology Tools, and Techniques (SoMeT_14), held in Langkawi, Malaysia with the collaboration of Universiti Teknologi Malaysia (Johor Baharu, Malaysia), from September 22 to 24, 2014 (http://seminar.spaceutm.edu.my/somet2014/). This round of SoMeT_14 celebrated the 13th anniversary of SoMeT conference series, which is ranked as B+ among other high ranking Computer Science conferences worldwide.

These 27 papers carefully selected in this book were sorted based on their quality and contribution to the subject of the conference. All articles were reviewed and examined by the designated Program Committee and confirmed to have more new

---

[1] Previous related events that contributed to this publication are: SoMeT_02 (the Sorbonne, Paris, 2002); SoMeT_03 (Stockholm, Sweden, 2003); SoMeT_04 (Leipzig, Germany, 2004); SoMeT_05 (Tokyo, Japan, 2005); SoMeT_06 (Quebec, Canada, 2006); SoMeT_07 (Rome, Italy, 2007); SoMeT_08 (Sharjah, UAE, 2008); SoMeT_09 (Prague, Czech Republic, 2009); SoMeT_10 (Yokohama, Japan, 2010), and SoMeT_11 (Saint Petersburg, Russia), SoMeT_12 (Genoa, Italy), IEEE-SoMeT_13 (Budapest, Hungary, 2013), SoMeT_14 (Langkawi, Malaysia, 2014)

results and updates compared to their previous revision presented in the SOMET_2014. Each article had more than three referees, who carefully reviewed these papers and it was later revised by the respective authors for better soundness, relevance, significance, and clarity.

The book was classified into eight chapters organized in relation to the articles features, covering:

Chapter 1 "Artificial Intelligence Techniques in Software Engineering"
Chapter 2 "Requirement Engineering, High-Assurance System"
Chapter 3 "Intelligent Software Systems Design"
Chapter 4 "Creative and Arts in Interactive Software Design"
Chapter 5 "Software Methodologies for Reliable Software Design"
Chapter 6 "Software Quality and Assessment for Business Enterprise"
Chapter 7 "Software Analysis and Performance Model"
Chapter 8 "Software Applications Systems"

On behalf of all authors who contributed to this book, the editors wish to thank the series editors of Communications in Computer and Information Science, in Springer for providing such an opportunity to publish post-proceedings of the 13th SOMET for the year 2014 in their series.

We also wish to express our gratitude to all the reviewers who devoted their time and expertise to validate these selected articles and provide variety of opinions and feedbacks that could assist authors in providing better revision for these articles.

We hope that practitioners and scientists may consider this book as reference to their studies in finding new ideas and simulation for their research and innovations.

Last but not least we would like to thank Springer publisher for allowing us to have the forthcoming SOMET series to be part of Communications in Computer and Information Science series.

January 2015   Hamido Fujita
                                                                                      Ali Selamat

Organization

Scientific Program Committee and Reviewers of Extended Best Articles
from the SOMET 2014
SOMET 2014 held in Langkawi, Malaysia
http://seminar.spaceutm.edu.my/somet2014/

General Chair

Hamido Fujita   Iwate Prefectural University,
Iwate, Japan

Program Chairs

Ali Selamat   Universiti Teknologi Malaysia,
Johor Bahru, Malaysia
Habibollah Haron   Universiti Teknologi Malaysia,
Johor Bahru, Malaysia

Program Committee

Abdul Syukor Mohamad Jaya   Universiti Teknikal Malaysia Melaka, Malaysia
Adzhar Kamaludin   Universiti Malaysia Pahang, Malaysia
Akram Zeki   International Islamic University, Malaysia
Alexander Vazhenin   University of Aizu, Japan
Ali Selamat   Universiti Teknologi Malaysia, Malaysia
Anna-Maria Di-Sciullo   University de Quebec de Montreal, Canada
Antoni Wibowo   Universiti Teknologi Malaysia, Malaysia
Aryati Bakri   Universiti Teknologi Malaysia, Malaysia
Azlan Mohd Zain   Universiti Teknologi Malaysia, Malaysia
Azrulhizam Shapii   Universiti Kebangsaan Malaysia, Malaysia
Azurah Abu Samah   Universiti Teknologi Malaysia, Malaysia
Balsam A. Mustafa   Universiti Malaysia Pahang, Malaysia
Beata Czarnacka-Chrobot   Warsaw School of Economics, Poland
Burairah Hussin   Universiti Teknikal Malaysia Melaka, Malaysia
Chawalsak Phetchanchai   Suan Dusit Rajabhat University, Thailand
Cheah Wai Shiang   Universiti Malaysia Sarawak, Malaysia
Claudio De Lazzari   National Research Council, Italy
Clemens Schaefer   Universiti Teknologi Malaysia, Malaysia
Dayang Norhayati Abang Jawawi   Universiti Teknologi Malaysia, Malaysia
Dewi Nasien   Universiti Teknologi Malaysia, Malaysia
Domenico Pisanelli   National Research Council, Italy
Md. Asri Ngadi   Universiti Teknologi Malaysia, Malaysia

Edwin Mit	Universiti Malaysia Sarawak, Malaysia
Elke Pulvermueller	University of Osnabrueck, Germany
Fernando Barbosa	Universidade do Porto, Portugal
Guido Guizzi	University of Naples Federico II, Italy
Habibollah Haron	Universiti Teknologi Malaysia, Malaysia
Hamido Fujita	Iwate Prefectural University, Japan
Hamzah Asyrani Sulaiman	Universiti Teknikal Malaysia Melaka, Malaysia
Hassan Chizari	Universiti Teknologi Malaysia, Malaysia
Hazura Zulzalil	Universiti Putra Malaysia, Malaysia
Hector Perez-Meana	National Polytechnic Institute, Mexico
Hishamuddin Asmuni	Universiti Teknologi Malaysia, Malaysia
Igor Kotenko	Institute of Informatics System, Russia
Imran Ghani	Universiti Teknologi Malaysia, Malaysia
Ismail Fauzi Isnin	Universiti Teknologi Malaysia, Malaysia
Johan Mohamad Sharif	Universiti Teknologi Malaysia, Malaysia
Jun Sasaki	Iwate Prefectural University, Japan
Kamal Zuhairi Zamli	Universiti Malaysia Pahang, Malaysia
Khairuddin Omar	Universiti Kebangsaan Malaysia, Malaysia
Love Ekenberg	Stockholm University, Sweden
Mahadi Bahari	Universiti Teknologi Malaysia, Malaysia
Maheyzah Md Siraj	Universiti Teknologi Malaysia, Malaysia
Marite Kirikova	Riga Technical University, Latvia
Masaki Kuremtsu	Iwate Prefectural University, Japan
Masitah Ghazali	Universiti Teknologi Malaysia, Malaysia
Maznah Kamat	Universiti Teknologi Malaysia, Malaysia
Md. Nazrul Islam	Universiti Malaysia Sabah, Malaysia
Mohamad Shukor Talib	Universiti Teknologi Malaysia, Malaysia
Mohammad Razzaque	Universiti Teknologi Malaysia, Malaysia
Mohammad Nazir Ahmad	Universiti Teknologi Malaysia, Malaysia
Mohd Naz'ri Mahrin	Universiti Teknologi Malaysia, Malaysia
Mohd Fahmi Mohamad Amran	Universiti Industri Selangor, Malaysia
Mohd Murtadha Mohamad	Universiti Teknologi Malaysia, Malaysia
Mohd Soperi Mohd Zahid	Universiti Teknologi Malaysia, Malaysia
Mohamed Mejri	Laval University, Canada
Mortaza Zolfpour	University of Marvdasht, Iran
Muhammad Khurram Raza Hameed	COMSATS, Pakistan
Narayanan Kulathuramaiyer	Universiti Malaysia Sarawak, Malaysia
Nazri Kama	Universiti Teknologi Malaysia, Malaysia
Nikolay Mirenkov	University of Aizu, Japan
Noor Maizura Mohamad Noor	Universiti Malaysia Terengganu, Malaysia
Noorfa Haszlinna Mustaffa	Universiti Teknologi Malaysia, Malaysia
Nor Azizah Ali	Universiti Teknologi Malaysia, Malaysia
Nor Erne Nazira Bazin	Universiti Teknologi Malaysia, Malaysia
Nor Haizan Mohamed Radzi	Universiti Teknologi Malaysia, Malaysia

Reviewers of the Extended Version of the Best Selected Articles from the SOMET_2014 Published in this Volume are

Reviewers

Abdul Syukor Mohamad Jaya	Universiti Teknikal Malaysia Melaka, Malaysia
Adzhar Kamaludin	Universiti Malaysia Pahang, Malaysia
Akram Zeki	International Islamic University Malaysia, Malaysia
Alexander Vazhenin	University of Aizu, Japan
Ali Selamat	Universiti Teknologi Malaysia, Malaysia
Anna-Maria Di-Sciullo	University de Quebec de Montreal, Canada
Antoni Wibowo	Universiti Teknologi Malaysia, Malaysia
Aryati Bakri	Universiti Teknologi Malaysia, Malaysia
Azlan Mohd Zain	Universiti Teknologi Malaysia, Malaysia
Azrulhizam Shapii	Universiti Kebangsaan Malaysia, Malaysia
Azurah Abu Samah	Universiti Teknologi Malaysia, Malaysia
Balsam A. Mustafa	Universiti Malaysia Pahang, Malaysia, Malaysia
Beata Czarnacka-Chrobot	Warsaw School of Economics, Poland
Burairah Hussin	Universiti Teknikal Malaysia Melaka, Malaysia
Chawalsak Phetchanchai	Suan Dusit Rajabhat University, Thailand
Cheah Wai Shiang	Universiti Malaysia Sarawak, Malaysia
Claudio De Lazzari	National Research Council, Italy
Clemens Schaefer	Universiti Teknologi Malaysia, Malaysia
Dayang Norhayati Abang Jawawi	Universiti Teknologi Malaysia, Malaysia
Dewi Nasien	Universiti Teknologi Malaysia, Malaysia
Domenico Pisanelli	National Research Council, Italy
Md Asri Ngadi	Universiti Teknologi Malaysia, Malaysia
Edwin Mit	Universiti Malaysia Sarawak, Malaysia
Elke Pulvermueller	University of Osnabrueck, Germany
Fernando Barbosa	Universidade do Porto, Portugal
Guido Guizzi	University of Naples Federico II, Italy
Habibollah Haron	Universiti Teknologi Malaysia, Malaysia
Hamido Fujita	Iwate Prefectural University, Japan
Hamzah Asyrani Sulaiman	Universiti Teknikal Malaysia Melaka, Malaysia
Hassan Chizari	Universiti Teknologi Malaysia, Malaysia
Hazura Zulzalil	Universiti Putra Malaysia, Malaysia
Hector Perez-Meana	National Polytechnic Institute, Mexico
Hishamuddin Asmuni	Universiti Teknologi Malaysia, Malaysia
Igor Kotenko	Institute of Informatics System, Russia
Imran Ghani	Universiti Teknologi Malaysia, Malaysia
Ismail Fauzi Isnin	Universiti Teknologi Malaysia, Malaysia
Johan Mohamad Sharif	Universiti Teknologi Malaysia, Malaysia
Jun Sasaki	Iwate Prefectural University, Japan
Kamal Zuhairi Zamli	Universiti Malaysia Pahang, Malaysia

Contents

Creative and Arts in Interactive Software Design

Software Methodologies for Reliable Software Design

Software Quality and Assessment for Business Enterprise

Software Analysis and Performance Model

Software Applications Systems

Artificial Intelligence Techniques
in Software Engineering

Public Participatory Decision Making

Love Ekenberg[1,2](✉)

[1] International Institute of Applied Systems Analysis,
IIASA, Schlossplatz 1, 2361 Laxenburg, Austria
[2] Department of Computer and Systems Sciences,
Stockholm University, Stockholm, Sweden
lovek@dsv.su.se

Abstract. Within the realm of e-government, the development has moved towards testing new means for democratic decision-making, like e-panels, electronic discussion forums, and polls. Although such new developments seem promising, they are not problem-free, and the outcomes are seldom used in the subsequent formal political procedures. Nevertheless, more formalized process models offer a promising potential when it comes to structuring and supporting transparency of decision processes in order to facilitate the integration of the public into decision-making procedures in a reasonable and manageable way. This presentation presents an outline for an integrated framework for public decision making to: (a) provide tools for citizens to organize discussion and create opinions; (b) enable governments, authorities, and institutions to better analyse these opinions; and (c) enable governments to account for this information in planning and societal decision making by employing a process model for structured public decision making.

Keywords: Decision analysis · Participatory decision making · Societal planning · Regional development · Democracy

1 Introduction

Public participation plays different parts in different democracy models, and consequently, the role of a public decision support system (PDSS) differs depending on the model. The underlying idea behind this has been to introduce various kinds of support tools to increase the democracy in one or another setting and enable a broader participation as well as provide new communication channels for more public opinion formation and decision making. During policy making processes several instruments have been used in order to enable interaction between actors such as decision-makers and citizens. Such instruments have often been discussed separately in the field of e-participation, both regarding interactions with the general public, between politicians, as well as between politicians and administrators. Since the contexts for such interactions differ, both methods and technologies to support them are expected to vary. Generally, democratic decision making is often described as a staged cyclic policy making model, where the initial step of each cycle is based on the outcome of preceding rounds. In a, so called, strong democracy model, the public should participate in

© Springer International Publishing Switzerland 2015
H. Fujita and A. Selamat (Eds.): SoMeT 2014, CCIS 513, pp. 3–12, 2015.
DOI: 10.1007/978-3-319-17530-0_1

all stages, and is often engaged in some way at each stage. The PDSS in a such would then take the role of an interactive tool to facilitate public discussion throughout most of the stages in, e.g., a policy making model where the public is supposed to be invited and (usually very informally) discuss the importance of certain criteria and, at best, have some possibility to study the effects of stating various preferences. In a thin model, the public is normally only consulted in the policy creation and monitoring stages, where the PDSSs would have a different character, depending of the domain under consideration. In both these cases, components such as citizen involvement and transparency issues challenge the decision-making process and the designs of adequate PDSSs. There are for instance still participatory issues that heavily troublesome from a democratic perspective, mainly concerning the usual issue of representativeness. Many support tools incorporate peer-communication and discussions as a way of reaching consensus, but despite a vast amount of such tools and methods, very little in the literature provides any reports of successful use of inclusive decision processes, in particular when it comes to more elaborated tool support. Furthermore, social media are, not more than other places, neutral, where participants are treated equally even when disregarding the obvious problems regarding availability to participate in collaborative works. Rather, they are places where discrimination regarding gender, age and ethnicity are just as common as in other social contexts [1]. Most tools are also seldom combined with any reasonable means to enable a deliberative democratic process in which relevant facts from multiple points of view are taken into consideration, making them as fallacious as more common types of debates.

Public participatory decision-making is thus for many reasons and not surprisingly a complex process, balancing on the borders of inclusion, structure, precision and accuracy, while trying to incorporate citizens' input in various processes in more or less structured formats. To simply enable more participation will obviously not yield enhanced democracy, but adequate mechanism for participation exercises is nevertheless vital regardless of the democracy model and must be addressed. And reasonable structures must be imposed here as well. Except for the need for clarity and interaction, the problems with formal modelling per se, and in particular with modelling the consequences of applying certain preferences, have so far received comparatively little interest within the e-democracy debate.

Despite the various aspects addressed above, collaborative information sharing and deliberative structured discussions on various platforms seem to have the potential of being vital parts of democratic processes and the benefits of more systematized tools should be substantial if the problems herein were better understood and handled. And in any case, people not only need the opportunity to participate in politics and the decision making, they also need information and insights into how government decision are reached, even when they are not personally affected or want to participate.

Therefore, we have during some years been working with various aspects of this and trying to design a realistic process model for public decision making. By combining two fields, e-participation and decision support and analysis, we have been addressing both the problem of communication, internally within the governmental body and externally to citizens, and that of modelling and analysis of decision alternatives, while handling issues regarding processes and tools for public participation in a much broader sense than usual. Except for usual preference elicitation techniques, the public has been invited by various means, including art projects, flash polls, and various means for dialogues providing background information that to a large extent can be processed by various decision analytical tools.

This article describes some important aspects of this work. Next section discusses tool support for public decisions and Section three problematizes this in a broader participatory context. Section four describes some features to be considered when designing systems of this kind as well as provides some recommendations regarding this and Section five discuss some validation studies that we have done during this work. The last section provides some concluding remarks.

2 Tool Support for Public Decisions

Many general process models, decision making methods, and accompanied tools for participation involving web-based platforms, supporting public decision making processes in an informative and participatory manner, have been suggested in the past [2]. These typically and more or less successfully collect and present debate and information perceived to be of relevance for an issue at hand. Generally these do not provide structuring tools for the actual decision process or decision evaluation. On the other hand, the various specialised support tools for formalised decision making require, to a large extent, idealised and unrealistic assumptions as well as using too simplified aggregation mechanisms, particular in multi-stakeholder situations, where there normally is a lot of uncertainty involved in the elicitation of the stakeholders' preferences. Methods from the related field of risk analysis has been proposed, but since that literature is rooted in different communities, integrated frameworks seem to be lacking even though the decision process and the risk analysis process are tightly connected in practice. More advanced computer based methods for risk and decision analysis using formal problem modelling suitable for use in societal decision making are typically implemented in the paradigm of graphical computing, which has also implied few possibilities to elicit the level of undesirability of different options from the perspectives of citizens and businesses and by doing so incorporating societal values and preferences in a structured way, so the current state-of-the-art does not provide a ready solution.

Thus, except for the actual participation in the various processes, a crucial part in this is the actual elicitation of information, where much uncertainty is involved, and the relaxation of precise importance judgments has been found to be advantageous in order to reduce the gap between the various theoretical models and their practical importance. Besides providing a more realistic representation that are less demanding for users, another advantage with methods based on more approximate judgments is that the decision support process can become more interactive, and in turn lead to improved decision quality, as well as, being especially suitable for group decision making processes as individual importance judgments can be represented by a union of the group's judgments. Furthermore, an approximate approach can be time and effort saving as one can iteratively conduct the analysis given imprecise input and test whether the input is sufficient for a final evaluation of alternatives.

It is sometimes stated that due to the relative robustness of linear decision models regarding weight changes, the use of approximate weights often yields satisfactory decision quality, but that the assumption of knowing the ranking with certainty is strong. Instead, there can be uncertainty regarding both the magnitudes and ordering of weights and that people can be quite confident that some differences in importance are greater than others. Nevertheless, although some weak form of cardinality may exist, cardinal importance relation information is seldom taken into account. As an alternative, if ordinal information, as well as, imprecise cardinality is taken into account, the resulting input seems to be more in line with a reasonable representation of significance, where imprecise weights, and mixing of ordinal and cardinal information as appropriate, taking both ordinal information as well as imprecise cardinal relation information of the importance of the attribute ranges into account. The criteria significance input can then be interpreted as regions of significance and the elicitation procedures can be divided into three main parts:

(a) extraction (extracting information through user input);
(b) representation (capturing the information in a formal structure); and
(c) interpretation (assigning meaning to the captured information).

To shortly sum the situation up, earlier methods have failed in providing reasonable decision processes for citizen participation that more systematically promote inclusion and transparency as well as providing useful tools for qualified decision analysis, that at least include:

(a) realistic but efficient elicitation processes, a utilization of a broad spectrum of modalities to enable as broad participation as possible;
(b) procedures for handling all relevant quantitative, qualitative, and structural information in decision situations; and
(c) reasonable and interactive decision rules that utilize the above information in a consistent framework that are computationally meaningful.

3   Coping with Democracy and Support Mechanisms

Even with adequate tool packages, an approach to democratic decision making processes must entail that the different views of citizens must be acknowledged as input; on the other hand available facts must be used to increase citizens' insights into the outcomes of applying different preferences as observed. This calls for a common model encompassing different points of view, different perspectives, multiple objectives, and multiple stakeholders using different methods for appraisals. In the case of planning decisions, this involves impact assessment methods such as life-cycle assessments, return-on-investment calculations, equality, and ethical assessments as well as political ideology alignment assessments through a multitude of participation channels, even in more innovative forms. Examples of the latter includes artistic performances such as described in [3–6], where we investigated whether art can form a basis for constructive dialogues and expressions of preferences for community development as well as finding more nuances beyond the prevailing hegemonic discourse and find new problem formulations and solutions (Fig. 1).

Fig. 1. From Rebecca Forsberg' s play Lise and Otto in collaboration with RATS Theatre and the Swedish national scene: the Royal Dramatic Theatre.

So solving the issues with democracy must be done not only by studying various web phenomena and adequate computational machineries, but by actually addressing the various issues by developing new tools, methods, and working cultures. The developments of concern should:

(a) operationalize the citizen interaction and discourse and
(b) provide on-demand feedback from the evaluation methods, while enabling processes for the construction of formal decision models.

The latter should include web based technologies, e.g., in the form of web-based questionnaires explicitly designed so that the preference statements provided by the stakeholders can be exploited for decision evaluation and aggregated in a meaningful way, both conceptually and computationally, where decision evaluation interests can also include, e.g., which alternatives are promoted by a specific group of stakeholders or how far different stakeholder groups are from each other with respect to preferences.

4 Designing a Decision Making Model

Assuming that the participatory aspects can be covered, the input must be handled and an adequate process model should carry a decision from agenda setting and problem awareness to feasible courses of action via objectives formulations, alternative generation, consequence assessments, and trade-off clarifications. The formal decision mechanism is of course usually problematical, both regarding hidden agendas and the lack of capacity of decision-makers in general.

Also generally, elicitation is a significant problem and normally a precise numerical weight is assigned to each criterion in a decision situation to represent the information extracted from the user. Thus, even having access to engaged stakeholders and adequate background data, a well-known and significant problem is to actually elicit preferences and utilise this for a structured trade-off management. With respect to elicitation, there exist various weighting methods that use various questioning procedures to elicit weights. In the literature, a number of methods have been suggested for assessing criteria weights and other values using exact numbers. These ranges from relatively simple ones, like the commonly used direct rating and point allocation methods, to somewhat more advanced procedures, generalised into be useful under impreciseness and vagueness as well.

Such methods are however extremely sparsely used and most do not contain adequate support for realistic decision making, despite it becomes very strong in these settings and is necessary for the use of dynamic decision making abilities in general. In this context, it is furthermore important to utilise means for enrichment of the content communicated between decision-makers, various stakeholders, and the general public; something that is basically not utilised at all.

Whether the scenarios are structured or not, in most decision situations involving various stakeholders also conflict situations arise. This is not necessarily a problem, but can rather be utilised in fruitful ways, provided there are reasonable instruments available for conflict resolution. Important parts in multi stakeholder situations are therefore modules for systematic negotiations and tools for analysing trade-off effects. The potential mutual benefits of structured negotiation processes are often severely underutilised in real settings, despite, e.g., the field of game and decision theory have provided very useful results in this context. In the models we have developed, we utilise decision structuring and evaluation procedure as extensions to earlier decision analytic method and tools combined with elicitation and negotiation models.

These have been used in several large decision problems involving many stakeholders, such as, e.g., the design of a flood insurance system for Hungary, deposition of nuclear fuel, purchasing decisions at the Swedish Rail Administration, investment decision analyses in industry, flood management, emergency management, energy pricing, demining, regional planning, and many others. A participatory model, initially developed in [7] has recently been further enhanced in [8] by studying how groups of political decision-makers desire to express values and priorities, but at the same time,

(a) does not require substantial formal decision analysis knowledge;
(b) is not cognitively too demanding by relaxing precision requirements to accommodate unknown parameters;
(c) is not too time-consuming;
(d) makes use of the information the decision-maker is able to supply; and
(e) provides means for aggregating imprecise weight statements from different stakeholders.

The objective of such a model is to enable the use of a process model for public decision making, specifically aimed at the inclusion of many stakeholders and possibly

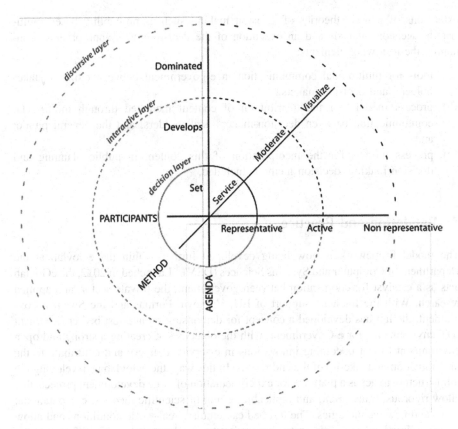

Fig. 2. An e-participatory map. From [9].

also many decision-makers integrating assessments made from a vast flora of methods and consigners. Figure 2 shows the different types of methods and approaches relative to each other, divided into three composite layers that contain different types of solutions.

(a) The discursive layer contains the deliberative process of setting the agenda, using a broad spectrum of multimodal tools to support organization and discussion, and using web statistics to clarify the representativeness of the information.

(b) The interaction layer contains interaction with affected stakeholders, organized stakeholder groups and citizens, using web-based techniques for interaction.

(c) The decision layer typically consists of the local government's administrative process making the investigations and assessments necessary for taking the process further and can be seen from the perspective from everything from the perspective of a large group to a single participant's perspective.

The layers also describe the different ontological and epistemological positions represented in our interdisciplinary research team and help us to create tools that constructively combine mixed, qualitative and quantitative methods. This has called for extensions of generic theories of decision making such as probability based multi-criteria decision analysis and an execution of the decision steps appropriately, containing the following elements:

(a) tools for multimodal communication in e-government between citizens, stakeholders, and decision-makers;
(b) process models for the distribution of content mediated through multimodal communication between decision-makers, stakeholders, and the general public; and
(c) process models for the incorporation of this content in public planning and decision making, decision methods included.

5   Validation and Practice

The model framework is now being developed further within the eGovlab at the Department of Computer and Systems Sciences (DSV).[1] Launched in 2012, the eGovlab acts as a catalyst for cooperation between government, the private sector, and applied research. With the financial support of EU, Vinnova, Formas and the Swedish government, the lab has developed a concept for demonstration and test bed environment (DT-environment) for e-Government, with the objective of creating a strong and open environment to test upcoming innovations in e-service delivery and contribute to the dissemination and take-up of the end results. In this way, the eGovlab is developing the infrastructure to act as a platform for experimentation of large development projects that allow rigorous, transparent, and replicable testing of scientific theories, computational tools, and new technologies. The test bed can emulate real-world conditions and allow everyone involved in public sector innovation to develop and test the different prototypes, concepts, products and services. The different tools for multimodal communication and public decision analysis proposed herein have two things in common. First, development proposals have created pronounced opinions (for or against) in civil society; among residents and other local stake holders. Second, decision-makers are faced with a situation in which a number of interests (to some extent coherent, to some extent contradictory) have to be considered in the decision-making process.

This will also use synergies with the EU FP7 project Sense4us[2] tool-kit as a socio-technical construct, where we adopt a semiotic analysis and a value sensitive design model to further unfold the meaning-making and decision support that such innovative tools offer (in the case of Sense4us – the extraction, analysis (semantic & sentiment) and visualisation of open data (social media) for policy makers. Furthermore we ask how simulation in such environments impacts the quality of decision making in e-governance. There are also strong connections to the Sida supported project Botswana Speaks,[3] where we have the ICT4D thematic outlook on how engagement by a widely

---

[1] http://egovlab.eu/.

[2] http://www.sense4us.eu/.

[3] http://www.botswanaspeaks.org/.

available technical platform enhances transparency and participation from civil society, within more traditional forms of governance in the developing world, as well as many others.

6 Conclusions

A decision theory without applications is meaningless. To use a such in a participatory setting, we must obviously take into account the complex issues of how governance arrangements and the formal planning process as such can be structured to effectively accommodate inputs from various citizens in a decision framework, including usable and transparent decision methods equipped for handling citizens and multiple decision-makers. This aspect focuses should focus more extensively on means and tools for how citizen content may be analysed, distributed and utilised by decision making authorities in public decision making and planning. The general need to facilitate the expression of views, concerns and opinions of general stakeholders is crucial not only to support decision-makers but to actually provide various groups to take part in the decision-making process, where decision rationales are clearly communicated to the citizens concerned. This means that the background information as well as the decision principles should be communicated together with means to understand and utilise them. In this context, the methods suggested above should be instrumental.

To conclude, public decision making is in a highly doubtful state and there is a large set of difficulties involved herein. The gains of initiatives of the type described here, could be a major step in the use of well-informed decision analysis for evaluation of critical societal issues and provide applicable and computationally meaningful public decision mechanisms, involving multiple-criteria, point-of-views, scenario analyses, uncertain appraisals of the decision parameters involved and visual formats for presentation of the relevant information. Hopefully, this would have a significant impact of the applicability of decision theory in participatory democracy and on modernizing the field of decision, policy, and societal risk analysis.

References

1. Glott, R., Schmidt, P., Ghosh, R.: Wikipedia Survey – Overview of Results. UNU-MERIT (2010)
2. Insua, R.D., Kersten, G.E., Rios, J., Insua, C., Grima, C., Ríos: Towards decision support for participatory democracy. Inf. Syst. E-Bussiness. Manage. 6(2), 161–191 (2007)
3. Forsberg, R., Milles, L., Barkhuus, L., Ekenberg, L., Sauter, W.: Women in Science. STYX, Stockholm (2013)
4. Forsberg, R.: Women in Science. The Royal Dramatic Theatre: mini festival with three plays (2013). http://ratsteater.se/en/production/theater/women-in-sience/
5. Hansson, K., Cars, G., Ekenberg, L., Danielson, M.: The importance of recognition for equal representation in participatory processes. Footpr. – Delft Archit. Theory J. 13, 81–98 (2013)
6. Ekenberg, L., Forsberg, R., Sauter, W.: Antigone's diary – A Mobile Urban Drama, a Challenge to Performance Studies, and a Model for Democratic Decision Making. Contemporary Theatre Review (to appear)

7. Danielson, M., Ekenberg, L., Riabacke, M.: A prescriptive approach to elicitation of decision data. J. Stat. Theory Pract. **3**(1), 77–88 (2009)
8. Riabacke, M., Danielson, M., Ekenberg, L.: State-of-the-art in prescriptive weight elicitation. Adv. Decis. Sci. **2012**, 1–24 (2012)
9. Hansson, K., Cars, G., Ekenberg, L., Danielson, M.: An e-participatory map over process methods in urban planning. In: Proceedings of CeDEM 2013: Conference for E-Democracy and Open Government (2013)

A New Selection Process Based on Granular Computing for Group Decision Making Problems

Francisco Javier Cabrerizo[1]([✉]), Raquel Ureña[2],
Juan Antonio Morente-Molinera[2], Witold Pedrycz[3],
Francisco Chiclana[4], and Enrique Herrera-Viedma[2]

[1] Department of Software Engineering and Computer Systems,
Universidad Nacional de Educación a Distancia (UNED), 28040 Madrid, Spain
cabrerizo@issi.uned.es
[2] Department of Computer Science and Artificial Intelligence,
University of Granada, 18071 Granada, Spain
{raquel,jamoren,viedma}@decsai.ugr.es
[3] Department of Electrical and Computer Engineering, University of Alberta,
Edmonton T6R 2T1, Canada
wpedrycz@ee.ualberta.ca
[4] School of Computer Science and Informatics, De Montfort University,
Leicester LE1 9BH, UK
chiclana@dmu.ac.uk

Abstract. In Group Decision Making, there are situations in which the decision makers may not be able to provide his/her opinions properly and they could contain contradictions. To avoid it, in this contribution, we present a new selection process to deal with inconsistent information. As part of it, we use a method based on granular computing to increase the consistency of the opinions given by the decision makers. To do so, each opinion is articulated as a certain information granule instead of a single numeric value, offering the necessary flexibility to increase the consistency. Finally, the importance of the decision makers' opinions in the aggregation step is modeled by means of their consistency.

Keywords: Group decision making · Selection process · Granular computing · Consistency · Aggregation

1 Introduction

Group Decision Making (GDM) is a situation where there is a set of alternatives, $X = \{x_1, x_2, \ldots, x_n\}$, to solve a problem and a group of decision makers, $E = \{e_1, e_2, \ldots, e_m\}$, $(m \geq 2)$, characterized by their own knowledge, trying to achieve a common solution. To do this, decision makers have to communicate their opinions by means of a set of assessments over the set of alternatives.

Preference relations are usually assumed to model decision makers' preferences in GDM problems [1]. According to the nature of the information expressed

© Springer International Publishing Switzerland 2015
H. Fujita and A. Selamat (Eds.): SoMeT 2014, CCIS 513, pp. 13–24, 2015.
DOI: 10.1007/978-3-319-17530-0_2

for every pair of alternatives, there exist many different representation formats of preference relations. In this contribution, we make use of fuzzy preference relations as they are one of the most employed because of their effectiveness as a tool for modelling decision processes and their utility and easiness of use when we want to aggregate decision makers' preferences into group ones [1,2].

The main advantage of pairwise comparison is that of focusing exclusively on two alternatives at a time, which facilitates decision makers when expressing their preferences. However, this way of providing preferences limits decision makers in their global perception of the alternatives and, as a consequence, the provided preferences could be not rational.

As consistent information, that is, information which does not imply any kind of contradiction, is more appropriate than information containing some contradictions, it is of great importance to provide decision makers with some tools that allow them to increase their level of consistency. To do so, information granularity may be used [3].

Information granularity is an important design asset offering to the decision makers some flexibility with the intent that their initial preferences can be adjusted in order to obtain a higher level of consistency. Assuming that each decision maker communicates his/her opinions using a fuzzy preference relation, this flexibility is brought into the fuzzy preference relations by allowing them to be granular rather than numeric. Therefore, the entries of the fuzzy preference relations are not considered plain numbers but information granules (fuzzy sets, probability density functions, rough sets, intervals, and so on).

The objective of this contribution is to present a new selection process based on granular computing for GDM. It is composed of three steps: (1) improvement of the consistency in the opinions given by the decision makers, (2) aggregation, and (3) exploitation. In the first step, an allocation of information granularity, as a key component to improve the consistency, is used. In such a way, some level of granularity is introduced in the realization of the granular representation of the fuzzy preference relations, supplying the required flexibility to increase the level of consistency. Then, assuming the choice scheme proposed in [4], aggregation following by exploitation, this new selection process is completed. On the one hand, the aggregation step consists in combining the decision makers' individual preferences into a collective one, which reflects the properties contained in all the individual preferences. On the other hand, the exploitation step transforms the global information about the alternatives into a global ranking of them. To do this, two quantifier-guided choice degrees of alternatives may be used: the dominance and the nondominance degree. The main advantages of this new selection process are that it supports the improvement of consistency, and it aggregates the decision makers' preferences giving more importance to the most consistent ones.

The rest of this contribution is set out as follows. Section 2 deals with how to obtain the level of consistency in a fuzzy preference relation. Section 3 provides a detailed description of the new selection process based on granular computing for GDM problems. An example of its application is shown in Sect. 4, and, finally, in Sect. 5, we point out some conclusions.

2   Obtaining the Consistency Level in a Fuzzy Preference Relation

In this section, we introduce both the definition of a fuzzy preference relation and a method to obtain its level of consistency.

Definition 1. *A fuzzy preference relation PR on a set of alternatives X is a fuzzy set on the Cartesian product $X \times X$, i.e., it is characterized by a membership function $\mu_{PR} : X \times X \to [0,1]$.*

A fuzzy preference relation PR may be represented by the $n \times n$ matrix $PR = (pr_{ij})$, being $pr_{ij} = \mu_{PR}(x_i, x_j)$ $(\forall i, j \in \{1, \ldots, n\})$ interpreted as the preference degree or intensity of the alternative x_i over x_j: $pr_{ij} = 0.5$ indicates indifference between x_i and x_j $(x_i \sim x_j)$, $pr_{ij} = 1$ indicates that x_i is absolutely preferred to x_j, and $pr_{ij} > 0.5$ indicates that x_i is preferred to x_j $(x_i \succ x_j)$. Based on this interpretation we have that $pr_{ii} = 0.5$ $\forall i \in \{1, \ldots, n\}$ $(x_i \sim x_i)$. Since pr_{ii}'s (as well as the corresponding elements on the main diagonal in some other matrices) do not matter, we will write them as '–' instead of 0.5 [5].

The previous Definition 1 dealing with a fuzzy preference relation does not imply any kind of consistency property and, thus, the preference values of the pairwise comparisons can be contradictory. Obviously, because of an inconsistent source of information is not as useful as a consistent one, it is quite important to be able to measure the consistency of the information provided by the decision makers. To do so, different properties to be satisfied with the fuzzy preference relations have been proposed in the literature [6,7].

In this contribution, we make use of the additive transitivity property which facilitates the verification of consistency in the case of fuzzy preference relations. As it was shown in [7], additive transitivity for fuzzy preference relations may be seen as the parallel concept of Saaty's consistency property for multiplicative preference relations [8]. The mathematical formulation of the additive transitivity was given by [1]:

$$(pr_{ij} - 0.5) + (pr_{jk} - 0.5) = (pr_{ik} - 0.5), \forall i, j, k \in \{1, \ldots, n\}. \tag{1}$$

Additive transitivity implies additive reciprocity. Indeed, because $pr_{ii} = 0.5$ $\forall i$, if we make $k = i$ in (1), then we have: $pr_{ij} + pr_{ji} = 1$, $\forall i, j \in \{1, \ldots, n\}$.

Equation (1) can be rewritten as follows:

$$pr_{ik} = pr_{ij} + pr_{jk} - 0.5, \forall i, j, k \in \{1, \ldots, n\}. \tag{2}$$

A fuzzy preference relation is considered to be "additively consistent" when for every three options encountered in the problem, say $x_i, x_j, x_k \in X$, their associated preference degrees, $pr_{ij}, pr_{jk}, pr_{ik}$, fulfil (2).

Given a fuzzy preference relation, (2) can be used to calculate an estimated value of a preference degree using other preference degrees. In fact, the following estimated value of pr_{ik} $(i \neq k)$ can be calculated in three different ways using an intermediate alternative x_j [5]:

- From $pr_{ik} = pr_{ij} + pr_{jk} - 0.5$, we obtain the estimated value $(epr_{ik})^{j1}$:

$$(epr_{ik})^{j1} = pr_{ij} + pr_{jk} - 0.5. \tag{3}$$

- From $pr_{jk} = pr_{ji} + pr_{ik} - 0.5$, we obtain the estimated value $(epr_{ik})^{j2}$:

$$(epr_{ik})^{j2} = pr_{jk} - pr_{ji} + 0.5. \tag{4}$$

- From $pr_{ij} = pr_{ik} + pr_{kj} - 0.5$, we obtain the estimated value $(epr_{ik})^{j3}$:

$$(epr_{ik})^{j3} = pr_{ij} - pr_{kj} + 0.5. \tag{5}$$

Then, the estimated value, epr_{ik}, of a preference degree, pr_{ik}, is calculated according to the following expression:

$$epr_{ik} = \frac{\sum_{\substack{j=1 \\ j \neq i,k}}^{n} \left((epr_{ik})^{j1} + (epr_{ik})^{j2} + (epr_{ik})^{j3} \right)}{3(n-2)}. \tag{6}$$

When information provided is completely consistent then $(epr_{ik})^{jl} = pr_{ik}$ $\forall j, l$. However, because decision makers are not always fully consistent, the assessment made by a decision maker may not verify (2) and some of the estimated preference degree values $(epr_{ik})^{jl}$ may not belong to the unit interval $[0, 1]$. We note, on a basis of (3)–(5), that the maximum value of any of the preference degrees $(epr_{ik})^{jl}$ $(l \in \{1, 2, 3\})$ is 1.5 while the minimum one is -0.5. In such a way, the error, εpr_{ik}, between a preference degree and its estimated one in $[0, 1]$ is computed as follows [5]:

$$\varepsilon pr_{ik} = \frac{2}{3} \cdot |epr_{ik} - pr_{ik}|. \tag{7}$$

This error can be used to define the consistency degree cd_{ik} associated to the preference degree pr_{ik} as follows:

$$cd_{ik} = 1 - \varepsilon pr_{ik}. \tag{8}$$

When $cd_{ik} = 1$, then $\varepsilon pr_{ik} = 0$ and there is no inconsistency at all. The lower the value of cd_{ik}, the higher the value of εpr_{ik} and the more inconsistent is pr_{ik} with respect to the rest of information.

Finally, the consistency degrees associated with individual alternatives and the overall fuzzy preference relation are defined as follows:

- The consistency degree, $cd_i \in [0, 1]$, associated to a particular alternative x_i of a fuzzy preference relation is defined as:

$$cd_i = \frac{\sum_{k=1; i \neq k}^{n} (cd_{ik} + cd_{ki})}{2(n-1)}. \tag{9}$$

- The consistency degree, $cd \in [0, 1]$, of a fuzzy preference relation is defined as:

$$cd = \frac{\sum_{i=1}^{n} cd_i}{n}. \tag{10}$$

When the fuzzy preference relation is given by a decision maker e_h, the consistency degree of the fuzzy preference relation is represented as cd^h.

3   A Selection Process Based on Granular Computing

In this section, we present the new selection process based on granular computing for GDM problems. It consists of three steps: (1) improvement of the consistency, (2) aggregation, and (3) exploitation. An allocation of information granularity, as a key component to increase the level of consistency in the fuzzy preference relations, is used in the first step. The aggregation phase defines a collective fuzzy preference relation indicating the global preference between every pair of alternatives, while the exploitation step transforms the global information about the alternatives into a global ranking of them.

3.1   Improvement of the Consistency

The improvement of consistency when the decision makers communicate their opinions by means of fuzzy preference relations becomes a very important aspect in order to avoid misleading solutions. As we have already aforementioned, the improvement of consistency calls for some flexibility exhibited by the decision makers with respect their initial opinions.

These changes of preferences are articulated through modifications of the entries of the fuzzy preference relations. That is, if the pairwise comparisons of the fuzzy preference relations are not managed as single numeric values, which are inflexible, but rather as information granules, it will bring the indispensable factor of flexibility.

The notation $G(PR)$ is here used to accentuate that we are interested in granular fuzzy preference relations. $G(.)$ represents the specific granular formalism which is used, say intervals, probability density functions, fuzzy sets, rough sets, and alike. In particular, in this contribution, the granularity of information is articulated through intervals. Therefore, $G(PR) = P(PR)$, where $P(.)$ denotes a family of intervals. The length of such intervals (entries of the fuzzy preference relations) is sought as a level of granularity α, which is treated as synonymous of the level of flexibility, facilitating the improvement of the consistency. The higher level of granularity is allowed to the decision maker, the higher the feasibility of arriving at a higher level of consistency.

This flexibility given by the level of granularity may be used to optimize a certain objective function in order to increase the level of consistency. In the interval-valued granular model of fuzzy preference relations, it is supposed that each decision maker feels equally comfortable when selecting any fuzzy preference relation whose values are placed within the bounds fixed by the level of granularity α. In such a way, the improvement of the consistency is effectuated at the level of individual decision makers using the following optimization index:

$$Q = \frac{1}{m} \sum_{h=1}^{m} cd^h. \tag{11}$$

Therefore, the overall optimization problem reads as follows:

$$\text{Max}_{PR^1, PR^2, ..., PR^m \in P(PR)} Q. \tag{12}$$

The aforementioned maximization is conducted for all acceptable interval-valued fuzzy preference relations because of the introduced level of granularity α. This fact is underlined by including a granular form of the fuzzy preference relations allowed in the problem, that is, PR^1, PR^2, ..., PR^m, are elements of the family of interval-valued fuzzy preference relations, namely, $\boldsymbol{P}(PR)$.

In this contribution, the optimization of the fuzzy preference relations, coming from the space of interval-valued fuzzy preference relations, is carried out by means of the Particle Swarm Optimization (PSO) framework [9]. PSO is here used because it is especially attractive given its less significant computing overhead in comparison with other techniques of global optimization [10]. However, other optimization mechanisms could be used as well.

The PSO is well documented in the existing literature with numerous modifications and augmentations. Refer to the generic flow of computing in which velocities and positions of the particles are updated. What is important in this setting is a formation of the particle. In our framework, each particle represents a vector whose entries are located in the unit interval. When it comes to the representation of the solutions, the particle is composed of "$m \cdot n(n-1)$" entries positioned in the $[0, 1]$ interval which corresponds to the search space.

Assuming a given level of granularity α (located in the unit interval) and starting with the initial fuzzy preference relation PR, provided by the decision maker, let us consider an entry pr_{ij} of PR. The interval of admissible values of this entry of $\boldsymbol{P}(PR)$ implied by the level of granularity α is equal to:

$$[a, b] = [\max(0, pr_{ij} - \alpha/2), \min(1, pr_{ij} + \alpha/2)]. \tag{13}$$

Considering that the entry of interest of the particle is x, an entry pr_{ij} is transformed linearly according to the expression $z = a + (b - a)x$. For instance, suppose that pr_{ij} is equal to 0.3, the admissible level of granularity α is equal to 0.1, and the corresponding entry of the particle is $x = 0.7$. According to it, the corresponding interval of the granular fuzzy preference relation calculated as given by (13) becomes equal to $[a, b] = [0.25, 0.35]$. Therefore, $z = 0.32$, and the modified value of pr_{ij} becomes equal to 0.32.

Finally, it is important to note that the overall particle is composed of the individual segments, where each of them is concerned with the optimization of the parameters of the fuzzy preference relations. Hence, the fitness function, f, associated with the particle is defined as $f = Q$, being Q the optimization index presented previously. The higher the value of f, the better the particle is.

3.2   Aggregation

Once the consistency of the fuzzy preference relations has been increased, a collective fuzzy preference relation $PR^c = (pr_{ij}^c)$ must be obtained by aggregating all of the m individual fuzzy preference relations $\{PR^1, \ldots, PR^m\}$. Here, each value $pr_{ij}^c \in [0, 1]$ will represent the preference of the alternative x_i over the alternative x_j according to the majority of the most consistent decision makers.

A logical assumption in the resolution process of a GDM problem is that of associating more importance to the decision makers who provide the most consistent opinions. Approaches for the inclusion of these values of importance in the aggregation process involve the transformation of the preference values under the importance degree by means of a transformation function to generate a new value [11,12]. In this contribution, we apply an alternative approach consisting of using consistency levels as the order inducing values of the Induced Ordered Weighted Averaging (IOWA) operator [13] to be applied in the aggregation step of the selection process.

Definition 2. *An IOWA operator of dimension n is a function $\Phi_W : (\mathbb{R} \times \mathbb{R})^n \to \mathbb{R}$, to which a set of weights or weighting vector is associated, $W = (w_1, \ldots, w_n)$, with $w_i \in [0,1]$, $\sum_i w_i = 1$, and it is defined to aggregate the set of second arguments of a list of n two-tuples $\{\langle u_1, p_1 \rangle, \ldots, \langle u_n, p_n \rangle\}$ according to the following expression:*

$$\Phi_W(\langle u_1, p_1 \rangle, \ldots, \langle u_n, p_n \rangle) = \sum_{i=1}^{n} w_i \cdot p_{\sigma(i)}, \tag{14}$$

being σ a permutation of $\{1, \ldots, n\}$ such that $u_{\sigma(i)} \geq u_{\sigma(i+1)}$, $\forall i = 1, \ldots, n-1$, i.e., $\langle u_{\sigma(i)}, p_{\sigma(i)} \rangle$ is the two-tuple with $u_{\sigma(i)}$ the i-th highest value in the set $\{u_1, \ldots, u_n\}$.

In the above definition, the reordering of the set of values to be aggregated, $\{p_1, \ldots, p_n\}$, is induced by the reordering of the set of values $\{u_1, \ldots, u_n\}$ associated with them, which is based upon their magnitude. Due to this use of the set of values $\{u_1, \ldots, u_n\}$, Yager and Filev called them the values of an order inducing variable and $\{p_1, \ldots, p_n\}$ the values of the argument variable [13].

An essential question in the definition of the IOWA operator is how to obtain the associated weighting vector. To do so, the approaches proposed to calculate the weighting vector of an Ordered Weighted Averaging (OWA) operator can be applied [14].

Definition 3. *An OWA operator of dimension n is a function $\phi_W : \mathbb{R}^n \to \mathbb{R}$, which has a set of weights or weighting vector associated with it, $W = (w_1, \ldots, w_n)$, with $w_i \in [0,1]$, $\sum_i w_i = 1$, and it is defined to aggregate a list of n values $\{p_1, \ldots, p_n\}$ according to the following expression:*

$$\phi_W(p_1, \ldots, p_n) = \sum_{i=1}^{n} w_i \cdot p_{\sigma(i)}, \tag{15}$$

being $\sigma : \{1, \ldots, n\} \to \{1, \ldots, n\}$ a permutation such that $p_{\sigma(i)} \geq p_{\sigma(i+1)}$, $\forall i = 1, \ldots, n-1$, i.e., $p_{\sigma(i)}$ is the i-th highest value in the set $\{p_1, \ldots, p_n\}$.

In the process of quantifier-guided aggregation, given a collection of n criteria represented as fuzzy subsets of the alternatives X, the OWA operator is used to implement the concept of fuzzy majority in the aggregation phase by means of a fuzzy linguistic quantifier [15], indicating the proportion of satisfied criteria "necessary for a good solution" [16]. This implementation is done by using the quantifier to calculate the OWA weights. According to it, in the case of a regular increasing monotone (RIM) quantifier Q, the procedure to evaluate the overall satisfaction of Q criteria (or decision makers) by the alternative x_j is carried out calculating the IOWA weights as follows:

$$w_i = Q(i/n) - Q((i-1)/n), \quad i = 1, \ldots, n. \tag{16}$$

When a fuzzy linguistic quantifier Q is used to compute the weights of the above aggregation operators, then it is symbolized by Φ_Q and ϕ_Q, respectively.

Definition 2 allows the construction of many different IOWA operators. Here, we use an IOWA operator in which the ordering of the preference values to be aggregated is induced by ordering the decision makers from the most to the least consistent one. Therefore, the collective fuzzy preference relation is obtained as:

$$pr_{ij}^c = \Phi_Q(\langle cd^1, pr_{ij}^1 \rangle, \ldots, \langle cd^m, pr_{ij}^m \rangle), \tag{17}$$

where Q is the fuzzy linguistic quantifier used to implement the fuzzy majority concept and, using (16), to compute the weighting vector of the IOWA operator.

3.3 Exploitation

At this point, in order to select the alternative(s) "best" acceptable for the majority (Q) of the most consistent decision makers, two quantifier-guided choice degrees of alternatives can be employed [17]: a dominance degree ($QGDD$), and a nondominance degree ($QGNDD$).

– $QGDD_i$: This quantifier-guided dominance degree evaluates the dominance that the alternative x_i has over all the others in a fuzzy majority sense. It is computed as follows:

$$QGDD_i = \phi_Q(pr_{i1}^c, pr_{i2}^c, \ldots, pr_{i(i-1)}^c, pr_{i(i+1)}^c, \ldots, pr_{in}^c). \tag{18}$$

– $QGNDD_i$: This quantifier-guided nondominance degree gives the degree in which the alternative x_i is not dominated by a fuzzy majority of the remaining alternatives. It is calculated as follows:

$$QGNDD_i = \phi_Q(1 - p_{1i}^s, 1 - p_{2i}^s, \ldots, 1 - p_{(i-1)i}^s, 1 - p_{(i+1)i}^s, \ldots, 1 - p_{ni}^s), \tag{19}$$

where $p_{ji}^s = max\{pr_{ji}^c - pr_{ij}^c, 0\}$ represents the degree in which x_i is strictly dominated by x_j.

The application of the above choice degrees of alternatives over X may be carried out according to two different policies: (1) sequential policy, and (2) conjunctive policy [5]. On the one hand, in the sequential policy, one of the choice degrees is selected and applied to X according to the preference of the decision makers, obtaining a selection set of alternatives. If there is more than one alternative in this selection set, then, the other choice degree is applied to select the alternative of this set with the best second choice degree. One the other hand, in the conjunctive policy, both choice degrees are applied to X, obtaining two selection sets of alternatives. The final selection set of alternatives is obtained as the intersection of these two selection sets of alternatives. The latter conjunction selection process is more restrictive than the former sequential selection process because it is possible to obtain an empty selection set.

4 Illustrative Example

In this section, we present an illustrative example which helps quantifying the performance of the selection process proposed in this contribution.

Let us suppose that the supermarket manager wants to buy 500 bottles of Spanish wine from among four possible brands of wine: $\{x_1 =$ Marqués de Cáceres, $x_2 =$ Los Molinos, $x_3 =$ Somontano, $x_4 =$ René *Barbier*$\}$. The manager decide to inquire four decision makers, $E = \{e_1, e_2, e_3, e_4\}$, about their opinions on what Spanish wine should be bought. The decision makers provide the following fuzzy preference relations:

$$PR^1 = \begin{pmatrix} - & 0.60 & 0.30 & 0.50 \\ 0.10 & - & 0.70 & 0.70 \\ 0.80 & 0.10 & - & 0.10 \\ 0.10 & 0.40 & 0.60 & - \end{pmatrix} \quad PR^2 = \begin{pmatrix} - & 0.20 & 0.50 & 0.10 \\ 0.40 & - & 0.20 & 0.80 \\ 0.50 & 0.40 & - & 0.90 \\ 0.90 & 0.10 & 0.40 & - \end{pmatrix}$$

$$PR^3 = \begin{pmatrix} - & 0.20 & 0.20 & 0.70 \\ 0.30 & - & 0.60 & 0.90 \\ 0.10 & 0.40 & - & 0.30 \\ 0.10 & 0.40 & 0.70 & - \end{pmatrix} \quad PR^4 = \begin{pmatrix} - & 0.70 & 0.10 & 0.50 \\ 0.50 & - & 0.50 & 0.30 \\ 0.90 & 0.70 & - & 0.40 \\ 0.30 & 0.70 & 0.70 & - \end{pmatrix}$$

Once the decision makers have expressed their opinions, the selection process is applied in order to rank the Spanish wines from best to worst.

4.1 First Step: Improvement of the Consistency

Proceeding with the details of the optimization environment, in this contribution, a generic version of the PSO is used. The parameters in the update equation for the velocity of the particle were set as $c_1 = c_2 = 2$, as these values are usually encountered in the existing literature. The size of the swarm consists of 100 particles, and the algorithm was run for 200 generations (or iterations). These values were selected as a result of intensive experimentation.

Considering a given level of granularity α, Table 1 shows the performance of the PSO quantified in terms of the fitness function. To put the achieved optimization results in a certain context, we report the performance obtained when no granularity is allowed ($\alpha = 0$), that is, when considering the entries of the fuzzy preference relations are single numeric values. In such a case, the corresponding consistency degrees of the four fuzzy preference relations are: $cd^1 = 0.73$, $cd^2 = 0.76$, $cd^3 = 0.82$, and $cd^4 = 0.81$. Therefore, the value of the fitness function f is 0.78.

Table 1. Performance of the PSO for selected values of α

	$\alpha = 0.2$	$\alpha = 0.4$	$\alpha = 0.6$	$\alpha = 0.8$	$\alpha = 1.0$	$\alpha = 1.2$	$\alpha = 1.4$	$\alpha = 1.6$	$\alpha = 1.8$	$\alpha = 2.0$
cd^1	0.73	0.77	0.79	0.83	0.88	0.93	0.96	0.98	1.00	1.00
cd^2	0.76	0.78	0.82	0.85	0.88	0.91	0.94	0.97	1.00	1.00
cd^3	0.83	0.84	0.86	0.89	0.91	0.94	0.97	0.99	1.00	1.00
cd^4	0.82	0.83	0.85	0.88	0.91	0.94	0.97	0.98	1.00	1.00
f	0.79	0.80	0.83	0.86	0.90	0.93	0.96	0.98	1.00	1.00

Comparing with the values obtained by the PSO, the fitness function f takes on now lower values. As we can see in Table 1, the higher the admitted level of granularity α, the higher the values obtained by the fitness function f. It is logical, as the higher the level of granularity α, the higher the level of flexibility introduced in the fuzzy preference relations and, hence, the possibility of achieving higher level of consistency. Furthermore, when each entry of the granular preference relation is treated as the whole $[0, 1]$ interval ($\alpha = 2.0$), the value of the fitness function is 1, the maximum one. Nevertheless, in this case, we have to take into account that whether the level of granularity is very high, the values of the entries of the fuzzy preference relation could be very different in comparison with the original ones given by the decision maker and, hence, he/she could reject them.

Following with the example, we are going to consider that the level of granularity α is equal to 0.6 and, therefore, the consistency level achieved among all the decision makers is 0.83 which is better than the consistency obtained when no granularity is admitted (0.78). Then, using this level of granularity, the new fuzzy preference relations obtained using the PSO are:

$$PR^1 = \begin{pmatrix} - & 0.30 & 0.10 & 0.20 \\ 0.10 & - & 0.40 & 0.40 \\ 0.50 & 0.10 & - & 0.10 \\ 0.10 & 0.10 & 0.30 & - \end{pmatrix} \qquad PR^2 = \begin{pmatrix} - & 0.26 & 0.52 & 0.21 \\ 0.42 & - & 0.26 & 0.76 \\ 0.52 & 0.42 & - & 0.81 \\ 0.81 & 0.21 & 0.42 & - \end{pmatrix}$$

$$PR^3 = \begin{pmatrix} - & 0.19 & 0.19 & 0.63 \\ 0.23 & - & 0.53 & 0.75 \\ 0.15 & 0.33 & - & 0.23 \\ 0.15 & 0.33 & 0.63 & - \end{pmatrix} \qquad PR^4 = \begin{pmatrix} - & 0.56 & 0.10 & 0.36 \\ 0.36 & - & 0.36 & 0.16 \\ 0.70 & 0.56 & - & 0.26 \\ 0.16 & 0.56 & 0.56 & - \end{pmatrix}$$

4.2   Second Step: Aggregation

Once the consistency of the fuzzy preference relations have been increased, we aggregate them by means of the IOWA operator presented in Sect. 3.2. We make use of the linguistic quantifier "most of", represented by the RIM quantifier $Q(r) = r^{1/2}$, which applying (16) generates a weighting vector of four values to obtain each collective preference value pr_{ij}^c. As example, the collective preference value pr_{12}^c is calculated in the following way:

$$w_1 = Q(1/4) - Q(0) = 0.5 - 0 = 0.5$$
$$w_2 = Q(2/4) - Q(1/4) = 0.71 - 0.5 = 0.21$$
$$w_3 = Q(3/4) - Q(2/4) = 0.87 - 0.71 = 0.16$$
$$w_4 = Q(1) - Q(3/4) = 1 - 0.87 = 0.13$$
$$cd^1 = 0.79, \ cd^2 = 0.82, \ cd^3 = 0.86, \ cd^4 = 0.85$$
$$\sigma(1) = 3, \ \sigma(2) = 4, \ \sigma(3) = 2, \ \sigma(4) = 1$$
$$pr^c_{12} = w_1 \cdot pr^3_{12} + w_2 \cdot pr^4_{12} + w_3 \cdot pr^2_{12} + w_4 \cdot pr^1_{12} = 0.21$$

Then, the collective fuzzy preference relation is:

$$PR^c = \begin{pmatrix} - & 0.21 & 0.17 & 0.45 \\ 0.27 & - & 0.43 & 0.58 \\ 0.37 & 0.36 & - & 0.31 \\ 0.25 & 0.33 & 0.54 & - \end{pmatrix}$$

4.3 Third Step: Exploitation

Using again the same linguistic quantifier "most of" and (16), we obtain the following weighting vector $W = (w_1, w_2, w_3)$:

$$w_1 = Q(1/3) - Q(0) = 0.58 - 0 = 0.58$$
$$w_2 = Q(2/3) - Q(1/3) = 0.82 - 0.58 = 0.24$$
$$w_3 = Q(1) - Q(2/3) = 1 - 0.82 = 0.18$$

Using, for example, the quantifier-guided dominance degree, we obtain the following values: $\{QGDD_1 = 0.34, QGDD_2 = 0.49, QGDD_3 = 0.36, QGDD_4 = 0.44\}$. Then, applying, for instance, the sequential policy, the following ranking of alternatives is obtained: $x_2 \succ x_4 \succ x_3 \succ x_1$. Using this information, the supermarket manager should buy 500 bottles of Los Molinos wine.

5 Conclusions

In this contribution, we have presented a new selection process based on granular computing to be used to solve GDM problems. As main novelty, it incorporates a first step in order to increase the consistency achieved by the decision makers in their opinions. To do so, we have proposed the concept of granular fuzzy preference relation and we have emphasized a role of information granularity as a conceptual vehicle to facilitate admissible changes to the results of pairwise comparisons. It has offered a badly needed flexibility to increase the consistency. In addition, the aggregation of the opinions provided by the decision makers has been carried out by giving more importance to the most consistent ones.

Acknowledgments. The authors would like to acknowledge FEDER financial support from the Projects FUZZYLING-II Project TIN2010-17876 and TIN2013-40658-P, and also the financial support from the Andalusian Excellence Projects TIC-05299 and TIC-5991.

References

1. Tanino, T.: Fuzzy preference orderings in group decision making. Fuzzy Sets Syst. **12**(12), 117–131 (1984)
2. Meng, F., Chen, X.: A new method for group decision making with incomplete fuzzy preference relations. Knowledge-Based Syst. **73**, 111–123 (2015)
3. Pedrycz, W.: Granular Computing: Analysis and Design of Intelligent Systems. CRC Press/Francis Taylor, Boca Raton (2013)
4. Fodor, J., Roubens, M.: Fuzzy Preference Modelling and Multicriteria Decision Support. Kluwer Academic Publishers, Dordrecht (1994)
5. Herrera-Viedma, E., Chiclana, F., Herrera, F., Alonso, S.: Group decision-making model with incomplete fuzzy preference relations based on additive consistency. IEEE Trans. Syst. Man Cybern. Part B Cybern. **37**(1), 176–189 (2007)
6. Chen, S.-M., Lin, T.-E., Lee, L.-W.: Group decision making using incomplete fuzzy preference relations based on the additive consistency and the order consistency. Inf. Sci. **259**, 1–15 (2014)
7. Herrera-Viedma, E., Herrera, F., Chiclana, F., Luque, M.: Some issues on consistency of fuzzy preference relations. Eur. J. Oper. Res. **154**(1), 98–109 (2004)
8. Saaty, T.L.: Fundamental of Decision Making and Priority Theory with the AHP. RWS Publications, Pittsburg (1994)
9. Kennedy, J., Eberhart, R.C.: Particle swarm optimization. In: Proceedings of the IEEE International Conference on Neural Networks, pp. 1942–1948 (1995)
10. Li, Y., Jiao, L., Shang, R., Stolkin, R.: Dynamic-context cooperative quantum-behaved particle swarm optimization based on multilevel thresholding applied to medical image segmentation. Inf. Sci. **294**, 408–422 (2015)
11. Mesiar, R., Špirková, J., Vavríková, L.: Weighted aggregation operators based on minimization. Inf. Sci. **178**(4), 1133–1140 (2008)
12. Špirková, J.: Weighted operators based on dissimilarity function. Inf. Sci. **281**, 172–181 (2014)
13. Yager, R.R., Filev, D.P.: Induced ordered weighted averaging operators. IEEE Trans. Syst. Man Cybern. Part B Cybern. **29**(2), 141–150 (1999)
14. Yager, R.R.: On ordered weighted averaging aggregation operators in multicriteria decision making. IEEE Trans. Syst. Man Cybern. **18**(1), 183–190 (1988)
15. Zadeh, L.A.: A computational approach to fuzzy quantifiers in natural languages. Comput. Math. Appl. **9**(1), 149–184 (1983)
16. Yager, R.R.: Quantifier guided aggregation using OWA operators. Int. J. Intell. Syst. **11**(1), 49–73 (1996)
17. Herrera, F., Herrera-Viedma, E., Verdegay, J.L.: A sequential selection process in group decision making with a linguistic assessment approach. Inf. Sci. **85**(4), 223–239 (1995)

Easy and Concise Programming for Low-Level Hybridization of PSO-GA

Suraya Masrom[1]([✉]), Siti Zaleha Zainal Abidin[2], and Nasiroh Omar[2]

[1] Faculty of Computer and Mathematical Sciences, Universiti Teknologi MARA,
Ipoh, Perak, Malaysia
suray078@perak.uitm.edu.my
[2] Faculty of Computer and Mathematical Sciences, Universiti Teknologi MARA,
Shah Alam, Malaysia
{zaleha,nasiroh}@tmsk.uitm.edu.my

Abstract. Responding to the difficulties of implementing Low-Level Hybridization (LLH) of meta-heuristics, this paper introduces a reusable software for the algorithm design and development. This paper proposes three implementation frameworks for the LLH of Particle Swarm Optimization (PSO) and Genetic Algorithm (GA). Then, with attempt to support a more effective programming environment, a set of scripting language constructs based on the proposed implementation frameworks is developed. For evaluation, twelve algorithms that composed of nine LLHs and three single PSO have been coded and executed with the scripting language. The results demonstrate that the scripting language is anticipated for enabling of an easier and more concise programming for effective rapid prototyping and testing of the algorithms.

1 Introduction

The research on meta-heuristics has widely discussed how hybridization works better than a single implementation [4,28,31]. Similarly, research on the PSO hybridization is gaining attention until recently [22,25,36]. This especially makes sense in the context of hybridizing PSO with GA, due to the speciality of GA operators that able to control the exploitation and exploration search ability of the algorithm [13,23]. The single PSO is commonly known with good exploitation, but less explorative, thus the GA operators can be adapted for improving the PSO search ability. However, despite the interest of PSO-GA hybrid is very progressing, knowledge that supports the implementation by means of implementation framework and software tool is lacking.

As meta-heuristics, the hybridization techniques between PSO and GA can be categorized as High-Level Hybridization (HLH) or Low-Level Hybridization (LLH). The level of hybridization reflects to the degree or strength of the combination [27,30]. The strength of the combination in HLH is lesser than LLH. Thus, the different meta-heuristics in HLH can be independently executed without any internal cooperation. In most approaches, different algorithms in HLH establish their communication through a well defined interface or protocol [27].

© Springer International Publishing Switzerland 2015
H. Fujita and A. Selamat (Eds.): SoMeT 2014, CCIS 513, pp. 25–38, 2015.
DOI: 10.1007/978-3-319-17530-0_3

With the algorithms interfaces, the implementation of HLH involves no internal structure modification.

On the contrary, the techniques of LLH are implemented without any interaction interfaces among the different hybrid algorithms. In other words, the LLH techniques involve in creating a new meta-heuristic with the combination of different components or functions from the different meta-heuristics. As a result, in most cases, implementing the LLH requires internal structure modification of the different hybrid algorithms. Therefore, the implementation of LLH tends to be more difficult than HLH. As all the different components are strongly connected in LLH, they must be accurately combined to ensure that the hybrid algorithm is suitable and effective for solving a specific kind of optimization problem. In case of PSO, the inclusion of GA components has increased the number of parameters used, which demands longer time for the algorithm setting and testing. To ease the tasks, it is anticipated in this research that the utilization of implementation framework and reusable software are highly beneficial for the users.

The objectives of this paper is to propose implementation frameworks for the LLH of PSO-GA and to introduce a rapid software for the implementation frameworks. The software consists of a set of scripting language constructs that enables an easy and concise programming for the algorithms development. In the evaluation part of this paper, the scripting codes will be measured with regards to the easiness and conciseness.

2   Research Background

2.1   Reusable Software for Meta-heuristics

Software reusability is a practice that reusing third-party software (program codes) to create another software. By using a reusable software, the users can rapidly develop and testing the meta-heuristics algorithms. This part reviews the functionality of the existing reusable software for meta-heuristics by means of the meta-heuristics paradigms (**Single, HLH, LLH**) as presented in the following Table 1.

As single paradigm is simpler than meta-heuristics hybrids, many of the existing software tools were designed to be more applicable for easy implementation of single meta-heuristics. Some of the software are *TEA* [11], *JEO* [3], *EAML* [32], *iOpt* [29], *EASEA* [7], *JSwarm* [24], *SwarmOps* [18] and *ESDL* [9]. Some software provides more than one meta-heuristics but each of them is independently executed without any sense of interactions that can enable meta-heuristics hybridization. For example *iOpt* support different meta-heuristics implementation including GA, DE, Local Search and Simulated Annealing.

Furthermore, most of the reusable software that support easy programming for meta-heuristics hybridization are more useful for HLH rather than LLH. A notable examples for the software that enable HLH are *GAlib* [35], *Mallba* [1], *EasyLocal++* [16], *Distributed Beagle* [10], *HeuristicLab* [34], *OPT4J* [20], *JCLEC* [33] and *ECJ* [21]. It is found that only three of the listed software tools have enable easy programming for the LLH, which are *Hotframe* [14], *ParadisEO* [5] and

Table 1. Meta-heuristics software tools

Software name	Single	HLH	LLH
iOpt	✓	x	x
Hotframe	✓	✓	✓
Mallba	✓	✓	x
JEO	✓	x	x
EasyLocal++	✓	✓	x
HeuristicLab	✓	✓	x
JSwarm	✓	x	x
MDF	✓	✓	✓
TEA	✓	x	x
GAlib	✓	✓	x
ParadisEO	✓	✓	✓
Opt4J	✓	✓	x
Distributed Beagle	✓	✓	x
JCLEC	✓	✓	x
EASEA	✓	x	x
PPCEA	✓	x	x
ESDL	✓	x	x
EAML	✓	x	x
ECJ	✓	✓	x
DGAFrame	✓	✓ (Homogeneous)	x

MDF [19]. The three software tools have been designed with a very generic software framework that enables easy meta-heuristics modelling for the hybridization. The modelling codes are still difficult to comprehend while the implementation codes totally rely on $C++$ programming language, which is complex and lengthy. The HLH support in *DGAFrame* software [12] is specifically useful for the GA only that employed homogeneous search cooperation.

2.2 Evaluation Approaches of the Meta-heuristics Reusable Software

Although many research have been carried out on the reusable software for meta-heuristics, no single study exists that adequately conducts evaluation of the important aspects concern in this research, which are easy and concise programming. Major evaluation focused on the performance aspect that showed the optimization results of the proposed software [5,19]. Differently, researchers in [15] have measured six popular software tools for Evolutionary Algorithms (EAs) specifically over six proposed criteria of flexibility, namely representation, fitness, operation, evolutionary model, parameter management and configurable output. The researchers introduced a quantitative software generic analysis that defined the measurement for each flexible criterion in three scales such as 2 as complete generic, 1 as partial generic and 0 for no generic. Furthermore, an extensive assessment of several meta-heuristics software tools has been conducted in [26]. However, the selected criteria were rather focused on functionality and usability aspects for instances meta-heuristics types, algorithm structure, hybridization characteristic, software platform, user interface, stopping condition, documentation and so forth. Also, since the reviewed software were founded with a common limitation of LLH, only the HLH criterion has been considered.

One important aspect that has been addressed for the meta-heuristics program is concise [9]. Besides easy, concise program provides benefits to users in the algorithm presentation or documentation, which is significant for the algorithm reproduction [9]. Concise codes increase user comprehension to the codes although with less and simple codes. The conventional or general purpose programming language like *C, C++* and *JAVA* are very lengthy. It is rather impossible to include the lengthy program codes for documentation or publication. Therefore, while many success report have been written for meta-heuristics, very few that provide detail information beyond the programming language. Without the program codes, other users who intend to replicate the algorithm have to redeveloped the algorithm in different program structure or in different program platform. In this way, the users face a problem in achieving the expected results as presented in the referred paper. As the awareness of concise aspect is still new, no measurement has been proposed for the conciseness of meta-heuristics software tools. To summarize, Table 2 lists some of the meta-heuristics reusable software with respects to its software evaluation metrics (**easy, concise**) and the **evaluation approach**.

Only the software with the evaluation report is listed in the Table 2. Across all software, majority of evaluation approach demonstrates application development that describes and explains the operations and codes for solving the related optimization problem. In most cases, this approach is used to qualitatively measure the easiness. Also, the capability of producing good optimization results has also been used to indirectly present the functionality of the software. Differently, researchers in [8] used Line of Codes (LOC), Word of Codes (WOC) and Character of Codes (COC) for evaluating the ESDL. In software engineering, Line of Code (LOC) metric has been widely used for measuring the easiness of development software. Nevertheless, the utilization of LOC for measuring the easiness among the meta-heuristics software tools is very lacking. Besides, among the evaluation approaches, there is no formal method or formula has been established for measuring the conciseness in quantitatively.

3   Implementation Frameworks

In general, Fig. 1 illustrates the implementation frameworks for the LLH of PSO-GA.

The dotted box represents that the inclusion of GA components (crossover and mutation) is an optional. In other words, the PSO can be included either

Table 2. Evaluation approaches of meta-heuristics reusable software

Software name	Easy	Concise	Evaluation approach
iOpt	✓	x	Application demonstration (Qualitative)
Hotframe	✓	x	Application demonstration (Qualitative)
Mallba	✓	x	Application demonstration (Qualitative)
			Optimization results observation (Quantitative)
JEO	✓	x	Application demonstration (Qualitative)
			Optimization results observation (Quantitative)
EasyLocal++	✓	x	Application demonstration (Qualitative)
			Optimization results observation (Quantitative)
HeuristicLab	✓	x	Application demonstration (Qualitative)
			Optimization results observation (Quantitative)
MDF	✓	x	Application demonstration (Qualitative)
			Optimization results observation (Quantitative)
TEA	✓	x	Application demonstration (Qualitative)
			Optimization results observation (Quantitative)
GAlib	✓	x	Application demonstration (Qualitative)
ParadisEO	✓	x	Application demonstration (Qualitative)
			Optimization results observation (Quantitative)
Open Beagle	✓	x	Application demonstration (Qualitative)
Distributed Beagle	✓	x	Application demonstration (Qualitative)
			Mathematical analysis (Quantitative)
JCLEC	✓	x	Application demonstration (Qualitative)
PPCEA	✓	x	Application demonstration (Qualitative)
			Optimization results example
ESDL	✓	✓	Application demonstration (Qualitative)
			Optimization results observation (Quantitative)
			LOC, WOC, COC (Quantitative)
			Conciseness is directly measured with easiness
DGAFrame	✓	x	Optimization results observation (Quantitative)
ECJ	✓	x	Application demonstration (Qualitative)
jMetal	✓	x	Application demonstration (Qualitative)
			Optimization results observation (Quantitative)

by a crossover or a mutation or both crossover and mutation. Therefore, based on the figure, three implementation frameworks have been proposed, which are named as *Sequential Global Crossover (SGCrossover)*, *Sequential Global Mutation (SGMutation)* and *Sequential Global Crossover and Mutation (SGCrossMutation)*. The implementation frameworks are also developed with several

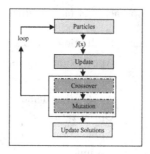

Fig. 1. Flowchart for the implementation frameworks

limitations that need further research extension. First, as stated in the frameworks name, the frameworks are applicable for sequential implementation from the PSO update to GA components. Second, they are governed for one global problem without solutions constraints, which also defined by the term *Global*. Third, it is a one-way LLH where PSO always be the master-metaheuristic. In addition, to support flexibility in creating variation of crossover and mutation operators to the LLH is not yet the main concern of this research. For the inclusion of both crossover and mutation, the process is presented in the Algorithm 1.

Algorithm 1. Crossover and Mutation

---

1 **foreach** *particle $x_i \in$ population* **do**
2 $\quad$ calculate crossover probability C_p
3 $\quad$ calculate mutation probability M_p

4 set r to a uniform random number $[0,1]$;
5 set d to a uniform random integer $[0, dim]$;
6 set $d1$ to a uniform random integer $[0, dim]$;
7 choose $pbest1, pbest2$ uniformly randomly among all n particles;
8 **foreach** *particle $x_i \in$ population* **do**
9 $\quad$ **if** $r < C_p$ **then**
10 $\quad\quad$ $x_{id1} = x_{id1} + \frac{pbest1_{d1} + pbest2_{d1}}{2}$;
11 $\quad$ **if** $r < M_p$ **then**
12 $\quad\quad$ $x_{id} = x_{id} + gaussian(\alpha)$;

All the LLHs with crossover perform crossover operation between two particles which are chosen probabilistically according to *uniform random* selection. Each position between the first and the maximum are then swapped according to the specific approach crossover rate C_p which can be constant or dynamically changed. This crossover operator was originally inspired by the *pbest* crossover introduced by Chen [6] which attempts to increase explorative search in PSO. The threshold value r is set to a random number in the interval $[0,1]$. It is compared to each particle's probability C_p of crossover to decide whether this particle's randomly chosen position d should be altered using *pbest* crossover. As proposed in Chen [6], the adjustment to dimension d is made using an average of two particles' relevant *pbest* values. For each particle being mutated in probability to mutation rate, randomly chosen particle's position d should be altered using specific mutation operator. In this work, mutation operator with random number from *gaussion* distributions [2,17]. The Gaussian function returns a random value from the range of the particle dimension.

4   Evaluation

The scripting language has to be evaluated with regards to the easiness and conciseness. Therefore, this section demonstrates several optimization applications written with the proposed scripting language. Each set of applications employs *SGCrossMutation*, *SGCrossover* and *SGMutation* implementation frameworks. In total, there are three group of application with nine LLHs are developed. First group of application is LLH with adaptive parameterizations, second is LLH with time-vary parameterizations and last group is LLH with constant parameterizations. For each set, single PSO with inertia weight in relation to the type of parameterizations is used as a benchmark algorithm. Therefore, for all experiments, there are twelve algorithms have to be developed with the scripting language. In order to test the performance of each algorithms that were written with the scripting language, all of the twelve algorithms were tested on a set of six well-known benchmark functions. The functions are listed in Table 3.

The experiments in every set of applications was repeated 30 times with 2000 iterations. The number of particles is set to 40 with 30 dimensions. Therefore, regardless of each algorithm, each of the 30 trials was allowed an equal number of 80000 function evaluations. The value for the personal and social learning rate (c1 and c2) is 2.0 respectively. The results are presented in Sect. 4.5. As to describe the scripting language components, two examples of scripting codes are given in the following part.

4.1   LLHs with Adaptive Parameterization

The name of each LLH application with adaptive parameterizations is **ACR** for adaptive *SGCrossover*, **AMR** for adaptive *SGMutation*, **ACMR** for adaptive

Table 3. Benchmark functions used in the experiments

Function name	Formula
Sphere	$f_1(x) = \sum_{i=1}^{D} x_i^2$
Rosenbrock	$f_2(x) = \sum_{i=1}^{D-1}(100(x_i^2 - x_{i+1})^2 + (x_i - 1)^2)$
Rastrigin	$f_3(x) = \sum_{i=1}^{D}(x_i^2 - 10cos(2\pi x_i) + 10)$
Levy	$f_4(x) = sin^2(\pi y_1) + \sum_{i=1}^{D-1}((y_i - 1)^2$ $(1 + 10sin^2(\pi y_i + 1))] + (y_D - 1)^2(1 + sin^2(2\pi y_D))$ $y_i = 1 + \frac{x_i - 1}{4}$
Griewank	$f_5(x) = \frac{1}{4000}\sum_{i=1}^{D} x_2^i - \prod_{i=1}^{D} \cos(\frac{x_i}{\sqrt{x_i}}) + 1$
Ackley	$f_6(x) =$ $-20exp(-0.2\sqrt{\frac{1}{30}\sum_{i=1}^{D} x_i^2}) - exp(\frac{1}{D}\sum_{i=1}^{D}(\cos 2\pi x_i) + 20 + \exp(1)$

SGCrossMutation and **AIW** for Single PSO with adaptive inertia weight. For examples, the scripting codes of the LLH with *SGCrossMutation* are written as in the following scripting codes 1. Each Crossover() and Mutation() statement is not included in the LLH that uses the *SGCrossover* and *SGMutation* implementation frameworks respectively. For the **(AIW)**, both Crossover() and Mutation() statements are not included.

Scripting Codes 1. Adaptive Parameterization of a LLH of SGCrossMutation

---

```
1 LLH(SGCrossMutation,ACMR, 30, 2000, 40);
2 SEARCHSPACE(particle,30);
3 PROBLEM(Rosenbrock,min);
4 Update(inertia[const 0.4], c1[const 0.2], c2[const 0.2],MaxP  10,
  MinP -5,MaxV  10,MinV  -5 );
5 Crossover( rate[ adaptive  ISA  0.9  0.3], operation[pbest],
  selection [uniform]);
6 Mutation( rate[ adaptive  ISA  0.9  0.3], operation[Gaussian]);
```

4.2   LLHs with Time-Vary Parameterizations

Each of the LLH with time-vary parameterization is named as **TCR** for time-vary *SGCrossover*, **TMR** for time-vary *SGMutation*, **TCMR** for time-vary *SGCrossMutation* and **TIW** for Single PSO with time-vary inertia weight. Regardless to each LLH with time-vary attributes, the scripting codes of the relevant statements can be written as the following examples of the scripting codes 2.

Scripting Codes 2. Time-vary Parameterization of a LLH of SGCrossMutation

---

```
1 LLH(SGCrossMutation,TVCMR, 30, 2000, 40);
2 SEARCHSPACE(particle,30);
3 PROBLEM(Rosenbrock,min);
4 Update(inertia[const 0.4], c1[const 0.2], c2[const 0.2],MaxP  10,
  MinP -5,MaxV  10,MinV  -5 );
5 Crossover( rate[ time-vary  LD  0.9  0.4], operation[pbest],
  selection [uniform]);
6 Mutation( rate[ time-vary  LD  0.9  0.4], operation[Gaussian]);
```

4.3   Easiness Test

The easiness test is valuable to indicate the effort in creating and reading the programs or algorithm descriptions. It uses volumetric measures which identify the **line of codes (LOC)** in the programs of eight algorithms that used adaptive and time-vary parameterizations. Each scripting codes of the algorithms is compared with the relevant *JAVA* source codes that were manually developed in the extended *JSwarm* software framework. Only codes that an end user would need to write is included while compilers and predefined operators, comments as well as begin and end symbols () are not assessed. **LOC** consists of any line containing letters or numbers either ended with semicolon or without semicolon (such as *for, while* and *if* statements), which is called as **physical LOC**. The results are depicted in Table 4. Across all algorithms, the scripting language codes consistently have shown less code than the main JAVA codes. This implies that to use the scripting language requires less effort to create and read the programs.

Table 4. Line of Codes (LOC)

Algorithms	Scripting language	Main JAVA
TMR	7	97
TCR	7	103
TCMR	8	108
TIW	6	89
AMR	7	96
ACR	7	99
ACMR	8	105
AIW	6	86

4.4 Conciseness Test

Referred to Oxford dictionary, conciseness means *"giving a lot of information in a few words"* or *"brief but comprehensive"*. In this paper, conciseness of a programming language is defined as less of codes but able to produce the desired output. In general, the conciseness can be directly presented from the language simplicity [8]. However, to provide quantitative measurement would be more valuable in indicating the conciseness aspect. In this work, conciseness is measured by calculating the total ratio of characters in relation to each group of desired task or functionality. Following are the lists the relevant statements used by the scripting language constructs and the main JAVA to achieve the program tasks that employed *SGCrossMutation* with constant parameterization or **CCMR**.

1. **Program Specifications**
   - Scripting language - There is only one keyword have to be written with the scripting language to begin and define the program which is *JACIE*.
   - main JAVA - The relevant codes for specifying a program in JSwarm are:
     1. *import net.sourceforge.jswarm_pso.*;*
     2. *import java.io.*;*
     3. *public class classname*
     4. *public static void main(String[] args).*

2. Experiment Specifications

- Scripting language - The related codes for experiment configurations is $SGCrossMutation(Name\ CCMR, ENum\ 30, Iter\ 2000, PSize\ 40);$.
- main JAVA - At least, the most relevant codes in JSwarm are:
  1. $int\ numof experiments = 30;$
  2. $double[]\ chibestf = new\ double[numof experiments];$
  3. $double\ bestf = 0.0;\ double\ stddev = 0.0;$
     $double\ ch = 0.0; int\ conv = 0; int\ avgconv = 0;\ int\ totalconv = 0;$
  4. $for(int\ z = 0; z < numof experiments; z + +)$
  5. $double[]\ convergencearray = new\ double\ [numberOf Iterations];$
  6. $System.out.println("bestfitness :" + c + "" + chibestf[c]);$
  7. $bestf + = chibestf[c];$
  8. $System.out.println("Totalbestfitness :" + bestf);$
  9. $System.out.println("Average\ bestfitness\ :" + bestf/numof experiments);$
  10. $stddev + = Math.pow(chibestf[K] - (bestf/numof experiments), 2);$

3. General Components Specifications

- Scripting language - The few codes are:
  1. $SEARCHSPACE(particle, 30);$
  2. $PROBLEM(Rosenbrock, min);$
- main JAVA - Some of the relevant codes are:
  1. $package\ net.source forge.jswarm\_pso.rosenbrock;$
  2. $Particle\ particles[];$ 3. $ParticleUpdate\ particleUpdate;$
  4. $Swarm\ swarm = new\ Swarm(30, new\ MyParticle(), new\ MyFitness$
     $Function());$
  5. $public\ MyFitnessFunction()\ super(false);$
  6. $swarm.initialization();$

4. Update Specifications

- Scripting language - The only codes to update solutions is
  $Update(inertia[const\ 0.4], c1[const\ 2],$
  $c2[const\ 2], MaxP\ 10.0, MinP\ -5.0, MaxV\ 10.0, MinV\ 5.0);$
- main JAVA - Some of the relevant codes are:
  1. $swarm.setInertia(0.9);$
  2. $swarm.setGlobalIncrement(2.0);$
  3. $swarm.setParticleIncrement(2.0);$
  4. $swarm.setMaxPosition(10);$
  5. $swarm.setMinPosition(-5);$
  6. $swarm.setMaxMinVelocity(10);$
  7. $swarm.evaluate();$
  8. $for(intj = 0; j < numof particle; j + +)$
  9. $swarm.update();$

5. Crossover Specifications

- Scripting language - The only statement for crossover specifications is:
  $Crossover(Crate[const\ 0.8], Coperation[pbest], Soperation[rouletewheel]);$

- main JAVA - The most relevant codes are:
  1. *Crossover crossover*;
  2. *Particle particle1, particle2, Offstring*;
  3. *selection = newSelection(swarm)*;
  4. *particle1 = selection.rouletewheel()*;
  5. *particle1 = selection.rouletewheel()*;
  6. *crossover = new pbestcrossover(particle1, particle2)*;
  7. *doublecprob = crossover.probability(0.2)*;
  8. *Offstring = crossover.crossoverallposition(cprob)*;

6. **Mutation Specifications**
   - Scripting language - The codes for mutation specifications can be written as:
     Mutation(Mrate[const 0.25], Moperation[Gaussian]);
   - main JAVA - The codes can be written as:
     1. *Mutator mutator*;
     2. *mutator = newGaussianmutator(swarm)*;
     3. *double x = mutator.probability(swarm, 0.25)*;
     4. *mutator.mutatorallposition(swarm, x)*;

There seems to be no formal method or formula has been established for measuring conciseness. In this work the conciseness is simply defined as the following equation.

$$C = \sum_{task=1}^{n} \frac{1}{h} \tag{1}$$

where C is the total conciseness of all tasks described above and h is the total number of non-space characters exist in the codes. The following Table 5 presents the calculation results.

Table 5. Language conciseness

Specification task	Scripting language	Main JAVA
Program	0.2000	0.0100
Experiment	0.0200	0.0021
General	0.0204	0.0046
Update	0.0120	0.0044
Crossover	0.0143	0.0034
Mutation	0.0208	0.0080

The total conciseness C of the scripting language and main JAVA is 0.29 and 0.03 respectively. This measurement indicates that the scripting language has better conciseness than the main JAVA codes.

4.5   Performance Test

From the performance aspect, the results of LLH algorithms in a different set of experiments have also revealed that the software framework with the scripting language is able to generate acceptable results for all the tested functions. As presented in the following Fig. 2, most LLH algorithms largely with *SGMutation*, produce very small range of mean best fitness (between $1.0E-52$ to $1.0E-01$) than the single PSO (between $1.0E-8$ to more than $1.0E+00$). The results reveal that the hybridization mechanisms used by the reusable software are effective and reliable.

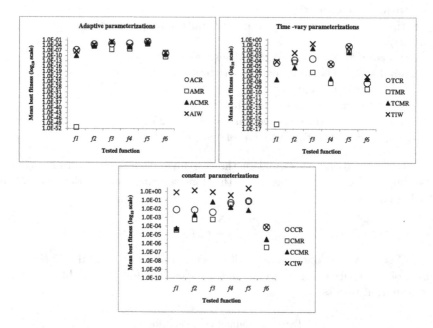

Fig. 2. Comparison mean best fitness between LLHs (ACR, AMR, ACMR, TCR, TMR, TCMR, CCR, CMR, CCMR) and Single PSO (AIW, TIW, CIW)

5   Conclusions

This work is an exposition of LLH for meta-heuristics, its associated conceptual and execution models through scripting language programming platform. Any works on continuous optimization such as experimental analysis, parameter tuning and control, applications development can all benefit from the proposed scripting language. The language can reduce the effort required from both the researcher and those who later make use of that research. At present, the scripting language supports two well-known meta-heuristics to be hybridized namely PSO and GA. Besides the easiness and conciseness aspects, the future evaluation of the scripting language can be conducted on the flexibility programming.

References

1. Alba, E., et al.: MALLBA: a library of skeletons for combinatorial optimisation. In: Monien, B., Feldmann, R.L. (eds.) Euro-Par 2002. LNCS, vol. 2400, pp. 927–932. Springer, Heidelberg (2002)
2. Alireza, A.: PSO with adaptive mutation and inertia weight and its application in parameter estimation of dynamic systems. Acta Automatica Sin. **37**(5), 541–549 (2011)
3. Arenas, M.G., Dolin, N., Marelo, J.J., Castillo, P.A., de Viana, I.F., Schonauer, M.: JEO: JAVA evolving objects. In: The Genetic and Evolutionary Computation Conference (GECCO) (2002)
4. Blum, C., Roli, A.: Hybrid metaheuristics: an introduction. In: Blum, C., Aguilera, M.J.B., Roli, A., Sampels, M. (eds.) Hybrid Metaheuristics. SCI, vol. 114, pp. 1–30. Springer, Heidelberg (2008)
5. Cahon, S., Melab, N., Talbi, E.: ParadisEO: a framework for the reusable design of parallel and distributed metaheuristics. J. Heuristics - Spec. Issue New Adv. Parallel Meta-Heuristics Complex Probl. **10**, 357–380 (2004)
6. Chen, S.: Particle swarm optimization with pbest crossover. In: 2012 IEEE Congress on Evolutionary Computation, pp. 1–6, June 2012
7. Collet, P., Lutton, E., Schoenauer, M., Louchet, J.: Take it EASEA. In: Schoenauer, M., Deb, K., Rudolph, G., Yao, X., Lutton, E., Merelo, J., Schwefel, H.P. (eds.) PPSN VI. LNCS, vol. 1917, pp. 891–901. Springer, Heidelberg (2000)
8. Dower, S.: Disambiguating evolutionary algorithms: composition and communication with ESDL. Ph.d. thesis, University of Swinburne (2011)
9. Dower, S., Woodward, C.J.: ESDL: a simple description language for population-based evolutionary computation. In: Proceedings of the 13th Annual Conference on Genetic and Evolutionary Computation (GECCO 2011), pp. 1045–1052 (2011)
10. Dubreuil, M., Parizeau, M.: Distributed BEAGLE: an environment for parallel and distributed evolutionary computations. In: 17th Annual International Symposum on High Performance Computing Systems and Applications (2003)
11. Emmerich, M., Hosenberg, R.: TEA: a C++ library for the design of evolutionary algorithms. Technical report (2001)
12. Escuela, G., Cardinale, Y., Gonzalez, J.: A java-based distributed genetic algorithm framework. In: Proceedings of the 19th IEEE International Conference on Tools with Artificial Intelligence, ICTAI 2007, vol. 1, pp. 437–441 (2007)
13. Feng-jie, S., Ye, T.: Transmission line image segmentation based GA and PSO hybrid algorithm. In: 2010 International Conference on Computational and Information Sciences (ICCIS), pp. 677–680, December 2010
14. Fink, A., Voß, S.: Hotframe: a heuristic optimization framework. In: Voß, S., Woodruff, D.L. (eds.) Optimization Software Class Libraries. Operations Research/Computer Science Interfaces Series, vol. 18, pp. 81–154. Springer, US (2002)
15. Gagné, C., Parizeau, M.: Genericity in evolutionary computation software tools: principles and case-study. Int. J. Artif. Intell. Tools **15**(02), 173–194 (2006)
16. Gaspero, L.D., Schaerf, A.: EASYLOCAL++: an object-oriented framework for flexible design of local search algorithms. Softw. -Pract. Experience **33**, 733–765 (2003)
17. Higashi, N., Iba, H.: Particle swarm optimization with gaussian mutation. In: IEEE Swarm Intelligence Symposium, pp. 72–79 (2003)
18. Hvass Pedersen, M.E.: SwarmOps for Java. Technical report, June 2011

19. Lau, H.C., Wan, W.C., Halim, S., Toh, K.: A software framework for fast prototyping of meta-heuristics hybridization. Int. Trans. Oper. Res. **14**(2), 123–141 (2007)
20. Lukasiewycz, M., Glaß, M., Reimann, F., Teich, J.: Opt4J - A modular framework for meta-heuristic optimization. In: Proceedings of the Genetic and Evolutionary Computing Conference (GECCO 2011), Dublin, Ireland, pp. 1723–1730, 12–16 July 2011
21. Luke, S.: The ECJ Owners Manual, 21st edn. Department of Computer Science, George Mason University, May 2013
22. Mahmoodabadi, M.J., Salahshoor Mottaghi, Z., Bagheri, A.: Hepso: high exploration particle swarm optimization. Inf. Sci. **273**, 101–111 (2014)
23. Martínez-Soto, R., Castillo, O., Aguilar, L.T., Rodriguez, A.: A hybrid optimization method with pso and ga to automatically design type-1 and type-2 fuzzy logic controllers. Int. J. Mach. Learn. Cyber. **6**, 175–196 (2013)
24. Pabl, C.: JSwarm-PSO. http://jswarm-pso.sourceforge.net/
25. Pan, I., Das, S.: Design of hybrid regrouping PSO GA based sub-optimal networked control system with random packet losses. Memetic Comput. **5**(2), 141–153 (2013)
26. Parejo, J.A., Ruiz-Cortés, A., Lozano, S., Fernandez, P.: Metaheuristic optimization frameworks: a survey and benchmarking. Soft Comput. **16**(3), 527–561 (2012)
27. Raidl, G.R., Puchinger, J., Blum, C.: Metaheuristic hybrids. In: Pardalos, M., Panos, H., Van, P., Milano, M. (eds.) Handbook of Metaheuristics, vol. 45, pp. 305–335. Springer, New York (2010)
28. Raidl, G.R., Puchinger, J.: Combining (integer) linear programming techniques and metaheuristics for combinatorial optimization. In: Blum, C., Aguilera, M.J.B., Roli, A., Sampels, M. (eds.) Hybrid Metaheuristics. SCI, vol. 114, pp. 31–62. Springer, Heidelberg (2008)
29. Dorne, R., Voudouris, C.: HSF: The iOpt's framework to easily design metaheuristic methods. In: Dorne, R., Voudouris, C. (eds.) Metaheuristics: Computer Decision-Making. Applied Optimization, vol. 86, pp. 237–256. Springer, US (2004)
30. Talbi, E.G.: Metaheuristics: From Design to Implementation. Wiley, New York (2009)
31. Thangaraj, R., Pant, M., Abraham, A., Badr, Y.: Hybrid evolutionary algorithm for solving global optimization problems. In: Corchado, E., Wu, X., Oja, E., Herrero, Á., Baruque, B. (eds.) HAIS 2009. LNCS, vol. 5572, pp. 310–318. Springer, Heidelberg (2009)
32. Veenhuis, C., Köppen, M.: XML based modelling of soft computing methods. In: Benötez, J., Cordón, O., Hoffmann, F., Roy, R. (eds.) Advances in Soft Computing, pp. 149–158. Springer, London (2003)
33. Ventura, S., Romero, C., Zafra, A., Delgado, J.A., Hervás, C.: JCLEC: a Java framework for evolutionary computation. Soft Computing - A Fusion of Foundations, Methodologies and Applications **12**, 381–394 (2008)
34. Wagner, S., Affenzeller, M.: The Heuristiclab optimization Environment (2004)
35. Wall, M.: GAlib: A C++ Library OF Genetic Algorithm Components. MIT, Cambridge (1996)
36. Zhang, H.: A new method of cooperative pso: multiple particle swarm optimizers with inertia weight with diversive curiosity. In: Ao, S.I., Castillo, O., Huang, X. (eds.) Intelligent Control and Innovative Computing. LNEE, vol. 110, pp. 149–162. Springer, US (2012)

A Framework for a Decision Tree Learning Algorithm with K-NN

Masaki Kurematsu[✉], Jun Hakura, and Hamido Fujita

Faculty of Software and Information, Iwate Prefectual University,
Sugo, 152-52, Takizawa, Iwate 020-0611, Japan
{kure,hakura,issam}@iwate-pu.ac.jp

Abstract. In this paper, we proposed a modified decision tree learning algorithm. We tried to improve the conventional decision tree learning algorithm. There are some approaches to do it. These methods have a modified learning phase and a decision tree made by them includes some new attributes and/or class label gotten by modified process. As a result, It is possible that exists modified decision tree learning algorithm degrade of the comprehensibility of a decision tree. So we focus on the prediction phase and modified it. Our proposed approach makes a binary decision tree based on *ID3*, which is one of well-known conventional decision tree learning algorithms and predicts the class label of new data items based on *K-NN* instead of the algorithm used in *ID3* and most of the conventional decision tree learning algorithm. Most of the conventional decision tree learning algorithms predicts a class label based on the ratio of class labels in a leaf node. They select the class label which has the highest proportion of the leaf node. However, when it is not easy to classify dataset according to class labels, leaf nodes includes a lot of data items and class labels. It causes to decrease the accuracy rate. It is difficult to prepare good training dataset. So we predict a class label from k nearest neighbor data items selected by *K-NN* in a leaf node. We implemented three programs. First program is based on our proposed approach. Second program is based on the conventional decision tree learning algorithms and third program is based on *K-NN*. In order to evaluate our approach, we compared these programs using a part of open datasets from UCL learning repository. Experimental result shows our approach is better than others.

Keywords: Decision tree learning algorithm · K-NN · ID3 · Min-max normalization · z-score standardization · The machine learning repository

1 Introduction

A decision tree learning algorithm [1] is one of well-known supervised machine learning algorithms. We use this algorithm to make a decision tree from the transaction dataset and predict a class label of the new data item using the decision tree. A decision tree shows the set of classification rules which show how to decide a class label of each data item based on attribute values. Though there are some statistical methods or machine learning algorithms to make classifiers from dataset, for example, SVM (support vector machine [2]), ANN (Artificial Neural networks [3]), analysts and

© Springer International Publishing Switzerland 2015
H. Fujita and A. Selamat (Eds.): SoMeT 2014, CCIS 513, pp. 39–51, 2015.
DOI: 10.1007/978-3-319-17530-0_4

researchers use this algorithm to make rules from dataset and predict a class of a new data item. One of reasons for using this algorithm is that it is easy to understand a decision tree made by this algorithm. The other reason is that there are some tools based on this algorithm, for example, Weka [4], R [5] and SPSS [6]. So this algorithm is used in many research filed, such as marketing, psychology and medical [7, 8].

A decision tree is considered to be appropriate if the tree can classify the unlabeled data items accurately and the size of the tree is small. We need good training dataset in order to make an appropriate decision tree because the performance of a decision tree depends on training dataset. However, it is not easy to prepare good training dataset in advance. So we need to improve a decision tree learning algorithm to manage the impact of the training dataset. There are some researches to improve a decision tree learning algorithm. There are two big streams, one is to make a multitude of trees and the other is to preprocess dataset.

First approach makes some difference decision trees and predicts using them. Random Forest [9] is one well-known method in first approach. Random forests are an ensemble learning method for classification that operate by constructing a multitude of decision trees at training time and outputting the class that is the mode of the classes output by individual trees. The training algorithm for random forests repeatedly selects a random sample with replacement of the training dataset and makes a decision tree for each sample. After training, predictions for unseen samples can be made by averaging the predictions from all the individual regression trees. We tried to make decision trees for each class label [10]. Before making a decision tree, we make the dataset for each class label. There are two class labels in each dataset. One class label shows the target class label and the other class label shows remaining class labels. We make a decision tree from each dataset. We predict a class label of the new data item by these decision trees and select the class label which has the maximum predict score.

Second approach adds extra information to dataset before learning. For example, Treabe et al. proposed a novel approach that the knowledge on attributes relevant to the class is extracted as association rules from the training data [11]. The new attributes and the values are generated from the association rules among the originally given attributes. They elaborate on the method and investigate its feature. The effectiveness of their approach is demonstrated through some experiments. Liang focused on the current automotive maintenance industry and combining K-means method and decision tree theory to analyze customer value and thus promote customer value [12]. This investigation first applies the K-means method to establish a customer value analysis model for analyzing customer value. By the results of the K-means method, the customers are divided into high, middle and low value groups. Moreover, further analysis is conducted for clustering variables using the LSD and Turkey HSD tests. Subsequently, decision tree theory is utilized to mine the characteristics of each customer segment. Gaddam et al. presented "K-Means + ID3," a method to cascade k-Means clustering and the ID3 decision tree learning methods for classifying anomalous and normal activities in a computer network, an active electronic circuit, and a mechanical mass-beam system [13]. The K-Means clustering method partitions the training instances into k clusters using Euclidean distance similarity. On each cluster, representing a density region of normal or anomaly instances, they build an ID3 decision tree. The decision tree on each cluster refines the decision boundaries by learning the subgroups within the cluster. To obtain a final decision on classification, the decisions of the *K-Means* and ID3 methods are combined using two rules: the Nearest-neighbor rule and the Nearest-consensus rule. We also proposed modified decision tree learning algorithms [13, 14]. Our proposed approach classified given dataset by a conventional decision tree learning algorithm and cluster analysis. Our proposed approach selected these algorithms according to information gain.

Though there are some approaches to try to improve a decision tree learning algorithm, they have advantage and disadvantage. One of big disadvantage is that these algorithms make the comprehensibility of a decision tree worse. Some algorithms use additional attributes made by them. Users don't know these additional attributes. So it becomes difficult for users to understand these decision trees. Other algorithms make multiple decision trees. That is, users have to understand more than one decision tree. Understanding multiple decision trees need more time than understanding a decision tree. So we should continue to improve a decision tree learning algorithm.

On the other hand, the number of available data increases recently. In addition to, the size of data and the dimension of data increase. Recently, we call these huge data as "Big Data" and we have to operate big data. Decision tree learning algorithm is one of the well-known methods to do. However, the size of a decision tree made from big data because big data has the big dimensions. And the comprehensibility of the decision tree becomes worse. So we have to control the size of a decision tree when we make it from big data.

In this paper, we propose a new approach to improve a decision tree learning algorithm. A decision tree learning algorithm consists of a learning phase and a prediction phase. Exists approaches tried to modify a learning phase. On the other hand, we focus on a prediction phase in this paper. We propose a framework for integrating a decision tree learning and *K-Nearest Neighbors* algorithm (*K-NN* for short) [16] in order to improve the accuracy rate of this algorithm. The framework makes a decision tree using a conventional decision tree algorithm in a learning phase. In s prediction phase, it selects k nearest neighbor data items in a leaf node using *K-NN* and predicts the class label form them.

Next section describes our approach in detail. Section 3 describes the experiment for evaluation our research. We also describe discussion about our approach according to the experimental result and future works in this section. Finally, we conclude this paper in Sect. 4.

2 A Framework for a Decision Tree Learning Algorithm with K-NN

2.1 Overview of Our Approach

A decision tree learning algorithm consists of a learning phase and a prediction phase. In order to improve the accuracy rate of this algorithm, researches tried to modify a learning phase in previous researches. They added extra information training dataset or make multi decision trees. However, a decision tree made by these approaches has modified attributes which doesn't appear in the original data item. It is not easy for user to understand these new attributes. It is possible to degrade the comprehensibility of a decision tree. That is, one of the strength points of a decision tree learning algorithm may become weak. So we focus on the prediction phase. We don't change the learning phase, so we think we can keep the comprehensibility of a decision tree. In the prediction phase, a decision tree learning algorithm identifies attributes of a new unlabeled data item to every paths of a decision tree made in a learning phase and finds the leaf node. Next, it returns the class label with the prediction score. The prediction score means the confidence of prediction about the class label. A decision tree learning algorithm calculates this value based on the ratio of class labels in the leaf node. If the border of class labels is not clear, data items which have similar attribute values and different class label are appropriated the leaf node. It causes to decrease the accuracy rate of the algorithm. So we focus and modify the prediction phase.

Our idea is simple. We try to predict the class label of a new data items from a leaf node based on k nearest data items instead of all data items in the leaf node. In order to select k nearest data items, we use K-NN algorithm. We think that our approach can reduce some noise data items in the leaf node and improve the accuracy rate.

The strength point of this approach is as the following. One is that improving the accuracy rate of a decision tree learning algorithm with maintenance of the comprehensibility of a decision tree. This approach does not change training dataset and attributes. A decision tree made by our approach is same as one made by a conventional algorithm. So the comprehensibility of the decision tree made by our approach is same as the comprehensibility of the decision tree made by a conventional approach. The other point is that the computational effort of this approach is smaller than the computational effort of K-NN. Of course, we need the computational effort for making a decision tree. However, we think the difference of the computational effort becomes small so that there is much quantity of new data items. Next, we show the proposed our approach in detail.

2.2   Making a Decision Tree by the Conventional Decision Tree Learning Algorithm

Our approach makes a binary decision tree from training dataset based on the *ID3* algorithm [17]. The *ID3* (Iterative Dichotomiser 3) algorithm is an algorithm invented by Ross Quinlan. This algorithm is one of well-known algorithm to make a decision tree from a dataset. It is typically used in the machine learning and natural language processing domains. Our approach makes a binary decision tree by *ID3* based algorithm in this section. Before explanation our approach, we define some variables. D shows a training dataset. The training dataset D has n data items. We show each data item as d_i where i shows the index of data item, i.e., d_i shows i-th data item in D. Each data item consist of m attributes and one class label. We show j-th attributes as $atr_{i,j}$ and the class label as c_i. And we show k-th test data item as t_k. t_k has m attributes and one class label. That is, $D = \{d_1, d_2, ..., d_n\}$, $d_i = \{atr_{i,1}, atr_{i,2}, ..., atr_{i,m}, c_i\}$ and $t_k = \{atr_{k,1}, atr_{k,2}, ..., atr_{k,m}\}$. We explain our algorithm using these variables.

In the first step, our approach begins with the original training dataset D as the root node. Next, our approach iterates through every attribute of the dataset D and calculates the information gain $IG(atr_{i,j})$ by the Eq. (1a) and (1b).

$$IG(atr_{i,j}) = H0 - \sum_{l=1}^{c} \frac{|\{d_x|c_x = c_l\}|}{|D|} \left(\sum_{x=1}^{n} -\frac{|\{d_x|atr_{x,j} < atr_{i,j}\}|}{|\{d_x|c_x = c_l\}|} \log_c \frac{|\{d_x|atr_{x,j} < atr_{i,j}\}|}{|\{d_x|c_x = c_l\}|} \right.$$

$$\left. + \sum_{x=1}^{n} -\frac{|\{d_x|atr_{x,j} \geq atr_{i,j}\}|}{|\{d_x|c_x = c_l\}|} \log_c \frac{|\{d_x|atr_{x,j} \geq atr_{i,j}\}|}{|\{d_x|c_x = c_l\}|} \right)$$

$$\tag{1a}$$

$$H0 = -\sum_{l=1}^{c} \frac{|\{d_l|c_l = c\}|}{|D|} \log_c \frac{|\{d_l|c_l = c\}|}{|D|} \tag{1b}$$

After that, our approach selects the attribute which has the largest information gain value and splits the given dataset D by the selected attribute (e.g. $atr_{x,j} < atr_{i,j}$, $atr_{i,j} \leq atr_{x,j}$). Our approach produces subsets of the given dataset. This approach continues to recurse on each subset until the entropy value of the given dataset is more than the threshold given by a user. We calculate the entropy value of the given dataset by the Eq. (1b). Though *ID3* makes a decision tree whose degree is more than one and use each attributes once to make it, our approach makes a binary decision tree by using each attribute more than once.

2.3 Predicting a Class Label by a Binary Decision Tree

We predict a class label of new unlabeled data item using the binary decision tree made from the training dataset. Next, we describe how to predict a class label.

At first, our approach applies every paths of the decision tree to the attributes of the new unlabeled data item and identifies one leaf node which is satisfied by the new data item.

Next, our approach extracts k nearest neighbors of the new data item in the leaf node instead of all data items. This is the different point between our approach and conventional decision tree algorithms. Conventional decision tree algorithms select the class label which has the highest proportion of the leaf node and return the class label with the prediction score. These algorithms divide the number of the class label in the leaf node by the number of all data items in the leaf node to get the prediction score. However, our approach select the class label which has the highest proportion of k nearest neighbors of the new data item in the leaf node and divides the number of the class label in the leaf node by the number of k nearest neighbors in the leaf node to get the prediction score. In order to select k nearest neighbors, we use *K-NN* algorithm. This algorithm is one of well-known optimization problem for finding closest points. At first, it calculates the distance between the new data item and each data item in given dataset. It identifies the top k nearest neighbors based on the distance and decides the class label which has the highest proportion of k nearest neighbors. Our approach also calculates the distance between the new data item and each data item in given dataset. We use Euclidean distance as the distance between data items. We get this distance by Eq. (2).

$$dis(t_k, d_i) = \sqrt{\sum_{j=1}^{m} (atr_{k,j} - atr_{i,j})^2} \tag{2}$$

It identifies the top k nearest neighbors based on the distance. In this approach, we define k is same as the number of class labels in advance. However, when it cannot identifies the top k nearest neighbors, for example, there are more than k nearest neighbors which have the shortest distance, it changes k to the number of all nearest neighbors. After that, it calculates the prediction score of each class label. It divides the number of data items which have the class label by the number of all data items in the leaf node to get the prediction score. Finally, it returns each class label with the prediction score.

The distance among each data item are influenced by the difference among the range of attributes. If the difference of the range is big, the distance tends to depend on a few attributes. In order to avoid this effect, we normalize attribute values in advance. In our approach, we try to normalize attribute values using the min-max normalize and z-score standardization. Equation (3) shows how to get the min-max normalization,

$$atr_{k,j}^{+} = \frac{atr_{k,j} - \min\{atr_{1,j}, \cdots, atr_{n,j}\}}{\max\{atr_{1,j}, \cdots, atr_{n,j}\} - \min\{atr_{1,j}, \cdots, atr_{n,j}\}} \tag{3}$$

where $min\{atr_{1,1}, ..., atr_{n,j}\}$ shows the minimum value of $\{atr_{1,1}, ..., atr_{n,j}\}$ and $max\{atr_{1,1}, ..., atr_{n,j}\}$ shows the maximum value of $\{atr_{1,1}, ..., atr_{n,j}\}$.

Equation (4) shows how to get the z-score standardization

$$atr_{k,j}^{++} = \frac{atr_{k,j} - mean\{atr_{1,j}, \cdots, atr_{n,j}\}}{SD\{atr_{1,j}, \cdots, atr_{n,j}\}} \tag{4}$$

where $mean\{atr_{1,1}, ..., atr_{n,j}\}$ shows the mean value of $\{atr_{1,1}, ..., atr_{n,j}\}$ and SD$\{atr_{1,1}, ..., atr_{n,j}\}$ shows the standard deviation.

3 Experiments

3.1 Overview of Our Experiments

In order to evaluate our approach, we did experiments using open dataset. We will explain the overview of our experiments.

First, we explain about dataset. We use a part of "Wine Quality Dataset" [18] as dataset. We can download this dataset from the machine learning repository in UCI's web site. Each data item has 12 attributes: fixed acidity, volatile acidity, citric acid, residual sugar, chlorides, free sulfur dioxide, total sulfur dioxide, density, pH, sulphates, alcohol and quality. Quality is output variable based on sensory data and other attributes are input variables based on physicochemical tests. Though the quality is between 0 and 10, the quality used in dataset is from 3 to 8, that is, there are 6 class labels. There is bias for the number of class labels. However, there are some real data has the bias of class labels so we don't modify this bias. We use the quality as the class label in this dataset. There are 1599 data items. We select about 80 percent of data items as training dataset randomly and use remain data items as test dataset. We make 5 pair of training dataset and test dataset.

Next, we explain how to evaluate our approach using above-mentioned. In order to validate our approach, we implemented three programs by JAVA programming language. We made first one based on our approach. We call this program as "*ID3K*". Second one is based on a conventional decision tree algorithm. We call this program as "*ID3b*". A binary decision tree made by *ID3b* is same as a decision tree made by *ID3K*. However, *ID3b* program gets the prediction score based on the proportion of the leaf node. We made the third program based on *K-NN*. We call this program as "*Knnb*". *Knnb* divides the number of data items with the target class label in k nearest neighbors by all data items in k nearest neighbors to get the prediction score and returns it. If the number of nearest neighbors is more than k, *Knnb* changes k to the number of all nearest neighbors. We compare the predicate score of the collect class label given each program. If the prediction score given by *ID3K* is better than the prediction score given by other programs, we can say that there is advantage of our approach over the conventional decision tree learning algorithm and *K-NN*. We made 5 pair of training and test dataset, so we get the prediction score from every pairs and compare the mean and the standard deviation of the prediction score. In addition to, we set the threshold for making a decision tree as 0.1, 0.3, 0.5, 0.7 and 0.9. We make 5 types decision trees and compare 3 programs using them.

3.2 The Result of Experiments

Table 1 shows the features of decision trees made in experiments. "Threshold" shows the threshold for making a decision tree. "# of Nodes" shows the number of nodes in a decision tree and nodes include root node, leaf nodes and other nodes. "Depth" means the deepest of the depth in a decision tree and "# of Paths" means the number of paths in it. *ID3K* makes the decision tree from dataset, so the decision tree made from one dataset differs from the decision tree made from other dataset. We made 5 dataset and made a decision tree from each dataset, so "Mean" is the mean value of 5 decision trees and "SD" is the SD value of 5 trees. The smaller the threshold is, the bigger the decision tree is. When the threshold is 1.0, *ID3K* does not make a decision tree.

We show the essence of the result of experiments as Table 2(a), (b) and (c). These tables show the result of *ID3K*, *ID3b* and *Knnb*. Table 2(a) shows the result, when we used original values to predict the class label. Table 2(b) shows the result, when we used min-max normalized values to predict the class label. Table 2(c) shows the result, when we used the z-score standardization to predict the class label.

We will describe each row in each table. "Program" shows the using program name. "Threshold" shows the threshold for making a decision tree. However, *Knnb* does not make a decision tree. So, we don't show any values. The smaller the threshold

Table 1. The outline of the decision trees made by *ID3K* and *ID3b*

Threshold	0.1		0.3		0.5		0.7		0.9	
Criteria	Mean	SD	Mean	SD	Mean	SD	Mean	SD	Mean	SD
# of Nodes	221.60	4.92	154.20	3.43	30.20	2.64	1.00	0.00	1.00	0.00
Depth	18.20	2.04	17.40	1.74	8.80	0.98	1.00	0.00	1.00	0.00
# of Paths	222.60	4.92	155.20	3.43	31.20	2.64	2.00	0.00	2.00	0.00

is, the bigger the decision tree is. "Set 1", "Set 2", "Set 3", "Set 4" and "Set 5" respectively show the mean value of the prediction score calculated from each dataset. "Mean" shows the mean value of the mean of the prediction score. In addition to, we counted up the number of data items which has the collect class label with the more than 0.6 prediction score, in each dataset. "Over 0.6" shows the mean value of this value counted up from each dataset.

We show some values in these tables by the boldface style. They show the maximum value in each row.

Experimental results show that *ID3K* is better than *ID3b* and *Knnb*. The smaller the threshold is, the bigger the mean of the prediction score is and the smaller the difference between the prediction score of *ID3K* and the prediction score of *ID3b*. Experiment results didn't show that the relationship between the prediction score and the threshold change by normalization. There is no big difference between original data and normalized data.

Table 2. (a) The result of *ID3K*, *ID3b* and *Knnb* (original value; not normalized)

Program	ID3K	ID3b	ID3K	ID3b	ID3K	ID3b	ID3K	ID3b	ID3K	ID3b	Knnb
Threshold	0.1	0.1	0.3	0.3	0.5	0.5	0.7	0.7	0.9	0.9	
Set 1	**0.804**	0.775	0.770	0.729	0.617	0.521	0.497	0.415	0.497	0.415	0.463
Set 2	**0.791**	0.755	0.742	0.694	0.597	0.517	0.460	0.401	0.460	0.401	0.456
Set 3	**0.782**	0.762	0.735	0.700	0.626	0.556	0.484	0.427	0.484	0.427	0.462
Set 4	**0.794**	0.773	0.746	0.708	0.617	0.520	0.498	0.416	0.498	0.416	0.477
Set 5	**0.790**	0.767	0.757	0.723	0.604	0.516	0.462	0.412	0.462	0.412	0.463
Mean	**0.792**	0.766	0.750	0.711	0.612	0.526	0.480	0.414	0.480	0.414	0.464
Over 0.6	**79.3%**	73.5%	76.8%	70.7%	59.2%	47.9%	37.0%	12.2%	37.0%	12.2%	33.6%

Table 2. (b) The result of *ID3K*, *ID3b* and *Knnb* (min-max normalization)

Program	ID3K	ID3b	ID3K	ID3b	ID3K	ID3b	ID3K	ID3b	ID3K	ID3b	Knnb
Threshold	0.1	0.1	0.3	0.3	0.5	0.5	0.7	0.7	0.9	0.9	
Set 1	0.772	**0.775**	0.729	0.729	0.580	0.521	0.498	0.415	0.498	0.415	0.508
Set 2	**0.772**	0.755	0.720	0.694	0.581	0.517	0.509	0.401	0.509	0.401	0.495
Set 3	**0.769**	0.762	0.715	0.700	0.617	0.556	0.518	0.427	0.518	0.427	0.510
Set 4	**0.774**	0.773	0.729	0.708	0.601	0.520	0.503	0.416	0.503	0.416	0.511
Set 5	**0.781**	0.767	0.751	0.723	0.602	0.516	0.503	0.412	0.503	0.412	0.507
Mean	**0.774**	0.766	0.729	0.711	0.596	0.526	0.506	0.414	0.506	0.414	0.506
Over 0.6	**75.8%**	73.5%	73.3%	70.7%	54.3%	47.9%	39.0%	12.2%	39.0%	12.2%	39.4%

Table 2. (c) The result of *ID3K*, *ID3b* and *Knnb* (z-score standardization)

Program	ID3K	ID3b	ID3K	ID3b	ID3K	ID3b	ID3K	ID3b	ID3K	ID3b	Knnb
Threshold	0.1	0.1	0.3	0.3	0.5	0.5	0.7	0.7	0.9	0.9	
Set 1	**0.794**	0.775	0.759	0.729	0.600	0.521	0.461	0.415	0.461	0.415	0.435
Set 2	**0.788**	0.755	0.743	0.694	0.593	0.517	0.457	0.401	0.457	0.401	0.435
Set 3	**0.791**	0.762	0.748	0.700	0.635	0.556	0.465	0.427	0.465	0.427	0.446
Set 4	**0.796**	0.773	0.741	0.708	0.597	0.520	0.451	0.416	0.451	0.416	0.442
Set 5	**0.809**	0.767	0.775	0.723	0.618	0.516	0.488	0.412	0.488	0.412	0.476
Mean	**0.796**	0.766	0.753	0.711	0.609	0.526	0.464	0.414	0.464	0.414	0.447
Over 0.6	**79.3%**	73.5%	77.3%	70.7%	58.9%	47.9%	36.9%	12.2%	36.9%	12.2%	33.3%

4 Discussion

According to the experimental results, *ID3K* is better than *ID3b*. The mean of the prediction score by *ID3K* is better than the prediction score by *ID3b* in many cases. So we say predicting a class label from k nearest neighbor data items in a leaf node can improve the conventional decision tree algorithm. Our idea is simple, so we can apply this idea to other decision tree learning algorithms. However, the advantage of *ID3K* became small as the size of a decision tree is big. In order to know this reason and evaluate our approach in detail, we calculated the ratio that *ID3K* improved the prediction score and the ratio that *ID3K* degraded the prediction score. Table 4 shows the result. In this table, "UP" shows the ratio that *ID3K* is better than *ID3b* and "DOWN" shows the ratio that *ID3K* is worse than *ID3b*. The smaller the threshold is, the smaller the ratio that *ID3K* degraded the prediction score. However, the ratio that *ID3K* improved the predict rate is the bigger than other cases. According to these result, *ID3K* run well as the size of a decision tree is small (Table 3).

The experimental results show ID3K improves and degrades the prediction score. So, we should select *ID3K* or *ID3b* based on criteria. In order to find criteria, we calculated the Pearson product-moment correlation coefficient between the number of data items in each leaf nodes and the value that subtracted the prediction score by *ID3b* from the prediction score by *ID3K*. We also calculated the Pearson correlation coefficient between the prediction score by *ID3b* and the value that subtracted the prediction score by *ID3b* from the prediction score by *ID3K*. Table 4 shows these correlation coefficients. These correlation coefficient show the correlation relation between the advantage of *ID3K* and the number of data items is weak. We think the prediction score of ID3 as the ratio of the collect label in a leaf node. So, the correlation relation between the advantage of *ID3K* and the ratio of the collect label is week, too. We cannot use these values as criteria for selecting *ID3K* or *ID3b*.

We used min-max normalization and z-score standardization in experiments. However, the difference of the prediction score using min-max normalization and the prediction score using original values and the difference of the prediction score using z-score standardization and the prediction score using original values are small. So, we cannot say that normalization is good for a decision tree learning algorithm according to experiments.

Table 3. The ratio that *ID3K* increases and decreases the prediction score

Threshold		0.1		0.3		0.5		0.7	
Normalize		UP	DOWN	UP	DOWN	UP	DOWN	UP	DOWN
original	Set1	37.2%	18.2%	50.0%	26.2%	72.0%	25.6%	67.3%	32.7%
	Set2	39.7%	16.0%	55.4%	26.7%	67.8%	31.3%	59.0%	41.0%
	Set3	33.1%	20.3%	51.5%	31.1%	62.6%	36.4%	56.4%	43.6%
	Set4	34.8%	18.4%	54.6%	27.3%	69.3%	29.9%	54.6%	45.4%
	Set5	32.6%	20.0%	48.2%	27.9%	59.7%	38.2%	56.8%	43.2%
	Mean	35.5%	18.6%	51.9%	27.8%	66.3%	32.3%	58.8%	41.2%
min-max	Set1	29.5%	24.4%	39.0%	36.0%	66.7%	30.7%	67.6%	32.4%
	Set2	33.9%	21.8%	49.8%	34.5%	64.5%	34.9%	67.4%	32.6%
	Set3	28.2%	25.9%	41.6%	41.0%	58.7%	40.0%	63.0%	37.0%
	Set4	27.6%	25.3%	48.9%	33.6%	64.4%	34.5%	56.3%	43.7%
	Set5	31.8%	22.1%	47.1%	30.6%	62.9%	35.6%	67.6%	32.4%
	Mean	30.2%	23.9%	45.3%	35.1%	63.4%	35.1%	64.4%	35.6%
z-score	Set1	33.0%	21.7%	47.3%	28.6%	69.0%	28.6%	64.0%	36.0%
	Set2	38.1%	17.9%	56.0%	27.7%	66.8%	32.2%	59.6%	40.4%
	Set3	34.4%	21.0%	51.5%	33.4%	63.9%	35.7%	51.1%	48.9%
	Set4	36.8%	16.7%	53.7%	29.0%	64.7%	34.2%	47.1%	52.9%
	Set5	36.8%	15.0%	49.7%	25.6%	69.7%	27.6%	67.1%	32.9%
	Mean	35.8%	18.5%	51.6%	28.9%	66.8%	31.7%	57.8%	42.2%

Table 4. The pearson product-moment correlation coefficient

	The # of Data Items in a Leaf Node				The Prediction score by *ID3b*			
Threshold	0.1	0.3	0.5	0.7	0.1	0.3	0.5	0.7
original	0.199	0.128	-0.009	-0.019	-0.294	-0.213	-0.095	-0.130
min-max	0.046	0.018	0.019	0.034	-0.179	-0.117	-0.117	-0.219
z-score	0.187	0.132	0.038	0.015	-0.289	-0.213	-0.085	-0.110

We compare *ID3K* and *Knnb* in experiments. The mean of the prediction score given by *ID3K* is better than *Knnb* in all cases according to experimental results. So, we say that *ID3K* was better than *Knnb*. We guess that *ID3K* could reduce the noise data items. We can regard a decision tree made by *ID3K* as the class set of data items. Each class shows most of data items with same class. If a data item A is in a class and a data item B is in other class, the data item A has a low degree of probability for having the same class label as the data item B. When a data item is in a class does not include the target data item, *ID3K* does not calculate the distance between these data items though the data item is near the target data item. *ID3K* can reduce the noise data items from nearest neighbors for the target data items. So, *ID3K* show better performance than *Knnb*. This point says we can use our approach for preprocess to *K-NN* in order to improve it.

We can see the advantage of our approach. Experimental result show *ID3K* based on our approach could increase the prediction score in many new data items. However, there are some new data items which *ID3K* degrades the prediction score. So, we should decide to use our approach based on the feature of a leaf node. One of our future works is to define selecting method of our approach in a decision tree learning algorithm. Therefore, we will analyze these experimental results. We will focus on the number of data items and the ratio of them. We think this problem is same as choosing an appropriate *k* for *K-NN*. We try to use some methods for this problem and modify to a decision tree. Now, we think the modify idea that we change *k* based on the future of a leaf node dynamically. We will implement this idea and validate this idea. The other future work is that we consider improving other decision tree learning algorithm using our approach. It is not difficult to add our approach to other algorithms, because our approach is simple. Our approach has a possibility of improving other algorithms and keeping the comprehensibility of a decision tree. We should validate this point.

5 Conclusion

In this paper, we proposed a modified decision tree learning algorithm. We tried to improve the conventional decision tree learning algorithm. There are some approaches to do it. These methods have a modified learning phase and a decision tree made by them includes some new attributes and/or class label gotten by modified process. As a result, It is possible that exists modified decision tree learning algorithm degrade of the comprehensibility of a decision tree. So we focus on the prediction phase and modified it. Our proposed approach makes a binary decision tree based on *ID3*, which is one of well-known conventional decision tree learning algorithms and predicts the class label of new data items based on *K-NN* instead of the algorithm used in *ID3* and most of the conventional decision tree learning algorithm. Most of the conventional decision tree learning algorithms predicts a class label based on the ratio of class labels in a leaf node. They select the class label which has the highest proportion of the leaf node. However, when it is not easy to classify dataset according to class labels, leaf nodes includes a lot of data items and class labels. It causes to decrease the accuracy rate. It is difficult to prepare good training dataset. So we used *K-NN* to predict a class label from data items in a leaf node. In order to evaluate our approach, we did an experiment using a part of open datasets from UCL learning repository. We compared the program, *ID3K*, based on our proposed approach to the program, *ID3b*, based on the conventional decision tree learning algorithms and the other program, *Knnb*, based on *K-NN* in this experiment. Experimental result shows our approach is better than others. However, there are some cases which *ID3K* degrades the prediction score. So we think our approach has the condition of using. In future, we have to evaluate experimental results and process in detail. We have to ascertain the cause of error. And we consider how to modify our approach to correct errors. We try to use other distance in the prediction phase. We also consider a learning phase. There are some approaches to make a decision tree. We use these approaches with *K-NN*. In addition to, we have to evaluate our new approach using some open datasets.

Acknowledgment. This work was supported by Japan Society for the Promotion of Science, Grant-in-Aid for Scientific Research (C):24500121. We would like to thank Ms. Saori AMA-NUMA who has completed a master's course of the graduate school of Iwate Prefectural University.

References

1. Breiman, L., Friedman, J.H., Olshen, R.A., Stone, C.J.: Classification and Regression Trees. Wadsworth Statistics/Probability. CRC-Press, Boca Raton (1984)
2. Corinna, C., Vladimir, N.V.: Support-Vector Networks. Mach. Learn. **20**(3), 237–297 (1995). Kluwer Academic Publishers, Hingham
3. Rosenblatt, F.: Principles of Neurodynamics: Perceptrons and the Theory of Brain Mechanisms. Spartan Books, Michigan (1962)
4. Weka 3 - Data Mining with Open Source Machine Learning Software in Java. http://www.cs.waikato.ac.nz/ml/weka/. Accessed 12 March 2014
5. The R Project for Statistical Computing. http://www.r-project.org/. Accessed 12 March 2014
6. IBM SPSS software. http://www-01.ibm.com/software/analytics/spss/. Accessed 12 March 2014
7. Bach, M.P., Ćosić, D.: Data mining usage in health care management: literature survey and decision tree application. Medicinski Glas. **5**(1), 57–64 (2008). Bosnia and Herzegovina
8. MacQueen, J. B.: Some methods for classification and analysis of multivariate observations. In: Proceedings of 5th Berkeley Symposium on Mathematical Statistics and Probability, pp. 281–297. University of California Press, Berkley (1967)
9. Breiman, L.: Random forests. Mach. Learn. **45**(1), 5–32 (2001). Kluwer Academic Publishers, Hingham
10. Kurematu, M., Hakura, J., Fujita, H.: An extraction of emotion in human speech using speech synthesize and each classifier for each emotion. WSEAS Trans. Inf. Sci. Appl. **3**(5), 246–251 (2008). World Scientific and Engineering Academy and Society, Greece
11. Terabe, M., Katai, O., Sawaragi, T., Washio, T., Motoda, H.: Attribute generation based on association rules. Knowl. Inf. Syst. **4**(3), 329–349 (2002). Springer, Heidelberg
12. Liang, Y.-H.: Combining the K-means and decision tree methods to promote customer value for the automotive maintenance industry. In: IEEE International Conference on Industrial Engineering and Engineering Management 2009, pp.1337–1341. IEEE, Hong-Kong (2009)
13. Gaddam, S.R., Phoha, V.V., Balagani, K.S.: K-Means+ID3: a novel method for supervised anomaly detection by cascading k-Means clustering and ID3 decision tree learning methods. IEEE Trans. Knowl. Data Eng. **9**(3), 345–354 (2007). IEEE, Washington
14. Kurematsu, M., Amanuma, S., Hakura, J., Fujita, H.: An extraction of emotion in human speech using cluster analysis and a regression tree. In: Proceedings of 10th WSEAS International Conference on Applied Computer Science, pp. 346–350. World Scientific and Engineering Academy and Society, Greece (2010)
15. Amanuma, S., Kurematsu, M., Fujita, H.: An idea of improvement decision tree learning using cluster analysis. In: The 11th International Conference on Software Methodologies, Tools and Techniques, pp.351–360. IOS Press, Amsterdam (2012)

16. Cover, T.M., Hart, P.E.: Nearest neighbor pattern classification. IEEE Trans. Inf. Theory **13** (1), 21–27 (1967). IEEE, Washington
17. Quinlan, J.R.: Induction of decision trees. Mach. Learn. **1**(1), 81–106 (1986). Springer, Heidelberg
18. UCI Machine Learning Repository. http://archive.ics.uci.edu/ml/datasets/. Accessed 29 March 2014

Requirement Engineering, High-Assurance System

Intelligent Content for Product Definition in RFLP Structure

László Horváth[✉] and Imre J. Rudas

John von Neumann Faculty of Informatics, Institute of Applied Mathematics,
Óbuda University, Budapest, Hungary
horvath.laszlo@nik.uni-obuda.hu, rudas@uni-obuda.hu

Abstract. This paper introduces a new contribution to high level abstraction assisted product definition methodology. The aim is enhanced knowledge representation for high level concept driven definition of multidisciplinary industrial products. The background of the proposed method is product definition in the requirement, functional, logical, and physical (RFLP) structure. This is the basis of four level abstraction based new generation of product lifecycle modeling. The problem to be solved by the proposed method is definition of content, control, and connections of R, F, L, and P elements. Usual dialogues at user surfaces require too complex thinking process which motivated research in intelligent assistance of RFLP element generation at the Laboratory of Intelligent Engineering Systems (LIES), Óbuda University. As preliminary result, abstraction on five levels was conceptualized and published at the LIES for product definition six years ago. The emergence of RFLP structures in leading PLM systems motivated refurbishing this abstraction for the new requirements. The result is the initiative, behavior, context, and action (IBCA) structure which organizes multiple human influence request originated content for the generation of RFLP structure elements and connects request definition with RFLP structure element and conventional feature generation through its four levels. Self adaptive product model concept was extended. Consequently, the IBCA structure driven model reconfigures and updates itself for new situations and events. This paper introduces recent relevant results in human controlled product model development. Following this, changes caused by RFLP structure in PLM model, the IBCA structure and its driving connections, and embedding IBCA structure in PLM model are discussed. Integration of IBCA structure in typical PLM model structure and implementation are issues in the rest of the paper.

Keywords: Product lifecycle management (PLM) · Multidisciplinary product definition · Adaptive product model · Generation of RFLP structure and its elements · IBCA structure

1 Introduction

Engineering activities have been integrated for complex products in their lifecycle. The environment which organizes these activities is product lifecycle management (PLM) system. In the background, self adaptive product model was one of the most important innovations in engineering during the first decade of this new century. This new

© Springer International Publishing Switzerland 2015
H. Fujita and A. Selamat (Eds.): SoMeT 2014, CCIS 513, pp. 55–70, 2015.
DOI: 10.1007/978-3-319-17530-0_5

achievement in product modeling required essential development in representation and accumulation of engineering knowledge [1]. It established new generations of comprehensive, integrated, consistent, and knowledge enriched lifecycle management of product information in PLM systems. One of the classical publications [2] defined PLM as a new 21st century paradigm. Currently, PLM systems are main environments for product engineering and rely upon sophisticated product representation.

The above development was grounded by the work for the integrated product information model (IPIM). IPIM based product model was standardized by the International Organization for Standardization (ISO) in the ISO 10303 and was implemented at many leading companies in car and other industries and used engineering area dependently standardized application protocols (AP) [3] during the nineties.

During the early second decade of this century, strong request for multidisciplinary PLM model enforced application of high level abstraction in order to establish unified conceptual model representation for different areas such as mechanical, electrical, electronic, hardware, and software product engineering. Leading PLM systems introduced the requirement, functional, logical, and physical (RFLP) structure of product model [4]. RFLP structure is known methodology in systems engineering (SE). Although advanced dialogues are available for RFLP element definition, the emerged complex decisions and generation of these elements require new dedicated intelligent methodology in the future PLM systems. Because RFLP structure means involving SE in PLM modeling, discussing SE in the context of product representations is actual and important in order to improve decision making [26]. Moreover, interacting systems specific problems will require system of systems engineering (SoSE) methods in PLM modeling in the future. Paper [23] outlines and discusses the problematic of SoSE assisted product modeling as initial result in this area at the Laboratory of Intelligent Engineering Systems (LIES). LIES is dedicated laboratory in development of new concepts and methods for industrially proven recent PLM models. LIES is active within the organization of the Institute of Applied Mathematics, John von Neumann Faculty of Informatics at the Óbuda University, Budapest, Hungary. As laboratory industrial PLM modeling environment for future research, Dassult Systemes V6 PLM product is under installation at the LIES.

This chapter introduces recent results at the LIES in the initiative, behavior, context, and action (IBCA) structure for knowledge driven generation of RFLP elements. Work for IBCA structure was grounded by five leveled content based abstraction. This abstraction was developed and published [6] at the LIES during first decade of this century. Beyond new RFLP structure based model, IBCA structure also supports intelligent generation of conventional feature based PLM model.

After introduction of recent results in human controlled product model development and changes caused by RFLP structure in PLM model, this paper explains the IBCA structure and its driving connections including embedding IBCA structure in PLM model and substructures on IBCA levels. The rest of paper discusses integration of IBCA structure in typical PLM model structure and implementation issues. Terms feature, context, element, and connections are applied in this paper as they were defined for RFLP based PLM modeling [4].

2 Human Controlled Adaptive Product Model Development

Real time and offline communication between engineers who define a product and control product data generation procedures is critical problem area from the beginning of model mediated engineering. After early recognition of this problem and importance of human intent modeling at product definition, authors of this paper published their results in [7, 10]. In [10], it was stated that undefined human source and decision background generated new problems at representation of product information for lifecycle especially where work of extensive engineer group should be organized in a project. Paper [7] analyzed human control on product model information and proposed modeling of human intent and human intent based definition of content which is behind product information.

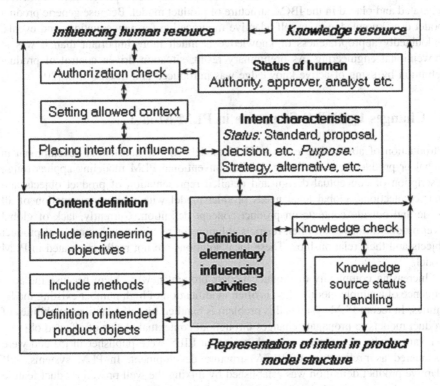

Fig. 1. Influence by human intent and its content

Figure 1 summarizes influence by human intent and its content on product definition as initial concept for IBCA structure based product definition. Resources which have influence on the product definition are communicating humans and knowledge sources. Knowledge sources are applied under human control in accordance with the personal context and mandatory knowledge which are effective in the actual PLM project. Authorization check uses stored information for authority, design engineer, approver, analyst, and other states of influencing humans. When personal context allows it, human place own intent as influence on the product model under construction, supervision, etc. Intent characteristics are locally defined and assist intent placing. Status of intent is standard, proposal, decision, opinion, experience, etc. Purpose of intent at product definition may be strategy, alternative, allowable range of a parameter, etc. Placing of intent is done in the form of elementary influencing activity definition. Content definition serves representation of engineering objectives, engineering methods, and intended product objects in order to answer questions, why, how, and what, respectively. The driving knowledge is checked in the course of knowledge source status handling. Influence of knowledge should be refused when it or its source produced erroneous result formerly, proved inappropriate for the task, or failed at multi aspect verification.

When checks of human authority and knowledge allow it, representation of intent is generated and placed in the IBCA structure of product model. Because generic product model uses knowledge at its self adaptive modification for new situations and events, undoubtedly appropriateness of knowledge is much more important than it was at conventional engineering. As preliminary result, situation driven control of product definition by using of active knowledge was introduced and discussed in [20].

3   Changes by RFLP Structure in PLM Model

Introduction of abstraction levels in PLM model requires substantial development in global or product level modeling. While conventional PLM modeling applies rough description of conceptual design and detailed representation of product objects and their connections, global level needs product model with wide representation of all inside and outside contexts on product concept definition. Currently, lack of global level product information often restricts solution for relative small number of product objects and their relationships. These local solutions are not really integrated in PLM model.

Increasing complexity of product models brought new problem because the consequence of a simple modification is often modification of high number existing model entities. In recent PLM systems this problem is handled by self adaptive capabilities of product models to propagate changes throughout contextual chains of affected objects. Relevant results of a former research project at LIES were publisher in [5] and were considered as preliminary of IBCA structure development. In PLM systems, self adaptive product definition was established by mixing the well proven product feature driven and a new knowledge feature driven product definitions during the first decade of this century. Feature modifies an existing model by contextual connections of its parameters with parameters of affected existing features. The result of mixing was defined as classical product model (CPM) in [6]. CPM concept was extended to representation of human thinking, engineering objectives and influences, definition of behaviors, and change propagation [14] as initial results in global level product modeling at LIES.

Definition process for CPM is explained in Fig. 2. Authorized engineer controls feature object generation procedures through feature definition dialogue. Product and knowledge features are defined then represented and placed in the PLM model. Product feature drives affected product feature (D_{PF}) and knowledge feature (D_{KF}) representations in the CPM models. Affected knowledge feature fires and drives (D_{KF}) relevant product features. In this way, self adaptive CPM model is constantly updated. Lifecycle product definition placed new emphasis on downstream applications of product feature. Paper [19] discusses this problem and proposes extended life cycle definition of feature.

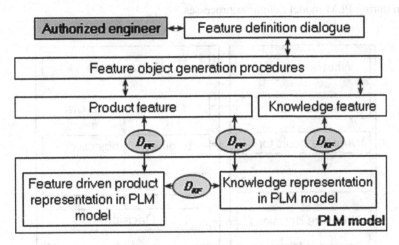

Fig. 2. Classical (CPM) way of product definition

As one of preliminaries of IBCA structure, abstraction in [6, 7] was motivated by unanswerable questions regarding the content which is behind previously defined features. This content is not represented in CPM model. Former decisions in a complex CPM model can not be interpreted in the absence of this content making new decisions very difficult and badly conditioned. The starting concept was identification of these questions and placing the answers on abstraction levels of product model (Fig. 3). Contextual chain of these levels designates the way from human intent to decision on product objects. New knowledge and experience, background definition, product behavior, context and statement, and adaptive action model representations are placed on human intent, meaning of concepts, engineering objectives, contexts, and decisions levels of abstraction, respectively. Usual behavior definition was extended to represent all product characteristics which can be considered as behavior [10]. Representations were connected with CPM model by mapping. Because including RFLP structure in PLM model proved the concept in Fig. 3, this five levels model of abstraction redefined in order to its application at content driven generation of R, L, F, and P elements using IBCA structure. As initial result, coordinated request based product modeling (CRPM) [13] supported collecting, organizing, and coordinating of corporate knowledge.

Integrated methodology for requirements engineering, functional-logical concepts, and physical representation was needed for the realization of the RFLP structure in the leading product V6 PLM of the Dassault Systèmes [4]. The RLFP implementation in [4] facilitates behavior representation in any F and L level elements. In this way, authors of

[8] emphasize that current SE approaches can not consider all required constraints for their integration and simulation in PLM and propose a framework including organized simulations and relevant product behaviors to bridge the gap between model based SE (MBSE) and currently applied PLM modeling. Although it uses more PLM system integrated modeling, objective of the IBCA structure is similar. Similarly, it is emphasized in [9] that SE methodology is required in PLM to achieve successful multidisciplinary collaboration at system level and better understanding of the modeled system during PLM model definition processes.

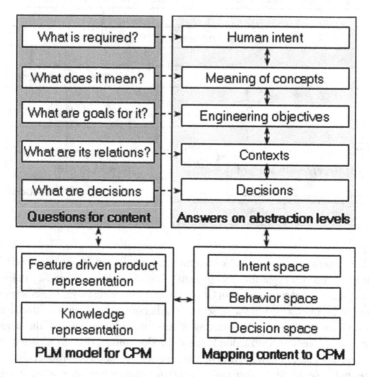

Fig. 3. Abstraction levels as proposed in [6, 7].

RFLP structure includes three new abstraction levels for engineering requirements to be fulfilled (level R), product functions which are selected in order to fulfill these requirements (level F), and logical connections within the PLM model (level L). Product structure objects first appear on the physical level (P) where product and knowledge features are defined. A level is a structure itself. Entities inside level structure are called as elements. Arbitrary elements can be connected in the RFLP structure (Fig. 4) regardless of level. In Fig. 4, elements F_{Xa} and F_{Xb} are connected by the relationship C_{xab} on the level X of the RFLP structure. An element may receive and transmit model data through information (I_{ca} and I_{cb}) and control (C_{ca} and C_{cb}) connections. IBCA structure uses structure and connections similar to as in RFLP structure in order to better integration in PLM model.

In order to prepare work in abstraction, authors of [11] organized and defined main concepts in CPM model based problem solution in engineering. They gave early definition and characterization of virtual engineering space concept towards which engineering was being developed in [12].

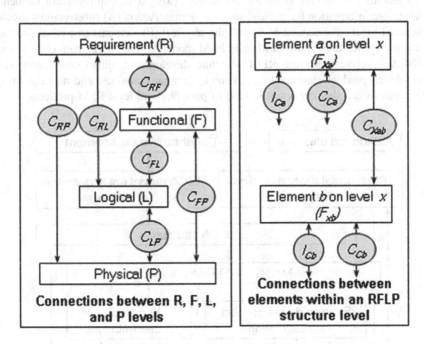

Fig. 4. Connections in the RFLP structure

4 Embedding IBCA Structure in PLM Model

It is important to state that IBCA method was established as contribution to RFLP structure based virtual technology which well proven in leading PLM systems [4]. It represents a new chapter in engineering methodology for sophisticated industrial PLM. Consequently, IBCA is extension and it requires specific model element definition dialogues and representations in PLM system organization. Levels in the IBCA model are intellectual initiative (I) for given product definition activity by engineer, definition of product behaviors (B), organized contextual connections in the PLM model (C), and action for the driving of physical level product representations (A).

Place of IBCA structure in PLM model is explained in Fig. 5. IBCA structure is created in an alternative but integrated way and supports model definition. Engineer communicates using PLM model entity definition dialogue for the definition of RFLP structure elements. On the P level of the RFLP structure, feature driven product representations are defined while knowledge representations also act driving features using same mechanism. On the F and L levels of the RFLP structure, behavior definitions can be placed in elements. Recent trend is integration coordinated simulation and model definition process representations in PLM model.

The IBCA structure builds up by interconnected substructures. In the connection of IBCA and RFLP structure representations (Fig. 6), initiative (I) substructure elements are in connection with requirement (R) structure elements. Behavior (B) substructure elements are connected with function (F) and logical (L) structure elements because these elements can receive behavior definitions. Context (C) substructure elements accommodate information for the logical (L) structure. Action (A) substructures should be prepared for the connection both with the physical (P) elements as well as product and knowledge features in the CPM level PLM model. Although the main objective of the IBCA structure is serving RFLP structure development, direct connection with feature driven product representations, knowledge representations, and manufacturing representations are also important in case of pure physical level PLM products.

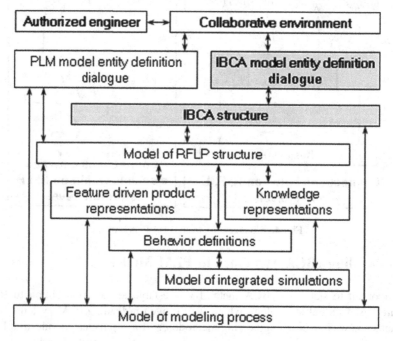

Fig. 5. Place of IBCA structure in PLM model

5 Substructures on IBCA Structure Levels

Because IBCA structure level is not as homogenous as RFLP structure level, IBCA level is divided into thematic substructures. RFLP and IBCA inter level connections are between elements. Driving connection carries contextual definitions (C) in the direction of arrow. For example, FI substructure element is defined in the context of DI substructure element. Connection often represents knowledge.

Initiative (I) substructures are available for the definition of engineer (design) intent. Definition (DI) substructure organizes initiatives. When IBCA structure receives different intents from different engineers for same or overlapped product definition, initiatives should be reviewed and coordinated. Accepted, verified but abandoned so that inactive initiatives are often valuable contributions to IP of company. At the same time, changed circumstances in the relevant situation substructure (SB) may result change inactive status of an abandoned initiative. Initiative process and model by LIES is one of the attempts to organize and utilize human contribution offers.

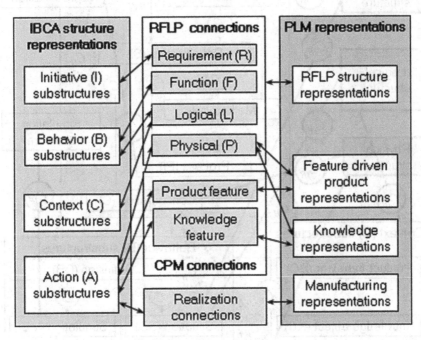

Fig. 6. Connections of IBCA structure with RFLP structure.

Function (FI) substructure elements consider specification (SI) within I substructures. SI element depends on function and includes all object and parameter wishes in intent. Method (MI) element includes knowledge for the definition of relevant product objects. It depends on relevant FI and SI elements. Modeling process (PI) and product configuration (CI) are also defined as initiative. I level IBCA process is active in lifecycle of product completing lifecycle initiatives by always actual decisions.

Behavior (B) substructures are controlled by definition (DB) for behaviors. Actual behaviors are generated in the context of active initiatives. Situations are organized in substructure SB. Additional substructure serves organized simulations (MB) in order to verify and analyze behavior. Execute (EB) substructure elements drive product object definition (OA) and knowledge object (KA) action (A) substructure elements for the control of action execution. Modeling process and simulation structures are defined in the context of PI and MB substructures, respectively. Context (C) substructures include organized contextual definitions for product behaviors (BC), knowledge objects (KC), and product objects (PC). They can be used among others at the construction of the proven object impact graph in PLM systems.

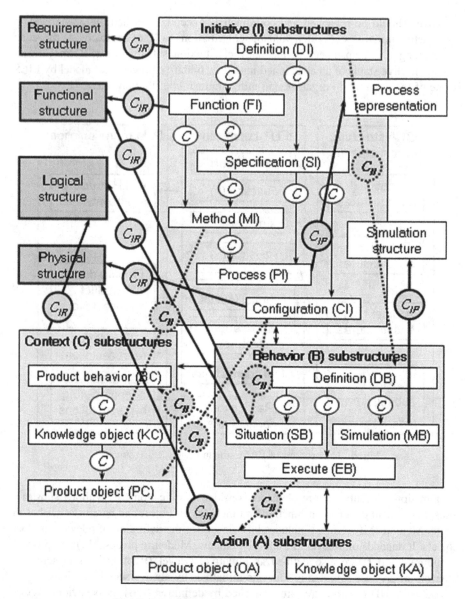

Fig. 7. Main connections of IBCA substructures

Driving contextual connections between IBCA and RFLP elements as well as IBCA elements and model definition processes and simulation structures are denoted by thick lines in Fig. 7. The C_{IR} contextual connection refers to connection between IBCA and RFLP elements.

R structure element is defined in the context of DI substructure elements. F structure element is contextual with FI and SB substructure elements. SB context is included because behavior is defined here. Contextual connection for driving L structure element is composed by information from SB and all relevant C substructure elements. P structure elements are driven by A substructure elements. In the meantime, CI substructure provides information for this connection.

C_{IP} refers to connection between IBCA and modeling process and organized simulation structure representations Connections C_{II} between different level IBCA substructures in Fig. 7 explain the main operating mechanism of the IBCA modeling. In order to generate behaviors from initiatives, DB substructure elements are defined in the context of DI substructure elements. Situation (SB) substructure element is composed by information in elements from all of the initiative substructures. This is not detailed in Fig. 7. BC, KC, and PC context substructure elements are defined in the context of elements in SB, MI and CI substructures, respectively. Action (A) substructure elements are defined in the context of EB substructure elements. Information is provided for the action by substructures in initiative (I) and behavior (B). Connections are also provided between elements within a substructure.

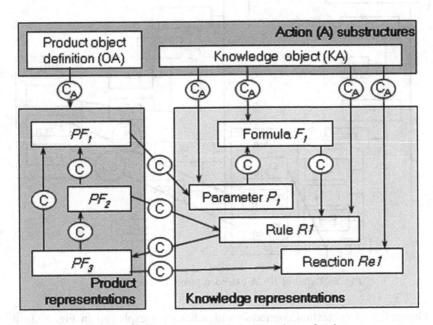

Fig. 8. Physical level contextual connections of actions

Connections in Fig. 7 ensure flexible representation of relationships in PLM model. LIES conceptualized IBCA mechanism similar to mechanism of RFLP structure in possible host PLM systems. For its connections (Fig. 4), RFLP element has port for information (I) to fill content and control of the element (C), and for connection between elements in different levels and substructures (C_{IL}) in the solution which is cited in [4]. Connections within IBCA substructures are similar to connections between RFLP elements in their structure. Element in the structure in a level of RFLP structure may exchange I and C information with an engineer directly. This source is not included in the IBCA structure. Dialogue which is available in PLM system is applied for this communication. For IBCA drive of RFLP element, actual element of RFLP structure exchanges I and C information with relevant element in a substructure on a level of the IBCA structure.

As it was mentioned above, action (A) substructure elements can drive contextual physical level elements or CPM features in the PLM model. Product and knowledge CPM features are defined in the context of action substructure elements. There are two way of this control as it is introduced in Fig. 2. One way is direct definition of product features by elements in product object definition (OA) action substructure. The other way is define knowledge objects (KA) on the A level in accordance with the knowledge features already defined in order to realize knowledge driven generation of product representations.

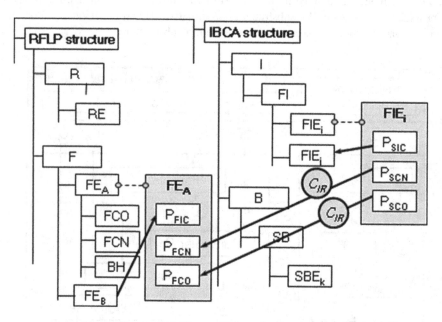

Fig. 9. Detail of IBCA extended product model structure.

Physical level contextual connections of actions are explained in Fig. 8. In this example, product representations include three contextual product features (PF_1-PF_3). Knowledge representations act as features and drive feature driven product representations using contextual connections between product and knowledge feature parameters. Action elements for knowledge object action drive simple engineer understandable knowledge representation features. These features are formula F_1, parameter P_1, rule R_1, and reaction Re_1. At the same time, F_1 is also driven by P_1. For this purpose, F_1 includes P_1 as its variable. Rule R_1 is fired when F_1 or result of its computation change. R_1 also fires when relevant parameter of PF_2 changes. Firing F_1 changes relevant parameter of PF_3. Reaction Re_1 is activated when relevant event is experienced at the definition of PF_3. For example, Re_1 is activated when activation status of PF_3 changes. Related product features, circumstances and events are adaptively modified, accordingly. This may be generation of instance from generic product model using the above self adaptive model characteristics. Relevant model change problem is studied in [24] in case of PLM model which includes intelligent computing related entities. Paper [25] studies human intent and knowledge modeling in order to conclude appropriate method for the management of changes.

Some more relevant publications are cited in the following. As preliminaries of knowledge driving by IBCA structure, knowledge related findings and definitions are explained in book chapter [18]. Knowledge representations may include soft computing [17] where the problem is characterized by tolerance for imprecision and uncertainty. Capabilities of fuzzy logic, genetic algorithm, and artificial neural network for engineering problem solving are discussed in [21]. Authors of [21] conclude high potential of soft computing in engineering. Paper [22] analyzes information aggregation for its application at intelligent engineering problem solving and proposes special procedures in order to identify aggregation function which best fit to field data. As future research, possible role and integration of soft computing in IBCA structure is planned to analyze at the LIES.

6 Integrated Model Structure

Detail of a typical RFLP structure based PLM model structure illustrates integration of IBCA structure in Fig. 9. It must be noted that contextual connections between structure elements are defined in parameter connections of those elements and are not visualized in this product structure. IBCA element communication uses the same mechanism as applied at the RFLP structure (See Fig. 4). RFLP element receives and transmits model data through information (I_c) and control (C_c) connections. In Fig. 9, function level structure element FE_A includes element specific information content (FCO) and special information for behavior (BH). It also includes actual control information (RCN). FE_A has three communication ports. One port is for the inter element connection with the element FE_B (P_{FIC}). Two additional ports serve the driving information from the function substructure level element FIE_i. Driving information is transmitted from the ports P_{SCO} and P_{SCN} for content and control purposes, respectively. Element FE_A receives this content and control at the ports P_{FCO} and P_{FCN}, respectively. Port P_{SIC} serves inter substructure element connection with the element $FIEj$.

Human is placed in a planned context which determines the area of allowed influence. Human decides on request definition directly, or applies or defines expertise as knowledge. New expertise definition may act as part of knowledge resource in future and enhances company intelligent property. In order to achieve initial verification, expertise definition is included in intelligent property in coordination with company experience. Human applies and defines company experience as knowledge resource. Requests are placed in multiple request structure. Initiative (I) substructures in the IBCA structure are active in the context of multiple request structure.

7 Implementation Issues and Future Research

Contexts and aspects of IBCA structure implementation in a host PLM system are discussed above in this paper together with relevant problems. PLM modeling environments are well prepared for their development at industrial environments where local knowledge, expertise, and experience are applied for research level definition of new model objects and related procedures. Experimental IBCA structure is planned to be configured and developed in the organization of appropriate object oriented modeling environment using user configuration and object definition communication surfaces. Where this is not enough, programming through application programming interface (API) will be considered.

Besides sophisticated representation of physical space objects, virtual space is increasingly integrated with physical world in engineering. When physical and virtual spaces are applied in a mixed configuration, we say that it is augmented or extended space. Development of IBCA structure is planned in this direction.

Other important issue is including intelligence in physical spaces by virtual element driven special purpose physical objects. These special virtual elements will be applied in connection with virtual spaces in order to access more virtual capabilities in the future. The above purposes increase significance of physical-virtual and virtual-virtual connections between cooperating systems in a SoSE environment.

Research for implementation of the IBCA structure will require elaboration of experimental connection of IBCA elements with PLM model in a representative industrial PLM system. This is facilitated by recent research purposed functionalities and model representation capabilities of PLM systems. Demand for generic product models increases [15] because this is the only way to cope with requirements such as short innovation cycle and reuse of knowledge in product model. Generic model of flexibly configurable product needs development towards product level application of IBCA structure concept and methodology. Generic PLM model is converted into instances in course of self adaptive session. This method makes repeated work on an earlier solved problem partly even fully avoidable. IBCA methodology and current advanced potential host PLM technology are inherently generic. IBCA structure inherently assists development of complex PLM model structures.

Within the work which is reported in this paper, intelligent modeling principles and methods are conceptualized and developed at LIES as possible contribution to the rapidly developing PLM modeling technology. One of the recent relevant concepts to enhance intelligent company property (IP) within PLM model is smart virtual product definition for virtual prototyping [16]. Activity at LIES is intended to follow this trend in the future.

8 Conclusions

This chapter is about new research results in human influence driven generation of elements on levels of the RFLP structure. Its main contribution is introduction of the IBCA structure and its integration in PLM modeling systems mainly for RFLP element and conventional physical level feature generation. IBCA structure is a contribution to efforts in representation and application of intelligent content at RFLP structure based product definition. Model of human influence at control of the product feature generation is proposed considering its role at development of model representation of engineer intent and its content. IBCA structure was targeted to drive both PFLP structure and based PLM models. IBCA structure levels and elements are integrated in the structure of accommodating PLM system by using of API programmed new objects, processing procedures, and communications. Intelligent engineering aspect of IBCA structure enriches knowledge property of company.

Acknowledgment. The authors gratefully acknowledge the financial support by the Óbuda University research fund.

References

1. Cross, N.: Expertise in design: an overview. Des Stud **25**(5), 427–441 (2004)
2. Stark, J.: Product Lifecycle Management: 21st Century Paradigm for Product Realisation. Birkhäuser, Heidelberg (2004)
3. Jardim-Goncalves, R., Figay, N., Steiger-Garcao, A.: Enabling interoperability of STEP Application Protocols at meta-data and knowledge level. Int J Technol Manage **36**(4), 402–421 (2006)
4. Kleiner, S., Kramer, C.: Model based design with systems engineering based on RFLP Using V6. In: Abramovici, M., Stark, R. (eds.) Smart Product Engineering. LNPE, pp. 93–102. Springer, Heidelberg (2013)
5. Horváth, L., Rudas, I.J.: Human intent description in environment adaptive product model objects. J. Adv. Comput. Intell. Intell. Inform. Tokyo **9**(4), 415–422 (2005)
6. Horváth, L., Rudas, I.J.: A new method for enhanced information content in product model. WSEAS Trans. Inf. Sci. Appl. **5**(3), 277–285 (2008)
7. Horváth, L., Rudas, I.J.: Human intent representation in knowledge intensive product model. J. Comput. **4**(10), 954–961 (2009)
8. Vosgien, T., Nguyen Van, T., Jankovic, M., Eynard, B., Bocquet, J.-C.: Towards simulation-based design in product data management systems. In: Rivest, L., Bouras, A., Louhichi, B. (eds.) PLM 2012. IFIP AICT, vol. 388, pp. 612–622. Springer, Heidelberg (2012)
9. Ambroisine, T.: Mastering increasing product complexity with Collaborative Systems Engineering and PLM. In: Proceedings of the Embedded World Conference, Nürnberg, Germany, pp. 1–8 (2013)
10. Horváth, L., Rudas, I.J.: New approach to knowledge intensive product modeling in PLM systems. In: Proceedings of the IEEE International Conference on Systems, Man and Cybernetics, Montreal, Canada, pp. 668–673 (2007)
11. Horváth, L., Rudas, I.J.: Modeling and Problem Solving Methods for Engineers, p. 330. Elsevier, Academic Press, New York (2004)
12. Horváth, L., Rudas, I.J.: Virtual intelligent space for engineers. In: Proceedings of the 31st Annual Conference of IEEE Industrial Electronics Society, pp. 400–405, Raleigh, USA (2005)
13. Horváth, L., Rudas, I.J.: Requested behavior driven control of product definition. In: Proceedings of the 38th Annual Conference on IEEE Industrial Electronics Society, pp. 2821–2826, Montreal, Canada (2012)

14. Horváth, L., Rudas, I.J.: Decision support at a new global level definition of products in PLM systems. In: Precup, R.-E., Kovács, S., Preitl, S., Petriu, E.M. (eds.) Applied Computational Intelligence in Engineering. TIEI, vol. 1, pp. 301–320. Springer, Heidelberg (2012)

15. Brière-Côté, A., Rivest, L., Desrochers, A.: Adaptive generic product structure modelling for design reuse in engineer-to-order products. Comput. Ind. **61**(1), 53–65 (2010)

16. Choiand, S.H., Cheunga, H.H.: A versatile virtual prototyping system for rapid product development. Comput. Ind. **59**(5), 477–488 (2008)

17. Zadeh, L.A.: Soft computing and fuzzy logic. Software **11**(6), 48–56 (1994)

18. Horváth, L., Rudas., I.J.: Knowledge technology for product modeling. In: Knowledge in Context – Few Faces of thess Knowledge Society, Chapter 5, pp. 113–137. Walters Kluwer (2010)

19. Sy, M., Mascle, C.: Product design analysis based on life cycle features. J. Eng. Des. **22**(6), 387–406 (2011)

20. Horváth, L., Rudas, I.J.: Active knowledge for the situation-driven control of product definition. Acta Polytechnica Hungarica **10**(2), 217–234 (2013)

21. Saridakis, K.M., Dentsoras, A.J.: Soft computing in engineering design. A review. Adv. Eng. Inf. **22**(2), 202–221 (2008)

22. Rudas, I.J., Pap, E., Fodor, J.: Information aggregation in intelligent systems: An application oriented approach. Knowl. Based Syst. **38**, 3–13 (2013)

23. Horváth, L., Rudas, I.J.: Towards interacting systems in product lifecycle management. In: Proceedings of the 8th International Conference on System of Systems Engineering (SoSE), pp. 267–272, Maui, Hawaii, USA (2013)

24. Horváth, L., Rudas, I.J., Bitó, J., Hancke, G.: Intelligent computing for the management of changes in industrial engineering modeling processes. Comput. Inform. **24**, 549–562 (2005)

25. Horváth, L., Rudas, I.J.: Emphases on human intent and knowledge in management of changes at modeling of products. WSEAS Trans. Inf. Sci. Appl. **3**(9), 1731–1738 (2006)

26. Horváth, L., Rudas, I.J.: New product model representation for decisions in engineering systems. In: Proceedings of 2011 International Conference on System Science and Engineering (ICSSE 2011), pp. 546–551, Macau, China (2011)

The Adoptions of USEPs in Identifying Usability Requirements in SSM-Based Framework: A Case Study

Chian Wen Too[✉] and Sa'adah Hassan

Faculty of Computer Science and Information Technology,
Universiti Putra Malaysia, 43400 Serdang, Selangor, Malaysia
cwtoo@yahoo.com, saadah@upm.edu.my

Abstract. Nowadays, user demand for quality software product have been increased and developers have to make sure that their products are able to meet the user's need in order to compete in the market. Usability, which is a kind of software quality, became an important factor to determine the success or failure of a software product in this challenging market. Unfortunately, lack of attention given to usability requirements especially during the early stage of software development process and therefore increase the cost of fixing usability problems and causes the final software products are poor in quality. Therefore, this paper aimed to identify usability requirements at the requirement stage of software development by using the SSM-based analysis framework. We have conducted a case study by applying a usability elicitation pattern, USEPs, into the framework. From the result of our study, it has shown that this pattern is useful to assist the stakeholders in identifying usability requirements along with the functionality of a system. Besides, we have also made some enhancement and extensions to the framework based on our findings from the study.

Keywords: Soft system methodology · Usability elicitation patterns · Usability requirements

1 Introduction

Usability, has been defined by the standard ISO 9241-11, is the "extent to which a product can be used by specified users to achieve specified goals with effectiveness, efficiency and satisfaction in a specified context of use" [1]. It has been pointed as the most important type of Non Functional Requirement (NFR) for guaranteeing software quality [2]. Lack of usability is common causes for failed software products. However from a software perspective, there is still a lack of effort in integrating usability features into software development process [3]. Usability features are often not adequately specified or rarely documented in software requirement specification (SRS). But usability implies significant constraints and requirement on the system architecture. It may arise later in the development cycle and can result in additional functionality to be implemented [4]. As a result, the software architecture and design did not meet the requirements, usability issues only detected during testing and deployment.

© Springer International Publishing Switzerland 2015
H. Fujita and A. Selamat (Eds.): SoMeT 2014, CCIS 513, pp. 71–82, 2015.
DOI: 10.1007/978-3-319-17530-0_6

This is a case study conducted by using an Online Air-Ticketing System to demonstrate the adoption of Usability Elicitation Patterns (USEPs) proposed by N. Juristo et al. in 2007 [5]. The main purpose of this work is to find out the practicability of USEPs in identifying usability features that have major implication for functionalities of a system. Additionally, we aimed to enhance and improve the Soft System Methodology (SSM) based analysis framework [6], especially the activities involved in the 'analysis' phase of the proposed conceptual model to further detail the descriptions of the identified usability features. Thus, this is a continuous effort to explore further and find out a way on how to properly specify and incorporate usability features for particular functionality of a system at the early stage of requirements engineering.

2 Background

2.1 Usability Elicitation Patterns (USEPs)

USEPs, generated from an approach based on developing specific guidelines in the usability features elicitation and specification process was proposed by Juristo [5] in 2007. It was the outcome of source of information from Human Computer Interaction (HCI) literature and has been analyzed from development perspectives. This pattern was refined from the method guidelines and heuristic analysis of the Usability Engineering Lifecycle (UEL) by Nielsen [7]. It consists of a set of issues to be discussed with stakeholders and addresses usability requirement as functional requirement during requirement engineering stage [8].

A list of Functional Usability Features (FUF), produced based on the guidelines provided in the usability literature has been used as a starting point for identifying usability features with an impact on system functionality. Each usability features in the pattern was denoted into different subtypes called usability mechanisms. Each usability mechanisms have been defined with its own elicitation and specification guidelines respectively. Table 1 shows an example of a usability feature, Feedback which denoted into four different subtypes (called usability mechanism): System Status, Interaction, Warning and Long Action Feedback. Table 2 shows part of the details of usability elicitation pattern of a usability mechanism: Long Action Feedback.

2.2 SSM-Based Analysis Framework

SSM, an approach used to clarify the objectives in complex and dynamic problem situations was developed at Lancaster University for more than 30 years [9,10]. It has been applied in software engineering discipline since 1980s and continues to grow until recent studies has been found useful in requirement engineering field. Lopez and Niu [11,12] conducted an exploratory case study to investigate the usefulness of SSM in identifying all the flaws in requirement engineering practices. The result from their study had proved that SSM could uncover a relatively complete set of flaws during the

Table 1. Example of a usability feature: feedback (adapted from USEPs [5])

Usability feature	Usability mechanism	HCI Authors' Label	Goal
Feedback	System Status	Modeless Feedback Area Status Display	To inform users about the internal status of the system
	Interaction	Interaction Feedback Modeless Feedback Area Let Users Know What is Going On	To inform users that the system has registered a users interaction, i.e. that the system has heard users
	Warning	Think Twice Warning	To inform users of any action with important consequences
	Long Action Feedback	Progress Indicator Show Computer is Thinking Time to Do Something Else Progress Modeless Feedback Area Let Users Know What is Going On	To inform users that the system is processing an action that will take some time to complete

practices. Besides that, their suggestions for the improvement changes to an organization's context had also been shown that contributed positively to the organization's requirement engineering activities.

Recently, Hassan. S [6] has explored the potential benefits of SSM in identifying usability requirement at the requirement phase by demonstrating the use of SSM approach in a Mobile Tourist Guide (MTG) application. In their study, they have conducted few main activities as defined in SSM: (a) Analyzing a problem statement, (b) building purposeful activity models based on root definitions and conceptual models, (c) compare the model with problem situation to identify ideas for improvement. From their findings, a SSM-based analysis framework with a conceptual model as stated in Fig. 1 has been proposed. They have elaborated and categorized the activities into two main "sub-processes": **Elicitation** and **Analysis**. The activities involved in the framework were used to identify usability features that complement with functional requirement.

3 Case Study

In our study, we have chosen an Online Air Ticketing System to demonstrate the usage of USEPs to assist software developer in specifying usability features of functionality. Firstly, we have conducted a preliminary analysis and following by applying the USEP patterns.

Table 2. Part of a usability mechanism: long action feedback (adapted from USEPs [5])

IDENTIFICATION
Name: Long Action Feedback
Family: Feedback
PROBLEM
Which information needs to be elicited and specified in order to provide users with information related with the evolution of the requested tasks.
CONTEXT
When a time-consuming process interrupts the UI for longer than two seconds or so on.
SOLUTION

Usability Mechanism Elicitation Guide

HCI Recommendation	Issue to be discussed with stakeholders
1. For on-going processes that take more than 2 seconds: If the process is critical, users should not be allowed to do anything else until this task is completed. If the task is not critical and takes over 5 seconds, users should be allowed to run another operation if they so wish. Users should be informed when the on-going operation finishes.	i. Which tasks are probably to take more than 2 seconds, and which of them are critical.
	ii. How will the user be informed when the process has finished.
2. Show an animated indicator of how much progress has been made. Either verbally or graphically (or both). Tell the user: • What's currently going on • What proportion of the operation is done so far, • How much time remains, and • How to stop it (or cancel it) if the time remaining is longer than 10 seconds	i. How the user will be informed about the progress of the different tasks, which information would be desired for each one.

3.1 Preliminary Analysis

According to the authors [5], the pattern needs to be instantiated in order to suit each particular application context. It is necessary to conduct a preliminary analysis of functional requirement first so that both developers and users can have a common understanding of the system and provide an insight into looking for improvement on how to identify the usability requirements in the functionalities. Another words, it reflects a rich picture of the context development which helps to identify the possible viewpoints that can be used to produce insight into the problem situation [6]. Thus, all the functional requirements (e.g. check flight availability, booking flight, make payment/purchase booking, manage/modify booking) have been identified and listed in advance before we apply the pattern. Figure 2a shows one of the documented functional requirements, Purchase/Payment for booking in Online Air Ticketing System, resulted from the preliminary analysis.

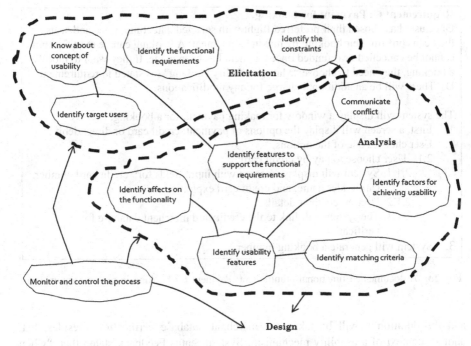

Fig. 1. SSM-based analysis framework model (adapted from [6])

3.2 Apply the USEPs Pattern

After the preliminary analysis, we have adopted the USEPs to our preliminary version of software requirements generated. Firstly, we tried to identify and select all the Usability Mechanisms that are related to our system functionality based on their usability features group and general goal stated. From each of the selected usability mechanisms, we studied their identification part of the pattern to find out all the general information available like their names, family of usability feature it belongs to and etc. Next, we checked the context section of the pattern carefully to find out which mechanisms are suitable to be adopted into the functionality of our system based on the descriptions and examples given.

Furthermore, we worked with the solution part of the pattern. This section is divided into two elements: Usability Mechanism Elicitation Guide and Usability Mechanism specification Guide. In the Usability Mechanism Elicitation Guide section, there are some recommendations from HCI experts (for developer guidance) and a list of issues used by developers to discuss with users. Figure 2b shows one of the expanded requirement descriptions after applying the usability patterns into our preliminary version of functionality, Payment for booking in Fig. 2a. As an example from Table 2, the context of a usability mechanism, Long Action Feedback stated that, "when a time-consuming process interrupts the UI for longer than two seconds or so on." has been applied to one of our system functionality, payment for booking as stated in Fig. 2b to inform user that the selected credit card merchant page is being connected

---

Requirement C: Payment for booking
Once user has chosen their preferred flight with selected date, time, price and seats, they can confirm their booking by making a payment. A booking can be modified but cannot be cancelled or refunded once payment has been made. If they want to modify a booking, they need to choose "Manage/Modify booking" (as stated in requirement D). There will be an additional charge for any modifications.

The system will display a window for making payment for a booking.
1.   First, a screen will display the options of payment: credit card or direct debit
2.   User chooses one of the options.
   2.1. User choose to pay by credit card:
      2.1.1. System will display a screen with input fields for: credit card number, cardholder name, and credit card expiration date.
      2.1.2. User enters their details.
      2.1.3. The system will link to the credit card merchant database for verification.
3.   System will generate a booking number.

Fig. 2a. A documented functional requirement: Payment for booking in preliminary analysis

and the duration it will be taken for merchant database verification. Besides that, another context of a usability mechanism, System Status Feedback stated that, "when changes/failures that are important to the user occur during task execution or because of external resources are not working properly" has also been applied to the payment for booking as stated in Fig. 2b to inform user whether their transaction in payment is successful or not.

In addition, we have also documented our discussions into an issue/functionality/ requirement table as suggested by the authors. Although this step is optional and could be skipped, but we wanted to avoid overlook any details in the problem domain. All the discussed issues, effect of usability features to the system functionality, the existing functional requirements affected or any possible new requirements emerged are documented into the table. Table 3 shows an example of the table for a Usability mechanism, Long Action Feedback which has been applied into our system.

4   Discussion

We have elaborated our findings into different sessions for discussion. In this section, we will discuss about the benefits and limitations in applying USEPs and further discuss about the enhancements of activities to our proposed framework.

4.1   Benefits of Applying USEPs

Based on the results, we can see that USEPs has provided a good guidance to help developers to carry out their requirement analysis task. Compared to Fig. 2a, the

Requirement C: Payment for booking

Once user has chosen their preferred flight with selected date, time, price and seats, they can confirm their booking by making a payment. A booking can be modified but cannot be cancelled or refunded once payment has been made. If they want to modify a booking, they need to choose "Manage/Modify booking" (as stated in requirement D). There will be an additional charge for any modifications.

The system will display a window for making payment for a booking. This window contains the information described below with **three options: back, next and cancel** (Abort Operation, Go Back)

1. First, a screen will display **two options of payment: by *credit card* or *direct debit* (Structured Text Entry)**

2. User chooses one of the 2 options.

    2.1. User choose to pay by credit card:

        2.1.1. System will display a screen with input fields for: credit card number, cardholder name, and credit card expiration date. **(Structured Text Entry)**

        2.1.2. **User enters their details as requested. If user does not complete all the necessary fields, system will redisplays the input fields with the input data and a note highlighted that certain required data is incorrect/ missing (Warning).**

        2.1.3. **Another window will display the information/ details about the booked flights and asking user either to confirm/cancel the operation. This window will then warn the user that once payment has been made, it cannot be cancelled or refunded. (Warning).**

        2.1.4. The system will link to the credit card merchant database for verification. While the selected credit card merchant page is being linked, **system will display a non-obstructive window and an indicator to inform user that the selected credit card merchant page is being connected and the duration it will be taken to finish (Long Action Feedback). If user choose to cancel, system will go back to the screen with options of payment (Abort operation)**

        2.1.5. **At the last stage of purchase/payment process, system will display a window to inform user whether the operation is done or undone. A dialogue box with the necessary information will be displayed obstructively (System Status Feedback).For failure operation, the possibilities are: the booking time limits is exceeded or there was a problem with the credit card merchant server/database connection.**

3. System will display **a confirmed booking status and a booking number will be generated. (System Status Feedback)**

Fig. 2b. The expansion of a functional requirement, Payment for booking after applying USEPs.

requirements documented in Fig. 2b has been expanded and added with more details information describing how to apply and integrate the usability features involved into our system functionality (highlighted in bold face). Each of the functionality in the

Table 3. An issue/functionality/requirement table for a usability mechanism: long action feedback for an online ticketing system

Source: Usability Elicitation Guide	Source: Discussion with stakeholders		Source: Developer	
Issue for Discussion	Is it applicable to the system	Affected Functionalities	Existing Requirements affected	New Requirement
LONG ACTION FEEDBACK				
1.1 Which tasks are probably to take more than 2 seconds, and which of them are critical?	A) When an image to display a seating plan is being loaded B) when the selected credit card merchant page/selected payment bank page is being linked (Critical)	-booking flight -payment for booking	Requirement B, C, D, F	–
1.2 How will the user be informed when the process has finished.	A) An image of the flight seating plan with input options will be displayed B) A confirmed booking status with a booking number will be displayed.	-booking flight -payment for booking	Requirement A, B, C, D, E, F	–
2.1 How the user will be informed about the progress of the different tasks, which information would be desired for each one	A) A non-obstructive window with an indicator will be displaying to inform user that an image is being loaded and the time remaining B) A non-obstructive window with an indicator will be displaying to inform user that the selected credit card merchant page/ selected payment bank's page is being loaded and the time remaining	-booking flight -payment for booking	Requirement B, C, D, F	–

system has been properly specified with its usability feature. This work has eased the following stage of software development activities and prevents the rework to be happened.

Most of the guidelines provided in the pattern are well explained, easy to understand and can be used without the existence of HCI experts. From the economic perspectives, it is cost efficient as many small-to-medium software companies are not affordable to hire HCI experts due to limited budgets. Besides that, this approach also encouraged the involvement of users during the issue discussions session. Users can get the opportunity to explore and understand the usability features of their system in the early stage of development.

In addition, documenting the discussions between stakeholders in an issue/functionality/requirement table as shown in Table 3 can help developers to understand the effect of usability features to the system and identify which requirement will be affected. This concept is similar with the factors and effect concept proposed by [6] in their model where the usability features will be identified by considering on the factors in achieving usability and its effects or benefits on the functionality. This table helps the developers to specify the fit criterion using standardized sentences and using the results of the table to fill in the specification. The dependencies among different functionalities of the system can be explicitly documented in the table. It is very useful especially for those inexperienced developers to do a quantitative analysis to understand the dependencies between other functional requirements and avoid missing out any details in the problem context [8].

4.2   Limitations in USEPs

However, we have found some limitations in this pattern based on our study:

Firstly, it is not so suitable to be used by inexperienced users because it requires the involvement of users to discuss the issues. It seems like their needs would not be captured correctly if they do not have a high level of knowledge or experience to help the developers to find out the correct answers based on the issues discussed.

Secondly, it did not sufficiently take user feedback into consideration as there is lack of iterative design and further participation of users. Although this approach is time efficient as it is only a one time task and did not require users to follow up after the discussion, this will affect the user acceptances especially when come to the later stage of development.

In addition, there is few usability mechanisms from the pattern did not provided with detail information. For instances, Structured Text Entry Mechanism, the issues to be discussed with stakeholders listed in the Usability Feature Configuration Guide are limited with only two issues and it is hard for those developers who are lack of knowledge in HCI to ask the right questions during the elicitation process. Lastly, some of the methods used are hard to be applied into the current software development process where extra efforts are needed for the adoption purposes.

4.3   Proposed Enhancements and Extensions to the SSM-Based Analysis Framework

Based on the result from our case study, it has shown that adopting USEPs at the requirement stage can be a useful way of helping software developer in eliciting and identifying usability features of particular system functionality. Usability patterns are common in HCI community for more than a decade. A catalogue of usability pattern is useful to describe proven and reusable solutions and to support software developer in selecting appropriate usability features of a system. It included the HCI recommendations which provide the rationale as guidance to developers to understand the reason they need to discuss the issues stated in the pattern with users.

As we know, usability which is a kind of non functional requirement (NFR) is hard to specify and characterize compare to functional requirement (FR) [13]. Thus, without using a tool or pattern as guideline especially for developers or users who are lack of knowledge and understanding in usability, it is not an easy task to identify all the important information to specify usability features. Although there are some weaknesses in the pattern as discussed earlier, but this pattern, in overall, is very useful in helping developer to specify usability features to the functional requirements of a system context.

As the result of our findings, we have revised the activities that should be taken in the development process of SSM-based analysis framework [6]. The enhancement that we have made involves the extension to the two main "sub-processes": Elicitation and Analysis in order to identify usability features that support the functional requirements as illustrated in Fig. 1 with the following activities:

1. Elicitation
   (a) Identify the functional requirement and constraints of the system
   (b) Conduct a preliminary analysis to the elicited functional requirements
2. Analysis - use all the input from elicitation process and:
   (c) Apply the USEP patterns to the functional requirements generated from preliminary analysis based on the following steps:
       i. Study the identification part of the pattern to find out all the general information of the available usability features.
       ii. Check the context of the pattern to find out which usability features are suitable to be adopted into the functional requirements.
       iii. Refer to the solution part of the pattern which consists of recommendations from HCI experts and a list of issues used by developers to discuss with users for each usability features.
       iv. Documenting the findings in a table.
       v. Review the table to consider the effect/benefits of particular usability features to the functionality or the entire system to ensure the equation.
   (d) Perform a trade-off analysis of all the features and constraints to avoid any conflict.

5 Conclusions and Future Works

NFR such as performance, security and usability have highly impact on the quality of software product. Empirical reports consistently indicate that improper dealing with NFR leads to project failures, long delays or significant increases in cost [13]. Nowadays, software engineering research community has the awareness that it is important to pay significant attention to the treatment related to NFR.

Due to this reason, our work has focused on dealing with usability at the early stage of software development process. Our case study has shown the practicability and usefulness of pattern based approach in identifying usability features of an application domain. It proved that this pattern, USEP is suitable to be adopted into our proposed frameworks and can help to enhance the analysis phase's activities to specify and incorporate usability features for particular functionality properly.

However, some modifications are needed to extend the existing pattern's information by specifying additional issues to be discussed during elicitation process for certain mechanisms [14]. Besides that, user feedback need to be taken into consideration after the discussions to ensure that the all the features captured meet the user needs. Thus, there is a need to clearly identify the responsibilities of all the stakeholders into our framework in future.

Our next task is to develop a software tool in order to support the elicitation process of usability requirement along with functional requirement while adopting the USEPs into the tool to provide guidance to the stakeholders. We hope that our proposed work can help to improve the quality of software product, in terms of the usability requirements and at the same time, solve the problem of late identification of usability requirement which is commonly happen in software development process.

Lastly, we need to highlight that this work aims to illustrate an example of USEPs adoption to identify usability requirement during the early stage of software development. We do not intend to adhere or promote to a particular software process model or standard. The software process activities discussed here are generic and based upon the generally accepted software engineering terminology classification. Therefore, our proposed approach is useful for any organization, regardless of the particular method taken for developing their process activities.

References

1. ISO 9241-11: Ergonomic requirements for office work with visual display terminals (vdts). The international organization for standardization (1998)
2. Rivero, L., Barreto, R., Conte, T.: Characterizing usability inspection methods through the analysis of a systematic mapping study extension. Lat. Am. Cent. Inform. Stud. Electron. J. **16**(1), 12 (2013)
3. Catarci, T., Perini, A., Seyff, N., Rukh, S., Ahmed, N.: First International Workshop on Usability and Accessibility focused Requirements Engineering (UsARE 2012) -Summary Report (2012)
4. Roder, H.: Specifying usability features with patterns and templates. In: UsARE 2012, Zurich, Switzerland, pp. 6–11 (2012)
5. Juristo, N., Moreno, A.M., Sanchez, M.: Guidelines for eliciting usability functionalities. IEEE Transa. Softw. Eng. IEEE Comput. Soc. **33**(11), 744–758 (2007)
6. Hassan, S., Too, C.W., Kesava, P.R.: An analysis framework for identifying usability requirement in mobile application development. J. Next Gener. Inf. Technol. (JNIT) **4**(4), 32–40 (2013)
7. Nielsen, J.: The usability engineering life cycle. IEEE Comput. **25**(3), 12–22 (1992)

8. Trienekens, J.J.M., Kusters, R.J.: A framework for characterizing usability requirement elicitation and analysis methodologies (UREAM). IARA **2012**, 308–313 (2012)

9. Checkland, P., Scholes, J.: Soft Systems Methodology in Action. John Wiley, Chichester (1990)

10. Checkland, P.B.: Systems Thinking, Systems Practice. Wiley, Chichester (1981)

11. Lopez, A.Y., Niu, N.: Software systems in requirement engineering: a case study. In: 22nd International Conference on Software Engineering and Knowledge Engineering (SEKE 2010). San Francisco Bay, California, USA, 1–3 July 2010, pp. 38–41. KSI Press (2010)

12. Niu, N., Lopez, A.Y., Cheng, J.R.C.: Using soft systems methodology to improve requirements practices: an exploratory case study. IET Softw. **5**(6), 487–495 (2011)

13. Too, C.W., Hassan, S., Din, J., Ghani, A.A.: Towards improving NFR elicitation in software development. In: Proceedings of 2nd ICAISED, Kuala Lumpur, 12–13 January 2013, pp. 33–44 (2013)

14. Marianella, A., Moreno, A.M.: Responsibilities in the usability requirements elicitation Process. J. Syst. Cybern. Inform. **6**(6), 54–60 (2008)

Requirements Engineering of Malaysia's Radiation and Nuclear Emergency Plan Simulator

Amy Hamijah binti Ab. Hamid[1(✉)], Mohd Zaidi Abd Rozan[1],
Roliana Ibrahim[1], Safaai Deris[2], Ali Selamat[2],
and Muhd. Noor Muhd. Yunus[3]

[1] Department of Information Systems, Faculty of Computing,
Universiti Teknologi Malaysia (UTM), 81310 Johor Bahru, Johor, Malaysia
amyhamijah@gmail.com,
amyhamijah@nuclearmalaysia.gov.my
[2] Department of Software Engineering, Faculty of Computing,
Universiti Teknologi Malaysia (UTM), 81310 Johor Bahru, Johor, Malaysia
[3] Research and Technology Development Program,
Malaysian Nuclear Agency (NM), 43000 Bangi, Kajang
Selangor, Malaysia

Abstract. Responses to disastrous radiation and nuclear meltdown incidents require a large and complex emergency health and social care capacity planning framework. Incompleteness, inconsistency, and infeasibility of the provided requirements of the proposed planning framework might create unnecessary conflicts during the system development. In this paper, we propose the requirements engineering of an emergency preparedness and response simulation model for the Malaysian radiation and nuclear emergency plan simulator. This simulator development refers to an empirical interpretive approach following the pragmatism view. This approach involves the construction of the dedicated simulator by interpreting insights and document analysis relevant to the stakeholders in the respective emergency plan in order to plan and manage responses to emergencies and disasters. Dedicated process models (overall process map and workflow diagram) explain that, those organisations unable to define and identify the disaster coordinator roles and responsibilities, resources and equipment may contribute 65.63 % of emergency plan disorder and severe calamities. Those models are able to materialise the structure of a simulation workflow in order to demonstrate in training the emergency response prerequisites rather than intervention principles alone. It is likely that, this approach is significantly useful and justifies a mixture of tacit and explicit knowledge among the emergency plan experts. Therefore, a strategic, simplified and prevailing radiation and nuclear emergency plan simulator can be attained, though it is certainly as complex.

Keywords: Emergency plan · Simulation · Business process · Requirements engineering · Theory building

© Springer International Publishing Switzerland 2015
H. Fujita and A. Selamat (Eds.): SoMeT 2014, CCIS 513, pp. 83–97, 2015.
DOI: 10.1007/978-3-319-17530-0_7

1   Introduction

The Malaysian government initiated a nuclear power plant program as part of the creation of a sustainable energy platform dealing with energy security and efficiency. In conjunction with that, the Malaysian nuclear power plant deployment required a demanding legal, regulatory and safety framework. This framework enabled the government to reduce public fears leading to a better public acceptance towards the nuclear power program rather than being oppose to it. Prior resolutions guide us to develop the radiation and nuclear emergency plan (RANEP) as a radiological trauma triage capacity planning simulator based on a radiation and nuclear (RN) emergency preparedness and response plan. The RANEP framework was developed and divided into an integrated business process model and simulation system development. By doing so, the emergency preparedness and response plan model (EPRM) shall be established, tested and approved by the authorities via stakeholders. RANEP is essentially a tool developed to test and validate the workability and effectiveness of the plans prior to drill emergency exercises. Hence, the RANEP simulator contributes the execution of the requested severe accident management. This study provides a primary guideline dealing with those untoward circumstances in order to solve these prominent problems, as follows:

1. The disorganized situation during the early phase of emergency due to lack of coordination between the people and organizations as well as coordination of information and message [1].
2. Many projects neglected development procedures leading to problems in launching the product since it does not meet the user requirement [2].

The guideline has proven the effective combination of the work system theory and business process modelling in constructing coordination in the research context (stakeholders and investigated organisations) in the prior process models, (refer to Figs. 1 and 2). Therefore, this action created a connection flow of information and message in the respective emergency plan. This coordination was positioned according to user requirements and included empirical confirmation and assumptions (stated experience and knowledge). Those process models were further evaluated using several methods and techniques which were then constructed as a simulated process model. Further evaluation was requested to avoid and reduce any outstanding problems dealing with the launch of the product since it does not match the user requirement [3]. This circumstance was caused by the lack of understanding of the concerned high-level businesses including non-functional and user requirements [4]. Those scenarios relate to the inability of stakeholders to recognise or appreciate the needs highlighted by others. In addition, the stakeholders may understand the problem domain, but being unable to characterise the available solutions and initiatives that should be met [5]. Moreover, sometimes those user requirements are misunderstood by researchers through the misinterpretations of the stakeholders' perceptions during the requirements gathering process (elicitation) [3]. Several challenges must be overcome during the informal process of the requirements elicitations in order to avoid the emergence of incorrect, incomplete, inconsistent and unclear requirements among all the stakeholders. These challenges include unexpected conflicts between the stakeholders and the requirements due to inconsistencies in the system's goal. Furthermore, the generated requirements of the stakeholders might be vague, lack specifics and being intolerant towards measurements or tests [5].

Consequently, the methodological approach is an integration of the thematic synthesis and the process flow and capacity measurement analysis which were applied to the prior process models in order to avoid and/or reduce those highlighted encumbrances. Therefore, the objectives of this paper are to further develop, test and validate the feasibility of the dedicated process models, namely, overall process map and workflow diagram accordingly.

2 Related Works in Applied Requirements Engineering

Requirements Analysis. RANEP is a process model representation of an emergency health and social care capacity planning framework simulator in the large and complex scale of a sociotechnical system [6, 7]. This study focused on the process of finding out, analysing, documenting and checking services and constraints in the relevant emergency plan known as requirements engineering (RE) [4]. As a systematic process, this method iteratively developed RANEP requirements in order to analyse the problem, document the resulting observations in various formats of representations, and check the accuracy of the system understanding gained [8]. RE is a framework of engineering processes of requirements analysis, namely, elicitation, specification, and validation [3, 4, 8, 9]. Elicitation is concerned with understanding a problem to be solved, specification is concerned with formally describing a problem, and validation focuses on the concern of attaining agreement on the nature of the problem [8].

Viewpoint-Oriented Requirements Definition (VORD) Method. Figures 1 and 2 depict what is needed in the RANEP framework. These figures provide a clear, precise, consistent and unambiguous statement of the problem to be resolved. Chiefly, the next task is to take the system environment which reflects certain requirements and actual needs of the simulation components. In other words, the action of constraining the environment can decrease the complexity of the system component [10]. The organisation of those requirements has to pass through a negotiation process (member checking sessions) whereby any changes can be worked and set accordingly. The resolution requirements are listed as the agreed requirements (see Fig. 3). The analysis consisting of this method that was adopted in this study is standardised and covers several techniques. Reflecting on these findings, based on Figs. 1 and 2, the development and analyses were related to the prioritised key concepts [11]. The following process of the requirements analysis was constructed according to the simulation capacity planning and analysis. Associated processes combined with the configuration of the process flow and capacity measurement analysis are discussed in the next section.

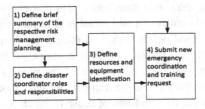

Fig. 1. Overall process map of the proposed RANEP simulator

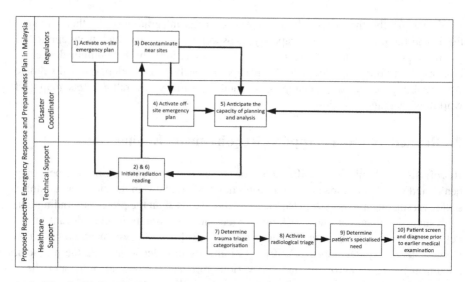

Fig. 2. High swim lane workflow diagram corresponding to proposed simulator

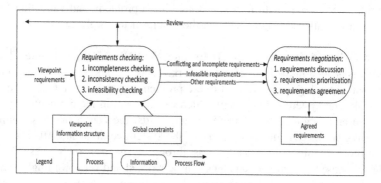

Fig. 3. VORD requirements analysis process

3 Materials and Methods

Data collection of the case studies was divided into the interpretation of the research context and the maturation of the structured models of the current simulator [6, 7, 12]. The case studies refer to a limited group of Malaysian stakeholders and existing phenomena regarding the respective emergency plan and energy program as a socio-technical system. Both data collection and member checking sessions were conducted in accordance with formalised permissions and ethical considerations. Through these activities, the preceding process models were made. However, Figs. 1 and 2 have to be reassessed in order to determine the association of the process components and proposed key concepts. Thus, they could be transformed into another simulation framework. Figure 4 presented the distributions of those research participants respectively.

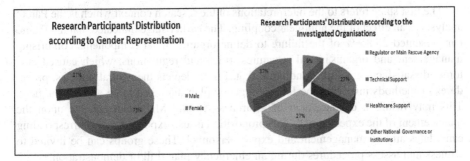

Fig. 4. Participants' distribution is corresponding to the synthesis of this study

4 Requirements Feasibility Validation and Synthesis

This section discusses the results achieved through several steps of validation and synthesis as follows: (1) conceptualisation of the thematic synthesis through the VORD approach and (2) process flow and capacity measurement analysis. Hence, the member checking transcriptions were validated and synthesised with reference to the conceptualisation synthesis [7, 12]. The baseline and case based simulation model argumentations and analyses were conducted as the second part of the validation [11–13].

4.1 Conceptualization of the Thematic Synthesis Through the VORD Approach

The critical elements of the RANEP simulator were sequentially and iteratively analysed into interpretive junctures and structured process models. The research context delivered requirements elicitations; meanwhile, the maturation of the structured process models comprised of the requirements specifications and validation. Those results provided a list of the prioritised functional and non-functional requirements of the simulator.

Briefly, the VORD supplies the different types of requirements needed [3]. Above all, indirect viewpoints normally provide domain characteristics and constraints that apply to the system. This viewpoint was analytically interpreted and structured as the fishbone diagrams (Figs. 5 and 6). Those figures were transmuted into Figs. 1 and 2. This functional requirement provides statements of services in the system to be reacting as particular inputs of the system's behaviour. Those diagrams highlight potential factors causing an overall effect in this case, together with issues and challenges in the respective phenomenon within the components of the sociotechnical system and information systems design theory and development key concepts [11, 12]. Previous studies have acknowledged that these theories and key concepts will optimise a system output, such as a safety precaution if well implemented. Every cause or reason behind the root causes of the fishbone diagrams identifies a defective source of variation related to job hazard analysis. Through this analysis, Figs. 5 and 6 were correlated to the preceding affinity, contingency and Pareto analysis as the following statement [7, 12]. Those analyses are briefly described below.

The first stage refers to the interpretations of the research context which is the Pareto analysis as an effect of the nonlinear coupling. The earlier stage indicated that the Pareto bar presented 25.85 % of the failure to define organisational components comprising management and organisational structures, rules and regulations, which caused customer dissatisfaction. Corresponding to that, Fig. 5 depicts the central policies, procedures or methods involving the RN, emergency plan that need to be applied publicly. This may result in enhancement of awareness among Malaysian citizens upon the management of the expected risk. This proposition is also exposed for the corresponding candidates among management and expert personnel. These groups can be invited to witness and assess procedures during an emergency plan drill or demonstration.

Fig. 5. Causes affecting the respective phenomenon

Further, a good RN, emergency plan must be both structured and thorough. It refers to standard laws and regulations emphasising the clear definition of roles and commands which indeed are indications of a good management procedure. These mechanisms, as noted in the diagram, circulate through various regions in order to both fix and enhance the characteristics of the stakeholders' work or projects. Therefore, they are knowledgeable and well-trained to be able to protect the community, environmental and other constituents during RN emergencies and disasters.

The second stage signified the organisation of the structured process models corresponding to the reduction in the issues and challenges in the event by 80 %. As a consequence, the Pareto bar accounted and accumulated 65.63 % of the failure to define disaster coordinator roles and obligations as well as to identify resources and equipment, which caused customer dissatisfaction. Clients in the Malaysian RN emergency plan work system are internal and external radiation workers and radiation related workers. Most of those appointed workers signify the stakeholders identified. Customers are also among the population surrounding RN related facilities and infrastructures. In addition, which is a new finding, patients in clinics and hospitals are also identified as customers, and most likely need to be rescued before any RN disasters, and emergencies occur [6, 12]. The finalised and main root causes in Fig. 6 could be addressed by conducting a practical and applied emergency preparedness and response plan mechanism. This mechanism must legitimately display direction, priorities and useful goals to be achieved. In addition, this mechanism might be focused on both radiation and nuclear as well as a medical emergency response plan. Those stakeholders also commented that the RANEP simulator is a useful project that should be implemented as soon as possible. These root causes suggested adequate corrective actions proposed by the experts. These findings were significantly related to the composition of nuclear safety implications. The finalised causes and reasons that were analytically generalised within the respective themes are illustrated in Fig. 6.

Next, interactor viewpoints are focused on as the higher-level organisational requirements and constraints in the development of the process and standards, which are shown in Figs. 1 and 2. These non-functional requirements evolved into the organisation and product, and also the external surroundings of the system. These requirements were constructed from a work system snapshot as described in [6, 12].

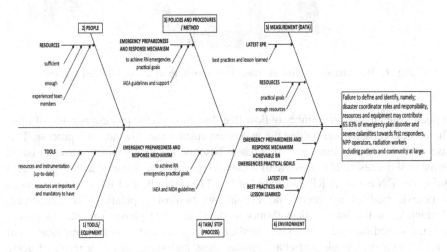

Fig. 6. Ishikawa (fishbone) chart is corresponding to the finalised root causes

In this finding, the domain viewpoints are the improvised process flow chart and baseline simulation interface, which are Figs. 7 and 8 (in the next section), respectively. Domain requirements usually consist of functional and non-functional requirements. Figures 5 and 6 were developed and depicted as an overall baseline simulation for this emergency plan. Most probably, concerned activities will need to be added later to the actual user interface. The concerned activities were derived from the outcome of the Ishikawa chart, Fig. 6, as stated by [11, 12]. Practical mechanism can be applied according to best practices and lessons learned from previous RN disasters and emergencies which show the direction, priorities and useful goals to be achieved.

4.2   Process Flow and Capacity Measurement Analysis

Jeston and Nelis (2008), and Anupindi et al. (2006) suggested process modelling of the RANEP simulator due to the investment of time, human resources, equipment and other terms of capacities involved among organisations or stakeholders in emergency planning [14, 15]. These process activities were linked within the chosen themes in Figs. 1 and 2. These figures are validated according to the documented outcomes as the running process simulations. By engaging these simulations, a stable process can be

Fig. 7. Baseline simulation interface corresponding to the highlighted themes

implied from an average number of flow that flow through the process per unit of time. The process capacity highlighted the maximum sustainable flow rate of a process. This case study tested and simulated the present baseline RANEP simulation model based on medical (inclusive of radiological) trauma triage capacity planning as it is prioritised during any RN events [CRP 2001 cited in 16]. The early phase of RN disaster (minutes to hours), medical treatment and decontamination of populations is anticipated. Meanwhile, in the intermediate (hours to days) and late phases (months to years), designated medical care is executed. Medical triage is described as the identification of radiation exposure levels and characteristic signs and symptoms as a result of acute radiation poisoning. The medical triage is presented in Table 1 [16–19]. Furthermore, this study purposefully aimed at the prevention of chaos during pre-hospital care and increasing the casualties' chance of survival due to the hospital care treatment. On-site and off-site emergency plans are provided for RN preparedness and anticipated response of health and social care [20]. The verification of those characteristics is based on those who are believed to have been exposed only, contaminated only, to have been both contaminated and exposed and neither been contaminated nor exposed. Medical treatment consists of complex medical management of radiation injury [21]. In addition, dosimetry must be provided in order to determine the dose of the radiation to which responders and the public have been exposed, according to certain methods (namely, calculation based on physical measurements, predicted values and use of biological markers). In conjunction, one study proposed people empowerment to enable citizens to maintain independence and to increase public awareness of any emergencies, thus a 72 h personal preparedness plan is crucial [22].

The requirements feasibility analysis is an appropriate mechanism for the radiological and medical emergency preparedness and response that is significantly needed. Estimation of each data point involves research study, observation and document analysis from prior radiological accident reports [20]. The point of entry is at the instant a patient enters the healthcare facility and the injury inspection of the appointed teams until the point of exit. The point of exit is divided into several scenarios, depending on whether the patient exits the trauma triage (Process 2) or is discharged and transferred to another zone seeking hospital treatment. The unit of flow is a patient (radiologically-affected casualty) and their categorisation, as shown in Table 1 [16–19]. A random sample of 357 patients was analysed over a one month period to determine the flow time by referring to the hospital database (regarding the entry and exit of each patient) within the process. The average of the 25 data points was 83 minutes and 40 seconds.

Table 1. Patient categorisation based on dose range and radiation sickness

Type of Patient	Triage Categorisation	Absorbed Dose Range (Gray)
P1	Severe	4–6
P2	Moderate	2–3
P3	Mild	< 0.75–2
P4	Very Severe	6–10

The process flow time in the entire process was examined in detail and broken down into constituent activities as shown in Table 2. Figure 8 is the improved process flow chart that depicts the activities and precedence relationships among them. For example, Process 2 must be completed before Activity 3 is accomplished. For each patient, the time required to perform each activity, as well as the number of repeats of that activity, were analysed. For instance, Activities 14–25 were repeated once for 98 % of the patients, and the average number of visits to these activities is 1.98 (Activities 14–15). The average work content for Activity 14 obtained by multiplying the activity time by 1.98. The rest of the selected activities were given an average number of visits accordingly in Table 2. This table presents summary of the data and computations as depicted in Fig. 8.

Consequently, Path 5 is the most critical path, yielding a theoretical flow time of the process as 772 min and 40 s. The process of Path 5 took about 65 min to take care of a patient, which is the longest duration of time identified. Next, the flow-time efficiency was measured to indicate the amount of waiting time associated with the process. The relationship between these two measures was defined as in (1) [15]:

$$\text{Flow-time efficiency} = \text{Theoretical flow time} / \text{Average flow time} \qquad (1)$$

As the actual flow time was measured at 83 min and 40 s and the theoretical flow time was at 772 min and 40 s, the flow time efficiency is expressed as in (2):

$$772{:}40/83{:}40 = 9{:}26 \text{ (hour:minutes) that equals } 926\% \qquad (2)$$

This means that waiting was roughly 9 times higher during any disaster, including day care basis. This scenario might happen as 10 simple data points were converted into 25 complicated data points as preparations to face the respective emergencies and disasters. Table 2 consolidates the activities required for each data point, with corresponding work content, and the allocated resources are restated in Table 3. All the resources were scheduled for daily operations of 8.00 am to 5.00 pm six days per week.

Table 2. Work content in RANEP process activities in Hospital XYZ

Activity/ Event		Type	Work content (Minutes per patient)
Patient entry	Start	Event: Start of process	NA
• Trigger on-site emergency plan	1	Activity: ITA	61.54
	2	Activity: ITA	2.4
	3	Activity: ITA	48.75
	End	Event: End of process	NA
• Activation of off-site emergency plan.	4	Activity: ITA	49.64
	5	Activity: ITA	65
• First activation of the radiological triage.	6	Activity: ITA	52
	7	Activity: RAT	25
• Activation of off-site emergency plan.	8	Activity: RAT	44.75
	9	Activity: RAT	25
• First activation of the radiological triage.	10	Activity: RAT	25
	11	Activity: RAT	30.25
	12	Activity: RAT	44.75
	End	Event: End of process	NA
• Second activation of the radiological triage.	13	Activity: HCT	34
	14	Activity: HCT	49.50
	End	Event: End of process	NA
• Second activation of the radiological triage.	15	Activity: HCT	52
	16	Activity: HCT	26.25
	17	Activity: HCT	25
	18	Activity: HCT	52
	19	Activity: HCT	25
	20	Activity: HCT	29
	21	Activity: HCT	45.25
	End	Event: End of process	NA
• Second activation of the radiological triage.	22	Activity: HCT	25
	23	Activity: HCT	52
	24	Activity: HCT	25
	25	Activity: HCT	29
	End	Event: End of process	NA
Legend:	ITA: Initial treatment area RAT: Reception area treatment HCT: Hospital care treatment		

During any disaster, this hospital will operate 24 h a day for seven days per week at least for the first 72 h [16]. Assume that the scheduled availability is 60 min per hour since all the processing is sequential, the load batch equals one. Referring to Table 2, we can compute the unit loads and theoretical capacity of the various resource units (see Table 3). The process throughput, R is the average number of flow units processed over time. This value is rarely equal to the theoretical capacity because of internal inefficiencies that lead to resource unavailability and idleness as well as external constraints such as the low outflow rate (due to low demand rate) or low inflow rate (due to low supply rate). Capacity utilisation is important in order to measure performance regarding the extent to which resources are effectively utilised in the process as in (3) [15]:

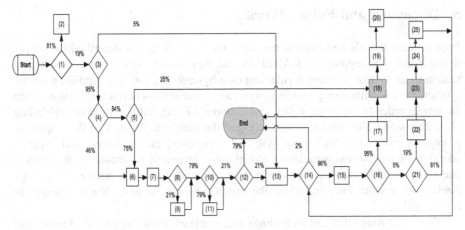

Fig. 8. Process flowchart corresponding to the proposed RANEP

$$\text{Capacity utilisation of resource pool } p = \text{Throughput/ theoretical capacity of resource pool } (p\rho_p = R/R_p) \tag{3}$$

The theoretical bottleneck of resources is the disaster coordinator with a capacity for processing only 0.33 patients per hour. Capacity utilisation of the process is defined as the capacity utilisation of the bottleneck resource pool. Finally, by analysing the process over a one month period, the study found that in the RANEP mechanism processes, on average, each patient is given 24 min of treatment per hour. Based on throughput, R = 0.24 patients per hour, we summarise the utilisation of resources in Table 3.

Table 3. Theoretical capacity of RANEP process activities

Resource Pool (p)	Unit Load (Minutes per patient, T_p)	Theoretical Capacity of Resource Unit (Patients per hour, $1/T_p$)	Number of Units in Resource Pool (Patients per hour, R_p)	Theoretical Capacity of Resource Pool (Patients per hour, R_p)	Capacity Utilization (%) ($\rho_p = R/R_p$)
First Aid Worker	61.54+48.75+49.64+65+52+34= 310.93	60/310.93= 0.19	2	0.19X2= 0.38	0.24/0.39= 62.19%
Paramedic	61.54+48.75+49.64+65+52+34= 310.93	60/310.93= 0.19	2	0.19X2= 0.38	0.24/0.39= 62.19%
Ambulance Personnel	61.54+48.75+49.64+65+52+34= 310.93	60/310.93= 0.19	2	0.19X2= 0.38	0.24/0.39= 62.19%
Physicist	48.75+49.64+65+52= 215.39	60/215.39 = 0.28	2	0.28X2= 0.56	0.24/0.56= 43.08%
Competent Technician	48.75+49.64+65+52+25= 240.39	60/240.39= 0.25	2	0.28X2= 0.50	0.24/0.50= 48.08%
Disaster Coordinator	49.64+65+52+25+44.75+25+25+30.25+ 44.75= 361.39	60/361.39 = 0.17	2	0.17X2= 0.33	0.24/0.17= 72.28%
Irradiation Plant	65+52= 117	60/117 = 0.51	1	0.51X1= 0.51	0.24/0.51= 46.80%
CBTF	25	60/25= 2.40	1	2.40X1= 2.40	0.24/2.40= 10.00%
Physician	44.75+25+25+39.25+44.75+26.25+45.25 = 250.25	60/250.25 = 0.24	2	0.48X2= 0.48	0.24/0.48= 50.05%
Surgeon	44.75+25+25+39.25+44.75+26.25+45.25 = 250.25	60/250.25 = 0.24	2	0.24X2= 0.48	0.24/0.48= 50.05%
Nurse	44.75+25+25+39.25+44.75+26.25+45.25 = 250.25	60/250.25 = 0.24	4	0.24X4= 0.96	0.24/0.96= 25.03%
Medical Assistant	44.75+25+25+39.25+44.75+26.25+45.25 = 250.25	60/250.25 = 0.24	2	0.24X2= 0.48	0.24/0.48= 50.05%
Appropriate Specialist	30.25	60/30.25= 1.98	1	1.98X1= 1.98	0.24/1.98= 12.10%
Registration Counter	34+49.50= 83.50	60/83.50 =0.72	1	0.72X1= 0.72	0.24/0.72= 33.40%
Clinical Lab Personnel	52+25+25+25+25= 152	60/152 = 0.39	1	0.39X1= 0.39	0.24/0.39= 60.80%
Inpatient Department	25+52= 77	60/77 = 0.78	1	0.78X1= 0.78	0.24/0.78= 30.80%
Ward Admission	29+29= 58	60/58 = 1.03	1	1.03X1= 1.03	0.24/1.03= 23.20%
Outpatient Department	52	60/52 = 1.15	1	1.15X1= 1.15	0.24/1.15= 20.80%
Legend:	CBTF: Community based treatment facility				

5   Discussion and Future Work

Prior process models and present baseline simulation diagrams described the output determinants that support the RANEP logical view which consists of a radiological trauma triage system covering regular and case-by-case care [16, 17]. Applied thematic synthesis and qualitative regression analysis are valuable tools to test and validate those models in order to support the key contributions of successful simulation modelling [22]. This study also supported and engaged the main stakeholders of the respective emergency plan. With their prior skill and experience, the usefulness and accurate adoption of the present simulation model were increased regarding to the present phenomenon. This statement is supported and correlated with the prior 89 % average (with a 99 % confidence index) of the experts' agreement towards the elements in Figs. 1 and 2.

This study found that certain findings are correlated, even though concurrently and constantly compared to the previous one. Occasionally, the provided analytical procedures establish theoretical integration prior to the preceding theories [23]. Constant comparison is executed to guide further data collections as inductive analysis to specify contexts or conditions in which any theories may apply, or reveals discrepancies between data samples that need clarification [24]. Those remarkable results represent the workflow diagram of that expertise. In other words, any requirements conflicts were resolved through negotiation during the member checking session. In addition, this study proposed an improved process flowchart significantly related to those categories in broader themes (see Fig. 8 and Table 2). Foremost, process modelling is also inductive coding that complements qualitative and interpretive research methods [24].

The definition and identification of disaster coordinator roles and responsibilities, resources and equipment is exceedingly challenging in Malaysia and deficiencies in defining and identifying these components contributed nearly 70 % of the severe RN circumstances. As shown in Table 3, the bottleneck in the RANEP process activities contributed to over utilisation of 72.28 % of the disaster coordinator and took a huge delay of 33 min in an immediate rescue action. Thus the theoretical capacity setting engaged each patient treatment within 24 min, also indicating rather slim chances of survival. Regarding that, the average flow time of approximately 1 h and 40 min signified the relative success of those activities, compare to prior reports indicating that the first 1 h and 15 min are the early phase rescue and an average of 48 h rescue for such condition [25].

Subsequently, multiple and integrated methodological approaches provided difficult analytical procedures. However; they did represent those requirements adequately. In short, these procedures did support requirements engineering processes in an efficient and consistent manner. Those analyses significantly determined the user needs and system requirements so as to match those with one another. In addition, those analyses anticipated requirements discovery, classification and organisation [6, 7, 12]. Requirements prioritisation, negotiation and documentation were also successfully initiated to propose a theory which engages with other preceding theories. This action is equal to the preceding methods so as to transform the unstructured elicitations of requirements into organised clusters. The elicitation related to sociotechnical components described each requirement by reference to its own meaning within the context (time, place and situation) in which they were observed [8]. Thus, this sociotechnical requirements elicitation involved primary technical problems and processes that should be carried out within a social context. These elicitations were applied with the optimal involvement of the stakeholders during member checking sessions. The social issues that are integrated in the systems are inevitably interdependently related to the technical ones. This scenario is also proven to be correlated to the current and preceding outcomes of the affinity analysis [7, 11, 12]. In regard to the system's limitations, it remain necessary to establish and address time control as this was not fully accommodated and was difficult to define in the present study.

6 Conclusions

Resolutions for the RANEP simulator or any emergency plan mechanism must be practical and achievable apart from the adequate provision of such equipment (daily or routine events and during emergencies). Those answers will decrease the incidence of injuries and disorders, especially among the first responders, radiation workers, clinical patients and above all, the neighbouring community. The simulation of benevolent radiation and nuclear emergency reports and cases will be proven in the near future. This action requires further computerised experimentations in order to justify whether it is worthwhile to construct as such models in order to ensure the minimisation of mortality and the maximisation of survival enhancement in the proposed scenario.

Acknowledgements. We wish to extend our gratitude to Prof. Dr. Maman Djauhari for his outstanding qualitative regression analysis technique. We are also grateful to the support granted by the Research Management Centre, Universiti Teknologi Malaysia under the Exploratory Research Grant Scheme (Vote No. QJ130000.7828.4L051) as well as Dr. Faridah Mohamad Idris for her guidance.

References

1. Niculae, C., French, S., Carter, E.: Emergency management: does it have a sufficiently comprehensive understanding of decision-making, process and context? Radiat. Prot. Dosimetry. **109**, 97–100 (2004)
2. Crick, M., McKenna, T., Buglova, E., Winkler, G., Martincic, R.: Emergency management in the early phase. Radiat. Prot. Dosimetry. **109**, 7–17 (2004)
3. Parviainen, P., Tihinen, M., Lormans, M., van Solingen, R.: Requirements engineering: dealing with the complexity of sociotechnical systems development. In: Mate, J.L., Hershey, S.A. (eds.) Requirements Engineering for Sociotechnical Systems. Information Science Publishing (an imprint of Idea Group Inc.) (2005)
4. Sommerville, I.: Software Engineering, 8th edn. Addison-Wesley Publishers Limited, England (2007)
5. Coulin, C., Zowghi, D.: Requirements elicitation for complex systems: theory and practice. In: Mate, J.L., Hershey, S.A. (eds.) Requirements Engineering for Sociotechnical Systems. Information Science Publishing (an imprint of Idea Group Inc.) (2005)

6. Hamid, A.H.A., Rozan, M.Z.A., Deris, S., Ibrahim, R.: Business process analysis of emergency plan using work system theory. J. Inf. Syst. Res. Innov. (JISRI) **3**, 37–43 (2013)
7. Hamid, A.H.A., Rozan, M.Z.A., Ibrahim, R., Deris, S., Muhd Yunus, M.N.: Framing a nuclear emergency plan using qualitative regression analysis. J. Nucl. Relat. Technol. (JNRT) **11**(1), 27–45 (2014)
8. Loucopoulos, P., Karatostas, V.: Systems Requirements Engineering. The McGraw-Hill International Series in Software Engineering, London (1995)
9. Sommerville, I., Sawyer, P.: Requirements Engineering: A Good Practice Guide. Wiley, Chichester (1997)
10. Kotonya, G., Sommerville, I.: Requirements engineering with viewpoints. In: Technical Report: CSEG/10/1995. Edited by Group CSE. Lancaster University, Lancaster, pp. 1−26 (1995)
11. Hamid, A.H.A., Rozan, M.Z.A., Ibrahim, R., Deris, S., Selamat, A., Yunus, M.N.M.: Requirements engineering of Malaysia radiation and nuclear emergency plan simulator. In: Fujita, H., Selamat, A., Haron, H. (eds.) New Trends in Software Methodologies, Tools and Techniques: The Proceedings of the Thirteenth SoMeT_14, pp. 476–492. IOS Press, Langkawi (2014)
12. Hamid, A., Rozan, M., Ibrahim, R., Deris, S., Nik Rushdi, H., Muhd Yunus, M.: Understanding and designing business process modelling for emergency plan. In: 3rd International Conference on Research and Innovation in Information Systems - 2013 (ICRIIS 2013). Universiti Tenaga Nasional (UNITEN), Kajang. p. 6, 27−28 November 2013
13. Aguilar-Saven, R.S.: Business process modelling: review and framework. Int. J. Prod. Econ. **90**(2), 129–149 (2004)
14. Jeston, J., Nelis, J.: Management by Process: A Roadmap to Sustainable Business Process Management. Elsevier Ltd., Armsterdam (2008)
15. Anupindi, R., Chopra, S., Deshmukh, S.D., Mieghen, J.A.M., Zemel, E.: Managing Business Process Flows: Principles of Operations Management, 2nd edn. Pearson Education, Inc., New Jersey (2006)
16. Hamid, A.H.B.A., Wah, L.K., Majid, H.A., Samah, A.A., Abdullah, W.S.W.: Towards the development of an absorbed dose range detection and treatment simulation system to manage the healthcare consequences of a nuclear accident in Malaysia. In: Operational Research Society Simulation Workshop 2012 (SW12), Worcestershire, United Kingdom, 27–28 March 2012
17. Hamid, A.H.B.Ab., Samah, A.A., Majid, H.A., Anwar, S., Rozan, M.Z.A., Deris, S., Ibrahim, R., Hashim, S.: Recommended factors for triage categories using simulation modelling. In: International Conference on Research and Innovation in Information Systems (ICRIIS 2011), Seri Pacific Hotel, Kuala Lumpur. p. 479, 23–24 November 2011
18. Hamid, A.H.B.A., Rozan, M.Z.A., Deris, S., Ibrahim, R., Samah, A.A., Hashim, S.: Triage categories for vulnerable groups using system dynamics simulation modelling. In: Sixth International Symposium on Radiation Safety and Detection Technology (ISORD-6), Awana Porto Malai, Langkawi, Kedah, Malaysia 12–14 July 2011
19. Pidd, M.: Tools for Thinking: Modelling in Management Science. Wiley, Chichester (2009)
20. Pidd, M.: Mixing other methods with simulation is no big deal. In: Proceedings of the 2012 Winter Simulation Conference. IEEE (2012)
21. Waller, E., Millage, K., Blakely, W.F., Ross, J.A., Mercier, J.R., Sandgren, D.J., Levine, I. H., Dickerson, W.E., Nemhauser, J.B., Nasstrom, J.S., et al.: Overview of hazard assessment and emergency planning software of use to RN first responders. Health Phys. Radiat. Saf. J. **97**(2), 145–156 (2009)

22. Kuljis, J., Paul, R.J., Stergioulas, L.K.: Can health care benefit from modeling and simulation methods in the same way as business and manufacturing has? In: Henderson, S. G., Biller, B., Hsieh, M-H., Shortle J., Tew, J.D., Barton, R.R. (eds.) 2007 Winter Simulation Conference, Washington, DC, USA, pp. 1449 – 1453, 9–12 December 2007
23. Urquhart, C.: Grounded Theory for Qualitative Research: A Practical Guide. Sage Publications, Los Angeles (2013)
24. Loonam, J., McDonagh, J.: A grounded theory study of enterprise systems implementation: Lessons learned from the Irish health services. In: Cater-Steel, A., Al-Hakim, L. (eds.) Information Systems Research Methods, Epistemology and Applications. IGI Global, Hershey (2009)
25. Mohd Zain, Z. (ed.): Pelan Tindakan Bencana HKL Edisi 2008, pp. 1–169. Hospital Kuala Lumpur, Kuala Lumpur (2008)

Intelligent Software Systems Design

Ontology COKB for Knowledge Representation and Reasoning in Designing Knowledge-Based Systems

Nhon V. Do[✉]

University of Information Technology, National University Ho Chi Minh City,
Ho Chi Minh City, Vietnam
nhondv@uit.edu.vn

Abstract. Knowledge Representation and Reasoning is at the heart of the great challenge of Artificial Intelligence, especially knowledge-based systems, expert systems and intelligent problem solvers. The models for knowledge such as logics, semantic networks, conceptual graphs, frames and classes are useful tools to design the above systems. However, they are not suitable to represent knowledge in the domains of reality applications. Designing of the knowledge bases and the inference engines of those systems in practice requires representations in the form of ontologies. For applications such as the intelligent problem solver in plane geometry, the knowledge contains a complicated system of concepts, relations, operators, functions, and rules. This situation motivates an ontology-based solution with such components. In this article, an ontology called Ontology of Computational Object Knowledge Base (COKB), will be presented in details. We also present a model for representing problems together reasoning algorithms for solving them, and design methods to construct applications. The above methodology has been used in designing many applications such as systems for solving analytic geometry problems, solving problems in plane geometry, and the expert system for diabetic micro vascular complication diagnosis.

Keywords: Knowledge representation · Ontology · Knowledge-based system · Intelligent problem solver

1 Introduction

Knowledge-Based Systems (KBSs) use knowledge-based techniques to support human decision-making, learning and action, solving problems. Knowledge representation methods play an important role in designing knowledge bases and inference engines of those systems. As mentioned in [1], first, general methods of knowledge representation and reasoning have been explored such as logics, semantic networks, conceptual graphs, rules of inference, frames and classes; and they can be found in [2–6]. These methods are useful, but they are very difficult to represent knowledge in domains of reality applications, because the complicated of knowledge domain. Second, researchers have developed specialized methods of knowledge representation and reasoning to handle core domains, such as time, space, causation and action. Third, researchers have tackled important applications of knowledge representation and reasoning, including query

© Springer International Publishing Switzerland 2015
H. Fujita and A. Selamat (Eds.): SoMeT 2014, CCIS 513, pp. 101–118, 2015.
DOI: 10.1007/978-3-319-17530-0_8

answering, planning, the Semantic Web and intelligent problem solvers (IPSs). These intelligent systems must have suitable knowledge base and they not only give human readable solutions but also present solutions as the way people usually write them.

For applications such as the intelligent problem solver in plane geometry, the knowledge contains a system of structured concepts, relations, operators, functions, and rules; besides, knowledge reasoning requires complex symbolic computations. The system can solve problems in general forms. Users only declare hypothesis and goal of problems base on a simple language but strong enough for specifying problems. The practical methods in [7–9] are difficult to use for designing this system. This situation motivates an ontology-based solution with such components.

Ontologies became popular in computer science. Gruber [10] defines an ontology as an "explicit specification of a conceptualization". Several authors have made small adaptations to this, and some of its definition can be found in [11–13] and [3]. The followings are common definitions of the terminology ontology:

- "The subject *ontology* is the study of *categories* of things that exist or may exist in some domain. The product of such a study, called *an ontology*, is a catalog of the types of things that are assumed to exist in a domain of interest D from the perspective of a person who uses a language L for the purpose of talking about D" (John F. Sowa, [3])
- For Artificial Intelligence researchers "an ontology describes a formal, shared conceptualization of a particular domain of interest. Thus, ontologies provide a way of capturing a shared understanding of a domain that can be used both by humans and systems to aid in information exchange and integration" (L. Stojanovic, [11]).

The article [14] address the dependency of the applications on the societies by separately defining process's ontology, the agent's knowledge, the society's ontology, and the society's knowledge. The proposed system can be applied to cloud computing platform. A semantic web application was presented in [15], in which the authors did a research on semantic search. A model proposed for the exploitation of ontology-based KBs to improve search over large document repositories. The approach includes an ontology-based scheme for the semi-automatic annotation of documents, and a retrieval system. In [16], authors presented some principles for organizing a library of reusable ontological theories which can be configured into an application ontology. This application ontology is then exploited to organize the knowledge acquisition process and to support computational design. Reference [17] proposed an extended model of the simple generic knowledge models, and used it for software experience knowledge. In [18], a knowledge-based system for the author linkage problem, called SudocAD, was constructed based on a method combining numerical and knowledge-based techniques. The ontology used in this system contains a hierarchy of concepts and a hierarchy of relations. Reference [19] presented an ontology-based method of supplementing and verifying information stored in a framework system of the semantic knowledge base. Development of applications in [15–19] was based on commonly used ontologies with simple concepts and relationships among them. In [20, 21] the author presented advanced topics of ontological engineering and showed us a couple of concrete examples. It provides us with conceptual tools for analyzing problems in a right way by which we mean analysis of underlying background of the problems as well as their essential properties to obtain more general and useful solutions.

Ontologies give us a modern approach for designing knowledge components of KBS. Practical applications such as the IPS in plane geometry expect an ontology consisting of knowledge components concepts, relations, relations, operators, functions, and rules that support symbolic computation and reasoning. In this article, we present an ontology called ontology of *Computational Object Knowledge Base* (COKB). It includes models, specification language, problems and deductive methods. The main approach for COKB is to integrate ontology engineering, object-oriented modeling [22] and symbolic computation programming [23]. This ontology was used to produce applications in education and training such as a program for studying and solving problems in plane geometry presented in [24], a system that supports studying knowledge and solving of analytic geometry problems presented in [25], and the expert system for diabetic micro vascular complication diagnosis in [26]. It can be used to represent the total knowledge and to design the knowledge bases. Next, computational networks (Com-Net) and networks of computational objects (CO-Net) in [27] can be used for modeling problems and for designing inference engine.

The rest of the paper is organized as follows. In Sect. 2, ontology COKB will be explained consisting the model and specification language. Section 3 presents computational networks and networks of computational objects. Based on the models presented in previous sections, reasoning methods for solving problems will be discussed in Sect. 4. We will discuss how to design knowledge base and inference engine in Sects. 5 and 6 gives some applications. Finally we conclude the paper in Sect. 7.

2   Ontology COKB

2.1   Model COKB

The model of computational objects knowledge bases, presented in [27], has been established from integration of ontology engineering, object-oriented modeling and symbolic computation programming.

Definition 1.1.   A computational object (Com-object) O has the following characteristics:

(1) The set consists of attributes, denoted by Attrs(O).
(2) There are internal computational relations among attributes of Com-object O. These are manifested in the following features of the object:

- Given a subset A of Attrs(O). The object O can show us the attributes that can be determined from A.
- The object O will give the value of an attribute.
- It can also show the internal process of determining the attributes.

The structure of computational objects can be modeled by (*Attrs, F, Facts, Rules*). *Attrs* is a set of attributes, *F* is a set of equations called computation relations, *Facts* is a set of properties or events of objects, and *Rules* is a set of deductive rules on facts.

Definition 1.2. The model of Computational Object Knowledge Base (COKB model) consists of six components:

$$(\mathbf{C}, \mathbf{H}, \mathbf{R}, \mathbf{Ops}, \mathbf{Funcs}, \mathbf{Rules})$$

C is a set of concepts of computational objects, and each concept is a class of Com-objects. **H** is a set of hierarchy relation (IS-A relation) on the concepts. **R** is a set of another relations on C, and in case a relation r is a binary relation it may have properties such as reflexivity, symmetry, etc. The set **Ops** consists of *operators* on C. The set **Funcs** consists of functions on Com-Objects. The set **Rules** consists of deductive rules. The rules represent for statements, theorems, principles, formulas, and so forth. Rules can be written as the form "if {facts} then {facts}".

Facts must be classified so that the knowledge component *Rules* can be specified and processed in the inference engine of KBSs and IPSs. There are 12 kinds of facts have been proposed from the researching on real requirements and problems in different knowledge domains:

- **Fact of kind 1**: states information about object kind or type of an object.
- **Fact of kind 2**: states determination of an object or an attribute of an object.
- **Fact of kind 3**: states determination of an object or an attribute of an object by a value or a constant expression.
- **Fact of kind 4**: states equality on objects or attributes of objects.
- **Fact of kind 5**: states dependence of an object on other objects by an equation.
- **Fact of kind 6**: states a relation on objects or attributes of the objects.
- **Fact of kind 7**: states determination of a function.
- **Fact of kind 8**: states determination of a function by a value or a constant expression.
- **Fact of kind 9**: states equality between an object and a function.
- **Fact of kind 10**: states equality between a function and another function.
- **Fact of kind 11**: states dependence of a function on other functions or other objects by an equation.
- **Fact of kind 12**: states a relation on functions.

The basic technique for designing deductive algorithms is the unification of facts. Based on the kinds of facts and their structures, there will be criteria for unification proposed. Then it produces algorithms to check the unification of two facts.

2.2 Specification Language and Knowledge-Based Organization

The language for ontology COKB is constructed to specify knowledge bases with knowledge of the form COKB model. This language includes the following:

- A set of characters: letter, number, special letter.
- Vocabulary: keywords, names.
- Data types: basic types and structured types.
- Expressions and sentences.

- Statements.
- Syntax for specifying the components of COKB model.

The followings are some structures of definitions for facts, and functions.

Definitions of facts:
    facts ::=   : fact-def+
    fact-def ::=   object-type | attribute | name | equation | relation | expression
    object-type ::=   cobject-type name) | cobject-type (name <, name>*)
    relation ::= relation (name <, name>+)
Definitions of functions – form 1:
    function-def ::= **FUNCTION** name;
                    ARGUMENT: argument-def+
                    RETURN: return-def;
                    [constraint]
                    [facts]
                    ENDFUNCTION;
    return-def   ::= name: type;
Definitions of functions – form 2:
    function-def ::= **FUNCTION** name;
                    ARGUMENT: argument-def+
                    RETURN: return-def;
                    [constraint]
                    [variables]
                    [statements]
                    ENDFUNCTION;
    statements   ::=   statement-def+
    statement-def ::=   assign-stmt I if-stmt I for-stmt
    asign-stmt   ::=   name := expr;
    if-stmt   ::=   **IF** logic-expr **THEN** statements+ **ENDIF**; I
                    IF logic-expr **THEN** statements+ **ELSE** statements+ **ENDIF**;
    for-stmt   ::=   **FOR** name **IN** [range] **DO** statements+ **ENDFOR**;

From the model COKB and the specification language, the knowledge-based organization of the system will be established. It consists of structured text files that stores the components concepts, hierarchical relation, relations, operators, functions, rules, facts and objects. The knowledge base is stored by the files listed below.

- File "CONCEPTS.txt" stores names of concepts. For each concept, we have the corresponding file with the file name "<concept name>.txt", which contains the specification of this concept.
- File "HIERARCHY.txt" stores information of the component H of COKB model.
- Files "RELATIONS.txt" and "RELATIONS_DEF.txt" are structured text files that store the specification of relations.
- Files "OPERATORS.txt" and "OPERATORS_DEF.txt" are structured text files that store the specification of operators.

- Files "FUNCTIONS.txt" and "FUNCTIONS_DEF.txt" are structured text files that store the specification of functions.
- File "FACT_KINDS.txt" is the structured text file that stores the definition of kinds of facts.
- File "RULES.txt" is the structured text file that stores deductive rules.
- Files "OBJECTS.txt" and "FACTS.txt" are the structured text files that store certain objects and facts.

3 Computational Network and Network of Computational Objects

Computational network (Com-Net) and network of computational objects (CO-Net) can be used to represent general problems in knowledge bases of the form COKB model. The methods and techniques for solving the problems on these networks will be useful tool for designing the inference engine of KBSs and IPSs.

3.1 Computational Network

Definition 3.1. A *computational network (CN)* is a structure (M, F) consisting of a set $M = \{x_1, x_2, ..., x_n\}$ variables and $F = \{f_1, f_2, ..., f_m\}$ is a set of computational relations over the variables in M. Each computational relation $f \in F$ has the following form:

(i) An equation over some variables in M, or
(ii) Deductive rule $f : u(f) \rightarrow v(f)$, with $u(f) \subseteq M$, $v(f) \subseteq M$, and there are corresponding formulas to determine (or to compute) variables in $v(f)$ from variables in $u(f)$. We also define the set $M(f) = u(f) \cup v(f)$.

The popular problem arising from reality applications is that to find a solution to determine a set $G \subseteq M$ from a set $H \subseteq M$. This problem is denoted by $H \rightarrow G$, H is the hypothesis and G is the goal of the problem.

Definition 3.2. Given a computational net $K = (M, F)$. For $A \subseteq M$, $f \in F$, denote $f(A) = A \cup M(f)$ be the set obtained from A by applying f. Let $S = [f_1, f_2, ..., f_k]$ be a list of relations in F, the notation $S(A) = f_k(f_{k-1}(... f_2(f_1(A)) ...))$ is used to denote the set of variables obtained from A by applying relations in S. We call S a *solution* of problem $H \rightarrow G$ if $S(H) \supseteq G$. Solution S is called a *good solution* if there is not a proper sublist S' of S such that S' is also a solution of the problem. The problem is *solvable* if there is a solution to solve it.

The following are some algorithms that show methods and techniques for solving the above problems on computational nets.

Algorithm 3.1: Find a solution of problem H→G on (M, F).
Step 1: Solution ← empty; Solution_found ← false;
Step 2: Repeat
          Hold ← H;   Select f ∈ F;
          while not Solution_found and (f found) do
              if (applying f from H produces new facts)
                  H ← H ∪ M(f); Add f to Solution;
              if (G ⊆ H)
                  Solution_found ← true;
              Select new f ∈ F;
          Until Solution_found or (H = Hold);

Algorithm 3.2. Find a good solution NewS from a solution S = [f$_1$, f$_2$, ..., f$_k$] of problem H→G.
Step 1: NewS ← []; V ← G;
Step 2: for i := k downto 1 do
              If (v(f$_k$) ∩ V ≠ ∅)
                  Insert f$_k$ at the beginning of NewS;
                  V ← (V − v(f$_k$)) ∪ (u(f$_k$) − H);

3.2   Network of Computational Objects

Definition 3.3.   A computational relation f between attributes or objects is called a *relation between the objects*. A network of Com-objects (CO-Net) consists of a set of Com-objects O = {O$_1$, O$_2$, ..., O$_n$} and a set of computational relations F = {f$_1$, f$_2$, ..., f$_m$}. This network of Com-objects is denoted by (O, F).

On network of Com-objects (O, F), we consider the problem that to determine attributes in set G from given attributes in set H. The problem is denoted by H → G.

Let M be a set of concerned attributes. Suppose A is a subset of M.

(a) For each f ∈ F, denote f(A) is the union of the set A and the set consists of all attributes in M deduced from A by f. Similarly, for each Com-object O$_i$ ∈ O, O$_i$(A) is the union of the set A and the set consists of all attributes (in M) that the object O$_i$ can determine from attributes in A.

(b) Suppose D = [t$_1$, t$_2$, ..., t$_m$] is a list of elements in F ∪ O. Denote A$_0$ = A, A$_1$ = t$_1$(A$_0$), . . ., A$_m$ = t$_m$(A$_{m-1}$), and D(A) = A$_m$.

We have A$_0$ ⊆ A$_1$ ⊆ . . . ⊆ A$_m$ = D(A) ⊆ M. Problem H → G is called *solvable* if there is a list D ⊆ F ∪ O such that D(H) ⊇ G. In this case, we say that D is a *solution* of the problem.

Algorithm 3.3. Find a solution of problem H→G on CO-Net (O,F).
Step 1: Solution ← empty list; Solution_found ← false;
Step 2: Repeat
        Hold ← H;   Select f ∈ F;
        while not Solution_found and (f found) do
          if (applying f from H produces new facts)
            H ← H ∪ M(f); // M(f) is the set of attributes in relation f
            Add f to Solution;
          if (G ⊆ H)
            Solution_found ← true;
          Select new f ∈ F;
        Until Solution_found or (H = Hold);
Step 3: if (not Solution_found)
        Select O_i ∈ O such that $O_i(H)$ ≠ H;
      if (the selection is successful)
          H ← $O_i(H)$; Add O_i to Solution;
          if (G ⊆ H)
            Solution_found ← true;
        else
          goto step 2;

Example 3.1   In a triangle ABC, suppose that AB = AC, the values of the angle A and the edge BC are given (hypothesis). ABDE and ACFG are squares (outside triangle ABC). Compute EG.

The problem can be considered on the network of Com-objects (O, F) as follows:
    O = {O_1: triangle ABC with AB = AC, O_2: triangle AEG, O_3: square ABDE, O_4: square ACFG }, and F = {f_1, f_2, f_3, f_4, f_5} consists of the following relations

    f_1 : $O_1.c = O_3.a$ {the edge c of triangle ABC = the edge of the square ABDE}
    f_2 : $O_1.b = O_4.a$ {the edge b of triangle ABC = the edge of the square ACFG}
    f_3 : $O_2.b = O_4.a$ {the edge b of triangle AEG = the edge of the square ACFG}
    f_4 : $O_2.c = O_3.a$ {the edge c of triangle AEG = the edge of the square ABDE}
    f_5 : $O_1.A + O_2.A = \pi$.

We have the problem H → G, with H = {$O_1.a$, $O_1.A$}, and G = {$O_2.a$};

$M(f_1)$ = {$O_1.c$, $O_3.a$}, $M(f_2)$ = {$O_1.b$, $O_4.a$}, $M(f_3)$ = {$O_2.b$, $O_4.a$},
$M(f_4)$ = {$O_2.c$, $O_3.a$}, $M(f_5)$ = {$O_1.\alpha$, $O_2.\alpha$},
M = {$O_1.a$, $O_1.b$, $O_1.c$, $O_1.A$, $O_2.b$, $O_2.c$, $O_2.A$, $O_2.a$, $O_3.a$, $O_4.a$}.

The above algorithms will produce the solution D = {f_5, O_1, f_1, f_2, f_3, f_4, O_2}, and the process of extending the set of attributes as follows:

$$A_0 \xrightarrow{f_5} A_1 \xrightarrow{O_1} A_2 \xrightarrow{f_1} A_3 \xrightarrow{f_2} A_4 \xrightarrow{f_3} A_5 \xrightarrow{f_4} A_6 \xrightarrow{O_2} A_7$$

with A_0 = A = {$O_1.a$, $O_1.A$},
    A_1 = {$O_1.a$, $O_1.A$, $O_2.A$},
    A_2 = {$O_1.a$, $O_1.A$, $O_2.A$, $O_1.b$, $O_1.c$ },

$A_3 = \{O_1.a, O_1.A, O_2.A, O_1.b, O_1.c, O_3.a\},$
$A_4 = \{O_1.a, O_1.A, O_2.A, O_1.b, O_1.c, O_3.a, O_4.a\},$
$A_5 = \{O_1.a, O_1.A, O_2.A, O_1.b, O_1.c, O_3.a, O_4.a, O_2.b\},$
$A_6 = \{O_1.a, O_1.A, O_2.A, O_1.b, O_1.c, O_3.a, O_4.a, O_2.b, O_2.c\},$
$A_7 = \{O_1.a, O_1.A, O_2.A, O_1.b, O_1.c, O_3.a, O_4.a, O_2.b, O_2.c, O_2.a\}.$

3.3 Extensions

There are domains of knowledge based on a set of elements, in which each element can be a simple valued variables or a function. For example, in the knowledge of alternating current the alternating current intensity $i(t)$ and the alternating potential $u(t)$ are functions. It requires some extensions of networks of computational objects such as *extensive computational objects networks* defined below.

Definition 3.4. An *extensive computational Object* (ECom-Object) is an object O has structure including:

- A set of attributes $Attrs(O) = M_v \bigcup M_f$, with M_v is a set of simple valued variables; M_f is a set of functional variables. Between the variables (or attributes) there are internal relations, that are deduction rules or the computational relations.
- The object O has behaviors of reasoning and computing on attributes of objects or facts such as: find the closure of a set $A \subset Attrs(O)$; find a solution of problems which has the form $A \rightarrow B$, with $A \subseteq Attrs(O)$ and $B \subseteq Attrs(O)$; perform computations; consider determination of objects or facts.

Definition 3.5. An *extensive network of computational objects* is a model **(O, M, F, T)** that has the components below.

- $O = \{O_1, O_2, ..., O_n\}$ is the set of extensive computational objects.
- M is a set of object attributes. We will use the following notations: $M_v(O_i)$ is the set of simple valued attributes of the object O_i, $M_f(O_i)$ is the set of functional attributes of O_i, $M(O_i) = M_v(O_i) \bigcup M_f(O_i)$, $M(O) = M(O_1) \bigcup M(O_2) \bigcup ... \bigcup M(O_n)$, and $M \subseteq M(O)$.
- F is the set of computational relations on attributes in M and on objects in O.
- $T = \{t_1, t_2, ..., t_k\}$ is set of operators on objects.

On the structure (O,T), there are expressions of objects. Each expression of objects has its attributes as if it is an object.

4 Problem Solving on COKB

In design process for KBSs, after representing knowledge and organizing the knowledge base, the inference engine has to be designed. To design the inference engine of a KBS for solving problems in general, with the knowledge base modeled by ontology COKB, we need to represent problems in general form. Problems can be modeled by using networks of computational objects, and the hypothesis of a problem has the form (O, F), in which O is a set of Com-objects, F is a set of facts on objects.

4.1 Modeling Problems

Definition 4.1. Model of problems on COKB has the form $(O, F) \rightarrow G$, and it consists of three sets: $O = \{O_1, O_2, \ldots, O_n\}$, $F = \{f_1, f_2, \ldots, f_m\}$, $G = \{g_1, g_2, \ldots, g_p\}$.

The CO-Net (O,F) is the hypothesis of the problem: O consists of n computational objects, F is the set of facts given on the objects. G consists of goals of the problem, each goal may be any facts such as determine an object or an attribute (or some attributes) of an object, prove a relation between objects, compute a value of a function relative to objects.

Definition 4.2. Give a problem $(O, F) \rightarrow G$ on model COKB, and the goal G is to determine (or compute) attributes; M is the set of attributes considered in the problem, $A \subseteq M$. Denote L be the set of facts in the hypothesis.

- Each $f \in$ Rules, each $O_i \in O$, we define:
  $f(A) = A \cup M_A(f)$, with $M_A(f)$ is set of attributes can be deduced from A by f.
  $O_i(A) = A \cup M_A(O_i)$, with $M_A(O_i)$ is set of attributes deduced from A by O_i.
- Suppose $D = [r_1, r_2, \ldots, r_m]$ is a list of elements r_j, $r_j \in$ Rules or $r_j \in O$. Denote:
  $L_0 = L$, $L_1 = r_1(L_0)$, $L_2 = r_2(L_1)$, $\ldots$ $L_m = r_m(L_{m-1})$ and $D(L) = L_m$
  A problem is called *solvable* if there is a list D such that $G \subseteq D(L)$. In this case, we say that D is a *solution* of the problem.

4.2 Reasoning Methods

The basic technique for designing deductive algorithms is the unification of facts. Based on the kinds of facts and their structures, there will be criteria for unification proposed. Then it produces algorithms to check the unification of two facts.

The forward chaining strategy can be used with some techniques such as usage of heuristics, sample problems. The most difficult thing is modeling for experience, sensible reaction and intuitional human to find heuristic rules, so that reasoning algorithms are able to imitate the human thinking for solving problems. We can use network of computational objects, and its extensions to model problems; and use above techniques to design algorithms for automated reasoning. For instance, a reasoning algorithm for model COKB with sample problems can be briefly presented below.

Definition 4.3. Given a model COKB $K = (C, H, R, Ops, Funcs, Rules)$, and a CO-Net (O, F) on this model. Denote L be the set of facts in the hypothesis. It is easy to verify that there exists an unique maximum set $\overline{L}$ such that the problem $(O, F) \rightarrow \overline{L}$ is *solvable*. The set $\overline{L}$ is called the *closure* of L.

Lemma: Given a COKB model $K = (C, H, R, Ops, Funcs, Rules)$, and a CO-Net (O, F) on this model, L is the set of facts in the hypothesis. By Definition 4.2, problem $(O, F) \rightarrow \overline{L}$ is solvable.

Then, there exists a list $D = [r_1, r_2, \ldots, r_k]$ such that $D(L) = \overline{L}$.

Theorem 4.1. Given a COKB model $K = (C, H, R, Ops, Funcs, Rules)$, and a problem $S = (O, F) \rightarrow G$ on this model. Denote L be the set of facts in the hypothesis. The following statements are equivalent.

(i) Problem S is solvable.

(ii) $G \subseteq \overline{L}$

(iii) There exists a list D such that $G \subseteq D(L)$

Proof:

    * The equivalent of (i) and (iii) can been checked easily. It is definition about solvable.

    * (i) => (ii): Problem S is solvable, but by Definition 3.4, $\overline{L}$ is a maximum set such that problem $(O, F) \rightarrow \overline{L}$ is solvable, so $G \subseteq \overline{L}$.

    * (ii) => (iii): Problem $(O, F) \rightarrow \overline{L}$ is solvable, by lemma, there exists an relation $D = [f_1, f_2, ..., f_k]$ such that $D(L) = \overline{L}$. But $G \subseteq \overline{L}$, so $G \subseteq D(L)$.

    Theorem 4.1 shows that forward chaining reasoning will deduce to goals of problems. So the effectiveness of the following algorithms would be ensure.

Definition 4.4. Give knowledge domain K = (C, H, R, Ops, Funcs, Rules), Sample Problem (SP) is a model on knowledge K, it consists of two components as $(\mathbf{H_p}, \mathbf{D_p})$. $\mathbf{H_p}$ is hypothesis of SP, and it has the following structure $H_p = (O_p, F_p)$, with O_p is the set of Com-Objects of Sample Problem, F_p is the set of facts given on objects in O_p. $\mathbf{D_p}$ is a list of elements can be applied on F_p.

A model of Computational Object Knowledge Base with Sample Problems (COKB-SP) consists of 7 components: (C, H, R, Ops, Funcs, Rules, Sample); in which, (C, H, R, Ops, Funcs, Rules) is knowledge domain which presented by COKB model, the Sample component is a set of Sample Problems of this knowledge domain.

    Algorithm 4.1: To find a solution of problem P modelled by (O,F)→G on knowledge K of the form COKB-SP.

        Solution← empty list; Solution_found← false;
        while (not Solution_found) do
            Find a *Sample Problem* can be applied to produce new facts;
            (heuristics can be used for this action)
            if (a sample S found)
                use the sample S to produce new facts;
                update the set of known facts, and add S to Solution;
                if (goal G obtained)
                    Solution_found ← true;
                continue;
            Find a *rule* can be applied to produce new facts or new objects;
            (heuristics can be used for this action)
            if (a rule r found)
                use r to produce new facts or objects;
                update the set of known facts and objects, and add r to Solution;
                if (goal G obtained)
                    Solution_found ← true;
        end do; { while }
        if (Solution_found)
            Solution is a solution of the problem;
        else
            There is no solution found;

Algorithm 4.2: To find a sample problem.

Given a set of facts H on knowledge K of the form COKB-SP. Find a sample problem that can be applied on H to produce new facts.

> SP ← Sample
> Sample_found←false
> Repeat
> > Select S in SP, then consider S as a rule;
> > (heuristics can be used for this action)
> > if (S can be applied on H to produce new facts)
> > > Sample_found ← true;
> > > break;
> > SP←SP – {S};
> Until SP = { };
> if (Sample_found)
> > S is a sample problem can be applied on H to produce new facts;
> else
> > There is no sample problem found;

Heuristic rules help finding solution quickly and giving a good human-readable solution. The followings are some useful heuristic rules we used:

1. Priority use of rules for determining objects and attributes.
2. Transform objects to objects at a higher level in the hierarchical graph if there are enough facts. For example, a triangle will become isosceles triangle if it has two equal edges.
3. Use rules for producing new objects that contains elements, which are not in existing objects.
4. Use rules for producing new objects that have relationship with existing objects, especially the goal, in necessary situations.
5. Try to use deduction rules to get new facts, especially facts that have relationship with the goal.
6. If we could not produce new facts or new objects then we should use parameters and equations.
7. There are always new facts (relations or expressions) when we produce new objects.

4.3   Extension

In Sect. 3, the extension of CO-Net (Definitions 3.4 and 3.5) is a model in which the concept of computational objects have functional attributes. Besides, objects have not only the inner computation relations but also the operators on objects.

Each expression of objects always has its attributes as if it is an object. Let E(Onet) is the set of expressions of objects on the network Onet = (O,M,F,T). We will use the following notations: M_E is set of attributes of expression E, E(r) is set of attributes in relation r of E(Onet), F_E is set of relations in E(ONet) or the relations attributes of the different objects. To solve problems modelled by using extensive CO-Net, we also define the concepts solutions and good solutions of problems. Then, the algorithm for solving problems is as follows:

Algorithm 4.3. Find a solution of the problem H→G.

Given Onet, E(ONet) and hypothesis $H \subseteq M \cup M_E$, $G \subseteq M \cup M_E$ that should be determined.

> Determine E(ONet) and new relation of E(ONet).
> Solution ← empty; Goal ← G;
> **Repeat** Hold ← H;
>> *< Search Function choices a r ∈ F with Heuristic's law> ;*
>> **while** (**not** Solution_found **and** (r found))
>>> **if** (Having a new r)
>>>> H ← H ∪ M(r);   Solution ← Solution ∪ {r};
>>> **if** $(G \subseteq H)$
>>>> Solution_found ← true;
>>> *<Search Function choice a r ∈ F with Heuristic's law >;*
>> **Until** Solution_found **or** (H = Hold);
>> **if** (**not** Solution_found)   <Not having a solution>;
>> **else** Solution is a solution of problem;

5   Designing Knowledge Base and Inference Engine

After collecting real knowledge, the knowledge base design includes the following tasks.

- The knowledge domain collected, which is denoted by K, will be represented or modeled based on the knowledge model COKB, CO-Net and their extensions or restrictions known. Some restrictions of COKB model were used to design knowledge bases are the model COKB lacking operator component (C, H, R, Funcs, Rules), the model COKB without function component (C, H, R, Ops, Rules), and the simple COKB sub-model (C, H, R, Rules). From Studying and analyzing the whole of knowledge in the domain, It is not difficult to determine known forms of knowledge presenting, together with relationships between them. In case that knowledge K has the known form such as COKB model, we can use this model for representing knowledge K directly. Otherwise, the knowledge K can be partitioned into knowledge sub-domains K_i (i = 1, 2, ..., n) with lower complexity and certain relationships, and each K_i has the form known. The relationships between knowledge sub-domains must be clear so that we can integrate knowledge models of the knowledge sub-domains later.
- Each knowledge sub-domain K_i will be modeled by using the above knowledge models, so a knowledge model $M(K_i)$ of knowledge K_i will be established. The relationships on $\{K_i\}$ are also specified or represented. The models $\{M(K_i)\}$ together with their relationships are integrated to produce a model $M(K)$ of the knowledge K. Then we obtain a knowledge model $M(K)$ for the whole knowledge K of the application.

- Next, it is needed to construct a specification language for the knowledge base of the system. The COKB model and CO-Nets have their specification language used to specify knowledge bases of these form. A restriction or extension model of those models also have suitable specification language. Therefore, we can easily construct a specification language L(K) for the knowledge K. This language gives us to specify components of knowledge K in the organization of the knowledge base.

From the model M(K) and the specification language L(K), the knowledge base organization of the system will be established. It consists of structured text files that stores the knowledge components: concepts, hierarchical relation, relations, operators, functions, rules, facts and objects.

The inference engine design includes the following tasks:

- From the collection of problems with an initial classification, we can determine classes of problems base on known models such as CO-Net, and its extensions. This task helps us to model classes of problems as frame-based problem models, or as CO-Nets for general forms of problems. Techniques for modeling problems are presented in Sect. 3. Problems modeled by using network of computational objects has the form (O, F) $\to$ Goal.
- The basic technique for designing deductive algorithms is the unification of facts. Based on the kinds of facts and their structures, there will be criteria for unification proposed. Then it produces algorithms to check the unification of two facts.
- To design reasoning algorithms for solving general problems, we can use the methods presented in Sects. 3 and 4. More works to do are to determine sample problems, heuristic rules (for selection of rules, for selection of sample problems, etc.).

6 Applications

The ontology COKB and design method for knowledge-based systems presented in previous sections have been used to produce many applications. In this section, we introduce some applications and examples about solutions of problems produced by the systems.

- The system that supports studying knowledge and solving analytic geometry problems. It consists of three components: the interface, the knowledge base, the knowledge processing modules or the inference engine. The program has menus for users searching knowledge they need and they can access knowledge base. Besides, there are windows for inputting problems. Users are supported a simple language for specifying problems. There are also windows in which the program shows solutions of problems and figures.
- The program for studying and solving problems in plane geometry. It can solve problems in general forms. Users only declare hypothesis and goal of problems base on a simple language but strong enough for specifying problems. The hypothesis

can consist of objects, facts on objects or attributes, and parameters. The goal can be to compute an attribute, to determine an object or parameters, a relation or a formula. After specifying a problem, users can request the program to solve it automatically or to give instructions that help them to solve it themselves. The program also gives a human readable solution, which is easy to read and agree with the way of thinking and writing by students and teachers.

Examples below illustrate the functions of the above systems for solving problems in general forms.

Example 6.1.   Given two points P(2, 5) and Q(5,1). Suppose d is a line that contains the point P, and the distance between Q and d is 3. Find the equation of line d.

Specification of the Problem:
   Objects = {[P, point], [Q, point], [d, line]}.
   Hypothesis = {DISTANCE(Q, d) = 3, P = [2, 5], Q = [5, 1], ["BELONG", P, d]}.
   Goal = [d.f].
Solution found by the system:
   Step 1: {P = [2, 5]} $\Rightarrow$ {P}.
   Step 2: {DISTANCE(Q, d) = 3} $\Rightarrow$ {DISTANCE(Q, d)}.
   Step 3: {d, P} $\rightarrow$ {2d[1]+5d[2]+d[3] = 0}.
   Step 4: {DISTANCE(Q, d) = 3} $\Rightarrow$ $\dfrac{|5d[1] + d[2] + d[3]|}{\sqrt{d[1]^2 + d[2]^2}} = 3$.

   Step 5: {d[1] = 1, 2d[1] + 5d[2] + d[3] = 0, $\dfrac{|5d[1] + d[2] + d[3]|}{\sqrt{d[1]^2 + d[2]^2}} = 3$ }

   $\Rightarrow$ {d.f = $(x + \dfrac{24}{7} y - \dfrac{134}{7} = 0)$, d.f = (x − 2 = 0)}.

   Step 6: {d.f = $x + \dfrac{24}{7} y - \dfrac{134}{7} = 0$, d.f = x − 2 = 0} $\Rightarrow$ {d.f}

Example 6.2.   Given the parallelogram ABCD. Suppose M and N are two points of segment AC such that AM = CN. Prove that two triangles ABM and CDN are equal.

Specification of the Problem:
Specification of the Problem:
      Objects = {[A, POINT], [B, POINT], [C, POINT], [D, POINT], [M, POINT],
            [N, POINT], [O1, PARALLELOGRAM[A, B, C, D],
            [O2, TRIANGLE[A, B, M]], [O3, TRIANGLE [C, D, N]]}.
      Hypothesis = { [« BELONG », M, SEGMENT[A, C]],
            [« BELONG », N, SEGMENT[A, C]],
            SEGMENT[A, M] = SEGMENT[C, N] }.
      Goal = { O2 = O3}.

Solution found by the system:
   Step 1: Hypothesis
      $\Rightarrow$ { O2.SEGMENT[A, M] = O3.SEGMENT[C, N],
         O2.SEGMENT[A, B] = O1.SEGMENT[A, B],
         O3.SEGMENT[C, D] = O1.SEGMENT[C, D]}.
   Step 2: Produce new objects related to O2, O3, and O1
      $\Rightarrow$ {[O4, TRIANGLE[A, B, C]], [O5, TRIANGLE[C, D, A]]}.
   Step 3: {[O1, PARALLELOGRAM[A, B, C, D]}
      $\Rightarrow$ {O4 = O5, SEGMENT[A, B] = SEGMENT[C, D]}.
   Step 4: { O2.SEGMENT[A, B] = O1.SEGMENT[A, B],
         O3.SEGMENT[C, D] = O1.SEGMENT[C, D],
         SEGMENT[A, B] = SEGMENT[C, D]}
      $\Rightarrow$ {O2.SEGMENT[A, B] = O3.SEGMENT[C, D]}.
   Step 5: {[«BELONG», M, SEGMENT[A, C]]} $\Rightarrow$ {O4.angle_A = O2.angle_A}.
   Step 6: {[«BELONG», N, SEGMENT[A, C]]} $\Rightarrow$ {O5.angle_A = O3.angle_A }.
   Step 7: {O4 = O5 } $\Rightarrow$ {O4.angle_A = O5.angle_A}.
   Step 8: { O4.angle_A = O2.angle_A, O5.angle_A = O3.angle_A ,
         O4.angle_A = O5.angle_A } $\Rightarrow$ { O2.angle_A = O3.angle_A}.
   Step 9: { O2.SEGMENT[A, M] = O3. SEGMENT[C, N],
         O2.SEGMENT[A, B] = O3.SEGMENT[C, D],
         O2.angle_A = O3.angle_A } $\Rightarrow$ {O2 = O3}.

7   Conclusion and Future Work

The ontology COKB can be used to design and to implement knowledge-based systems, especially expert systems and intelligent problem solvers. It consists of the model COKB, the specification language for COKB, the network of Com-Objects for modeling problems, algorithms for automated problem solving. It provides a natural way for representing knowledge domains in practice. By integration of ontology engineering, object-oriented modeling and symbolic computation programming it provides a highly intuitive representation for knowledge. These are the bases for designing the knowledge base of the system. The knowledge base is convenient for accessing and for using by the inference engine. The design of inference engine is easy and more effectively by using heuristics, sample problems in reasoning. So, the methods of modeling problems and algorithms for automated problem solving represent a normal way of human thinking. Therefore, systems not only give human readable solutions of problems but also present solutions as the way people write them.

Ontology COKB is a useful tool and method for designing practical knowledge bases, modeling complex problems and designing algorithms to solve automatically problems based on a knowledge base. It was used to produce intelligent softwares for e-learning. Besides applications were presented here, ontology COKB is able to use in other domain of knowledge such as physics and chemistry. Moreover, it also has been used to develop applications for e-government.

This ontology certainly has its limitation. Our future works are to develop the models and algorithms. First, Six related knowledge components in COKB model are complicated and not effective for representing simple knowledge domains. So, we need to investigate restriction models of COKB and their relationships and integration. Second, the concept Com-object should be extended so that attributes can be functional attributes. Third, the rules component of COKB model should have rules of the form equations to adapt more knowledge domains.

References

1. van Harmelen, F., Lifschitz, V., Porter, B.: Handbook of Knowledge Representation. Elsevier, Amsterdam (2008)
2. Russell, S., Norvig, P.: Artificial Intelligence – A Modern Approach, 3rd edn. Prentice Hall, Englewood Cliffs (2010)
3. Sowa, J.F.: Knowledge Representation: Logical Philosophical and Computational Foundations. Brooks/Cole, Boston (2000)
4. Luger, G.F.: Artificial Intelligence: Structures And Strategies For Complex Problem Solving. Addison Wesley Longman, Inc., Boston (2008)
5. Baral, Chitta: Knowledge Representation, Reasoning and Declarative Problem Solving. Cambridge University Press, UK Cambridge (2003)
6. Lakemeyer, G., Nebel, B.: Foundations of Knowledge representation and Reasoning. Springer-Verlag, Berlin Heidelberg (1994)
7. Wu, W.-T.: Mechanical Theorem Proving in Geometries. Springer, Berlin, Heidelberg (1994)
8. Chou, S.C., Gao, X.S., Zhang, J.Z.: Machine Proofs in Geometry. Utopia Press, Singapore (1994)
9. Pfalzgraf, J., Wang, D.: Automated Practical Reasoning. Springer, Heidelberg (1995)
10. Gruber, T.R.: Toward principles for the design of ontologies used for knowledge sharing. Int. J. Hum. Comput. Stud. 43, 907–928 (1995)
11. Stojanovic, L., Schneider, J., Maedche, A., Libischer, S., Suder, R., Lumpp, T., Abecker, A., Breiter, G., Dinger, J.: The role of ontologies in autonomic computing systems. IBM Syst. J. 43, 598–616 (2004)
12. Gómez-Pérez, A., Férnandez-López, M., Corcho, O.: Ontological Engineering. Springer, Heidelberg (2004)
13. Guarino, N.: Formal ontology, conceptual analysis and knowledge representation. Int. J. Hum. Comput. Stud. 43, 625–640 (1995)
14. Fathalipour, M., Selamat, A., Jung, J.J.: Ontology-based, process-oriented, and society-independent agent system for cloud computing. Int. J. Distrib. Sens. Netw. 2014, 17 (2014)
15. Vallet, D., Fernández, M., Castells, P.: An ontology-based information retrieval model. In: Gómez-Pérez, A., Euzenat, J. (eds.) ESWC 2005. LNCS, vol. 3532, pp. 455–470. Springer, Heidelberg (2005)
16. Van Heijst, G., Schreiber, A.T.H., Wielinga, B.J.: Using explicit ontologies in KBS development. Int. J. Hum. Comput. Stud. 45, 183–292 (1997). Academic Press Limited
17. Abdulmajid, H.: Mohamed, sai peck lee, siti salwah salim, an ontology-based knowledge model for software experience management. Int. J. Comput. Internet Manage 14(3), 79–88 (2006)
18. Chein, M., Leclere, M., Nicolas, Y.: Sudocad: a knowledge-based system for the author linkage problem. In: Huynh, V.N., Denoeux, T., Tran, D.H., Le, A.C., Pham, S.B. (eds.) Knowledge and Systems Engineering, vol. 1, pp. 65–83. Springer International Publishing, Switzerland (2014)

19. Krotkiewics, M., Wojtkiewicz, K.: An introduction to ontology based structured knowledge base system: knowledge acquisition Module. In: Selamat, A., Nguyen, N.T., Haron, H. (eds.) ACIIDS 2013. LNCS, vol. 7802, pp. 497–506. Springer, Heidelberg (2013)

20. Mizoguchi, R.: Advanced course of ontological engineering. New Gener. Comput. 22(2), 193–220 (2004). Ohmsha Ltd. and Springer-Verlag, 2004

21. Mizoguchi, R.: What ontological engineering can do for solving real-world problems. In: Huynh, V.N., Denoeux, T., Tran, D.H., Le, A.C., Pham, S.B. (eds.) Knowledge and Systems Engineering, vol. 1, p. 3. Springer International Publishing, Switzerland (2014)

22. Berge, J.M., Levia, O., Rouillard, J.: Object-Oriented Modeling. Kluwer Academic Publishers, Netherlands (1996)

23. Bernadin, L., et al.: Maple Programming Guide. Maplesoft, a division of Waterloo Maple Inc, Waterloo (2012)

24. Van Nhon, D.: A program for studying and solving problems in plane geometry. In: Proceedings of International Conference on Artificial Intelligence, Las Vegas, USA, pp. 1441–1447 (2000)

25. Van Nhon, D.: A system that supports studying knowledge and solving of analytic geometry problems. In: 16th World Computer Congress 2000, Proceedings of Conference on Education Uses of Information and Communication Technologies, Beijing, China. pp. 236–239 (2000)

26. Thi, T.L.N., Van Do, N.: An expert system for diabetic microvascular complication diagnosis. J. Comput. Sci. Issues 10(4), 308–316 (2013). No 2

27. Van Do, N.: Model for knowledge bases of computational objects. Int. J. Comput. Sci. 7(3), 11–20 (2010). No 8

Dynamic WLAN Fingerprinting RadioMap for Adapted Indoor Positioning Model

Iyad H. Alshami$^{(\boxtimes)}$, Noor Azurati Ahmad, and Shamsul Sahibuddin

Advanced Informatics School (AIS), Universiti Teknolgi Malaysia (UTM),
Jalan Semarak, 54100 Kuala Lumpur, Malaysia
`hmaeyad2@mail.live.utm.my`, {`azurati,shamsul`}`@utm.my`

Abstract. As a result of Smartphone usage increment a sharp growth in demand for indoor environment computing especially for Location Based Services (LBS) has been occurred. The basic concept of LBS is to determine the mobile users' location, which is important for services such as tracking or navigation in Civil defense and Healthcare. Currently, there are many techniques used to locate a mobile user in indoor environment. WLAN is considered as one of the best choices for indoor positioning due to its low cost, simple configuration and high accuracy. Although the WLAN Received Signal Strength Indicator (RSSI) fingerprinting method is the most accurate positioning method, it has a serious drawback because it's Radio Map (RM) become outdated when environmental change occurs. In addition, recalibrating the RM is a time consuming process. This paper presents a novel adapted indoor positioning model which uses the path loss propagation model of the wireless signal to overcome the outdated RM. The experimental results demonstrate that the proposed adapted model is highly efficient in solving the problems mentioned especially in a dynamically changing environment.

Keywords: Indoor positioning · Fingerprinting · Radio map · Path loss model

1 Introduction

The recent decade witnesses a high demand for Location Based Services (LBS) in outdoor environments as well as indoor environments. LBS can be involved in several and critical systems in our daily life such as: Emergency services, healthcare, retailing, manufacturing, logistics and many other industries. Indoor positioning systems (IPS) gained in importance after the Global Positioning System (GPS) fails in determining a location accurately inside buildings (known as indoor environments) because the GPS receiver could not be in line-of-sight with the satellites. A lot of researches have been conducted to find other techniques to enable the LBS to provide its services in a closed environment. Although Wireless Local Area Network (WLAN) technology is a valuable technology to be used for IPS due to its low cost and simple configuration, achieving high accuracy still needs more investigation because the WLAN's has two main weaknesses. These weaknesses are multipath influenced by presence of obstacles and signal strength fluctuation during the day time [1, 2].

© Springer International Publishing Switzerland 2015
H. Fujita and A. Selamat (Eds.): SoMeT 2014, CCIS 513, pp. 119–133, 2015.
DOI: 10.1007/978-3-319-17530-0_9

This research presents new adapted WLAN-based IPS model and this model is able to estimate the location of mobile device in dynamic environment accurately, and this paper organized as follows: Sect. 1 presents a brief background which covers the Fingerprinting method and the path loss model. Section 2 discusses some of the related work, while in Sect. 3 the proposed model is introduced. Section 4 presents and discusses the experimental results followed by a conclusion and suggestions for future work.

2 Background

Location System, Geolocation System, Positioning System, and Localization System are alternative expressions to the same system [2–4]. This system has the ability to determine the current position/location of a specific object, mobile device, in a specific environment.

The need for positioning system is not new. Historically the ancient people built their own positioning system for navigation and the old positioning systems mainly depend on the location of the stars. The astronomical tables give the location of specific stars in the sky throughout the year. People in the recent days also have the same need as the ancient people but for many purposes beside navigation purpose.

The Global Positioning System (GPS) is a satellite navigation system that is able to provide the location of the GPS receiver device as tuple of Longitude and Latitude. The GPS receiver must be in line-of-sight with the satellite. The GPS was developed in 1973 for military use, but it has been allowed freely for civilian use but with a degraded performance [5]. Widespread use of the GPS shows that LBS has become a significant part of people's daily life [4]. LBS can be defined as services that integrate the mobile user's location with other information in order to provide valuable information to the user [6]. These services vary according to the characteristics of its targeted users such as; Military to track/determine target location; Civil defense to determine the appeal location; Marketing to help possible customers; Healthcare to find the current location of a doctor for emergency cases; and in Management to follow up the employee's location or location of objects.

2.1 Indoor Positioning Methods and Techniques

After the failure of GPS in determining the location in the indoor environments, a lot of researches have been conducted to find other methods or techniques to enable LBS systems to provide its services in such an environment. These methods can be divided into three general categories [2, 3, 7–9]: Proximity; Triangulation; and Scene Analysis. Figure 1 gives a clearer and closer view of the WLAN-based indoor localization techniques.

Proximity. Proximity is also known as connectivity based. The position of mobile device is determined by the coverage area of the transmitter (access point in WLAN case) – it is fixed in a known position and has limited range [2, 8]. The proximity method has a wide range of distance errors.

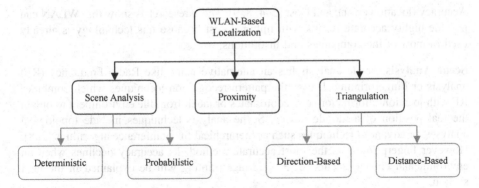

Fig. 1. WLAN-based localization techniques

Triangulation. Triangulation method uses the triangles' geometric properties of the radio frequency to locate the current location of the mobile device. It has two approaches: distance-based and direction-based. The distance-based (*Lateration*) approach converts the measurement of the propagation-time of the received signal into distance to estimate the mobile device location, as shown in Fig. 2 Triangulation Techniques: (a) Lateration (b) Angulation, where the Time of Arrival (ToA) has been used in [10] and the Round Trip Time (RTT) has been used in [3]; or based on converting the measurement of the receive signal strength (RSS) into distance such as in [11, 12]. On the other hand, the direction-based (*angulation*) approach estimates the location based on the angle of the received signal [2, 8] as shown in Fig. 2 Triangulation Techniques: (a) Lateration (b) Angulation.

Triangulation became a very rich research area since the radio frequency has a wide range of technologies such as: Radio Frequency Identification (RFID); Infrared Radiation (IR); Ultra Wide Band (UWB); Wireless LAN (WLAN); Ultrasound; and Bluetooth. The efficiency of these radio technologies have been examined, and the performance of these technologies have been measured by many metrics such as:

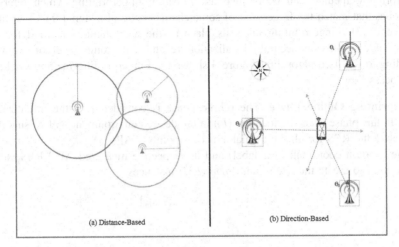

Fig. 2. Triangulation Techniques: (a) Lateration (b) Angulation

Accuracy (location error), and Cost [2–4, 8, 9]. These researches show that WLAN can provide highly accurate results with minimal cost because this technology is already used in most of the companies and institutions.

Scene Analysis. Scene analysis has an alternative name like Radio Frequency (RF) analysis or Fingerprinting. It uses the pattern recognition techniques which combines RF with location information, e.g. coordinates or label, from the environment to obtain the real position of a mobile device. Scene analysis techniques include topological analyses, or advanced techniques such as hierarchical fuzzy inference algorithms [2, 8]. However fingerprinting is the most accurate method, its accuracy declines when an environmental change occurs [2, 3, 7]. Fingerprinting will be explained in the next section.

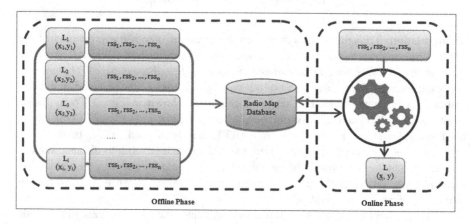

Fig. 3. Fingerprinting method's scheme

2.2 Fingerprinting

Fingerprinting method can be defined as "Location fingerprinting which refers to techniques that match the fingerprint of some characteristic of a signal that is location dependent" [3]. Fingerprinting takes its place as the most famous method for IPS because it can provide accurate localization result, with some level of variation according to the used algorithm. Figure 3 shows the Fingerprinting method's scheme and process flow.

Fingerprinting Offline Phase. The offline phase is considered as the initialization phase. In this phase each site location (L_i) in the desired environment will be surveyed to measure the RSS for all the available access points – APs- (S_i).

The location coordinates (or label) and its respective measured APs' RSS values will be used to create the site's radio map (RM) instances.

$$S_i = \{rss_{i1}, rss_{i2}, \ldots, rss_{in}\} \qquad (1)$$

where rss_{ij} refers to the signal strength of access point A_j in the location L_i. This means that the radio map can be expressed as:

$$RM = \{T_1, T_2, \ldots, T_m\} \tag{2}$$

where T_i is a tuple of (S_i, L_i) and m is the number of instances in the RM.

Fingerprinting Online Phase. The online phase is also known as run-time or positioning phase. In this phase the current location (L_c) of a mobile device, laptop or smartphone, is required to be determined based on the current measurement set of RSS (S_c).

$$S_c = \{rss_{c1}, rss_{c2}, \ldots, rss_{cn}\} \tag{3}$$

The process is done by searching the RM for the best matching of the signal strength part (S_i) of the stored tuples (S_i, L_i). The matching process can be performed by searching for the most similar signal pattern in RM, Euclidian Distance (4) used to measure the similarity between two patterns. The less distance is the most similar pattern and vice versa.

$$d_{ci}(S_c, S_i) = \sqrt{[2]\sum_{j=1}^{n}(S_{cj} - S_{ij})^2} \tag{4}$$

where d_{ci} is the distance between two RSS sets S_c and S_i.

The location coordinates or label (L_c) of the selected RM's instance, with the minimum Euclidian Distance, will be considered as the current location coordinates or label of that mobile device.

$$L_c(d_{ci}) = argmin\{d_{ci}(S_c, S_i) \forall S_i \in RM\}\} \tag{5}$$

Fingerprint Drawbacks. Although fingerprinting is the most valuable IPS' method due to its accurate location detection, its accuracy level dramatically decline in the case of environmental change occurrence [2, 3, 7, 9]. That change means the RM, bulky and time consuming process in offline phase, become outdated and it must be recreated again to include the effects of that environmental change in the scene analysis. The environmental change can be; adding/moving furniture, add/removing partition, adding/removing access points, and environmental expanding horizontally/ vertically.

Fingerprint's Matching Algorithms. There are two different approaches of algorithms which can be used to search for the best fingerprint matching; *Deterministic* and *Probabilistic* [2–4, 8, 9]. The *probabilistic approach* uses probability methods, such as Naïve Bayesian, to compute the probability characteristics of the RM instances to find the best match fingerprint to determine the current location of the mobile device. A lot of researches have been conducted in this area such as [13, 14]. On the other hand, the *deterministic approach* used scalar values such, as the mean and non-probabilistic methods to estimate the current location of the mobile device. A lot of researchers used K-Nearest-Neighbor (KNN) [15]; Artificial Neural Networks (NN) [16–18]; and Support Vector Machine (SVM) [17, 18], to estimate the current location of the mobile device as a deterministic method [7, 19, 20]. The deterministic approach is well established and has less computational cost since it does not require big RM as the probabilistic approach [21].

KNN is a simple and powerful classifier, widely used in indoor localization systems based on fingerprinting approach due to its high localization accuracy [15, 16, 22]. NN-based IPS is a high non-linear mapping between S_i and L_i. However NN-based IPS is limited by its slow convergence and easy trapping into local minimum. In addition, the NN model will fail when an environmental change occurs [23, 24]. In this research paper KNN and NN have been used in order to examine the accuracy of the proposed model.

2.3 WLAN Signal Propagation Path Loss Models

In order to get an accurate localization result, the predicted fingerprints must be as close to the real RSS values as possible. Goldsmith A. in [25] classifies the propagation models into two classes: deterministic and empirical. The prior one considers high complexity approach and it needs very precise information about the environment [7]. The first deterministic model was proposed by Hae-Won, S. and Noh-Hoon, M. [26] in 1999, but the most known deterministic model was proposed by Athanasiadou, G.E. et al. [27] in 2000.

On the other hand the first empirical path loss model appeared at the end of 1980 s [28]. A lot of researches have been conducted to enhance the RSS prediction in the empirical model such as [28–35]. Mardeni, R. and Solahuddin, Y. in [28] define the empirical path loss model as the experimental mathematical formulation which predicts radio wave propagation based on limited but essential parameters such as frequency, path loss exponent, distance, and physical blockings. Due to its lower computational cost and simple to design [7], the empirical study was selected to be our RSS prediction model. In the next section the most valuable four path loss propagation models will be provided.

One-Slope Model. One-slope model (OSM) [35] (1992) is the most commonly used path loss model, the RSS value decreases exponentially with the distance d, distance in meter, between the transceivers.

$$PL(d) = PL(d_0) + 10n \log\left(\frac{d}{d_0}\right) \qquad (6)$$

where the $PL(d_0)$ is the free space propagation loss at reference distance d_0, typically 1 meter, and n is the slope factor (power decay index) which becomes 2 for free space and 6.5 for obstructed space [33, 35]. The term free space means that the receiver can be in line-of-sight (LOS) with the transmitter.

Log-Normal Shadowing Model. The Log-Normal Shadowing Model is an extension of the One-Slope Model proposed in [35] (1992). Here, the effects of random shadowing due to varying levels of clutters are taken into account. The average path loss between a transmitter and its receiver is expressed as Eq. (7)

$$PL(d) = PL(d_0) + 10n \, \log\left(\frac{d}{d_0}\right) + X \tag{7}$$

where X is a zero-mean Gaussian distributed random variable proposed by Seidel, S.Y. and T.S. Rappaport in [35], to replace all the possible attenuation factors. However, using zero-mean random variable will make a big difference between the RSS values; thus, more attention for the attenuation factors will bring more systematic RSS prediction.

Multi-Wall Model. In addition of the free space path loss, Multi-Wall Model (MWM) [33] (2001) considers the penetration parameters such as the wall and floor attenuation factors Eq. (8).

$$PL(d) = PL(d_0) + 10n \, \log\left(\frac{d}{d_0}\right) + \sum_{i=1}^{I}\sum_{k=1}^{k_{wi}} L_{wik} + \sum_{j=1}^{J}\sum_{k=1}^{k_{fj}} L_{fjk} \tag{8}$$

where L_{wik} is considered the attenuation factor of all types of wall and L_{fik} is the attenuation factor of all types of floors, and I and J are the number of wall types and the number of floor respectively.

As evolution of MWM, COST231 MWM assumes that all walls have the same properties such as the material and thickness and the entire floor also have the same properties, Eq. (9).

$$PL(d) = PL(d_0) + 10n \, \log\left(\frac{d}{d_0}\right) + \sum WAF + \sum FAF \tag{9}$$

where WAF and FAF represent the wall attenuation factor and the floor attenuation factor respectively.

A combination between the MWM [33] and the zero-mean Gaussian distributed random variable, proposed in [35], will be used in this work as in the following equation Eq. (10):

$$PL(d) = PL(d_0) + 10n \, \log\left(\frac{d}{d_0}\right) + \sum WAF + X \tag{10}$$

3 Related Works

A lot of researches have been conducted in order to overcome the environmental change occurrence; these researches can be divided into two based on their approaches. The first approach uses extra hardware such as feedback devices or sensors, example of this approach can be found in [36–41]. On the other hand the second approach tries to use the signal propagation path loss model and such researches can be found in [22, 42–46]. This research falls under the second approach so the later related work will be discussed briefly in this section.

In 2000, Microsoft's researchers, Bahl, P. and Padmanabhan, N., proposed RADAR [22]. RADAR is considered the base of the WLAN fingerprinting IPS. RADAR operates by applying the basic concept of fingerprinting methods. It records and processes the WLAN' RSS of a UTP broadcast message from a mobile user collected by three fixed position stations, to determine the mobile user's location. RADAR also combines the RSS empirical measurements with signal propagation modeling Eq. (11), to fill the missing cells in the offline fingerprint measurement to provide more accurate localization.

$$PL(d) = PL(d_0) + 10n \ \log(d) + \begin{cases} nw * WAF & nw < C \\ C * WAF & nw \geq C \end{cases} \tag{11}$$

where n indicates the rate at which the path loss increases with distance, $PL(d)$ is the signal power at some reference distance d_0 and d is the transmitter-receiver (T-R) separation distance. C is the maximum number of obstructions (walls) up to which the attenuation factor makes a difference, nw is the number of obstructions (walls) between the transmitter and the receiver, and WAF is the wall attenuation factor. RADAR's experimental testbed is a floor of an area of 980 m^2, and includes more than 50 rooms. The experimental result shows the validity of using the WLAN's signals in the indoor positioning systems with distance error between 2 m to 3 m. However, from our point of view RADAR has some defect; the *first* one, it works on determining the mobile user location at the room level. That means the distance error measurement is not consistent with experimental testbed since the distance error relays the average of the distance differences by meter and the location unit here is 3 m^2, which is the room size in the experimental testbed; the *second* one, RADAR builds an offline fingerprint database which become outdated database because the RSS can fluctuate and environment change may occur; the *last* one, it uses signal propagation model to fill the missed RSS reading in the offline fingerprint database. It means if RSS value is constant in a specific point x on distance d, while in reality measuring the RSS value in a specific point x on distance d many times will show different values each time.

Liu et al. [43], in 2011, provided IPS based on combining the fingerprinting method and path loss models for multi floor environment, because most of the WLAN-based IPS did not consider the multi floor environment. Selected samples per floor have been selected to create the radio map and in the online phase the floor number is localized based on searching the radio map. After determining the floor, the mobile device location is determined by triangulation methods based on the APs location, estimated by the path loss model in Eq. (12).

$$PL(d) = PL(d_0) + 10n \ \log(d) + OAF \tag{12}$$

where OAF is all the obstacles which include walls and partitioning plates. The experimental result of the proposed solution shows that the floor positioning is highly accurate close to 100% and point localization precision is close to 1.6 m, with 5 m distance between each point. Although a high accurate result is important in floor positioning, in any fingerprinting systems the main drawback is that a database is usually required to rebuild for accurate localization if environmental change occurred.

In 2013, Narzullaev, A. et al. [44], proposed algorithm to handle the extensive and time-consuming RSS calibration process in designing the radio map for the indoor localization systems. The proposed algorithm combines the concept of the reference point (feedback point) and the one-slope- model (OSM), Eq. (12), pass loss signal prediction model (8) to get time-efficient calibration process. It starts by calibrating the RSS of the available APs by the feedback points, then it estimates the location of the APs with the strongest RSS based on the distance between the prediction point and it closes the feedback point where the RSS can be predicted by using OSM. However, the experiment results show the efficiency of the proposed algorithm in reducing the RSS calibration time without reducing the location prediction accuracy. From the author point of view, the proposed solution has few drawbacks. Firstly, it increases the cost of indoor positioning system by using a feedback point. Secondly, the algorithm increases the computational complexity by searching for the strongest APs and determining its locations. Thirdly, it uses the OSM model which assumes ideal wireless media which will not fluctuate nor attenuate due to many known and unknown reasons.

4   The Proposed Model

The proposed model consists of two modules the Room Localizer (RLOC) and Environment Descriptor (EDEC). RLOC is considered the main part of the model because its task is to determine the current location of the mobile device. RLOC contains the Radio Map Generator (RMG) and the Location Detector (LD). EDEC is a simple information store, this information describes the environment's layout and the used access points and its locations as shown in Fig. 4. RMG work is based on the information on EDEC to create RM and then the LD will be invoked to determine the mobile device location based on the generated RM. The RSS value will be computed based on Eq. (20).

In case of NN usage it will be built and trained based on the created RM. The architecture of the NN will be n input neurons, $(2n + 1)$ hidden neurons, and 1 output neuron. And in case of KNN usage the nearest five neighbors will be considered. In the positioning stage, RLOC will get the RSS tuple from the mobile device and pass this tuple to the LD model to provide room label as the current location of the mobile device.

5   Experiments & Result Discussion

5.1   Determining Test-Bed Environment

The eastern side on the third floor of the Menara Razak building, Universiti Teknolgi Malaysia (UTM) Kuala Lumpur, has been selected as testbed environment. This testbed has been gridded into 1 m x 1 m cell size as shown in Fig. 5. The dimension of the selected area is 370 m^2, and this area contains blocked area which means that there are around 300 different points are available for calibrations.

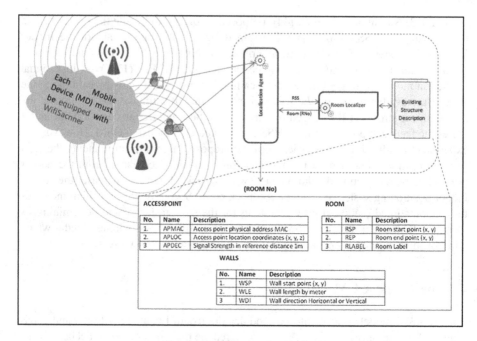

Fig. 4. Environment description

5.2 Manual Radio Map (RM) Creation

In order to calibrate the RSS values from the existing three CSICO WAP4410 N APs, WifiScanner application has been developed in two different platforms; Android OS 4.2 and MS Windows. WifiScanner has been configured to capture one WLAN beacon frame per second, and for each point in the environment grid it configured to capture ten different beacon frames. After fixing the APs locations, two rounds of the RSS collection have been conducted, and about ten hours were spent for each round. In order to create RM, each point is represented by the mean value of its RSS values and labeled by the point coordinate and the room number is then stored in CSV file. The final RM size is 1070 instances. This RM will be used in two different tasks: firstly to examine the accuracy for fingerprinting algorithms such as KNN and NN; secondly to use it as testing set in order to evaluate the proposed adaptive model.

Fig. 5. Gridding the selected environment

5.3   Examining the Accuracy of Fingerprinting Algorithms

This experiment has been conducted in order to compare the accuracy, for room level, of the KNN and the NN. The calibrated RM, 1070 instances, has been used in this experiment and it has been partitioned into 70% and 30% as training set and testing set respectively. The accuracy of the KNN by counting the majority of 5 neighbors was 93%, on the second hand the architecture of NN, with 3 input neurons; 7 hidden neurons; and 1 output neurons, achieved 94% as a regression value and 80% as accuracy. The number of hidden neurons in NN has been selected firstly to be double the input neurons, and then the approach of trial and error showed that 7 hidden neurons is the best one. Table 1 summarized this experiment.

Table 1.   KNN & NN accuracy based the structure

KNN			NN		
K Neighbors	MSE	Accuracy	H. Neurons	MSE	Accuracy
3	0.093458	90.75%	6	0.202492	79.98%
5	0.071651	92.94%	7	0.199377	80.16%
			8	0.224299	77.67%

The results came in this manner due to the small difference in RSS in each point, so that NN shows high regression between the input and the output but with high 0.2 as MSE. On the other hand KNN can distinguish between these too closed RSS values by simple technique as Euclidian Distance. Hence, KNN will be adopted as localization algorithm for the proposed model.

5.4   Predicted Radio Map for Indoor Positioning

This experiment has been conducted to prove the efficiency of the predicted radio map in the indoor positioning process. In this experiment the MWM path loss model and the shadowing zero-mean random variable, Eq. (10), will be adopted to build the radio map for the selected testbed environment as shown in Fig. 6. In order to generate an accurate dynamic RM based on the adopted model, the different parameters of the model must be determined carefully. Different experiment has been conducted to determine the proper value of these parameters as follow: Firstly, the distance (d) determined based on the APs in EDEC. Secondly, the path loss at 1 m distance $PL(d_0)$ has been found experimentally equals to -34 dBm for the used APs. Thirdly, the power decay index (n) has been determined to equal -2.1 dBm because the selected environment is simple structure environment. Fourthly, the wall attenuation (WAF) factor equals to -2 dBm as measured in [3333], as it has been proven experimentally. - Finally, random shadowing factor (X) is a random integer in [-3, 3].

In order to examine the efficiency of the proposed adapted model KNN algorithm, with K=5, has been used to estimate the room label for testing set based. The testing set consists of 34 in from the calibrated RM where as stars shown in Fig. 6, these points represent the rooms' centers and the main corridor. The selected testing set consists of

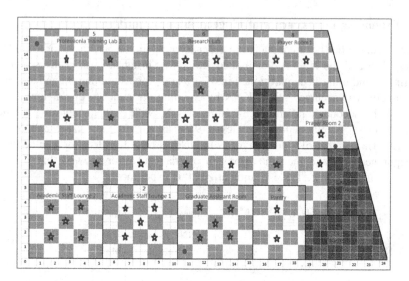

Fig. 6. Site radio map grid

986 instances. Then the mean RSS value of each point has been computed to produce a more reliable testing set with 34 instances. The experimental result shows high localization accuracy as shown in Table 2. This high accuracy occurs due to the accurate determination of the adopted path loss model parameters.

Table 2. Whole testing set vs averaged testing set

Testing Set	# instances	# Correct estimated	Accuracy
Whole	986	837	88.5%
Averaged	34	31	91.2%

6 Conclusion

The last few years showed a sharp increase in the mobile phone market and as a result there is a sharp growth in the demand for pervasive computing in indoor environment to achieve the benefits of the Location Based Services (LBS). Based on the mobile user location, LBS can provide different types of services such as tracking or navigation in important areas such as Healthcare; Civil defense; Marketing; and Management. Currently, WLAN technology is considered as one of the best choices for indoor positioning for many reasons such as low cost, simple infrastructure and high accuracy. Although the WLAN fingerprinting method is the most accurate positioning method its accuracy declines sharply when environmental change occurs. In addition recalibrating the fingerprinting Radio Map is a time consuming process. This paper provides a novel adapted indoor positioning model which is able to adapt the RM using the path loss signal propagation models to overcome the effects of the occurrence of environmental changes. The experimental results show that the proposed adapted model is highly efficient in solving the mentioned problem in dynamically changing environments.

References

1. Mantoro, T., CutifaSafitri, M.A., Ayu, E.: Optimization of cellular automata for user location determination using IEEE 802.11. In: 2012 International Conference on Indoor Positioning and Indoor Navigation, 13–15th November 2012 (2012)
2. Farid, Z., Nordin, R., Ismail, M.: Recent advances in wireless indoor localization techniques and system. J. Comput. Netw. Commun. 2013, 12 (2013)
3. Liu, H., et al.: Survey of wireless indoor positioning techniques and systems. IEEE Trans. Syst. Man, Cybern. Part C: Appl. Rev. 37(6), 1067–1080 (2007)
4. Liu, Y., et al.: Location, localization, and localizability. J. Comput. Sci. Technol. 25(2), 274–297 (2010)
5. Pace, S., et al.: The global positioning system: assessing national policies (1995). DTIC Document
6. Schiller, J., Voisard, A.: Location-Based Services. Elsevier, San Fransisco (2004)
7. Chen, P., et al.: Survey of WLAN fingerprinting positioning system. Appl. Mech. Mater. 380, 2499–2505 (2013)
8. Deak, G., Curran, K., Condell, J.: A survey of active and passive indoor localisation systems. Comput. Commun. 35(16), 1939–1954 (2012)
9. Yanying, G., Lo, A., Niemegeers, I.: A survey of indoor positioning systems for wireless personal networks. IEEE Commun. Surv. Tutorials 11(1), 13–32 (2009)
10. Zhang, D., et al.: Localization technologies for indoor human tracking. In: 2010 5th International Conference on Future Information Technology (FutureTech), IEEE (2010)
11. Gezici, S.: A survey on wireless position estimation. Wireless Pers. Commun. 44(3), 263–282 (2008)
12. Youssef, M.A., Agrawala, A., Udaya Shankar, A.: WLAN location determination via clustering and probability distributions. In: Proceedings of the First IEEE International Conference on Pervasive Computing and Communications, (PerCom 2003). IEEE (2003)
13. Youssef, M., Agrawala, A.: The horus WLAN location determination system. In: Proceedings of the 3rd International Conference on Mobile Systems, Applications, and Services, pp. 205–218. ACM, Seattle, Washington (2005)
14. Roos, T., et al.: A probabilistic approach to WLAN user location estimation. Int. J. Wireless Inf. Netw. 9(3), 155–164 (2002)
15. Cover, T., Hart, P.: Nearest neighbor pattern classification. IEEE Trans. Inf. Theor. 13(1), 21–27 (1967)
16. Lin, T.-N., Lin, P.-C.: Performance comparison of indoor positioning techniques based on location fingerprinting in wireless networks. In: 2005 International Conference on Wireless Networks, Communications and Mobile Computing, IEEE (2005)
17. Brunato, M., Battiti, R.: Statistical learning theory for location fingerprinting in wireless LANs. Comput. Netw. 47(6), 825–845 (2005)
18. Duda, R.O., Hart, P.E., Stork, D.G.: Pattern Classification. Wiley, New York (2012)
19. Shih-Hau, F., Tsung-Nan, L.: Indoor location system based on discriminant-adaptive neural network in IEEE 802.11 environments. IEEE Trans. Neural Netw. 19(11), 1973–1978 (2008)

20. Harle, R.: A survey of indoor inertial positioning systems for pedestrians. IEEE Commun. Surv. Tutorials **15**(3), 1281–1293 (2013)
21. Xiaoyong, C., Qiang, Y.: Reducing the calibration effort for location estimation using unlabeled samples. In: Third IEEE International Conference on Pervasive Computing and Communications, PerCom 2005 (2005)
22. Bahl, P., Padmanabhan, V.N.: RADAR: an in-building RF-based user location and tracking system. In: Proceedings of the INFOCOM 2000, Nineteenth Annual Joint Conference of the IEEE Computer and Communications Societies. IEEE (2000)
23. Di, W., Yubin, X., Lin, M.: Research on RSS based indoor location method. In: Pacific-Asia Conference on Knowledge Engineering and Software Engineering, KESE 2009 (2009)
24. Huang, G.-B., Zhu, Q.-Y., Siew, C.-K.: Extreme learning machine: a new learning scheme of feedforward neural networks. In: 2004 IEEE International Joint Conference on Neural Networks, Proceedings, IEEE (2004)
25. Goldsmith, A.: Wireless Communications. Cambridge University Press, Cambridge (2005)
26. Hae-Won, S., Noh-Hoon, M.: A deterministic ray tube method for microcellular wave propagation prediction model. IEEE Trans. Antennas Propag. **47**(8), 1344–1350 (1999)
27. Athanasiadou, G.E., Nix, A.R., McGeehan, J.P.: A microcellular ray-tracing propagation model and evaluation of its narrow-band and wide-band predictions. IEEE J. Sel. Areas Commun. **18**(3), 322–335 (2000)
28. Mardeni, R., Solahuddin, Y.: Path loss model development for indoor signal loss prediction at 2.4 GHz 802.11n network. In: Microwave and Millimeter Wave Technology (ICMMT) (2012)
29. Andrade, C.B., Hoefel, R.P.F.: IEEE 802.11 WLANs: a comparison on indoor coverage models. In: 2010 23rd Canadian Conference on Electrical and Computer Engineering (CCECE). IEEE (2010)
30. Akl, R.: Indoor Propagation Modeling at 2.4 GHz for IEEE 802.11 Networks. University Of North Texas, Denton (2005)
31. Borrelli, A., et al.: Channel models for IEEE 802.11 b indoor system design. In: 2004 IEEE International Conference on Communications. IEEE (2004)
32. Phaiboon, S.: An empirically based path loss model for indoor wireless channels in laboratory building. In: TENCON 2002 Proceedings of the 2002 IEEE Region 10 Conference on Computers, Communications, Control and Power Engineering. IEEE (2002)
33. Lott, M., Forkel, I.: A multi-wall-and-floor model for indoor radio propagation. In: IEEE VTS 53rd Vehicular Technology Conference, VTC 2001 Spring (2001)
34. Cheung, K.-W., Sau, J.-M., Murch, R.D.: A new empirical model for indoor propagation prediction. IEEE Trans. Veh. Technol. **47**(3), 996–1001 (1998)
35. Seidel, S.Y., Rappaport, T.S.: 914 MHz path loss prediction models for indoor wireless communications in multifloored buildings. IEEE Trans. Antennas Propag. **40**(2), 207–217 (1992)
36. Krishnan, P., et al.: A system for LEASE: location estimation assisted by stationary emitters for indoor RF wireless networks. In: INFOCOM 2004, Twenty-third Annual Joint Conference of the IEEE Computer and Communications Societies (2004)
37. Chen, Y.-C., et al.: Sensor-assisted wi-fi indoor location system for adapting to environmental dynamics. In: Proceedings of the 8th ACM International Symposium on Modeling, Analysis and Simulation of Wireless and Mobile Systems. ACM (2005)
38. Jie, Y., Qiang, Y., Ni, L.M.: Learning adaptive temporal radio maps for signal-strength-based location estimation. IEEE Trans. Mob. Comput. **7**(7), 869–883 (2008)
39. Segou, O.E., Mitilineos, S.A., Thomopoulos, S.C.A.: DALE: a range-free, adaptive indoor localization method enhanced by limited fingerprinting. In: 2010 International Conference on Indoor Positioning and Indoor Navigation (IPIN) (2010)

40. Lo, C.-C., Hsu, L.-Y., Tseng, Y.-C.: Adaptive radio maps for pattern-matching localization via inter-beacon co-calibration. Pervasive Mob. Comput. **8**(2), 282–291 (2012)
41. Atia, M.M., Noureldin, A., Korenberg, M.J.: Dynamic online-calibrated radio maps for indoor positioning in wireless local area networks. IEEE Trans. Mob. Comput. **12**(9), 1774–1787 (2013)
42. Ji, Y., Biaz, S., Pandey, S., Agrawal, P.: Dynamic indoor localization using wireless ethernet: the ARIADNE system. In: Braun, T., Carle, G., Fahmy, S., Koucheryavy, Y. (eds.) WWIC 2006. LNCS, vol. 3970, pp. 299–310. Springer, Heidelberg (2006)
43. Hung-Huan, L., Yu-Non, Y.: WiFi-based indoor positioning for multi-floor environment. In: IEEE Region 10 Conference TENCON 2011–2011 (2011)
44. Narzullaev, A., Park, Y.: Novel calibration algorithm for received signal strength based indoor real-time locating systems. AEU – Int. J. Electron. Commun. **67**(7), 637–644 (2013)
45. Fan, X., Shin, Y.: Indoor localization for multi-wall, multi-floor environments in wireless sensor networks. In: AICT 2013, The Ninth Advanced International Conference on Telecommunications (2013)
46. Shi, J., Shin, Y.: A low-complexity floor determination method based on WiFi for multi-floor buildings. In: AICT 2013, The Ninth Advanced International Conference on Telecommunications (2013)

Incorporating Users Satisfaction to Resolve Sparsity in Recommendation Systems

Shahid Kamal[1,2], Roliana Ibrahim[1(✉)], Imran Ghani[1], and Ziauddin[2]

[1] Faculty of Computing, Universiti Teknologi, 81310 Skudai, Johor, Malaysia
{roliana,imran}@utm.my
[2] Institute of Computing and Information Technology, Gomal University,
Dera Ismail Khan, Pakistan
{skamaltipu,ziag}@gmail.com

Abstract. Recommendation systems have shown great potential to help users in order to find interesting and relevant items from within a large information space. Information overload experienced a significant response because of huge amount of internet usage and also has been demonstrated by recommendation systems; that is, providing adapted information services. User preferences play a key role in formulating recommendations to search required information over the web. User feedback, both explicit and implicit, has proven to be vital for recommendation systems, with the similarity between users then able to be computed. In this paper we propose that traditional reliance on user similarity may be overstated. Nevertheless, there are many problems to be faced, specifically; sparseness, cold start, prediction accuracy, as well as scalability which can all result in a challenge of accuracy over the recommendation systems. A sparsity rate of 95 % is experienced in CF-based commercial recommendation applications. Furthermore, we discuss the manner in which other factors have significant effect in managing recommendations. Specifically, we propose that the issue of user satisfaction must be considered and incorporated with explicit feedback for improved recommendations. Supported by experimental results, our approach demonstrates better results while incorporating user satisfaction with the feedback.

Keywords: Recommendation system · Information access · Sparsity · Explicit feedback · User satisfaction

1 Introduction

Recommendation systems offer required information to users. These processes input information with the aim of obtaining related features, as well as information that can be viewed as a tool in order to improve the problem of information overload.

There are many things in our daily life which need to be selected, namely; which audio to listen to, which website to visit for interesting stories, and so on. RS also applies to the higher studies domain, specifically: which book to read, which research area to focus upon. For these purposes, we depend upon friends as well as on our professional colleagues. This can be in the form of gaining benefit from their experience, perusing articles written by renowned journalists and academicians, as well as

H. Fujita and A. Selamat (Eds.): SoMeT 2014, CCIS 513, pp. 134–146, 2015.
DOI: 10.1007/978-3-319-17530-0_10

discovering important and interesting information or services. RS supports a shortcut for the selection of suitable alternatives. Otherwise, the effort and costs typically required while using traditional methods is generally not considered to be worth the trouble [1].

In this era of technology, the Recommendation Systems (RS) are software applications that recommend certain articles/products to users who are involved in that area [2]. RSs have come about to help users by proposing items (images, products, books, etc.) that they might find useful. These programs have gained popularity due to increasing acceptance of Web 2.0 [3] and related information availability over the Internet.

A detailed definition of the recommendation system is given as *"Recommender systems or recommendation systems (sometimes replacing "system" with a synonym such as platform or engine) are a subclass of information filtering system that seek to predict the 'rating' or 'preference' that user would give to an item"*.[1] Moreover, in order to lessen the amount of available information, a Collaborative Filtering (CF) technique is commonly used in the recommendation systems [4, 5].

Besides, recommendation systems have been exposed to several following problems. Some of those are:

Data Sparsity- problem appears when a new user or item has just entered the system and he has not rated the information available. Hence, similarity between users and items cannot be calculated accurately which results in poor quality of recommendations [6].

Scalability- is associated with the condition when recommendations systems decreases calculation time by matching the interest profile of the user to its separated and even smaller training samples [7].

Synonymy- refers to the tendency of a number of the same or very similar items to have different names or entries. It has strong effects on the quality of search results [8].

Gray Sheep- refers to the users whose opinions do not consistently agree or disagree with any group of people. This problem reasons increased error rate in collaborating filtering based recommendation system [9].

Shilling attacks- In recommendation systems, shilling attacks refers to the situations when people may give lot of ratings of their own products and negative ratings for their competitors and effects the provision of accurate recommendations [10].

Collaborating filtering techniques use a database of preferences for items by users to calculate additional topics or products, a new user might like. In a typical CF scenario, there is a list of m users and a list of n items, and each user, u_j, has a list of l_{ui} items, which the user has to rate, or about which their preferences have been concluded through their behaviors. Thus, a decision regarding the quality of recommendation systems depends upon its collaborative filtering measures [11]. The authors of [12] claimed that CF algorithms are required to have the ability to deal with highly sparse data, to scale with the increasing numbers of users and items, to make satisfactory

---

[1] en.wikipedia.org/wiki/**Recommender system.**

recommendations in a period of time, and to deal with other problems like data noise, and privacy protection problems.

A well-known problem in recommendations system "cold start" addressed in [13] that involves a degree of automated data modelling. Prediction accuracy is investigated in the study [14]. Furthermore, the problem of scalability and trustworthiness of RS selection is addressed in the study [15]. In the past the Web of Trust scheme has been used to support the recommendation production; however, to the best of our knowledge, the sparsity problem has not yet been investigated in this regard [16].

Several collaborative filtering (CF) based recommendation systems experience the sparsity problem. It is defined as the ratio between the actual ratings and potential ratings. Usually a rate of more than 95 % sparsity is found in commercial applications. Different studies [17–19] have suggested diverse methods by which to overcome data sparsity, but still it is considered as a major challenge in CF-based recommendation systems.

A web service provides an interface which can be accessed via a network for functionality of application. It is developed by using standard technologies related to the Internet. Generally an evaluation relating to the Quality of Service (QoS) of the services is published by the service providers. The services are then evaluated and assessed by the consumers on the basis of these published QoS results. Therefore QoS has an important standing as a research subject in the domain of web services over current years [20, 21]. Thus, in this scenario, the QoS evaluation of services for personalized service requests becomes essential in service selection, ranking or composition [22]. There are two ways to capture user preferences; either implicit or explicit. The first is concerned with user actions or following some patterns; while in the second method, users are asked to provide ratings for items in which they are interested. In order to increase the value of recommendations systems, perceptions of accuracy and trustworthiness are considered as acceptance from users.

In this paper, we present an algorithm based on a de-noising algorithm [23] in which users are asked to once again rate previously-rated items. In addition, they are also asked to compute the ratings on the basis of satisfaction percentage previously provided by them. The remainder of this paper is organized in five sections as follows. Section 2 discusses the related work with this study on issues involved in missing values and sparsity problems. Section 3 describes the methodology adapted in this study. Section 4 presents an empirical analysis of the proposed methodology. Finally, Sect. 5 offers concluding remarks regarding this research and future intentions.

2 Related Work

In recommendation systems, sparsity because of inconsistent explicit user feedback has been known for some time. However, regardless of the large and growing bibliography in the area of recommendation systems and the importance of this issue in the design of effective strategies, there are not many references in the literature. Resolving the sparsity problem in recommendation systems is of prime importance from the user and system perspectives [24]. However, the approaches discussed in this section have their own limitations and provide strong foundation for our proposed methodology. In this section we concisely describe the several contributions that have been made for undertaking sparsity problem to improve the performance of recommendation systems.

Antonio Hernando et al. [2] introduced the concept of integrating reliability measure accompanying to the predictions made by recommender systems based on collaborating filtering. Furthermore, they have also given a method for obtaining specific reliability measures according to different specific needs of recommendation systems. Therefore, they have unwrapped a way for researchers to think about other concepts that can be incorporated with recommendation systems for better results like user satisfaction in our case.

In order to find successful solutions towards improved recommendations Pitsilis and Knapskog [16] proposed a hybrid scheme. They claimed that, even though the approach of using a Web-of-Trust scheme for assisting the recommendation production has been well -adopted, issues like the sparsity problem have not been explored adequately so far. They verified their hybrid scheme by using the existing ratings of users to calculate the hypothetical trust. The proposed scheme addressed the problem of sparsity as cold start problem as well. In different with this approach, we have put emphasis on the user ratings to be recalculated on the bases of user satisfaction provided explicitly by the users to get better performance.

The trustworthiness of web recommendation systems is commonly measured by the reputation of web services. This measurement depends on either the rating of the user experience [26] or on computed actual measurement of the conformance of execution QoS to Promised QoS [27]. The solution given in [26] suffers a fairness problem as well as sparsity because of user ratings for provided services, especially in cases where malicious users may give false ratings or subvert the reputation of services.

Huang, Chong-Ben et al. [18] addressed the sparsity of user's ratings as poor quality challenge in recommendation systems and to alleviate the issue by utilizing the popular same value and singular value decomposition techniques. Besides, they solved a new problem that can predict values of the null ratings in the candidates. Although, they claimed improved accuracy of the predicted values but they modified the existing ROUSTIDA to generate the ratings contrary to our approach, in which we rely on the user given ratings solely.

Yildirim, Hilmi, and Mukkai S. Krishnamoorthy [19] highlighted the sparsity problem by giving a novel item-oriented algorithm, Random Walk Recommender. It took into account the probabilities between items based on their similarities and modeled finite length random walks on the item space to compute predictions. Although the authors focused on resolving sparsity problem same like us but they considered item based similarities and used adjusted cosine based similarity measure. While, we compute the user ratings based on the user satisfaction given explicitly for resolving the issue of sparsity in order to achieve the better accuracy.

Given a user ratings as preferences, Amatriain, Xavier, et al. [23] used this concept by asking users for explicit item ratings. The authors raised the questions on the accuracy in result of user's inconsistent behavior in giving ratings and also introduced a non-negligible amount of natural noise that affects the accuracy as well. In order to quantitatively understand the impact of natural noise in order to resolve the sparsity problem, the authors first analyze the response of common recommendation algorithms to this noise. Next they proposed a novel algorithm to de-noise existing datasets by means of re-rating. The summary of the literature described above is given in Table 1.

Table 1. Summary of the related work

Author/ Year	Problem Focused	Methodology	Achievement	Limitations
Hernado, A. et al., (2013)	Prediction reliability, data sparsity	Using reliability measure associated with the predictions made by recommender system	Accuracy	Did not use user specific information
Pitsilis, G. et al., (2012)	Data sparsity	Hybrid Scheme	Accuracy	Inadequate for resolving sparsity problem
Huang, C.B. et al., (2008)	Data sparsity	Same value and singular value decomposition	Accuracy	Modified the existing approach to generate ratings
Yildirim, H. et al., (2008)	Data sparsity	Item based similarity and adjusted cosine similarity	Accuracy	Did not consider user ratings
Amatriain, X. et al., (2009)	Data sparsity	Common algorithm response to noise analysis	Accuracy	Did not consider inconsistency in re-rating procedure
L. Zeng, B.B. et al., (2004)	Data sparsity	Web services reputation measurement	Trustworthiness	Fairness as well as sparsity because of user ratings

We carried out our methodology to be tested by using small scale experiment described in following section.

3 Methodology

This study aims to develop a framework to improve performance and accuracy of web services recommendations. To achieve this objective, the framework is designed as shown in Fig. 1. This study consists of different steps in order to achieve the objectives mentioned above.

This study seeks to develop an accurate web services recommendation system in terms of resolving data sparsity problem. During Step 1, a literature review of previous research studies relating to recommendation systems has been conducted. Such that, planning activities such as problem formulation and research planning are to be performed in the first phase. The literature review which is performed is bi-directional. This means that the Recommendation System and QoS properties of the web service were measured at run time by the user. At the first point of the survey, the problem domain has been determined and different phases considered necessary for a recommendation system have been discovered.

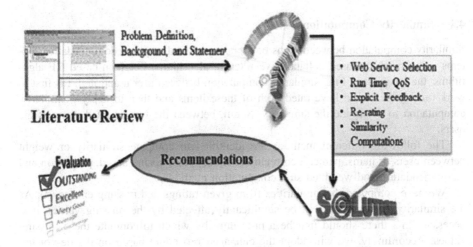

Fig. 1. Research framework with different phases

In Step 2, the problem of user's ratings is highlighted. The research directions are then formulated and examined by investigating different areas i.e. web service selection, dynamic QoS, feedback either explicit or implicit, ratings and re-rating procedures, similarity computations. Then after exploring the areas, the solutions are identified and provided to user in Step 3 that includes the procedure to be adopted in the run time of QoS values of the web services provided according to user requirements. In Step 4, an algorithm has been developed to work according to the desired research directions. The last step in this methodology is evaluation of the proposed approach which will be tested by application in different web-related domains.

Finally, in Step 5 we have evaluated the developed approach by conducting experiments in support of our concept of user satisfaction to resolve the data sparsity issue. Our experiments showed better performance and attained better accuracy to be compared with other approaches.

4 Empirical Analysis

The problem of recommendation is condensed into a question of giving ratings to services/items which remain unseen and not yet experienced. After estimating the user ratings for services or items, we can predict the ones that can be recommended in order to receive a high rating. Ratings play an important role in the recommendation process. These ratings can either be explicit, i.e., by having the user's opinion about a given product, or implicit, when the mere act of purchasing or mentioning of an item counts as an expression of appreciation. While implicit ratings are generally more superficial to collect, their usage indicates adding noise to the collected information. Sparsity problem occurs when the users either award high ratings intentionally or do not provide ratings to the selected/provided items.

4.1 Similarity Computation

Similarity computation between items or users is a critical step in recommendation systems using memory-based collaborative filtering algorithms. For item-based CF algorithms, the basic idea of the similarity computation between user u and item i is first to work on the users who have rated both of these items and then to apply a similarity computation to determine the similarity, Simui, between the two co-rated items of the users.

The following different methods are identified to compute similarity or weight between users or items, namely; correlation-based, vector cosine-based, prediction and recommendation and weighted sum computation methods.

We have computed the similarities from given ratings and missing entries (*). As the similarity computation will be significantly affected by the missing values, it is necessary that there should first be a procedure by which to compute these missing values. Accordingly, we will adopt the enhanced procedure based on the de-noising algorithm used by [23] for the re-rating of the items. The proposed re-rating algorithm will be based on the pseudo code given in Fig. 2.

Further, it will be used to write an algorithm which can be practically incorporated into the proposed methodology.

We used the Eq. (1) to compute similarity between users on the sample data given in Table 2; where X1 and X2 are two users. We are then required to compute similarity and there are five (5) items representing the web services i.e. I = 5.

$$Sim(x_1, x_2) = \frac{\sum_i r_{x1,i} \times r_{x2,i}}{\sqrt{\sum_i r_{x1,i}^2} \times \sqrt{\sum_i r_{x2,i}^2}} \tag{1}$$

We obtained the value -0.67, with the negative result showing less similarity between the users. It is caused by the missing entries represented as symbol (*) in Table 2.

In order to overcome the sparsity problem caused by the missing values in the rating matrix, the concept of C has been introduced by [25]; where C is 0.5. If one of the users has not rated the item otherwise; it is 1. Equation (2) is used to obtain the value of similarity using the data given in Table 3.

ALGORITHM.   *[Re-rating (Explicit Feedback)]*
{ This algorithm will compute ratings based on the satisfaction
percentage and then will compute the similarities among users and
their ratings}

Step 1   *Start*
Step 2:   *User will be provided with web services*
Step 3:   *User gives ratings (1.....5)*
Step 4:   *IF Not (rating) THEN*
                  Begin:
Step 5:   *Execute loop one time and goto step 3*
Step 6:   *INPUT ◄------ satisfaction percentage*
Step 7:   *COMPUTE new rating based on INPUT step 6*
Step 8:   *IF (new rating > old rating) THEN*
                  Begin
                  SWAP [ratings]
                  End if
Step 9:   *COMPUTE similarity*
                  End if
Step 10:   *End*

Fig. 2. Pseudo code of the algorithm

Table 2. User –item values

Items	X_1	X_2
1	2	*
2	3	2
3	*	3
4	5	*
5	2	1

Where * represents the missing entry.

$$\text{Sim}(x_1, x_2) = \frac{\sum_i r_{x_1,i} \times r_{x_2,i}}{\sqrt{\sum_i C \times r_{x_1,i}^2} \times \sqrt{\sum_i r_{x_1,i}^2}} \tag{2}$$

The similarity between users is computed as 0.41 representing positive value.

Detailed computations are given in Table 4 in order to provide the computations used in similarity measurements between users X1 and X2.

In order to gain the best value we used Eq. (3) and obtained a better value of 0.49 than by using Eq. (2); an enhancement in the strategy was given by [25]. This attempt aimed to overcome the sparsity problem caused in terms of missing values in the user item matrix.

$$Sim(x_1, x_2) = \frac{\sum_i r_{x_1,i} \times r_{x_2,i}}{\sqrt{\sum_i C \times r_{x_1,i}^2} \times \sqrt{\sum_i C \times r_{x_2,i}^2}} \tag{3}$$

Table 3. User-item values with computation of C

Items	X_1	X_2	C
1	2	0	0.5
2	3	2	1
3	0	3	0.5
4	5	0	0.5
5	2	1	1

Table 4. Computations performed

Items	Users							
	X_1	X_2	C	$X_1 * X_2$	X^2	Y^2	$(C * X_1^2)$	$(C * X_2^2)$
1	2	0	0.5	0	4	0	2	0
2	3	2	1	6	9	4	9	4
3	0	3	0.5	0	0	9	0	4.5
4	5	0	0.5	0	25	0	12.5	0
5	2	1	1	2	4	1	4	1
5	12	6		8	42	14	27.5	9.5

4.2   Sparsity Problem Experiment

Let us say we have five users U [1, 2, ..., 5] who are required to give explicit ratings about five web services, i.e. Ws1, Ws2, ... Ws5.

The Table 5 presents these ratings by users. Here, zero (0) means a missing value, i.e., a user has not provided a rating relating to a particular web service.

Table 5. User/web services rating

	WS_1	Ws_2	WS_3	WS_4	WS_5
User 1	2	1	0	3	1
User 2	0	1	4	5	1
User 3	3	2	3	2	2
User 4	4	2	3	4	0
User 5	1	0	2	3	0

Following this, we have computed the similarities among users by using the Pearson correlation co-efficient presented below in Table 6.

Based on the data presented in Table 6, Fig. 3 clearly shows a negative relationship between users resulting in a sparsity problem.

At this point, we examined the effect of the missing values and strengthened our study into the sparsity problem by incorporating satisfaction percentage data from users. We then replaced 0 by a randomly-generated satisfaction percentage as an experiment presented in Table 7.

Table 6. Users' similarities

	User 1	User 2	User 3	User 4	User 5
User 1		0.162	-0.32	0.498	0.437
User 2	0.162		-0.084	0.372	0.867
User 3	-0.32	-0.084		0.491	0.21
User 4	0.498	0.372	0.491		0.733
User 5	0.437	0.867	0.21	0.733	

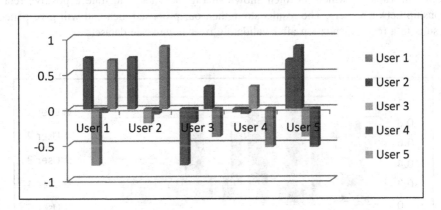

Fig. 3. User similarities using PCC

Table 7. Re-rating computations based on satisfaction percentage

Web Service	U1	S	Re-rating	U2	S	Re-rating	U3	SS	Re-Rating	U4	S	Re-Rating	U5	S	Re-rating
1	2	28	4	0	40	2	3	85	3	4	39	2	1	22	4
2	1	58	3	1	47	2	2	36	2	2	10	2	0	56	4
3	0	52	5	4	79	4	3	97	4	3	91	3	2	81	4
4	3	33	4	5	27	5	2	81	4	4	84	5	3	97	5
5	1	12	4	1	71	4	2	7	4	0	43	4	0	28	5

By doing so, we obtained the similarity values presented in Table 8, which are then shown in Fig. 4. The data presents evidence of a positive relationship between Users 1 and 3 as 0.791 instead of -0.32 as previously represented in Table 6. The purpose was to reduce the effect of missing values. These values were replaced with the new value of rating calculated on the basis of satisfactory percentages provided by the users.

Table 8. User Similarities after re-rating

	User 1	User 2	User 3	User 4	User 5
User 1		0.527	0.791	0.271	0
User 2	0.527		0.875	0.943	0.152
User 3	0.791	0.875		0.772	0.228
User 4	0.271	0.943	0.772		0.157
User 5	0	0.152	0.228	0.157	

After performing these computations, we acquired the similarity values presented above in Table 8, which are then shown in Fig. 4. These illustrate a positive relationship between users. The results strengthen our proposed idea and will give better results in a recommendation after validating over large-scale datasets.

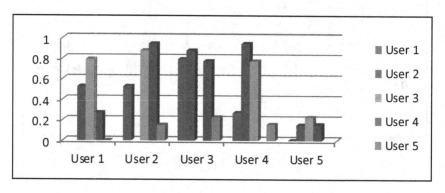

Fig. 4. User similarities applying PCC

5 Conclusion

In this study, we underlined the sparsity issue in recommendation systems that arise by uneven ratings (feedback) from the users. We introduced a concept of users' satisfaction to be incorporated into ratings given by them, so that accuracy of the recommendations systems can be measured. For this instance, we used users' satisfaction percentage in re-rating procedure associated with feedback collection. In the event of ratings of the provided items not being supplied, users will then be asked to give a satisfaction percentage based on the results provided to them. Following this, on the basis of satisfaction percentage, re-rating will then be initiated to overcome the sparsity issue in recommendations. The proposed methodology in this study is evaluated on a small scale data. It results positive outcome in similarity computation as well as in reducing the effect of sparsity found in the data, because of missing values in ratings given by users. We believe that the work presented in this paper opens up a new avenue of research in future. In addition, we will evaluate proposed methodology on public datasets for better support of our concept of incorporating user satisfaction percentage in explicit feedback given by user. We are assertive that our methodology will perform better when it will be compared with state of art approaches.

Acknowledgement. We would like to thank the Universiti Teknologi Malaysia and the Malaysia Ministry of Higher Education (MOHE) Research University Grant Scheme (Vot No. Q. J130000.2528.05H84) and also (Vot No: 4F315) for the facilities as well as support to conduct this research study. Moreover, we would also like to say thanks to the Higher Education Commission of Pakistan.

References

1. Bedi, P., Kaur, H., Marwaha, S.: Trust based recommender system for semantic web. In: Proceedings of the 2007 International Joint Conferences on Artificial Intelligence (2007)
2. Hernando, A., et al.: Incorporating reliability measurements into the predictions of a recommender system. Inf. Sci. **218**, 1–6 (2013)
3. Lin, K.J.: Building Web. Comput. **40**(5), 101–102 (2007)
4. Breese, J.S., Heckerman, D., Kadie, C.: Empirical analysis of predictive algorithms for collaborative filtering. Morgan Kaufmann, Massachusetts 43–52. Morgan Kaufmann, Massachusetts, pp. 43–52 (1998)
5. Tuzhilin, G.A.: Toward the next generation of recommender systems: a survey of the state-of-the-art and possible extensions. IEEE Trans. Knowl. Data Eng. **17**(6), 734–749 (2005)
6. Zhang, F., et al.: An adaptive recommendation method based on small-world implicit trust network. J. Comput. **9**(3), 618–625 (2014)
7. Bakshi, S., et al.: Enhancing scalability and accuracy of recommendation systems using unsupervised learning and particle swarm optimization. Appl. Soft Comput. **15**, 21–29 (2014)
8. Samet, H., et al.: Reading news with maps by exploiting spatial synonyms. Commun. ACM **57**(10), 64–77 (2014)
9. Ghazanfar, M.A., et al.: Leveraging clustering approaches to solve the gray-sheep users problem in recommender systems. Expert Syst. Appl. **41**(7), 3261–3275 (2014)
10. Gunes, I., et al.: Shilling attacks against privacy-preserving collaborative filtering. J. Adv. Manage. Sci. **1**(1), 54–60 (2013)
11. Jonathan, L., Herlocker, J.A.K., Borchers, A.l., Riedl, J.: An algorithmic framework for performing collaborative filtering. In: Proceedings of the 22nd ACM SIGIR (1999)
12. Su, X., Khoshgoftaar, T.M.: A survey of collaborative filtering techniques. Adv. Artif. Intell. **2009**(4), 1–19 (2009)
13. Fazeli, S., et al.: A trust-based social recommender for teachers. In: Proceedings of the 2nd Workshop on Recommender Systems for Technology Enhanced Learning (RecSysTEL 2012) (2012)
14. Codina, V., Ceccaroni, L.: A recommendation system for the semantic web. Distrib. Comput. Artif. Intell. **79**, 45–52 (2010)
15. Mehta, H., et al.: Collaborative Personalized Web Recommender System using Entropy based Similarity Measure. arXiv preprint arXiv: (2012)
16. Pitsilis, G., Knapskog, S.J.: Social Trust as a solution to address sparsity-inherent problems of Recommender systems. arXiv preprint arXiv:1208.1004 (2012)

146   S. Kamal et al.

17. Lekakos, G., Giaglis, G.M.: A hybrid approach for improving predictive accuracy of collaborative filtering algorithms. User Model. User-Adap. Inter. **17**(1–2), 5–40 (2007)
18. Huang, C.B., Gong, S.J., Employing rough set theory to alleviate the sparsity issue in recommender system. In: 2008 International Conference on Machine Learning and Cybernetics, pp. 1610–1614. IEEE (2008)
19. Yildirim, H., Krishnamoorthy, M.S.: A random walk method for alleviating the sparsity problem in collaborative filtering. In: Proceedings of the 2008 ACM conference on Recommender systems, ACM (2008)
20. Hadad, J., Manouvrier, M., Rukoz, M.: TQoS: Transactional and QoS-aware selection algorithm for automatic web service composition. IEEE Trans. Serv. Comput. **3**, 73–85 (2010)
21. Kritikos, K., Plexousakis, D.: Requirements for QoS-based web service description and discovery. IEEE Trans. Serv. Comput. **2**, 320–337 (2009)
22. Yang, R., Chen, Q., Qi, L., Dou, W.: A QoS Evaluation Method for Personalized Service Requests. In: Gong, Z., Luo, X., Chen, J., Lei, J., Wang, F.L. (eds.) WISM 2011, Part II. LNCS, vol. 6988, pp. 393–402. Springer, Heidelberg (2011)
23. Amatriain, X., et al.: Rate it again: increasing recommendation accuracy by user re-rating. In: Proceedings of the third ACM conference on Recommender systems. ACM (2009)
24. Tiwari, S., Kaushik, S.: A non functional properties based web service recommender system. In: Computational Intelligence and Software Engineering (CiSE) (2010)
25. Magureanu, S., et al.: Epidemic trust-based recommender systems. In: 2012 International Conference on and 2012 International Confernece on Social Computing (SocialCom) Privacy, Security, Risk and Trust (PASSAT), IEEE (2012)
26. Zeng, L., Benatallah, B., Ngu, A.H., Dumas, M., Kalagnanam, J.: Qos-aware middleware for web services composition. IEEE Trans. Softw. Eng. **30**(5), 311–327 (2004)
27. Limam, N., Boutaba, R.: Assessing software service quality and trustworthiness at selection time. IEEE Trans. Softw. Eng. **36**(4), 559–574 (2010)

Creative and Arts in Interactive Software Design

Redefining Game Engine Architecture Through Concurrency

Ali Mohebali and Thiam Kian Chiew(✉)

Department of Software Engineering, Faculty of Computer Science
and Information Technology, University of Malaya, Kuala Lumpur, Malaysia
tkchiew@um.edu.my

Abstract. Over the past 30 years, software developers have been conveniently taking advantage of hardware performance increase, giving little consideration to internal architecture changes of the hardware. However, hardware architectural changes like central processing unit will affect software architectures and can no longer be ignored. This is especially true for real-time applications, including computer games, which tend to push the limits of hardware and take the most advantage of available resources. By applying the concepts of concurrency, multithreading and multi-core Central Processing Unit (CPU) technology, this paper redefines the existing linear architecture of game engines as a generic concurrent and multi-core friendly architecture. Major game engine modules and their inter-dependencies are identified in order to design the new architecture. A sample game was developed to evaluate the performance of the proposed architecture. The comparison of the test results provided in this paper indicates noticeable improvements (5.1 % to 61.2 %) in the concurrent architecture over the conventional linear approach. User acceptance evaluation with several industry experts also showed encouraging feedback.

Keywords: Concurrency · Architecture · Game engine · Multi-core · Performance

1 Introduction

Over the past 30 years, hardware architects have improved performance in terms of clock speed, execution optimization, and cache; which are mainly focused on singular and linear execution. However, exponential growth in hardware performance as Moore predicted cannot continue forever before hard physical limits are reached. The growth in single core designs' clock speeds (frequency) is at the expense of faster growth rate in power consumption [1]. Sutter [2] noted that the clock race is already over due to several physical issues including heat, high power consumption, and leakage problems. He concluded that the performance gains in future are going to be accomplished in fundamentally different ways, driven by hyper threading, multi-core, and cache.

There are two main reasons to think about concurrency:

- To improve responsiveness especially for real-time applications as responsiveness is a major quality attribute of such applications [3].

© Springer International Publishing Switzerland 2015
H. Fujita and A. Selamat (Eds.): SoMeT 2014, CCIS 513, pp. 149–161, 2015.
DOI: 10.1007/978-3-319-17530-0_11

- To improve performance and scalability, which according Sutter and James [4], have not been widely investigated through parallelism and concurrency.

The two common reasons collectively seem to be valid for game applications. Nevertheless, games are inherently linear applications consisting of a series of cycles (or frames), making it not easily amendable to parallelization. Almost all the steps in game engine cycles, from retrieval of the end-user input to updating and processing AI and physics, and finally producing corresponding visual and audio outputs, need to be done in a linear fashion. This linear nature of game application processing makes it difficult to adapt to and utilize the performance advantage that concurrency could offered.

2 Background

A decent game engine cycle consists of input-output (IO), artificial intelligence (AI), physics, sound, scene and screen render processing, with tight coupling between the modules as depicted in Fig. 1.

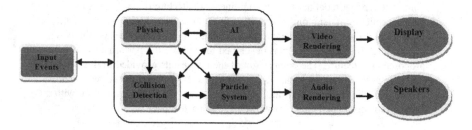

Fig. 1. Interaction of modules in a game engine.

Thus far, game applications have been pushing the boundaries of hardware through adaptation or optimization to increase efficiency in usage of available resources [4], without taking full advantage of available CPU power. In order to continually push the limits of hardware, they have no choice but adopting concurrency to utilize all parallel cores [5].

A parallel game server architecture has been proposed by [6] to support concurrency for online multi-player games. The architecture, however, neglects synchronization by assuming network latencies already exist and games are full of approximations. The concurrent video-game design pattern proposed by [7] supports only concurrency within frames, leaving inter-frame concurrency for future improvement. The limitation has been overcome by [8] but the proposed design pattern, namely Sayl, does not consider categorization of tasks in a typical game and their interdependencies. Identification of the interdependencies is essential in optimizing scheduling of tasks and thus concurrency, too. Researchers have also attempted to achieve concurrency through scripting [9], without an overall game engine. The overall limitation of these researches is that there is a lack of domain-specific (game) concurrent engine with necessary low level details, which the game developers seek. It is thus the intention of this paper to propose a domain specific generic concurrent game engine architecture that meets the needs of game developers.

3 Concurrency and Game Engines

Concurrent software development concept suffers from the shortage of reusable design patterns and concurrent framework definition [10]. The concurrent programming model is also difficult to understand and reason, than it is for sequential and linear control flow [2]. The ideal scenario of a concurrent application is where all tasks run entirely independent of each other and produce distinct outputs. However, that rarely is the case, and leads to another major difficulty in adoption of concurrency: the degree of coupling between tasks and operations in an application.

Another problem in concurrency is resource sharing and synchronization [5]. Synchronization of resources is traditionally done through locking techniques which introduce performance overheads. Additionally, poor design of resource sharing and locking will lead to data racing, and as a result data corruption, data inconsistency and dead-locks. Apart from deadlocks, synchronization locks also introduce other runtime issues such as performance slowdowns. These performance issues usually occur due to priority inversion and convoying [11]. Both priority inversion and convoying cause CPU power easily wasted.

While synchronization methods are used to solve low level parallelism issues, they will not be able to resolve concurrency's high level and architectural problems. In order for an application to perform efficiently in a multi-core and parallel environment, it has to be defined and architected as a set of appropriately granulated concurrent tasks with careful consideration given to data dependency among the tasks [12, 13].

Each module of a game engine has a well-defined and distinguishable task to perform, but it will produce data that other modules are dependent on and/or uses data produced by other modules. Thus, although the responsibilities (tasks) are distinguishable, the data consumed by each module causes the modules to be dependent on one another, making high level task and data decomposition a challenging effort.

Joselli et al. [14] claimed that a typical game loop can be divided into three general classes of tasks:

- Data acquisition tasks responsible for retrieving user commands.
- Data processing tasks responsible for updating the game state.
- Data presentation tasks responsible for presenting the results to the user.

Furthermore, based on runtime execution environment, the tasks are classified as either CPU task, GPU (graphics processing unit) task, or both. Thus, they proposed an adaptive loop model which represents a game loop implementation architecture that uses both CPU and GPU to perform and complete game engine tasks. This model, as depicted in Fig. 2, applies the idea of automatic task distribution. The architecture uses a set of heuristic algorithms to study the existing CPU and GPU attributes (e.g. speed) on the system at runtime, in order to perform task distribution between the processing units efficiently.

The adaptive loop model is based on this categorization and thus the main goal of the technique is the arrangement of the execution of tasks based on their category, in order to simulate parallelism. Even though the adaptive loop model defines a mathematical methodology to efficiently distribute and assign different tasks to different central and graphical processing unit, it does not define an appropriate generic methodology to categorize different tasks in different game engine modules. Furthermore, the technique is exceedingly hardware specific and might not be easily adapted to future hardware.

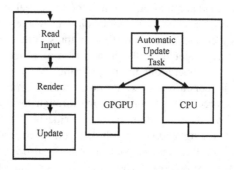

Fig. 2. Adaptive Loop Model [7]

4   Gaming Modules and Inter-dependencies

We studied a few game engines available in the market to identify typical modules among them. These included Unity (http://unity3d.com), NeoAxis (http://www. neoaxis.com), Blender (http://www.blender.org), CryEngine (http://www.cryengine. com), and id Tech 4 (http://www.idsoftware.com). Although some of the engines are designed or tailored for specific games, and it is almost impossible to design a generic, reusable, and extensible game engine for any games [15], the engines we studied do have six modules in common. The modules are rendering engine (renderer) for 2D or 3D graphics, physics engine (collision detection and collision response), sound module, scripting module, AI, networking and scene graph. A typical game engine loop, as depicted in Fig. 3, starts with the engine retrieves the input from the end user. The game play and AI logic then respond to the input correspondingly, changing states of the game environment. Next, the physics module resolves physics states and collision detection. After that, the scene graph selects and nominates visual objects for presentation to the end-user. Finally, the renderer updates the graphical screen while the audio plays the corresponding sound effects, collectively reflecting the game state.

Although this loop works perfectly in a single threaded engine, it causes architectural difficulties when dealing with multi-threaded and concurrent environments. In order to understand the interdependency between these modules which is required to design a concurrent game engine architecture, we carefully examined the relationships between these the modules to discover the possible data and operational coupling between each of them. The examination of individual modules shows that some

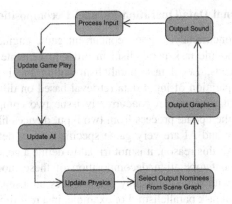

Fig. 3. Typical game engine loop

modules produce and modify most of the data while others only use the manipulated data. The game play and AI modules are the major data manipulators while graphics and audio mostly consume the generated data to produce outputs to the end user. Figure 4 depicts the overall inter-module coupling in a game engine. The direction of an arrow defines dependency on a module.

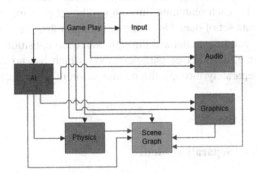

Fig. 4. Game engine modules inter-dependency

Because of scene graph's tight coupling with other modules, its data is the most manipulated/used data. As a result, the scene graph requires much optimized synchronization algorithm to avoid performance bottlenecks. On the other hand, input data is only used by game play module and it can be easily synchronize through simple locking algorithms. Game play and AI are the only modules to modify physics, audio and graphics and thus it seems to be a good decision to keep them running under the same thread rather than concurrently, to remove the need of physics, audio and graphics data synchronization.

4.1   Modules' Internal Data/Operation Parallel Decomposition

Apart from module concurrency, a good concurrent game engine must also provide support for internal module task parallelism in order to generate fine grains of concurrent operation threads. Local task parallelism within the input module can be introduced through separation of input data retrieval based on different input devices. For example, the input module can concurrently issue two completely separate and independent tasks for the update process from two input devices like a keyboard and a mouse. The game play and AI are very game specific as they define the logic incorporated in the game. For this reason, it is not trivial to define a generic methodology or approach for internal data/operation decomposition of these modules. As a rule of thumb, any operation within the game play that operates on a separate set of data is a good candidate for local task parallelism. For example, in a real-time strategy game, the AI logic running for two different AI agents (e.g. troops) operating on distant locations on the game terrain can run as parallel tasks.

In general, physics, scene graph, graphics and audio modules are good candidates of data parallelism. Most of the physics engines in recent days split the physical environment into multiple physical islands to minimize the calculations needed to resolve collisions and object interactions. Thus, it is possible for the physics module to operate on the data for each of these islands in a parallel manner. Scene graphs are inherently designed based on separation of data space. For example, an octree scene graph is a tree data structure used to partition a 3D space by subdividing it into eight octants in a recursive manner. Searching through an octree can therefore be defined as a set of concurrent tasks, each searching through a different partition of the tree and thus operating on a separate set of data. On the other hand, for graphic modules, any kind of graphical animation can be parallelized through data decomposition. For example, in a typical particle engine, each set of particles cloud which has no dependency on the others, is updated separately through the manipulation of a separate set of data.

5   The Architecture

5.1   Data/Operation Separation Model

Based on the examination of a typical game engine and its modules, the following points are crucial in terms of efficiency for a concurrent game engine:

- In order for a game engine to operate concurrently with minimum performance overhead, each module needs to operate locally in its own domain, limited to a minimum shared data access and as little interaction with other modules as possible.
- The engine must support module sub task parallelism, making it possible to have finer grains of operation concurrency and thus higher processing unit task allocation efficiency.

To accomplish the goals, we designed a data/operation separation model based on the concept of data server redundancy, where the engine modules will maintain a local copy of the shared data rather than access common data. This technique removes the cost of using lock methods and thus reduces performance overhead. To maintain consistency between the local data maintained by different modules, a state manager needs to be implemented. The change to shared data needs to be reported to the state manager, which in return will inform all the systems interested in the data change. It is also possible for multiple modules to modify the shared data at the same time. Rules are defined to synchronize the correct value after the changes.

This data/operation separation model requires implementation of a centralized scheduler which holds the master clock and is set at a pre-determined frequency. The responsibility of the scheduler is to submit underlying engine modules for execution, through the task manager for every clock tick. The scheduler will wait for all modules to complete execution according to the preset clock tick duration.

The task manager handles scheduling of a system's tasks within its thread pool. The thread pool creates one thread per processor to get the best possible multi-way scaling to processors and prevents over subscription, which in turn avoids unnecessary task switching within the OS. The task manager receives the list of tasks from the scheduler. Only one primary task is defined per system, although each primary task is allowed to generate as many sub-tasks as it needs to operate on its local data. Figure 5 illustrates the overall engine loop explained.

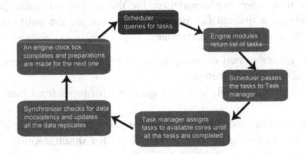

Fig. 5. Loop of the engine

5.2 Layered Architecture

The proposed concurrent engine architecture consists of three layers as depicted in Fig. 6:

- Framework layer
- Kernel layer
- Engine system layer

The framework layer provides OS level functionality such as thread creation, file operation, etc. The framework layer also defines memory management and object messaging used within the engine system. The engine kernel defines the generic engine operations such as object management, module management, data synchronization and task management. Besides providing generic concurrent engine management functionality, the kernel defines interfaces of engine objects and modules that can be implemented to extend engines functionality. The last layer, engine system, contains the actual engine functionality and game logic that is implemented on top of the kernel.

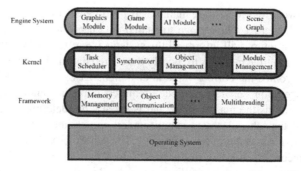

Fig. 6. Layers of the concurrent engine architecture

6 Performance Evaluation

A concurrent and a traditional game program with exact features were implemented to assess the performance and accuracy of the proposed engine. For the traditional game program, all modules are run in a linear fashion under single core implementation. In contrast, under multi-core implementation for the concurrent game program, each engine layer service is queried for available tasks that are the most computationally expensive for the next frame. In particular:

- 3D physics generates two or more tasks in each frame for processing collision detection and physics simulation.
- Game service generates only one task querying for input from user and updating game logic.
- Scene graph generates four tasks: one task for generating three scene object lists and three tasks for processing the three scene object list simultaneously.
- Renderer generates one task for rendering the previously generated render list.

   The games include a huge enclosed environment consisting of nine stacks of 125 (five rows, five columns and five levels) boxes each. Figure 7 depicts a screenshot of the physical environment within the programs.

Fig. 7. Screenshot of the test programs

A set of tests were performed on five CPUs representing different generations of multicore hardware architecture from 2006 to 2010 to analyze the performance of each program on the architectures. The performance for each test was measured using frames per second (FPS). A higher FPS indicates less time spent for execution of code in one frame of game program, denoting a more efficient execution. Each test result was sampled for the duration of one minute of game play, with the player moving around and shooting metal balls randomly (using a keyboard or mouse). While the test progressed, more objects (metal balls and boxes) were added to the scene. As a result, more collision calculation was required and more CPU resources were required to complete the additional calculations, leading to noticeable FPS drops toward the completion of the testing. FRAPS, a real time video capture and benchmarking application (http://www.fraps.com) was used to measure the FPS of the game at runtime.

The list of CPU models used is shown in Table 1. To reduce random factors in the measurements, the same graphic card and memory configuration were adopted for the tests.

Table 1. CPU models used in benchmarking

Family	Specific model	Core speed	Multi-core	Released
AMD 1.8	Athlon XP 2500+	1.833 GHz	No (1)	2003
Intel Core 2	E6600	2.4 GHz	Yes (2)	2006
Intel Core 2 DUO	T5250	1.6 GHz	Yes (2)	2007
Intel Core 2 DUO	P7550	2.26 GHz	Yes (2)	2009
Intel Core I3	i3-2100	3.2 GHz	Yes (2)	2010

For the first step of benchmarking, the traditional game program was run on the selected CPUs. Figure 8a depicts the results of the tests showing frame count changes as time progresses. In general, for all CPUs, the faster the clock speed, the higher the FPS. In addition, performance of all CPUs degraded as more objects in the scene were manipulated.

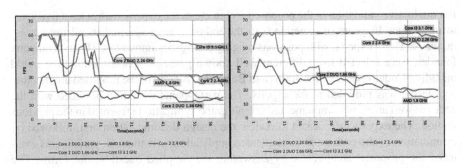

Fig. 8. a. Results on traditional engine **b.** Results on concurrent engine

For the second step of benchmarking, test results were sampled on the same set of CPUs using the proposed concurrent engine. The results are illustrated in Fig. 8b. The sampling results on the slowest CPU, Core 2 DUO 1.66 GHz, showed improvement as both cores on the CPU were utilized. In this case, FPS for Core 2 DUO 1.66 GHz was increased by almost ten frames for each sample. As for the higher end CPUs, the improvement was obvious. The latest architecture Core I3 showed almost no frame drop during the one minute sampling period, contrary to the first test result. For the other two CPUs, Core 2 DUO 2.26 GHz and Core 2 2.4 GHz, the frame drop was very minor.

The maximum frame rate on Core 2 DUO 1.66 GHz showed improvement of ten units. This is a good indication that the new architecture improves frame rate on low end multi-core architecture by removing calculation bounding on a single core and utilizing all cores available. On the other hand, the minimum frame rate for all the CPUs with multicore design has improved, with the change being more significant on older architectures. For Core 2 2.4 GHz CPU, the minimum frame rate has almost doubled. Meanwhile, FPS samplings on the AMD CPU for both traditional and concurrent game programs were very close. Thus, it shows that the proposed concurrent architecture does not affect performance on older single-core CPUs while increasing frame rate on newer multi-core CPUs. Table 2 summarizes the improvement by showing the average FPS measured from the benchmarking tests.

Table 2. Average FPS

CPU	Traditional program	Concurrent program	Improvement (%)
AMD 1.8	29.55	29.70	5.1
Intel Core 2 2.4 GHz	36.02	58.05	61.2
Intel Core 2 DUO 1.6 GHz	17.13	25.38	48.2
Intel Core 2 DUO 2.26 GHz	44.20	60.33	36.5
Intel Core I3 3.2 GHz	58.1	60.88	9.9

7   User Acceptance Evaluation

For qualitative validation of the proposed architecture, ten experts with at least five years to more than 15 years of experience in the industry were selected to fill up a questionnaire. These experts, with positions ranging from programmer to CTO and company founder, were selected from different well known game companies around the world including Codemasters, GameBrains and Boomzap. A copy of the proposed architecture and design was provided to the experts. The participants were also provided with the codes as well as the two implemented sample game application presented in the previous section. The experts were asked to review the design documentation first, followed by examination of the codes and implemented applications. At the end, participants evaluated the proposed architecture by answering the supplied questionnaire forms. The questionnaire consists of ten questions, separated into two sections:

- Architectural qualities (Questions 1–7, multi choice)
- Industry domain specific (Questions 8–9, multi choice)

The last question is an open-ended question for the participants to express their view about the strength and weakness of the proposed architecture. Table 3 summarizes the responses obtained from the questionnaire survey. The feedback obtained is very encouraging indeed.

Table 3. Summary of survey results

No	Aspect	Excellent (%)	Good (%)	Average (%)	Poor (%)
1	Intended functionality	60	40	0	0
2	Performance	20	80	0	0
3	Learnability	80	20	0	0
4	Portability	20	60	20	0
5	Reusability	100	0	0	0
6	Extensibility	50	50	0	0
7	Modifiability	70	30	0	0
8	Address industry's concern about concurrency	40	60	0	0
9	Practicality	80	N/A	20	0

Through the last question, the participants also indicated that the lockless architecture works very well for concurrency execution. They suggested that the proposed architecture may benefit many current technologies such as paging geometry, software hierarchical occlusion and dynamic batching/instancing. On the other hand, some participants commented that demonstrating a mix of platforms running the engine, e.g. Xbox 360 and PS3, would increase the confidence of the engineers to adopt the system. They also suggested that the architecture implementation could prove to be heavy on some mobile platforms and if required a lighter weight version of the design would be needed. A respondent highlighted that the number of threads and CPUs is not the only criteria that is important, indicating that platform specific operations can have significant improvement.

8 Discussion and Conclusion

Concurrency is still new to game development. Many game developers avoid parallelism due to difficulties related to synchronization and its effect on runtime performance. One of the difficulties in adopting concurrency is that game engines are inherently linear applications, where all the steps need to be done in a correct order. This research takes the initiative to review the existing concurrent software techniques that take advantage of the multithreading and synchronization concepts, such as lock free programming, to propose a generic, flexible, and scalable concurrent game engine architecture. This study has highlighted the need of undertaking the challenge to carefully examine the interrelations of game engine modules at low levels. The aim was to discover sections and operations appropriate for concurrency, while at the same time, maintaining and assuring the required sequence of consumption, process and production of data in a concurrent game engine cycle. Benchmarking and industry experts' assessment were adopted to validate and verify the proposed concurrent game engine architecture. Both of them have shown encouraging results.

As opposed to Adaptive Loop Model, a popular concurrent game architecture which merely addresses engine task concurrency, the architecture proposed in this research defines an appropriate generic methodology to concurrently handle task management as well as data sharing and synchronization. The architecture presented here does not require major change in the existing linear game architectures. The traditional engine step model has been preserved. Engine tasks are still performed within the engine step time frames with exception that the new architecture provides task concurrency on the same frame utilizing all the CPU cores available on an executing hardware.

Another strong point of the proposed architecture, as indicated in Sect. 5, is its compatibility with single core processor architectures. The provided design avoids usage of traditional data synchronization techniques (e.g. locks), which have proven to be resource intensive and introduce overheads. This was achieved through application of lock-free synchronization algorithms and data redundancy, which avoid overheads (introduced by older techniques) on single core architecture. For this reason, the number of cores available is transparent to the proposed architecture. The architectural design perceives available CPU resource as a computational unit with variable quantity of cores. In other words, from the proposed architecture point of view, older generation CPUs are just another multi-core processor, with only one core available. At the same time, the architecture does not limit the power of newer generation CPUs. The more cores available, the more tasks can be performed synchronously, leading to improved performance results.

Due to the lockless synchronization virtue of the proposed architecture, real-time creation of new objects by one service which are requested by another synchronous service is unlikely during the task performance phase. As its current state of design, the proposed architecture will only permit such operation during data synchronization phase. This can be seen as a major drawback for the games where the game play environment data are synchronously generated and destroyed seamlessly in a streaming manner. Thus, the streaming data loaded asynchronously might not be available until the next upcoming frame. As a result, frequent unnecessary downtime of game logic execution might be introduced, leading to underutilization of available CPU power. Meanwhile, as there are many game genres exists in the market and each game type imposes different styles of game play implementation, it is very important for the proposed architecture to be tested across various game types.

In addition, the proposed architecture has not been tested on platforms such as XBOX 360 and PS3, which are known to be the leading game consoles with superior processing power through specialized modern multi-core hardware architecture platforms and might need to be adjusted based on specific concurrency techniques available on each platform. Smartphones and tablets are other major platforms for game application that have gained popularity in recent years. Although improved greatly from the early predecessors, they are still very limited compared to personal computers and game consoles. As a result, handheld devices might lack some of the lockless techniques introduced in this research. Clouds is another platform which is gaining more pupularity in recent years and is worthwhile to be investigated, too.

References

1. Blake, G., Dreslinski, R.G., Mudge, T.: A survey of multicore processors. IEEE Signal Process. Mag. **26**(6), 26–37 (2009)
2. Sutter, H.: The free lunch is over: a fundamental turn toward concurrency in software. Dr. Dobb's J. **30**(3) (2005). http://www.gotw.ca/publications/concurrency-ddj.htm. Accessed 25 Feb 2013
3. Joselli, M., Clua, E., Montenegro, A., Conci, A., Pagliosa, P.: A new physics engine with automatic process distribution between CPU-GPU. In: Proceedings of the 2008 ACM SIGGRAPH Symposium on Video Games, pp. 149–156 (2008)
4. Sutter, H., James, L.: Software and concurrency revolution. Queue-Multiprocessors **3**(7), 54–62 (2005)
5. Pankratius, V., Schaefer, C., Jannesari, A., Tichy, W.F.: Software engineering for multicore systems: an experience report. In: Proceedings of the 1st International Workshop on Multicore Software Engineering, pp. 53–60 (2008)
6. Raaen, K., Espeland, H., Stensland, H.K., Petlund, A., Halvorsen, P., Griwodz, C.: A demonstration of a lockless, relaxed atomicity state parallel game server (LEARS). In: Proceedings of the 10th Annual Workshop on Network and Systems Support for Games (NetGames), pp. 1–3 (2011)
7. Best, M.J., et al.: Searching for concurrent design patterns in video games. In: Sips, H., Epema, D., Lin, H.-X. (eds.) Euro-Par 2009. LNCS, vol. 5704, pp. 912–923. Springer, Heidelberg (2009)
8. AlBahnassi, W., Mudur, S.P., Goswami, D.: A design pattern for parallel programming of games. In: Proceedings of the 14th International Conference on High Performance Computing and Communication, pp. 1007–1014 (2012)
9. Kehoe, J., Morris, J.: A concurrency model for game scripting. In: Proceedings of the 12th International Conference on Intelligent Games and Simulation, pp. 10–15 (2011)
10. Mattson, T., Wrinn, M.: Parallel programming: can we PLEASE get it right this time?. In: Proceedings of the 45th Annual Design Automation Conference, pp. 7–11 (2008)
11. Herlihy, M., Moss, J.E.: Transactional memory: architecture support for lock-free data structures. ACM SIGARCH Comput. Archit. **21**(2), 289–300 (1993)
12. Miller, A.: The task graph pattern. In: Proceedings of the 2010 Workshop on Parallel Programming Patterns (2010)
13. Manolescu, D-A.: A data flow pattern language. In: Proceedings of the 4th Pattern Languages of Programming (1997)
14. Joselli, M., Zamith, M., Clua, E., Montenegro, A., Leal-Toledo, R., Conci, A., Pagliosa, P., Valente, L., Feijó, B.: An adaptative game loop architecture with automatic distribution of tasks between CPU and GPU. Comput. Entertain. **7**(4) (2009) doi:10.1145/1658866. 1658869
15. Gregory, J.: Game Engine Architecture. CRC Press, Boca Raton (2009)

Educational Features of *AIDA Programs

Yutaka Watanobe[✉], Nikolay Mirenkov, and Mirai Watanabe

University of Aizu, Aizu-wakamatsu 965-8580, Japan
yutaka@u-aizu.ac.jp

Abstract. Programming in pictures is an approach whereby pictures and animation are used as super-characters for representing features of computational algorithms and data structures, as well as for explaining models and application methods involved. *AIDA is a language supporting programming in pictures. In this chapter, some features of *AIDA programs are discussed and how these features can be applied for educational goals oriented to users with little programming experience. Special attention is paid to new examples in which algorithmic dynamics is explained by animations and template programs supporting the implementation of this dynamics.

Keywords: *AIDA · Algorithmic cyber-scene · Educational materials

Introduction

Programming is a very useful skill but learning to program is a very difficult process. How to help novice programmers and end-users, what are behind abilities of expert programmers, and which experience is necessary to turn a novice into an expert? Such topics have been intensively studied for many years (see, for example, a review [1]). In addition, taking into account the currently vital role of computers and information resources available anywhere and at any time, a set of new initiatives in education and research has been promoted by ACM, IEEE-Computer society and individuals [2–4]. The goal of these initiatives is to prepare future generations for a truly digital world. Computer education is considered as an entryway to that world. Though, not everyone needs coding skills, the usefulness of understanding of how to think like a programmer can be really high in many disciplines. Ideas of computational thinking are supported as ways to learn how to apply abstraction, divide a problem into subproblems or compose components, develop cognitive ability, and obtain problem-solving skills. In other words, the role of computers in higher-order thinking and programming as the second literacy are hot topics again, as in the past [5,6]. Within these initiatives, special attention is paid to novice programmers and teaching programming in high school.

Acquiring knowledge about programming is based on a variety of cognitive activities and mental simulations related to program design, modifying, understanding, debugging, etc. Very often such acquiring is focused on composing

© Springer International Publishing Switzerland 2015
H. Fujita and A. Selamat (Eds.): SoMeT 2014, CCIS 513, pp. 162–177, 2015.
DOI: 10.1007/978-3-319-17530-0_12

loops, conditional statements and other basic constructs into computational plans. As a first step, the focus on program models is really important for novices to understand semantics of the language constructs and how programs work. However, taking into account application problem models and corresponding application algorithms has a deeper influence on understanding data types, data flow, hierarchical structures, mapping between layers, etc., as well as on understanding problem-solving processes as a whole. The novices not only lack the specific knowledge but also experience to apply the knowledge they possess. Existing programming environments are still complex for our users to access to previous decisions of others, to get support for quick perception and understanding these decisions, and obtain the confidence in making own decisions.

In this chapter, we briefly present *AIDA language (AIDA stands for Animation and Images to Develop Algorithms) and explain some features of programs in pictures which can be useful for learning how to program and understand algorithms. Our focus is users with little programming experience (of novice programmers to end-users level).

New examples for explanations of algorithms, animations involved in the explanations, and for the use of template programs, supporting the implementation of algorithmic scene dynamics, as well as for understanding C++ constructs are provided. This includes an extended set of super-characters, animations of row-by-row and zig-zag traversals, and a dynamics of Dijkstra's algorithm. In addition, some ideas for enhancing features of *AIDA programs to be more suitable for educational goals are also discussed.

1   Related Work

We are interested in programming environments where application programmers can present not only application requirements, specifications and program texts, but also various features of models applied, ideas behind, methods involved, etc. In other words, we promote an idea of programs as information resources [7] which can be used for different goals and based on the idea of comprehensive explanations and automatic generations of corresponding documents, presentation slides, executable codes, etc. In fact, such information resources can be the basis for a global environment of active knowledge which can be much easier to search, understand, and immediately reuse. They can also be a basis of educational materials of a new generation. Within such an approach, our research is related to works on algorithm visualization and explanation. This includes visual language constructs and how they can be represented in conventional languages. This is also related to how the visualization, explanation and representations mentioned can be useful for novices and end-users to acquire knowledge about algorithms and programming.

Algorithm visualizations are usually considered by instructors very positively for improving computer science education. However, in reality, the positive support of the idea does not match the practical use of it. So, special analysis of reasons and how to overcome various barriers for getting algorithm visualizations into the classroom are performed [8]. Among these efforts, sorting out examples of the good and poor quality visualizations and providing adequate information, about how the best can be used, are promoted [9]. Special efforts have been done to establish the AlgoViz portal [10], where the best practices are acquired by online educational community related to the algorithm visualization. A family of tools for supporting the learning of programming by university students is promoted in [11]. Papers on educational programming environments of Scratch and Alice types [12, 13] allowing novices to create simple programs are also works of our interests. Within these interests it is important to mention Lego Mindstorms Kits broadly applied for supporting modeling and learning processes related to programmable robots and embedded systems. RCX Code and ROBOLAB icon-based languages are a basis for wiring box programming (see, for example [14]); though a variety of other languages can also be involved.

Visual programming languages of domain-specific types, such as LabVIEW supporting electronic system specialists [15] (and above mentioned users interested in robotics) and Max/MSP oriented to digital music designers [16], are rich sources of how algorithms can be presented within the frameworks of a high level of abstraction. An overview of software engineering challenges, which are faced by end-users [17], provides existing practices related to corresponding languages, tool designs, domain specific adaptations, and educational tasks. In addition, programming by examples and programming by demonstrations [18, 19] representing some techniques to follow are within our ways of thinking.

Though visual languages and related environments are among of our primary interests, still there are many other types of online tutorials, courses, tools, mentoring systems, etc. which should be under our attention. They are based on conventional languages, visualization of programs in such languages, and on long-term experience of programming teaching acquired by instructors (see, for example, [20–22]).

2 Programming in Pictures

Programming in (algorithmic) pictures is an approach where pictures and moving pictures are used as super-characters for representing features of computational algorithms and data structures. Within this approach some "data space structures" are traversed by "fronts of computation" [23, 24] and/or some "units of activity" are traversed by flows of data [25, 26]. There are compound pictures to define algorithmic steps (called Algorithmic CyberFrames) and generic pictures to define the contents of compound pictures. Compound pictures are assembled into special series to represent some algorithmic features. The series are assembled into Algorithmic CyberScenes and CyberFilm. The generic/compound pictures and their series are developed and acquired in special galleries of an open type where supportive pictures of embedded clarity annotations are also included. *AIDA (Star-AIDA) is a modeling/ programming language supporting the programming in pictures.

A special feature of *AIDA language and its environment is that programs in pictures are developed as information resources not only for code generating,

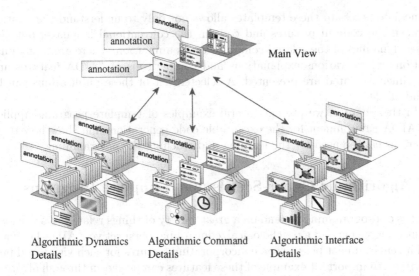

Fig. 1. Algorithmic CyberFilm format

but also for explaining application algorithms and models related. Another special feature is in the concept of super-characters allowing, if necessary, applying pictures within the frameworks of the text-type expressions and, in this way, combining simplicity and expressiveness of visual and text forms.

Algorithmic CyberFilm format (Fig. 1) has a hierarchical structure where on the top there is a series of CyberFrames representing a main (integrated) view of an algorithm.

To enhance the algorithm comprehension, each picture of the main view frames is supported by corresponding meaning annotation and/or by a series of frames of the bottom layer views. On the bottom layer there are algorithmic dynamics, command and interface views. In other words, perception, comprehension, and cognition of algorithmic steps depend on the interaction with, at least, a few different but mutually supplementing explanations of algorithmic pictures. Animation, other pictures, and text are involved for these explanations to clarify meaning of algorithmic dynamics, details of formulas, input/output operations, and data features. Usually, the users work with pictures of the main view and pictures/text related to the explanations are called only on special demand.

*AIDA language and its environment are developed and promoted as a testbed for various innovations in applying hybrid forms of information resources [23] where "self-explanatory" (multiple views) formats play an important role. A basis of the explanation is Main view of a corresponding *AIDA program supported by details on demand provided by other views and various annotations. A standard rule of *AIDA is in the use of annotations to a cover frame of Main view frames for explaining some features of the model as a whole. Another important point related to *AIDA is that template programs implementing repetitive processes of Algorithmic Cyber-scenes in C++ are available as annotations.

Immediate access to these templates allows not only to understand the relation between the code in pictures and code in the conventional language, but also to see dynamics of the related computation as animation. There are many publications where various explanations and comparisons of *AIDA features and experiments related are presented. A selected list of these publications can be found at [24].

In this chapter, we present several examples of template programs applied in *AIDA environment for the executable code generation, and show how these programs can be used for the learning and teaching the programming.

3   Algorithmic Cyber-Scenes and Template Programs

Studies of programming depend on a great variety of things related to a software engineering vision and a psychological/educational perspective. *AIDA language and its environment possess some incorporating features for such vision and perspective. An important example of these features can be shown through algorithmic cyber-scenes and template programs supporting the scene implementation and execution, as well as through multiple views and possible annotations.

An algorithmic cyber-scene is a traversal process on a space data structure (or a group of structures). Such a process is based on a partial order of the node structure scanning. Examples of super-characters which represent data structures imitating some physical regions (shapes) in 3-D space are depicted by Fig. 2.

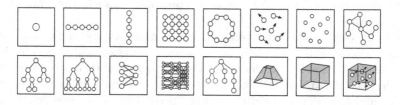

Fig. 2. Examples of super-characters representing space data structures

All structures are scalable and defined by corresponding structure parameters. For example, for a 2-D grid, the number of rows and columns can be specified as its parameters. Examples of super-characters representing traversal processes (of how computational activities come to the structure nodes) are depicted by Fig. 3.

Behind each super-character of this type, there is a template program implementing a correspondingly nested loop or a more complicated repetitive construct. (In fact, in *AIDA there are also diagram structures and data flow activities on them. However, in this paper, we focus only on space data structures).

To define computational steps imitating some real world processes, our user should select a space data structure and declare variables (application attributes) and their types on these structures. Then a traversal scheme on the structure

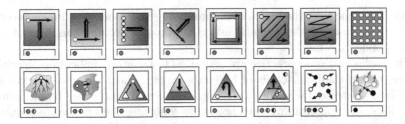

Fig. 3. Examples of super-characters representing traversal processes

and operations on structure nodes should be specified. In this approach, algorithms are represented by the structures, a series of traversal schemes on structures and corresponding operations involved in nodes of the traversal schemes. For each scene, to support its self-explanatory features, at least a few views (annotations) are created. These annotations can show dynamic aspects of algorithms involved, images of real objects, text-based explanation of methods applied, links to external explanations, etc. There are three types of annotations. The first type is related to algorithmic details views of the *AIDA program format and new scene pictures. These views and annotations are attached by developers when scenes and corresponding scene pictures are included in libraries and galleries. The second type is related to the joint activity of an editor of *AIDA environment and the user: the editor initiates an interaction by asking special questions and the user's answers are transformed into some annotations. Questions about units of measure and/or some features of initial data can be an example of the interactions. Finally, the third type is annotations prepared and attached by the user on his own initiatives. In such cases, balloon type micro-icons are appeared near some expressions or constructs. The annotations are hidden behind the Main view of *AIDA programs and called only on user's demands. For each scene, to support some efficiency of the code generation, a number of temple programs is prepared, and one of them can be selected within the code generation process. A set of such template programs is created if there is some necessity; often one template program is enough to efficiently represent scene activities. The end users usually do not create new scenes and their template programs but adapt the existing ones by changing their sizes, variable declarations, activity units as well as by introducing special masks (no activity zones), etc. Of course, the users can do it by submitting their forms and solutions; however, including them in galleries and libraries is possible only after a special refereeing procedure.

In addition to existing scenes based on embedded templates, there are scenes (first of all among those which are based on diagram structures) where template programs are generated automatically. For such scenes, after finishing the diagram drawing, a template program generator is called to generate templates. The templates produced are used as input for *AIDA compiler to generate an executable code in C++. Usually, the end users work on the super-character levels and there is no necessity for them to see template programs. However, at any moment these programs are available as special annotations for related scenes. In this paper, our interest is in how the development of individual programming skill of novices and end users can be supported. This should include, from one side, the basics of programming and good software engineering practice, and from another, mental aspects of program comprehension and relation to application models.

The basics and good practice are organized to focus on application algorithm features rather than on details of language syntax, and to acquire general and specialized strategies for problem solving. The mental aspects are based on multiple views and constraining the choices by following the knowledge acquired. Super-characters, pictures, and animations accompanied by various annotations are a basis for speeding-up the development of individual programming skill of novices and end users. Of course, programming ability is based on a foundation of knowledge about programming languages, supporting tools and computer architectures. Within *AIDA environment, an access to such a foundation is arranged through template programs in C++, codes generated, various annotations and links. Let us consider a few examples of relations between algorithmic cyber-scenes, their animations, and template programs.

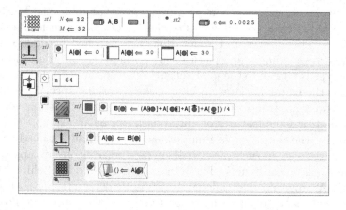

Fig. 4. A main view of an *AIDA program including four cyber-scenes

Figure 4 presents a simple program including four cyber-scenes defined by the three icons (super-characters) of the following types: (one cyber-scene is used twice, in rows 2 and 5).

Understanding these super-characters is not only about understanding semantics of the repetitive constructs, but also about understanding a place where they can be applied in algorithm representations. This is also about basic cognitive units used in program design (in composing a program plan). The first cyber-scene, related to super-characters, is based on formulas applying masks (to avoid the involvement of if-then-else operations). Three other cyber-scenes are inside a construct of the for-loop type.

To understand dynamics of the cyber-scene represented by , the user can click this super-character and see a tile view of this dynamics (Fig. 5). He can also see it as animation.

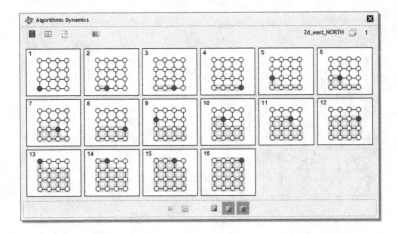

Fig. 5. A tile view of the first cyber-scene dynamics

Multiple views are promoted here as a basis for exercises on high-level program comprehension: given the picture-based text (super-text) and the users have to show some understanding of how it works.

The template program supporting super-character ⬛ is also a part of the multiple view and can be useful for exercises on program comprehension.

```
/** _st is a target 2d grid object where the computational scheme is performed.
 * The outer for loop corresponds to iteration processes in the 2d grid where
 * each row is traversed from the bottom to the top.
 * The inner for loop represents iteration processes in each row where
 * each column is traversed from the left to the right.
 * FORMULA_0_BODY is replaced by the specified formulas with _p which is
 * an index of the corresponding active node.
 */
void SCENE(Grid2D & _st) {
    Index _p = Index(&_st);
    for ( int _i = _st.numOfRow()-1; _i >= 0; _i-- ) {
        for ( int _j = 0; _j < _st.numOfCol(); _j++ ) {
            _p = _i*_st.numOfCol() + _j;
            /* FORMULA_0_BODY */
        }
    }
}
```

In addition, it is to demonstrate how a C++ program performs some task (a scanning process) and how the code generation integrates formulas of computational activity. It is also about an important aspect of the programming process: mapping from the problem domain into the programming domain. Rather than studying a program line by line, the users obtain a high-level vision of what is going on.

The effects are essentially enhanced by considering another super-character ▨, which is similar to the previous one, but with a different traversal process.

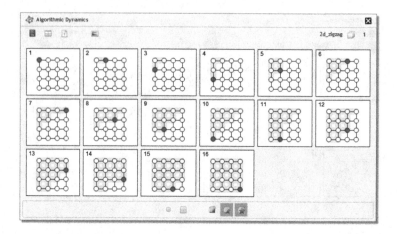

Fig. 6. A tile view of another cyber-scene dynamics

The users can see the animation of this process (Fig. 6) and a template program involved (see, hereafter). A comparison of two template programs is a ground for better confidence in obtaining the programming knowledge and skill.

```
/** _st is a target 2d grid object where the computational scheme is performed.
 * The outer for loop corresponds to iteration processes in the 2d grid where
 * each vertical line is traversed from the top-left to the bottom-right.
 * The inner for loop represents iteration processes in each line where
 * each vertical line is traversed from the bottom-left to the top-right or
 * from the top-right to the bottom-left.
 * FORMULA_0_BODY is replaced by the specified formulas with _p which is
 * an index of the corresponding active node.
 */
void SCENE(Grid2D & _st){
  Index _p = Index(&_st);
  for ( int _k = 0; _k < (_st.numOfCol() + _st.numOfRow()-1); _k++ ){
    int _bj = _k%2?min(_k, _st.numOfCol()-1):max(0, _k-_st.numOfRow()+1);
    int _bi = _k%2?max(0, _k-_st.numOfCol()+1):min(_k, _st.numOfRow()-1);
    int _d = _k<min(_st.numOfCol(), _st.numOfRow())?_k:_st.numOfCol()+_st.numOfRow()-_k-2;
    for ( int _l = 0; _l < _d+1; _l++ ){
      int _i = _bi + (_k%2?1:-1)*_l;
      int _j = _bj + (_k%2?-1:1)*_l;
      _p = _i*_st.numOfCol()+_j;
      /* FORMULA_0_BODY */
    }
  }
}
```

This can be extended by considering additional super-characters and performing additional comparisons. Let us do it for the third cyber-scene of the Fig. 4 example; it is represented by super-character ▨ which animation is presented by one frame only with simultaneous flashing of all nodes of the 2D structure (Fig. 7).

This parallel involvement of all nodes is applied for a collective operation which semantics is "taking values of a variable (in this case, it is **A**) from all

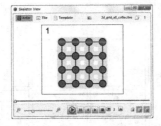

Fig. 7. One frame flashing dynamics of the third cyber-scene

nodes and use them as initial data for an operation specified (in this case, an output operation)." A sequential version of the template program supporting this super-character includes the following lines.

```
/** _st is a target 2d grid object where the computational scheme is performed.
 * _all is an object which includes all indices (nodes) in _st.
 * FORMULA_0_BODY is replaced by specified formulas which include operations
 * or functions taking _all as their parameter.
 */
void SCENE(Grid2D &_st){
    All _all = All(&_st);
    /* FORMULA_0_BODY */
}
```

The examples considered can be useful for preparing not only questions about the programs but also for preparing tasks to create templates for other types of traversal schemes. Results of such programming can be compared with template programs available in *AIDA environment. Applying super-characters, related animations, and template programs is an approach for enhancing the user's ability both to read a program and to write one. A step-by-step involvement of more complex examples adds new values to the approach. Let us step more in this direction.

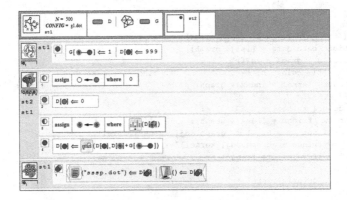

Fig. 8. A main view of *AIDA program specifying Dijkstra's shortest paths algorithm

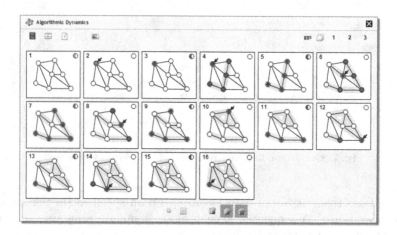

Fig. 9. Tile view of a cyber-scene dynamics related to Dijkstra's algorithm

```
/** _graph is a target graph object where the computational scheme is performed.
 * The scheme is implemented based on adjacency lists of the graph object and
 * some colors which represent states of each node during the traversal scheme.
 * WHITE is for non-visited nodes, GREEN is for visited nodes and BLUE is for
 * completed nodes. The colors depend on specified formulas to
 * FORMULA_2_ASSIGN_0_WHERE_0 as well as to FORMULA_0_BODY and FORMULA_1_BODY for
 * the initialization and FORMULA_2_BODY and FORMULA_3_BODY for operations on the
 * kernel (selected) node and on its fringe nodes respectively.
 */
void SCENE(Observer &_ob, Graph &_graph){
    int _color[_graph.size()];
    static const int COLOR_WHITE = 0;
    static const int COLOR_GREEN = 1;
    static const int COLOR_BLUE = 2;

    for ( int _i = 0; _i < _graph.size(); _i++ ) _color[_i] = COLOR_WHITE;
    Index _source = Index(&_graph, /* FORMULA_0_ASSIGN_0_WHERE_0 */);

    /* FORMULA_0_BODY */
    /* FORMULA_1_BODY */

    _color[_source] = COLOR_GREEN;

    for ( int _n = 0; _n < _graph.size(); _n++ ){
        List _candidate = List(&_graph);
        rep(_c, _graph.size())
            if( _color[_c] == COLOR_GREEN ) _candidate.push_back(_c);
        Index _kernel = Index(&_graph, /* FORMULA_2_ASSIGN_0_WHERE_0 */);
        /* FORMULA_2_BODY */
        _color[_kernel] = COLOR_BLUE;
        Index _fringe = Index(&_graph);
        for ( int _i = 0; _i < _graph.adj[_kernel].size(); _i++ ){
            _fringe = _graph.adj[_kernel][_i];
            if ( _color[_fringe] == COLOR_BLUE ) continue;
            /* FORMULA_3_BODY*/
            _color[_fringe] = COLOR_GREEN;
        }
    }
}
```

Figure 8 presents Dijkstra's algorithm for the shortest paths problem. Our focus is on a scene which is behind the super-character .

The dynamic of computation and a variety of operation types applied are depicted by Fig. 9 which is followed by a corresponding template program. This program provides a basis for preparing various questions and exercises.

4   A Usability Test

A lot of experiments, case studies and usability tests have been done within the process of *AIDA development. This has included the picture-based program compactness, understanding the programs and related algorithms, quality of the code generations, developing programming skill and cognitive adaptations of users, etc. (please, see Sect. 8 in [23] for a brief overview). Here we present a new usability test to start a deeper analysis of *AIDA programs as educational materials. Therefore, we decided to begin with a questionnaire related to the *AIDA tutorials [27]. A small part of the questionnaire is presented by Fig. 10 (the full version is available at [28]). Totally, it was 33 questions. Two teachers and four students answered them. Though the questions required different types of scores and marks, we summarized the answers in 12 categories and calculated average values based on different participant answers.

Understanding a-characters (algorithmic characters) and constructs

1. A-characters and constructs (in general) - very good, 55 %; good, 25 %, so-so, 20 %
2. A-characters and constructs (in special groups) - very good, 55 %; good, 25 %, so-so, 20 %
3. Declarations of space structures, variables and masks - very good, 55 %; good, 35 %, so-so, 10 %
4. Generic a-characters used for assignment statements and formulas -very good, 65 %; good, 25 %, so-so, 10 %
5. Scene a-characters - very good, 45 %; good, 35 %, so-so, 20 %

Understanding of three types of programs and recommendations on the improvement of the explanations

1. Very simple programs - very good, 65 %; good, 25 %, so-so, 10 %
2. Simple programs - very good, 55 %; good, 25 %, so-so, 20 %
3. Rather complex programs - very good, 30 %; good, 35 %, so-so, 35 %

Usefulness of cognitive aspects of programming in pictures for readability and understandability of the programs

1. Considering an algorithm as an activity in "space-time" - very good, 45 %; good, 35 %, so-so, 20 %
2. Animations of traversal schemes on the space structures - very good, 75 %; good, 25 %

3. Highlighting (flashing) nodes where computation is currently performed - very good, 35 %; good, 45 %, so-so, 20 %
4. Quality (attractiveness) of super-character designs - very good, 50 %; good, 50 %

A special question related directly to the paper topic

1. Do you support the idea that explaining conventional language constructs for beginners should be performed trough explaining corresponding *AIDA constructs and related template programs? All participants positively answered this question.

The results demonstrate a high level of understanding algorithmic characters, constructs, and program examples as a whole. It is important to note that this understanding is related to characters, constructs, and programs taken from the *AIDA environment without any enhancements oriented to educational tasks. On the other hand, essential numbers of "so-so" answers point where improvements and enhancements can be done (within the environment or educational material preparations). First of all, we see such improvements and enhancements in adding different annotations, example variations, etc.

Within the framework of this questionnaire, free style comments were also allowed. Two students pointed that animations are useful not only for demonstrating the dynamics of algorithm behavior, but also for engaging the learners. They also think that the possibility of applying one traversal scheme for different

1.   Understanding a-characters (algorithmic characters) and constructs (in general)

1.1.   For how many percentages (75%, 55%, 35%, 25%) of the items, sufficiency of the intuitive level can be recognized for understanding the meaning?

1.2.   For how many percentages (75%, 55%, 35%, 25%) of items, annotations provided by demand are necessary;

1.3.   How good is efficiency of super-character (glossary) explanations (very good, good, satisfactory, unsatisfactory);

1.4.   How do you evaluate factors (of 2, 5, 8, 10 times) decreasing the necessity of special efforts for memorizing a-characters and constructs;

1.5.   How useful are comparisons of *AIDA a-characters and constructs with similar things of conventional languages (very useful, rather useful, satisfactory, unsatisfactory);

1.6.   Which super-character (glossary) explanations should be improved (to point such explanations, copy and paste them or their parts).

2.   Understanding a-characters and constructs (in special groups)

2.1.   Declarations of space structures, variables and masks

2.1.1. Sufficiency of the intuitive level for (75%, 55%, 35%, 25%) cases;

2.1.2. Importance of annotations provided by demand for (75%, 55%, 35%, 25%) cases;

2.1.3. Efficiency of glossary explanations (very good, good, satisfactory, unsatisfactory);

Fig. 10. A beginning part of the questionnaire to the *AIDA tutorial materials

computational tasks is an important feature. The teachers involved pointed that *AIDA programs can be used for both the teaching and learning and can be incorporated into conventional lecture materials.

5   Conclusion and Future Work

In this chapter, we briefly presented some features of *AIDA programs and environment and tried to consider how they can be useful for learning the programming by users with little programming experience. Our focus was related to some explanations of algorithms, animations involved in the explanations, and to applying template programs, supporting the animations, to understand C++ constructs. Several examples were considered and a usability test was performed. The test demonstrated an educational goal attractiveness of *AIDA programs in the current status (as they are now) and also pointed directions to how the attractiveness can be extended by adding annotations, examples, etc. It is our first step and in future work we will consider in detail other features of *AIDA language and various aspects of data/knowledge acquisition within the *AIDA environment for developing the educational materials. This will be based on ours vision of why the features and acquisition can be useful for learning the programming:

1. Programs are usually written for a goal related to some problems or specifications. *AIDA programs help in some understanding the problem domain before the program writing.
2. *AIDA program is a cluster of multiple views demonstrating the relation between an application algorithm in pictures and how it can be implemented in C++.
3. *AIDA supports novices to understand basic patterns/schemas, hierarchy of components, as well as to minimize bugs associated with loops and conditionals. Initial course materials can be simple and systematically expanded as the users gain experience.
4. It is also to minimize the influence of the lack of the specific knowledge and skills and to increase a level of confidence. It is to simplify frustration and get "a feeling of success." This encourages the users to actively engage in exploring the programming processes in learning "by doing."
5. *AIDA is a basis for effective communication between teacher and student. It is to foster independent and life-long learners.

References

1. Robins, A., Rountree, J., Rountree, N.: Learning and teaching programming: a review and discussion. Comput. Sci. Educ. 13(2), 137–172 (2003)
2. Cerf, V.: Computer science education - revisited. Commun. ACM 56(8), 7 (2013)
3. McGettrick, A.: Education, always. Commun. ACM 57(2), 5 (2014)
4. Shein, E.: Should everybody learn to code? Commun. ACM 57(2), 16–18 (2014)

5. Patterson, J.H., Smith, M.S.: The role of computers in higher-order thinking. In: Jack Culbertson, J., Cunningham, L.L. (eds.) Microcomputers and Education, Part 1, pp. 81–108 (1986) ISSN:0077–5762
6. Culbertson, J.A.: Whither computer literacy? In: Jack Culbertson, J., Cunningham, L.L. (eds.) Microcomputers and Education, Part 1, pp. 109–131 (1986) ISSN:0077–5762
7. Watanobe, Y., Mirenkov, N., Terasaka, H.: Information resources of *AIDA programs, In: Proceedings of the IEEE Symposium on Visual Languages and Human Centric Computing, Melbourne, July–August 2014
8. Shaffer, C.A., Akbar, M., Alon, A.J.D., Stewart, M., Edwards, S.H.: Getting algorithm visualizations into the classroom. In: Proceedings of the 42nd ACM Technical Symposium on Computer Science Education, SIGCSE 2011, pp. 129–134. ACM, New York (2011)
9. Shaffer, C.A., Cooper, M.L., Alon, A.J.D., Akbar, M., Stewart, M., Ponce, S., Edwards, S.H.: Algorithm visualization: the state of the field. ACM Trans. Comput. Educ. **10**, 1–22 (2010)
10. AlgoViz.org: The algorithm visualization portal. http://algoviz.org/. (Accessed 26 March 2014)
11. Robling, G.: A family of tools for supporting the learning of programming. Algorithms **3**(2), 168–182 (2010)
12. Dann, W.P., Cooper, S., Pausch, R.: Learning To Program with Alice, 2nd edn. Prentice Hall Press, Upper Saddle River (2008)
13. Ford, J.L.: Scratch Programming for Teens. Course Technology Press, Boston (2008)
14. RCX Code Programming Language. http://robofest.net/academy/rcxcode4robofest.pdf
15. Bitter, R., Mohiuddin, T., Nawrocki, M.: LabView: Advanced programming techniques, 2nd edn. CRC Press, Boca Raton (2007)
16. Freed, A., MacCallum, J., Schmeder, A.: Dynamic, instance-based, object-oriented programming in MAX/MSP using open sound control message delegation. In: Proceedings of the ICMA Conference (2011). http://cnmat.berkeley.edu/system/files/attachments/102_FREED_ADRIAN_PAPER_CR.pdf
17. Ko, A.J., Abraham, R., Beckwith, L., Blackwell, A., Burnett, M., Erwig, M., Scaffidi, C., Lawrance, J., Lieberman, H., Myers, B., Rosson, M.B., Rothermel, G., Shaw, M., Wiedenbeck, S.: The state of the art in end-user software engineering. ACM Comput. Surv. **43**(3), 44 (2011). Article 21
18. Lieberman, H. (ed.): Your Wish is My Command: Programming by Example. Morgan Kaufmann Publishers, San Francisco (2001)
19. Cypher, A., Halbert, D.C., Kurlander, D., Lieberman, H., Maulsby, D., Myers, B.A., Turransky, A. (eds.): Watch what I do: Programming by Demonstration. MIT Press, Cambridge (1993)
20. Aleven, V., Leber, B., Sewall, J.: ITS authoring through programming-by-demonstration. In: Aleven, V., Kay, J., Mostow, J. (eds.) ITS 2010, Part II. LNCS, vol. 6095, pp. 438–438. Springer, Heidelberg (2010)
21. Farchi, E., Harrington, B.R.: Assisting the code review process using simple pattern recognition. In: Ur, S., Bin, E., Wolfsthal, Y. (eds.) HVC 2005. LNCS, vol. 3875, pp. 103–115. Springer, Heidelberg (2006)
22. Harms, K.J., Kerr, J.H., Ichinco, M., Santolucito, M., Chuck, A., Koscik, T., Chou, M., Kelleher, C.L.: Designing a community to support long-term interest in programming for middle school children. In: Proceedings of the 11th International Conference on Interaction Design and Children, NY, pp. 304–307 (2012)

23. Watanobe, Y., Mirenkov, N.: Hybrid intelligence aspects of programming in *AIDA algorithmic pictures. Future Gener. Comput. Syst. **37**, 417–428 (2014)
24. AIDA language. http://aida.u-aizu.ac.jp/aida/index.jsp
25. Watanobe, Y., Mirenkov, N.: Diagram scenes in *AIDA. In: IEEE Proceedings of 12th International Conference on Intelligent Software Methodologies, Tools and Techniques, Budapest, Hungary, pp. 209–215, 22–24 September 2013
26. Watanobe, Y., Mirenkov, N.: F-modeling environment: acquisition techniques for obtaining special-purpose features. In: Madaan, A., Kikuchi, S., Bhalla, S. (eds.) DNIS 2013. LNCS, vol. 7813, pp. 167–181. Springer, Heidelberg (2013)
27. AIDA tutorial materials. http://aida.u-aizu.ac.jp/aida/tutorial.jsp
28. http://aida.u-aizu.ac.jp/aida/paper/Questionnaire2014_1.pdf

An Intelligent Application for Outdoor Rendering Taking Sky Color and Shadows into Account

Hoshang Kolivand and Mohd Shahrizal Sunar[✉]

MaGIC-X (Media and Games Innovation Centre of Excellence) UTM-IRDA Digital Media Centre, Universiti Teknologi Malaysia, 81310 Skudai, Johor, Malaysia
shahrizal@utm.my

Abstract. It has been a long time since outdoor environments needed a package to avoid unnecessary concern regarding outdoor parameters such as the sun position, sky color and shadows in real-time rendering. An intelligence system is in order to control these main factors for outdoor rendering environments. Calculating and measuring shadows with respect to the sun position in any outdoor rendering environments is a challenging and heavy task. In this paper we try to explore a method of exerting shadows on other objects with respect to the sun position in any given location, date, and time by means of a real-time sky color generation. The sun position makes up an important part of outdoor environments. Sky color is also the main background for any outdoor environments. To create shadows and shadow volumes, stencil buffer and depth buffer are employed. By calculating the sun position in any specific date, time and location, shadow is cast accordingly. Length and angle of shadow are two parameters measured for building designs which are calculated in this real-time application. Therefore, the application can be used to investigate the behavior of the sun position and location of shadows for any outdoor games and outdoor rendering.

Keywords: Shadow generation · Real-time shadow · Sky color rendering · Outdoor rendering · Sun position

Introduction

The earth rotates around its axis (situational movement) once every 24 hours. Night and day occur due to this movement and are dependent on which side of the earth is facing the sun. Furthermore, because of this, time difference in different parts of the earth is produced. Rotating around the sun is another movement which takes up to one year and during its elliptical orbit, the earth turns (from west to east) around the sun. This movement is called the land transfer movement. A year on this motion is called a solar year (365 days 6 hours), a complete rotation around the sun.

Shadows, the sunlight, and sky color are important aspects of outdoor rendering environments. Shadows are important since they are everywhere and they

© Springer International Publishing Switzerland 2015
H. Fujita and A. Selamat (Eds.): SoMeT 2014, CCIS 513, pp. 178–190, 2015.
DOI: 10.1007/978-3-319-17530-0_13

have a lot of benefits. Shadows reveal the distance between objects as well as the complexity of objects. They also contribute towards architecture as well as making realistic image or games.

Sky color is the other significant factor for outdoor scenes. It needs to be generated in real-time to reduce the expenses and human energy.

An integration system to manage all these important factors for outdoor rendering is the ultimate goal of this research. A systematic technique is presented to combine these factors easily and robust enough. To achieve this aim the main objectives are presented as follow:

- To create a real-time sky color with respect to the sun position in specific location, date and time.
- To employ shadow volumes to cast shadows on arbitrary objects.
- To develop an intelligence outdoor rendering application sky color and shadows into consideration.

Previous Works

Various kinds of techniques have been proposed to create shadows such as drawing a dark shape same as the occluder on the ground. Although it is not so accurate, it was using in old computer games. Projection shadow algorithm is the simplest techniques that is still widely used in game programming. Projection shadow can create shadows only on flat surfaces. To create shadow on other objects more calculation is required [1]. Shadow volumes are one of the techniques that can be used to have a shadow on arbitrary objects [2]. Shadow maps [3] are another technique for casting shadows on other objects.

The sun and the sky are the main sources of natural illumination. The angle of the light source can be controlled by location, date, and time. The skylight is the most important outdoor illumination to make the scene as realistic as possible [25].

Shuling and Wang [13,14] are the the researchers who worked on simulation of the sun and sky in clear days. Shuling [13] focused on scattering based on Rayleigh scattering [15] using gradients map sampling. They have tried to simplify the Mie scattering of atmosphere. Wang [14] computed the sky light using an analytic sky model. They considered the light sources at night such as moonlight, starlight, zodiacal light, and airglow. Tone reproduction is a technique applied to render the sky.

Most real-time rendering techniques have focused on indoor rendering but the sophisticated part of lighting can be referred to outdoor rendering [16,17]. It is because the sky usually illuminates a point from almost all directions. A realistic sky scene greatly improves the reality of the outdoor virtual environment [18]. Generating sky color as a background for each outdoor scene is an essential factor to make it more realistic. Observing the sky has become a critical part of many building designers, so that the sky or a surrounding scene can be observed effectively through the building windows [19].

Many algorithms are proposed for shadow generation; Shadow volumes and shadow maps are such classic real-time shadow techniques. Shadow volumes are accurate enough but they are geometrically-based and require extensive calculations. Although shadow volumes are established in the gaming industry, they have two expensive phases; updating volume rendering passes, and silhouette detection to recognize the outline of occluders [7,20–23]. Silhouette detection requires a novel algorithm or an improvement on existing algorithm to reduce the rendering time in shadow volumes.

There are many applications to recognize the position of the sun and measure the length of shadows but our approach is for real-time application and can be used for any outdoor rendering.

More recently Kolivand et al. [5] worked on shadow projection with respect to the sun position. The main shortcoming of the technique was shadow cast on flat surfaces but they managed solved this inconvenience using a new shadow generation technique [4].

To sum this up: The significant factors in realistic outdoor environment rendering include the sun position, sky color, and shadows. Sky color and shadow generation are expensive for rendering individual cases, let alone their integration. Thus, they require more improvements not only in the case of rendering time but also in the case of realism.

The main steps to achieve the aim are as follows: To compute the sun position in case of real-time rendering using Julian date. To generate sky color with respect to the sun position based on Perez model [24]. To implement shadow volume and to provide a real-time platform of shadow generation with respect to the sun position.

Methodology

Shadow volume and shadow mapping are the best techniques available to construct shadow on arbitrary objects. In this paper we could create shadow volume with respect to the sun position. Julian date is the technique which is used to control the position of the light source in a specific location, date, and time while shadow volumes are employed to cast shadows on arbitrary objects.

Shadows

Shadow volumes are the convenient method that could generate shadows on other objects, proposed by Crow [2]. Shadow volumes are constructed based on geometrical techniques. In this technique silhouette detection of occluder [6] is the most important and expensive part of the shadow volume's algorithm. After recognition of the silhouette drawing a line from the light source to the outline of the occluder and continuing it to infinity, produces a pyramid. The truncate pyramid that is located between occluder and shadow receiver is called volumes that can be seen in Fig. 1(left). As the truncate continue to infinity, each object or part of object that is located in the truncated pyramid is present in shadow; otherwise it is lit.

Z-pass algorithm that recognizes whether a pixel is located inside the shadow or not uses stencil buffer. Z-pass algorithm is used where the point of view is located out of the shadows and Z-fail algorithm is used where the point of view is located in the shadows. Stencil buffer is the other buffer that is used to create real-time shadows. This kind of buffer is used to recognize the area that require to cast shadows. In other words: stencil buffer can help minimize the updating part for rendering. One of the convenient usages of the stencil buffer is when it combines with Z-buffer. Stencil values can automatically be increased or decreased for every pixel when depth test fails or passes. A redefinition of shadow volumes' algorithm can be seen in Algorithm 1.

Algorithm 1. Shadow volumes algorithm

---

1. Clear color-buffer and z-buffer.
2. Render the scene with only ambient and emissive lighting.
3. For all lights clear stencil-buffer, disable writing to color-buffer and z-buffer, set z-buffer test to less-than 0(zero).
4. Render all front facing shadow mesh triangles generated by l; increase the stencil value when the z-test passes.
5. Render all back facing shadow mesh triangles generated by l; decrease the stencil value when the z-test passes.
6. Re-enable writing to color-buffer, set z-buffer test to equal, set stencil test to pass when value is 0 and enable additive blending.
7. Render the scene with only diffuse and secular lighting.

In the case of multi-light sources, the first loop fills the z-buffer then the whole loop process is repeated for every one of the other light sources in the scene. Since the shadowed areas resulting from one light source are independent of those caused by other light sources completely, stencil buffer must be cleared before repeating the loop process for the subsequent light sources.

Sky Modeling

The sun position, sky modeling, and sky color generation are the main concepts in this section. To integrate these components a mathematical modeling of the dome is the first requirement. Then, the sun position is traced using the Julian dating. Finally, sky color is generated using Perez model and then applied to the constructed dome.

The most important effect of the sun position is on sky color and shadow orientation. Position of the sun depends on location, date, and time. Location depends on longitude and latitude but it differs on different day of the year.

Modeling of the sky dome is a platform for implementing the outdoor rendering. Although dome generation using 3D Studio Max, Maya and Rhino is easy and can be more realistic, mathematical design of sky dome can be more appropriate in the case of real time rendering [7]. Dome is like a hemisphere in Fig. 1(right) in which the view point is located inside.

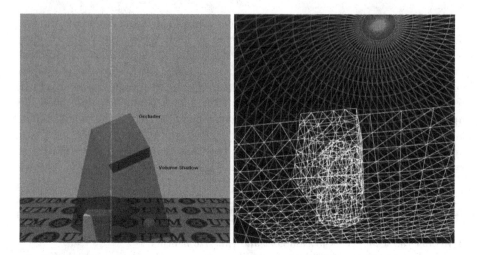

Fig. 1. Left: Shadow volumes on other objects, Right: Sky dome in wireframe

Before creating shadows in virtual environments, the sun position must be determined and this will be described in the following section.

The Sun Position

The principle calculation of the sun position is well known and old procedure needing exact data to work with. The ancient Egyptians were able to calculate the sun position. By digging a large hole inside one of the pyramids they managed to get the sun to shine on the dead pharaoh's grave, once a year on his birthday [8].

The sun position and the amount of sunshine required for any rendering procedure has been an important part of most of researchers historically. The earth oriented north - south line is not exactly perpendicular to the orbit. It has about 23.5° deviation. The diversion of earth during a turn in the orbit around the sun stays the same. When earth is located on the right side of the sun, the southern hemisphere, due to the slight deviation (23.5°) recieves more direct radiation from the sun. About six months later, when the earth goes to the other side of the sun, this radiation to the northern hemisphere is more vertical. Thus, in the northern hemisphere by changing the angle of surface radiation over the years, the earth becomes warmer or colder. Surrounding air being warm or cold will change the seasons [9]. Sunset and sunrise are produced by rotation of the earth.

Longitude and latitude are the two most important aspects to calculate the sun position. The other data that is required is Greenwich Mean Time (GMT). To determine the position of the sun in the created dome, zenith and azimuth are enough.

Calculation of the Sun Position

As mentioned before to calculate position of the sun, zenith and azimuth are enough. Specific location, date, and time are required to compute zenith and azimuth. Julian date is used for calculating the sun position.

$$t = t_s + 0.17\sin(\frac{4\pi(J - 180)}{373}) - 0.129\sin(\frac{2\pi(J - 8)}{355}) + 12\frac{SM - L}{\pi} \qquad (1)$$

where,
t: Solar time
t_s: Standard time
J: Julian date
SM: Standard meridian
L: Longitude

The solar declination is calculated as Eq. 2.

$$\delta = 0.4093\sin(\frac{2\pi(J - 8)}{368}) \qquad (2)$$

The time is calculated in decimal hours and degrees in radians. Finally, zenith and azimuth can be calculated as follows (Eqs. 3 and 4):

$$\theta_s = \frac{\pi}{2} - sin^{-1}(sinlsin\delta - coslcos\delta cos\frac{\pi t}{12}) \qquad (3)$$

$$\varphi_s = tan^{-1}(\frac{-cos\delta sin\frac{\pi t}{12}}{coslsin\delta - sinlcos\delta cos\frac{\pi t}{12}}) \qquad (4)$$

where θ_s is solar zenith, φ_s is solar azimuth and l is latitude. With calculation of zenith and azimuth the sun position is obvious.

Measurement of the horizontal shadow angle (HSA) is calculated using these formulas:

$$HSA = \rho = \varphi_s - W \qquad (5)$$

The vertical shadow angle (VSA) is calculated by:

$$VSA = \sigma = tan^{-1}(\frac{tan\theta}{cos\rho}) \qquad (6)$$

where W is the orientation of buildings.

With different Julian days from 1 to 365, at different times, the amount of HSA (Horizontal Shadow Angle) and VSA (Vertical Shadow Angle) were measured and the following results are obtained. Figure 2(left and right) illustrates that the center of the change is between 6:00 to 10:45 and 13:45 to 17:45.

Figure 2 is amount of horizontal and vertical shadow angle at different times of the day. Figure 2(left) illustrates that the highest VSA is in the first three

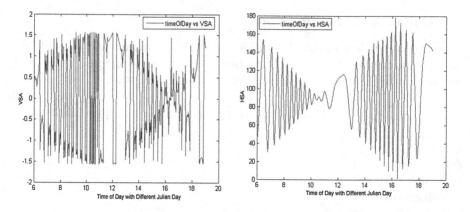

Fig. 2. HSA and VSA in different Julian day

quarters. Figure 2(right) shows that the highest HSA is in the third and final one-third. They can be used to position the orientation of a building.

With calculating the zenith (θ_s) and azimuth (φ_s) the sun position is accurately determined. In the case of shadow volumes, Cartesian coordinate is needed. Thus, to convert the spherical coordinate to Cartesian coordinate, the following function in MATLAB can be used.

$$[x, y, z] = sph2cart$$

The point (x, y, z) is the position of the sun and it is unique in every location, date, and time. This pixel in 3D is enough to show position of the shadows and calculate the length of shadows in any specific location, date, and time using the intelligence application.

Sky Color

Sky color changes during daytime due to the sun position and the levels of luminosity are also different around the same time on different days. Therefore, a suitable interface is required to control the sky color with respect to the sun position in any specific location, date, and time.

These researchers tried to model and simulate the atmospheric sky color including its wide range colors. The algorithms and the techniques suggested by these researchers are investigated. The most suitable technique for outdoor rendering, based on real atmosphere, is then decided.

Although most of the presented techniques are acceptable for generating sky color, rendering the sky using an analytic model is more convenient. Preetham's model [16] is chosen due to exaggerated sky color. This method is based on [24] model which considers the actual atmosphere. This can be handled with respect to the location, date, and time. At the end of this phase the method is implemented which forms one of the main requirements o the third objective.

There are a number of reasons why this method is selected. One of the reasons is the impressive results produced and proven by [16]. Moreover, the research is

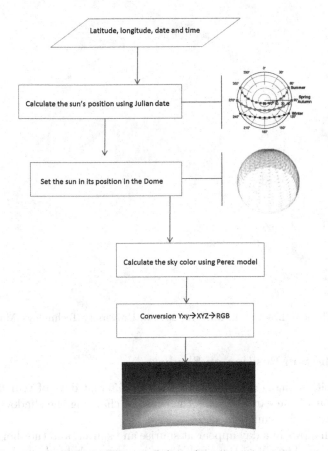

Fig. 3. Process of sky color generation

trying to achieve a real-time implementation. This will be possible by removing the calculation of aerial perspective, which is expensive in computation. Time can also be adjusted by a timer set in the GUI(graphic user interface) of the software. Therefore, the program will show the simulation of the sky color at any specific location.

Implementing Sky Color

In this part, the sky color is implemented with respect to the sun position. The implementation process is based on the flowchart illustrated in Fig. 3.

The calculation of sky color using Perez model will give distribution coefficients and zenith values for luminance Y, and chromaticities x and y [24]. Therefore, the value in Yxy space given by the calculation needs to be converted into RGB space. This is because the OpenGL API only supports the RGB space in displaying the color. For the color space conversion from CIE Yxy to RGB, this must be translated into CIE XYZ, and then converted to RGB space. This part of research outlines the implementation procedure for the color space conversion.

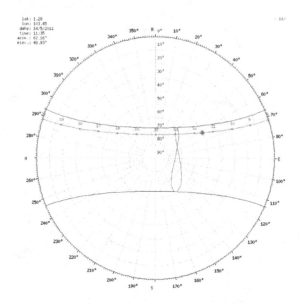

Fig. 4. The sun direction in May 14, 2014 in University Technology Malaysia

Effect of the Sun Position on Shadows

The sun position changes at the same time in different days of year because of elliptical orbit of the earth. This is the cause of changing the shadow length in different days at the same time.

Longer shadows in a day appear at sunrise and sunset; and the short shadows appear at noon. The tilt of the earth's axis is a reason behind why each part of earth can see more or less sun on the same day. Different seasons are results of the difference between the length of days and nights [10].

Amount and orientation of shadows depend on latitude, longitude, date, and time of the day (Fig. 4); as a result, direction of the sun in specific location is important [11,12].

Results and Discussion

Yxy space is another color space which is used in this research. This space determines the XYZ values in terms of x and y chromaticity co-ordinates. Equation 7 is used to convert XYZ space to Yxy co-ordinates.

$$Y = Y, x = \frac{X}{X+Y+Z}, y = \frac{Y}{X+Y+Z} \tag{7}$$

Conversely, Eq. 8 can be used to convert Yxy co-ordinates to XYZ.

$$X = \frac{x}{y}X, Y = Y, Z = \frac{1-x-y}{y}Y \tag{8}$$

The Z tri-stimulus value is not visible by itself and is combined with the new co-ordinates.

Perez Sky Model

The model is convenient to illuminate arbitrary point (θ_p, γ_p) of the sky dome with respect to the sun position. It uses CIE standard and could be used for a wide range of atmospheric conditions. Luminance of point (θ_p, γ_p) is calculated using the Eqs. 9 and 10:

$$L(\theta_p, \gamma_p) = (1 + Ae^{\frac{B}{\cos \theta_p}})(1 + Ce^{D\gamma_p} + E\cos^2 \gamma_p) \tag{9}$$

$$\gamma_p = \cos^{-1}(\sin\theta_s \sin\theta_p \cos(\varphi_p - \varphi_s) + \cos\theta_s \cos\theta_p) \tag{10}$$

where:
A: Darkening or brightening of the horizon
B: Luminance gradient near the horizon
C: Relative intensity of circumsolar region
D: Width of the circumsolar region
E: Relative backscattered light received at the earth surface

Essentially, to use Yxy space, the following three components are needed. In each point of view, the Y luminance is calculated by:

$$Y = Y_z \frac{L(\theta_p, \gamma_p)}{L(0, \theta_s)} \tag{11}$$

The chromaticity of x and y is calculated by:

$$x = x_z \frac{L(\theta_p, \gamma_p)}{L(0, \theta_s)} \tag{12}$$

$$y = y_z \frac{L(\theta_p, \gamma_p)}{L(0, \theta_s)} \tag{13}$$

To color each sky pixel, all of the pixels in the introduced formulae must be calculated iteratively. Involving date and time in specific locations enables the exact color reproduction of each pixel.

First of all the result of the sun position for sunrise and sunset is compared with the real sunrise and sunset using an online website which is accurate enough. The results of sky color is compared with the real sky color which are captured using web cameras station at famous landscapes. The generated sky color is compared in details about different parts of the sky.

Figure 5 (left) shows the direction of the sunshine and shadows at 9:15 am in Universiti Teknologi Malaysia on latitude 1.28 and longitude 103.45 on 14th May. The location, date, and time is determined using a user-friendly GUI which is provided in OpenGl Glui. The position of the sun is in accordance with the real one in the specific location, date, and time. Figure 5(right) illustrates the sky color and shadows with respect to the sun position in Universiti Teknologi

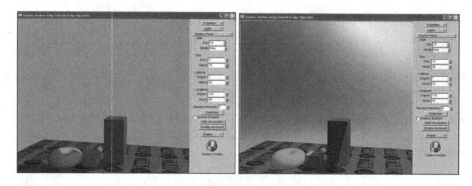

Fig. 5. Left: Result of application in Universiti Teknologi Malaysia (At 9:15 am, May 14, 2013), Right: Result of application in Universiti Teknologi Malaysia (At 10:40 am, May 14, 2013)

Fig. 6. Left: Real sky color in Universiti Teknologi Malaysia 15 June. Right: Result of the Sky Color application (UTM, 15 June)

Malaysia at 10:40 am on 14th May. Self-shadowing is another contribution which the algorithm supports as well as casting accurate shadows on others objects.

Figure 6(left) shows the real sky color and Fig. 6(right) shows virtual sky color generated by presented application on June 15th at Universiti Teknologi Malaysia, at 8:48 am in sunset.

Conclusion and Future Works

Shadows and sky color are the most attractive parts of any outdoor environments. In this study shadows and sky color with respect to the sun position in any specific location, date, and time is taken into consideration to make the rendered environments more realistic.

Although shadow maps are fast enough to cast shadows on other objects, shadow volumes are employed due to accurate enough silhouette.

The first objective of this research was achieved by generating sky color based on Perez model and Julian dating. The result of sky color is evaluated by comparing it to the real sky color captured at the same location, date, and time. The second objective is achieved using implementation of shadow volumes using stencil buffer. Finally, the intelligence application is created by integrating the sun position, sky color, and shadows.

The presented platform can be beneficial for any outdoor environments like outdoor games without worrying about the time of day and orientation of shadows in any day of the year.

This research is evaluated based on a real benchmarks as the manner of other researchers. Many pictures are captured and compared with the generated pictures using our software.

For the future works soft shadows and semi-soft shadow can be looked into. Soft shadows combined with sky color can make it as realistic as possible. Interaction between sky color and objects in outdoor environments will be more adamant regarding this matter.

References

1. Xiao, Y., Yicheng, J., Yong, Y., Zhuoyu, W.: GPU based real-time shadow research. In: 2006 International Conference on IEEE Computer Graphics, Imaging and Visualisation, pp. 372–377 (2006)
2. Crow, F.: Shadow algorithms for computer graphics. Comput. Graph. 11(2), 242–247 (1977)
3. Williams, L.: Casting curved shadows on curved surfaces. In: SIGGRAPH 78 vol. 12, no. 3, pp. 270–274 (1978)
4. Kolivand, H., Sunar, M.S.: Realistic outdoor rendering in augmented reality. Plos One 9(9), e108334 (2014). doi:10.1371/journal.pone.0108334
5. Kolivand, H., Sunar, M.S.: Covering photorealistic properties of outdoor components with the effects of sky color in mixed reality. Multimedia Tools Appl. 72(3), 2143–2162 (2014)
6. Kolivand, H., Sunar, M.S., Rehman, A.: Extended edge silhouette detection algorithm to create real-time shadow volume. Int. J. Acad. Res. 4(3), 209–218 (2012)
7. Kolivand, H., Sunar, M.S.: Real-time outdoor rendering using hybrid shadow maps. Int. J. Innovative Comput. Inf. Control (IJICIC) 8(10), 1355–1361 (2012)
8. Tadamura, K., Qin, X., Jiao, G., Nakamae, E.: Rendering optimal solar shadows with plural sunlight depth buffers. Vis. Comput. 17, 76–90 (2001)
9. Chang, T.P.: The sun apparent position and the optimal tilt angle of a solar collector in the northern hemisphere. Sol. Energy 83, 1274–1284 (2009)
10. Nabeel, A., Al-Rawi, A.: Simple accurate and reliable method for measuring the sun's elevation and orientation. Renew. Energy 1, 231–235 (1991)
11. SunErth (2012). http://www.sunearthtools.com. Cited 1st August 2012
12. Ismail, I., Kolivand, H., Sunar, M.S., Basori, A.H.: An overview on dynamic 3D character motion techniques in virtual environments. Life Sci. J. 10(3), 846–853 (2013)
13. Shuling, D., Cheng, R., Tizhou, Q.: Graphics real-time simulation of sky and sun in clear day. J. Comput.-Aided Des. Comput. 3, 305–310 (2009)

14. Wang, S., Wu, E., Liu, Y., Liu, X., Chen, Y.: Abstract line drawings from photographs using flow-based filters. Comput. Graph. **36**(4), 224–231 (2012)
15. Bucholtz, A.: Rayleigh-scattering calculations for the terrestrial atmosphere. Appl. Opt. **34**(15), 2765–2773 (1995)
16. Preetham, A.J., Shirley, P., Smits, B.: A practical analytic model for daylight. In: Proceedings of the 26th Annual Conference on Computer Graphics and Interactive Techniques, pp. 91–100. ACM Press/Addison-Wesley Publishing Co., (1999)
17. Rnnberg, S.: Real-time rendering of natural illumination. Ph.D dissertation, Master thesis (2004)
18. Wang, C.: Real-time rendering of daylight sky scene for virtual environment. In: Ma, L., Rauterberg, M., Nakatsu, R. (eds.) ICEC 2007. LNCS, vol. 4740, pp. 294–303. Springer, Heidelberg (2007)
19. Dobashi, Y., Nishita, T., Kaneda, K., Yamashita, H.: A fast display method of sky colour using basis functions. J. Vis. Comput. Anim. **8**(2), 115–127 (1997)
20. Raskar, R., Cohen, M.: Image precision silhouette edges. In: Proceedings of the 1999 Symposium on Interactive 3D Graphics, pp. 135–140. ACM (1999)
21. Assarsson, U., Akenine-Mller, T.: A geometry-based soft shadow volume algorithm using graphics hardware. ACM Trans. Graph. (TOG) **22**(3), 511–520 (2003)
22. Jung, S.K., Kwon, S.I., Kim, K.-J.: Real-time silhouette extraction using hierarchical face clusters. Department of Computer Engineering, pp. 1–8 (2004)
23. Billeter, M., Sintorn, E., Assarsson, U.L.F.: Real time volumetric shadows using polygonal light volumes. In: Proceedings of the Conference on High Performance Graphics, pp. 39–45. Eurographics Association (2010)
24. Perez, R., Seals, R., Michalsky, J.: All-weather model for sky luminance distribution-preliminary configuration and validation. Solar Energy **50**(3), 235–245 (1993)
25. Dobashi, Y., Kaneda, K., Yamashita, H., Nishita, T.: Method for calculation of sky light luminance aiming at an interactive architectural design. Comput. Graph. Forum **15**(3), 109–118 (1996)

The Simulation of Flow Shop Production System in PTO Environment Through a Matrix Approach in System Dynamics Logic

Piera Centobelli, Giuseppe Converso[✉], Mosè Gallo, Teresa Murino, and Liberatina C. Santillo

Department of Chemical, Materials and Industrial Production Engineering,
University Federico II, Naples, Italy
giuseppe.converso@unina.it

Abstract. This paper faces the problem of industrial production optimization through a simulation based approach and in a context of high rigidity production constraints. When an industrial plant is made by several work centers, operating in a typical flow shop configuration, its operation can be seen as a sequence of discrete events, whose optimization can be solved as a scheduling problem. The approach shown in this work is based on a System Dynamics simulation logic. In despite of an apparent greater complexity if compared to traditional discrete event simulation approaches, this logic allows to identify at each instant the position and the confluence of each single order and, moreover, to decide in a dynamic way operations planning at each work center. The simulation approach makes use of matrices to develop the model. In order to evaluate the efficacy of the proposed approach, we have applied it to a case study, considering a flow shop production system in a PTO environment.

Keywords: System dynamics · Modeling · Simulation · Process analysis · Scheduling · Production systems

1 Introduction

Over the past few years, a growing attention has been devoted to planning tools and, more specifically, to simulation techniques intended to modeling and analysis of systems and business problems. In particular, computer simulation has acquired a leading role among the tools to deepen and support the analysis of highly complex and dynamic managerial contexts. In this perspective, these tools are valuable aids for decision makers not only to better understand the managerial contexts under observation, but also to facilitate the decision-making and retrieval of information essential to the whole system of management control implemented in the company, especially if it has to be set up and implemented in a context of high turbulence.

The aim of this paper is to use computer simulation as a decision support tool in orders management for a generic flow-shop manufacturing system operating in a purchase to order (PTO) environment.

© Springer International Publishing Switzerland 2015
H. Fujita and A. Selamat (Eds.): SoMeT 2014, CCIS 513, pp. 191–207, 2015.
DOI: 10.1007/978-3-319-17530-0_14

The added value of this work is the universality of the model developed: the simulation model has been realized as general as possible, in order to make it suitable for any flow-shop production system using a logic PTO.

The System Dynamics (SD) logic has been used as it captures the dynamic behavior of the system. The SD logic allows to generate a model that describes the causal relationships between the variables of interest, thus providing a greater understanding of the dynamics underlying processes. In fact, it merges the systemic and dynamic approach of systems theory, with the dynamic and quantitative theory of simulation, resulting, therefore, a systemic, dynamic and quantitative approach for the study of complex problems. This approach is based on the assumption that the systems are more complex than the sum of their parts, so that the behavior of a system can not be explained by the behavior of its components. Rather it is necessary to analyze the interactions among these components. This assumption allows us to study complex systems with a high level of abstraction. The simulation, then, allow to take into account the variability of the system, as well as the stochastic nature of the process modeled. The reminder of this paper is organized as follows. In the second section a review of the relevant literature is provided. The third section presents the problem formulation. In the fourth and fifth sections model design and simulation have been developed. A case study has been presented in Sect. 6. Methodology validation with results analysis and scenario analysis are commented in Sects. 7 and 8. Finally Sect. 9 contains concluding remarks and future research directions.

2   The Literature Review

Production planning is becoming an increasingly important and strategic process to ensure companies the ability to compete with a better and reliable service. In a market that demands ever-shorter delivery times, it becomes essential the ability to optimize materials, resources and information management in order to minimize waste throughout the entire supply chain.

In this extremely complex market, it arises the need for a rational and organized management of the entire business system, basically realized through a careful and structured operations planning and programming [25].

A careful planning activity leads to the optimization of the production process efficiency through the identification and elimination of waste.

The goal is to reduce lead time along the supply chain resulting in a reduction of waiting times, costs and working capital and an increase in productivity, quality, service level and customer satisfaction.

In order to achieve these objectives a careful scheduling of activities is essential. The term scheduling refers to a wide class of problems, very different in complexity and structure [11]. Many authors have provided a summary of the methods developed over the last 30 years related to scheduling. This effort has produced many interesting results that allow us to classify many models in a systematic way and to unify some algorithmic approaches.

However, in contrast to other areas of combinatorial optimization, for scheduling problems it is not possible to prefer a single approach to solve them but each time can be more appropriate to use heuristics, enumeration or approximation algorithms [1].

In summary, the optimization techniques provide the best solution in relation to constraints and objectives and are always combined with examination of results. The modality with which it reaches the solution is different depending on the type of heuristic technique used, but in general, the goodness of the solution is certifiable only with experimental campaigns and not through demonstrations [4].

Although the simulation it is not a method for the resolution of operational scheduling problems, it represents a tool that allows the evaluation of solutions produced by other methods, for example the method of the priority lists (dispatching rules) [10].

Simulation is not an appropriate tool for problems solvable with easier methods, for example with analytical solutions of mathematical models or when the development and execution time, as well as costs, are prohibitive, or when it is not possible to validate the simulation model created.

Simulating a system means achieve a representative model of the real world in order to use it to study and analyze its behavior, performance and responses to different inputs.

A system can be defined as a set of identifiable entities, these components connected to each other through mutual relationships visible or defined by its observer. A characteristic element of a system is the overall balance among its parts. At each instant of time, a system is in a certain condition, said 'state', this state is defined through a set of individual conditions related to its components. The evolution of a dynamic system is described by the chronological sequence of its states [16].

System Dynamics modeling tool allows to understand the logic by which the relevant variables interact each other, the role that each of them plays, and the scenarios that emerge as a result of alternative hypotheses about the initial state of the system [26].

3   Problem Definition

In a PTO environment the order management process must fulfill customer requirements and planned delivery dates avoiding penalties due to delays. Therefore it is essential to manage this process as fast as possible.

In this paper a simulation model has been implemented in order to analyze and compare different scenarios based on the different dispatching rules adopted. The simulation model allows to choose the best dispatching policy.

In a flow shop context a job is processed by two or more machines and the sequence is fixed for each one. Before processing an order at a work center, it is necessary that all the previous operations must be completed.

Thus the problem is to define, for each station, the order with which the parts should be processed.

The accuracy of a scheduling algorithm is evaluated through three different aspects:

Compliance with the delivery dates;
Stations saturation (bottleneck phenomenon should be avoided);
WIP level (WIP level should be as low as possible).

We assume that orders arrive into the system in a stochastic way and they are collected in a list; everyday they are evaluated to define the amount and type of materials to be ordered. When raw materials arrive at warehouse the order is ready to be released to the shop and processed. If an order has a priority it released into shop floor before others. If during the process any non-compliance occurs, it will be blocked and the order will be placed in a buffer containing all orders not yet completed; once resolved the non-compliance the order is put back among orders available for processing.

If no non-compliance occurs the order is completed and then inserted into the buffer of completed orders and, therefore, among those available for further processing. This procedure is repeated for each work center until all the necessary operations are completed.

A system dynamics approach has been used for order management in order to identify the better dispatching rule. This choice is mainly due to the complexity of the system simulated, its operations, its behavior and the complexity of data collection mode.

Therefore, it is necessary to understand relationships among the various subsystems, the impact of a particular decision on the entire system and relationships among variables in order to evaluate the system status with different dispatching policies. This is guaranteed by the SD tool, describing the system through flow and level variables and events chain.

4 Model Design

In order to develop a model, as general as possible, a generic flow-shop system has been simulated, assuming that it operates in PTO (purchase to order) environment. We consider a system composed by n work centers. Each work center is composed by several buffers; before to be processed, the order is placed in a buffer and it is compared to all other orders present in the buffer in order to define which order should be processed as first. Obviously, this choice depends on dispatching policy adopted.

If during the order processing, a non-compliance occurs the order is moved into another buffer waiting for problem resolution. Once solved the problem, the order will be re-evaluated together with other orders and, according to a specific priority rule, it is released for processing.

For this reason, between two consecutive work centers, there is a buffer with a high enough capacity, to accommodate the orders waiting to be processed.

This model architecture requires that the each order is identifiable unmistakably. Moreover the dimension of system stocks cannot be scalar, but must be a matrix.

4.1 Order Scheduling

Each order is characterized by seven characteristics and it is represented as a row vector in which each column represents one of these characteristic.

The characteristics of the order are:

- Arrival date;
- Delivery date;
- Number of pieces;
- Discriminant;
- Number of pieces in 'stop';
- Customer type;
- Penalty.

Depending on the case study, is it possible add or delete some features.

Arrival Date: Represents the time of order generation.

Delivery Date: It is the day by which the order must be completed.

Number of pieces: It represents the number of pieces of which an order is composed by.

Discriminant: It is a numeric value assigned to each order and indicates the priority level of the specific order. The value of "discriminant" value depends on the case and on the dispatching policy adopted.

The value of the discriminant is calculated as follows:

$$D = P\left[\left(\sum i\, ncli * tucli\right) - (De)\right] \tag{1}$$

where:

ncli = WIP at the i-th workcenter;

tucli = work time unit at the i-th work center;

Dc = delivery date;

P = penalty.

Number of pieces stop: This value is generated randomly on the basis of historical data and it is a value between zero and the number of pieces related to the order considered. The characteristic "number of pieces in a stop condition" has considered for each work center.

Customer type: It indicates at which class of customer the order belongs (B2C or B2B). If this value is equal to one, it means that the company have to pay a penalty if delivery takes place over the due date; instead if this value is zero it means that there will be no penalty for delay.

Penalty: It indicates the value of the penalty. For B2B customers, this value is equal to a defined economic amount; for private clients the penalty refers to a company image damage.

5 Model Simulation

The simulation model has been developed with Powersim Studio 7. In order to model the first work center a system composed by several concatenated buffers has been developed. Each buffer is represented by a level variable indicating the amount of orders over time.

Each buffer is an array with a number of rows equal to the number of orders and a number of columns equal to the number order characteristics. These information are useful during the simulation process.

Figure 1 shows the order management model related to the first work center.

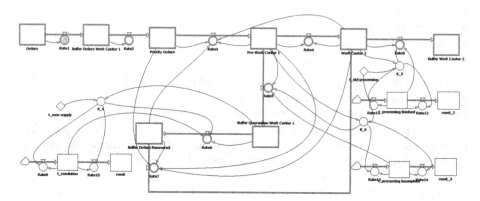

Fig. 1. The order management model related to the first work center.

The first level variable is *"Orders"*, which collects input orders; it is linked to another level variable *"Buffer Orders Work Center 1"* by the flow variable *"Rate1"*
The condition inside the Rate1 is the following:

$$FOR(i = 1..n; j = 1..m | IF(TIME > = Orders[i; 1]; Orders[i; j]; 0)) \qquad (2)$$

The variable *"Rate1"*, therefore, has to move the i-th order from the buffer *"Orders"* to the buffer *"work center orders"*, when the simulation time is exactly equal to the arrival date of the order i-th. The level variable *"buffer orders work center"* and the variable level *"Priority Orders"* are connected by the flow variable *"Rate2"*. The condition is as follows:

$$FOR(i = 1..n; j = 1..m | IF('Buffer\ Orders\ Work\ Center\ 1'[i; 3] = MAX('Buffer\ Orders$$
$$Work\ Center\ 1'[i; 3]; 'Buffer\ Orders\ Work\ Center\ 1'[i; j]; 0)) \qquad (3)$$

Then, the transfer of the i-th order from a variable level to another one occurs when there is an order in the *"buffer orders work center"* with a value of discriminant higher than others.

The level variable *"Priority Orders"* and the level variable *"Pre-Work center 1"* are connected by the flow variable *"Rate3"*.

The condition related to Rate3 is as follows:

$$FOR(i = 1..n; j = 1..m | IF('Pre - Work\ Center\ 1'[i; 1] = 0\ AND\ 'Priority$$
$$Orders'[i; 3] = MAX('Priority\ Orders'[i; 3]; 'Buffer\ Orders\ Recovered'[i; 3])AND \qquad (4)$$
$$'Work\ Center\ 1'[i; 1] = 0; 'Priority\ Orders'[i; j]; 0))$$

In the buffer Priority Orders, the order with the highest discriminant value is selected and, at the same time, machine state is evaluated. Obviously orders priority depends on the dispatching policy adopted.

Once selected the order with highest priority, manufacturing process can start. Following there are two centers: Pre-Work Center 1 and Work Center 1.

The situations that may occur are as follows:

Order does not present any nonconformity: In this case the order passes from the Pre-Work Center 1 to Work Center 1. When a job is in the Work Center 1, a "time counter" starts counting the time, the job is held in the work center until the time becomes equal to the time required to process its parts.

Order presents a nonconformity: The pieces stop for non-conformance in the *Pre - Work Center 1*, while others are processed in the Work Center 1. In fact, after working in the *Pre -Work Center 1* the order is moved to the *buffer quarantine orders* until the problem is solved. Also this transfer, from Pre - *Work Center 1* to *Buffer quarantine orders*, is regulated by a time counter.

In order to fix the problem it is necessary to wait a certain amount of time before the order is available for processing again, and the order waits in this buffer. The waiting time for problem resolution depends on the type of non-compliance occurred.

The flow variable *"Rate7"* is defined as follows:

$$FOR(i = 1..4; j = 1..4 | IF('Pre - Work\ Center\ 1'[i; 1] = 0\ AND\ 'Work\ Center\ 1'[i; 1] = 0\ AND$$
$$('Buffer\ Orders\ Recovered'[i; 3] = MAX('Priority\ Orders'[i; 3]; 'Buffer\ Orders \tag{5}$$
$$Recovered'[i; 3]; 'Buffer\ Orders\ Recovered'[i; j]; 0))$$

In this way the order with the highest value of discriminant highest among all orders is chosen. If the order comes from *"Buffer Orders Recovered"*, it must remain for the processing time of its pieces.

When the work center is released, it is available to process a new order.

The final part of the model is related to the first work center resulted in the displacement of the vector order, by the variable level 1 to the variable level Work Center Work Center Buffer 2. These two variables are connected by *"Rate8"*, in which the condition of switching between the two variables is defined:

$$FOR(i = 1..n; j = 1..m | IF('Work\ Center\ 1'[1, 4] = 0\ AND\ K\_5 < > 0\ AND$$
$$K\_5 =' t\_processing\ finished'; 'Work\ Center\ 1'[i; j]; 0)) \tag{6}$$

At the end the order arrives at the buffer Center 2; so all processes related to the work center 1 have been completed and the order is ready to be worked at the work center 2.

The structure of the model related to the work center 2 (Fig. 2) is the same as for work center 1, except for the level variable 'Orders' related to the generation of orders.

Generally if we denote by n the total number of work centers in the production system, the configuration has to be repeated $n-1$ times and the last work center should have the following structure (Fig. 3).

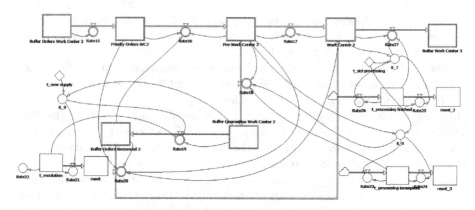

Fig. 2. Order management at the second work center.

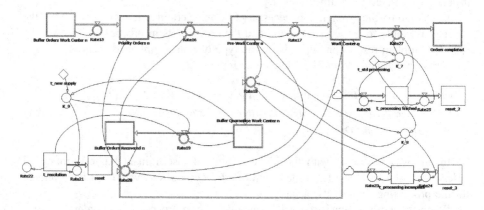

Fig. 3. N-th Work center configuration.

6 The Case Study

The Company under study (it will be called Company X), operating in the market of aluminum/wood and PVC, deals with all phases from design to installation.

Continuous innovation, top quality, customer orientation and high are the commercial strengths of the Company.

The solutions of Company X are designed based on a thorough analysis of market needs and are able to provide a complete and innovative response to any request. Aluminum, PVC, wood and glass are the input of the production process that allows for a wide range of products.

The Company X is part of a greater group. The company X, specialized and well established all over Italy with a wide sales network in the realization of aluminum frames, interior doors in glass both aluminum and wood, structural curtain wall, timely and ventilated, and everything in the world can apply for closures to be transparent, both in vertical and coverage. More than 200 people collaborate, including directors and employees.

The activities of Company X for product delivery begins with the order receipt by the commercial office until get the product installation and after-sales support.

The activities of the company X for the delivery of the product begin with the receipt of the order by the commercial office until get the product installation and after-sales support.

7 Validation Methodology and Results

After a deep data analysis the necessity for the Company to manage orders efficiently arises. The application of the simulation model described above should manage the production flow and improve its performance. This would have a positive effect on both customer satisfaction, thanks to the respect of delivery dates, and costs due to optimal management of orders characterized by non-compliance.

In the previous section a simulation model able to represent any flow shop production system that operates in purchase to order was carried out.

This model is perfect in order to manage Company X orders.

The Company X production system, as regard to the corresponding line to windows and door-windows in aluminum, is characterized by five work centers:

Area of cut (cut);
Area of assembly (assembly);
Area mounting hardware (installation);
Assembly area glass (glass);
Area packaging (packaging).

So, the model in this case is characterized by five work centers arranged in series and each work center has the same structure.

The various sub-models, corresponding to the various work centers, are connected according to what is the structure of the company production process.

The simulated scenarios in this case are three:

Scenario 1 "AS IS" is the current priority rule FIFO;
Scenario 2 "TO BE 1" is the one that takes into account penalties associated with delays in delivery;
Scenario 3 "TO BE 2" finally takes into account not only the delivery due date and the penalty, although the remaining processing time.

As previously mentioned, each order is represented by a row vector where columns correspond to the components depending on the characteristics that must be considered.

The features considered in this case are the following:

Arrival date: indicates the time when an order is confirmed; it is expressed in minutes because the simulation time step is "*minutes*". Every working day is eight hours per day, so each day is equal to 480 minutes.
Delivery date: indicates the date on which it is to be ready for order delivery. The company's policy ensures the implementation of the order within 30 days, therefore,

the delivery date is calculated by adding the date of arrival, 14.4 thousand minutes (i.e. 30 days).

Number of pieces: each order is characterized by a number of pieces, each piece needs a certain time for its realization.

Customer type: indicates the client category to which the order belongs, if the value is zero indicates a private client, if it is equal to one indicates a B2B company.

Penalty: indicates the value of the penalty; for B2B customers it is a cost that the company pays if incurs in any delays in delivery and it must take into account both the number of pieces of order (5 % of the total order) and the number of days of delay; in case of private clients, it takes into account the image loss in case of non-compliance with delivery dates.

Number of pieces in stop: indicates the number of pieces that were manufactured before a non-compliance occurs.

Discriminating 1: Indicates FIFO policy adoption for order scheduling.

Discriminating 2: a bigger weight has to be added to these orders involving additional costs if delivery is in late.

Discriminate 3: a bigger weight has been added to those orders that, considering in addition days late, considering also the number of completed pieces.

Depending on the simulated scenario, activate/deactivate the discriminant in the model. For this purpose were inserted combo box (Fig. 4):

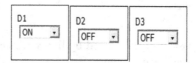

Fig. 4. Combo box related to the three discriminant.

For the validation phase historical data has been used for evaluation of the current company performance.

The time horizon is from January 2012 to June 2013. In this period there 228 orders arrive. The modeling and simulation software Powersim allows to import Excel files, so, order history has been organized in an Excel spreadsheet in which each row of the matrix represents an order and each column represents a feature.

The priority rule used takes into account only the orders arrival date. Thus, the discriminant to be activated is the discriminant 1 and, before starting the simulation, you must select the ON button on the combo box of the discriminant 1.

In order to validate the model, it is necessary to identify the key performance indicators used by the company X and compare them with those obtained by simulation.

The performance indicators used by the company are (Table 1):

Table 1. Performance indicators of Company X.

Indicator	Unit of measure
Average lead time	Day
Orders in late	N°
Contracts with penalties for delay	N°
Aggregate of days late	Day
The aggregate amount of days in the queue	Day
Aggregate of days with penalty	Day

In order to evaluate system performance some structure has been added to the simulation model (Fig. 5).

Lead Time

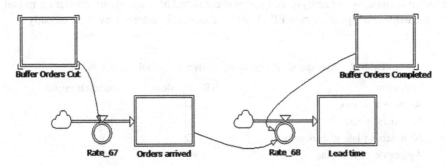

Fig. 5. Structure for the calculation of the lead time.

Rate_67 and Rate_68 contain respectively the following statements:

$$FOR(i = 1..228; j = 1..1/IF('Buffer\ Orders\ Cut'[i; 1] < >)0; 1; 0) \quad (7)$$

$$FOR(i = 1..228; j = 1..1/IF\ ('Buffer\ Orders\ Cut'[i; 1] = 0\ AND\ 'Orders \quad (8)$$
$$Arrived'[i; j] = 1; timestep *'\ Orders\ Arrived'[i; j]; 0))$$

The aggregate amount of days in the queue is shown in Fig. 6.
The condition inside Rate69 is the following:

$$FOR(i = 1..228; j = 1..1/IF('Pr\ iority\ Orders\ Cut'[i; 1] < > 0\ or' Buffetr\ Quarantine$$
$$cut'[i : j] < > 0\ or\ 'Buffer\ Orders\ Recovered\ cut')) \quad (9)$$

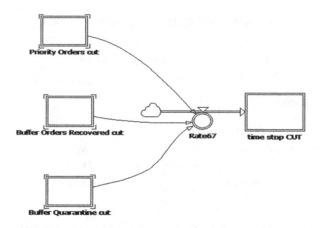

Fig. 6. Counter for days in queue.

Table 2 shows the comparison between the average values of real system performance (obtained by the analysis of historical data) and average of our simulation model results, made with priority rule FIFO, the one currently adopted by the company.

Table 2. Average results comparison over the whole time horizon.

Indicators	Real system	Simulation results
Average lead time	33,68	35,70
N° orders in late	89	85
N° orders in late with penalty	32	33
Aggregate of days late	1801	1905
Aggregate of days with penalty	613	675
Aggregate amount of days in the queue	3596	3716

Table 2 highlights that the model reproduces almost exactly company performance and, therefore, its suitability is demonstrated in order to represent the order management system of Company X.

8 Scenario Analysis

In order to evaluate the model performance with different dispatching policy, it is necessary to select some performance indicators.

In the literature, there are several indicators to evaluate the model performance; in this paper four measures have been identified.

Following a brief description of the indicators used in the model is outlined:

Mean Total Flow Time (MTFT): Indicates the time interval between the order arrival date (OCD) and its completion.

Mean Lateness (ML): The lateness indicates the delay/ advance of the scheduled delivery date of an *i-th* order:

If OCD < DD (Due Date), then the order is completed before the due date; if, however, occurs OCD > DD, then the order processing is completed in late.

Mean Tardiness (MT): The tardiness indicates the actual delay in the delivery of a generic order i; if the order is delivered on time, the tardiness is zero, otherwise it coincides with the lateness.

Percentage of Tardy Jobs (PTJ): Indicates the percentage of orders that terminate all the processes within the expected delivery date. In Table 3 summarizes the performance measures used in the simulation and their acronyms.

Table 3. Performance indicators and related acronyms.

MSFT	*Mean Shop Flow Time*
ML	*Mean Lateness*
MT	*Mean Tardiness*
PTJ	*Percentage of Tardy Jobs*

In addition to these performance indicators will be also analyzed the performance measures used by the company X.

The scenario "AS IS" refers to the order management policy used by the company X. The scenario "TO BE 1" refers to the priority rule that takes into account the penalty while the scenario "TO BE 2" takes into account the date of delivery, the time remaining for processing and penalties.

Table 4 reports a summary of all the indicators resulting from simulation scenarios:

Table 4. Summary table.

Indicators	AS IS	TO BE 1	TO BE 2
Number of orders in lateness	85	99	93
Number of orders in lateness with penalty	33	26	21
Aggregate days of lateness	1905	1765	1365
Aggregate days of lateness (orders with penalty)	675	454	358
Aggregate days of queue	3716	3331	2857
MTFT	35,70	33,03	30,74
Mean lateness	3,75	3,03	0,74
Mean tardiness	7,98	7,74	5,99
PTJ	41 %	47 %	43 %

The analysis of the values reported in Table 4 (where the "AS IS" column corresponds to the one named "SIMULATION RESULTS" in the Table 2) shows that the scenario "TO BE 1" is worse than "TO BE 2" scenario. It is useful compare the scenario "AS IS" and the scenario "TO BE 2".

In this case, the scenario "TO BE 2", despite having an increase in the number of late orders of 9.41 % compared to the scenario "AS IS", presents a significant improvement for all other performance considered. In particular:

Penalty for the number of orders in late has been reduce of 36.36 %;
Penalty for the aggregate of days delay for orders has been reduce of 46.96 %;
Aggregate of days in delay has been reduced of 28.35 %;
Days in queue have been reduced of 23.12 %.

9 Conclusions and Future Work

The main purpose of production planning is to link market demand with business constraints, in terms of production system potential, economic objectives and performance achievement. In particular for manufacturing companies, production planning is crucial to the achievement of a high level of customer satisfaction, as well as company success.

In this paper a simulation model has been developed in order to address scheduling problem and therefore to compare system performance with different priority rules adopted. The added value of this work is the methodology universality in the model developing: the simulation architecture has been built as general as possible (in such a way that it can be applied to different companies, which use flow-shop productive systems in PTO environment), and recurring to the less number of statistic (or, in general, not deterministic) simulation solutions.

The model main construct allows to manage the evolving elements of the system (the orders) strictly referred and related to the real factory history. Once defined these data, it is possible to identify the priority rule that provides the best solution in terms of performance.

Besides, using System Dynamics logic, it is possible to manage industrial phenomena that are subordinate respect to production process strictly considered (human behavior, materials flow, resources management, and so on), and that cannot be reproduced through discrete events simulation approaches. The simulation description of these interactions (which is done through actions and feedback applied on the different production states) determines a complex balance of the entire production system, marked in its rhythmic evolution by the constrained production flow, as well shown in our paper.

The future developments of this modeling logic consist in the implementation of the main construct, shown in this paper, n-times applied (in order to build the architecture binding of the production system) with the simultaneous interaction of different constructs based on the description of continuous evolution phenomena, typical of industrial production, which evolve in complex scenarios (presence of different production environments, linked in series or in parallel way, coexistence of opposite production logic, etc.).

References

1. Baker, K.R.: The effects of input control in a sample scheduling model. J. Oper. Manag. **4** (2), 99–112 (1984)
2. Baker, K.R.: Introduction to Sequencing and Scheduling. Franco Angeli, Milan (1974)
3. Betche, W.: Theory and practice of load-oriented manufacturing control. Int. J. Prod. Res. **35** (3), 375–420 (1988)
4. Bergamaschi, D., Cigolini, R., Perona, M., Portioli, A.: Order review and release strategies in a job shop environment: a review and a classification. Int. J. Prod. Res. **35**(2), 399–420 (1997)
5. Bertrand, J.W.M., Wortmann, J.C.: Production Control and Information Systems for Component-Manufacturing Shops (Dissertation) (1981)
6. Blackstone, J.H., Phillips, D.T., Hogg, G.L.: A state-of-the arte survey of dispatching rules for manufacturing job shop operations. Int. J. Prod. Res. **20**(1), 27–45 (1982)
7. Bragg, D.J., Duplaga, E.A., Watts, C.A.: The effects of partial order release and component reservation on inventory and customer service performance in an MRP environment. Int. J. of Prod. Res. **35**(3), 523–538 (1999)
8. Brandolese, A., Pozzetti, A., Sianesi, A.: Gestione Della Produzione Industriale. Hoepli, Milano (1991)
9. Castagna, R., Roversi, A.: Sistemi produttivi. Il processo di pianificazione, programmazione e controllo. Isedi, Torino (1990)
10. Chan, F.T.S., Chan, H.K., Lau, H.C.W., Ip, R.W.L.: Analysis of dynamic dispatching rules for a flexible manufacturing system. J. Mater. Process. Technol. **138**(1-3), 325–331 (2003)
11. Cheng, T.C.E., Gupta, M.C.: Survey of scheduling research involving due-date determination decision. Eur. J. Oper. Res. **38**(2), 156–166 (1989)
12. Cowling, P.I., Johansson, M.: Using real-time information for effective dynamic scheduling. Eur. J. Oper. Res. **139**, 230–244 (2002)
13. Fiorani, G.: System Thinking. System Dynamics e politiche pubbliche. Egea, Milano (2010)
14. Jayamohan, M.S., Rajendran, C.: New dispatching rules for shop scheduling: a step forward. Int. J. Prod. Res. **38**(3), 563–586 (2000)
15. John, S., Naim, M.M., Towill, D.R.: Dynamic analysis of a WIP compensated decision support system. Int. J. Manuf. Syst. Des. **1**, 289–297 (1994)
16. Kingsman, B.: Modeling input-output workload control for dynamic capacity planning in production planning systems. Int. J. Prod. Econ. **68**, 73–93 (2000)
17. Lauff, V., Werner, F.: Scheduling with common due-date, earliness and tardiness penalties for multimachine problems: a survey. Math. Comput. Model. **40**(5–6), 637–655 (2004)
18. Masturzi, A.: Organizzazione e gestione della produzione industriale, vol. III. Liguori Editore, Napoli (1990)
19. Modrák, V., Pandian, R.S.: Flow shop scheduling algorithm to minimize completion time. Tehnički vjesnik **17**(3), 273–278 (2010)
20. Ouelhadj, D., Petrovic, S.: A survey of dynamic scheduling in manufacturing systems. J. Sched. **12**, 417–431 (2009)
21. Patroklos, G., Charalampos, M.: Real-time production planning and control system for job-shop manufacturing: a system dynamics analysis. Eur. J. Oper. Res. **216**, 94–104 (2012)
22. Powersim Studio 2003 User's Guide, Powersim Software AS
23. Ragatz, M.: A simulation analysis of due date assignment rules. J. Oper. Manage. **5**, 27–39 (1984)
24. Roderick, L.M., Phillips, D.T., Hogg, G.L.: A comparison of order release strategies in production control systems. Int. J. Prod. Res. **30**(3), 611–626 (1992)

25. Silver, E.A., Pyke, D.F., Peterson, R.: Inventory Management and Production Planning and Scheduling. Wiley, New York (1998)
26. Sterman, J.D.: System dynamics modeling: Tools for learning in a complex world. Calif. Manage. Rev. **43**(4), 8–25 (2001)
27. Sterman, G.D.: Business Dynamics: Systems Thinking and Modeling for a Complex World. Irwin/McGraw-Hill, Boston (2000)
28. Vinod, V., Sridharan, R.: Simulation modeling and analysis of due-date assignment methods and scheduling decision rules in a dynamic job shop production system. Int. J. Prod. Econ. **129**, 127–146 (2011)
29. Wight, O.W.: A review of the order release policy research. Prod. Inventory Manag. **11**(3), 9–30 (1970)
30. Vollmann, T.E., Berry, W.L., Whybark, D.C.: Manufacturing Planning and Control Systems. Irwin/McGraw Hill, Boston (1997)
31. Manfredi, S., Santini, S.: An adaptive measurement fusion scheme for drifted and biased sensors fault isolation. Int. Rev. Autom. Control **6**(5), 552–557 (2013). ISSN:1746-6172
32. Fiengo, G., Santini, S., Glielmo, L.: Emission reduction during TWC warm-up: Control synthesis and hardware-in-the-loop verification. Int. J. Model. Ident. Control **3**(3), 233–246 (2008). doi:10.1504/IJMIC.2008.020122. ISSN: 17466172
33. Carotenuto, S., Iannelli, L., Manfredi, S., Santini, S.: Sensor fusion by using a sliding observer for an underwater breathing system. In: Proceedings of the 44th IEEE Conference on Decision and Control, and the European Control Conference, CDC-ECC 2005, art. no. 1583399, pp. 7662–7667 (2005). doi: 10.1109/CDC.2005.1583399. ISBN: 0780395689;978-078039568-8
34. Brancati, R., Montanaro, U., Rocca, E., Santini, S., Timpone, F.: Analysis of bifurcations, rattle and chaos in a gear transmission system. Int. Rev. Mech. Eng. **7**(4), 583–591 (2013). ISSN: 19708734
35. Sarghini, F., de Felice, G., Santini, S.: Neural networks based subgrid scale modeling in large eddy simulations. Comput. Fluids **32**(1), 97–108 (2003). doi:10.1016/S0045-7930(01)00098-6. ISSN 0045-7930
36. Manfredi, S.: A theoretical analysis of multi-hop consensus algorithms for wireless networks: Trade off among reliability, responsiveness and delay tolerance. Ad Hoc Netw. **13**, 234–244 (2014). ISSN:1570-8705
37. Manfredi, S.: Decentralized queue balancing and differentiated service scheme based on cooperative control concept. IEEE Trans. Industr. Inf. **10**(1), 586–593 (2014). doi:10.1109/TII.2013.2265879
38. Valente, A.S., Montanaro, U., Tufo, M., Salvi, A., Santini, S.: Design of a Platoon Management Strategy and its Hardware-In-the Loop validation. Accepted for publication in The Second International Workshop on Vehicular Traffic Management for Smart Cities (2014)
39. Beneduce, A.P., Gallo, M., Moscato, V., Picariello, A., Sansone, L.: A novel hybrid approach to semantic interoperability for logistic applications. In: Proceedings of the International Conference on Harbour, Maritime and Multimodal Logistics Modelling and Simulation 1, pp. 10–15 (2009)
40. Gallo, S.A., Melloni, R., Murino, T.: Simulation model to analyze transport, handling, temporary storage and sorting issues: a valuable way to support layout, system definition and configuration and scheduling decision. In: 25th European Modeling and Simulation Symposium, EMSS 2013, pp. 349–358 (2013)
41. Romano, E., Santillo, L.C., Zoppoli, P.: A static algorithm to solve the air traffic sequencing problem. WSEAS Trans. syst. **6**(7), 682–695 (2008)

42. Santillo, L., Converso, G., De Vito, L.: The role of innovation in industrial development system. A simulation approach for sustainability of global supply chain network. In: 25th European Modeling and Simulation Symposium, EMSS 2013, pp. 654–658 (2013)
43. Guerra, L., Gallo, M., Santillo, L.C.: Facility layout problem: formulations and solution methodologies. In: Proceedings - 13th ISSAT International Conference on Reliability and Quality in Design, pp. 400–405 (2007)
44. Murino, T., De Carlini, R., Naviglio, G.: An economic order policy assessment model based on a customized ahp. Front. Artif. Intell. Appl. **246**, 445–456 (2012)
45. Revetria, R., Catania, A., Cassettari, L., Guizzi, G., Romano, E., Murino, T., Improta, G., Fujita, H.: Improving Healthcare Using Cognitive Computing Based Software: An Application in Emergency Situation. In: Jiang, H., Ding, W., Ali, M., Wu, X. (eds.) IEA/AIE 2012. LNCS, vol. 7345, pp. 477–490. Springer, Heidelberg (2012)
46. Caputo, G., Gallo, M., Guizzi, G.: Optimization of production plan through simulation techniques. WSEAS Trans. Inf. Sci. Appl. **6**(3), 352–362 (2009)
47. Guizzi, G., Murino, T., Romano, E.: An innovative approach to environmental issues: the growth of a green market modeled by system dynamics. Front. Artif. Intell. Appl. **246**, 538–557 (2012)

Software Methodologies for Reliable Software Design

Highlighting Value and Effort Drivers Early in Business and System Models

Matthias Book[1]([⊠]), Simon Grapenthin[2], and Volker Gruhn[2]

[1] Department of Computer Science, University of Iceland, Reykjavík, Iceland
book@hi.is
[2] paluno – The Ruhr Institute for Software Technology,
University of Duisburg-Essen, Essen, Germany
{simon.grapenthin,volker.gruhn}@paluno.uni-due.de

Abstract. In complex business modelling and software development projects, we often observe that teams focus on those aspects of a system that are well understood or easy to resolve, while a blind eye is turned (consciously or subconsciously) to the actual value and effort drivers – i.e. those components that require higher effort due to their intrinsic value, risk, complexity or uncertainty. In this paper, we introduce a pragmatic approach for highlighting elements of high-level business and system models with visual annotations that mark particular issues, requirements or complexities that would otherwise not immediately meet the eye, and would thus present risks to a project's successful completion if uncovered too late.

Keywords: Models · Annotations · Value-driven software engineering

1 Introduction

In observations of industrial software development practice over the past ten years, we often observe that teams focus on those aspects of a system that are well understood, since it is easy to produce specifications and functioning artifacts for them. However, this often keeps the team's attention on the more trivial aspects of a system, while a blind eye is turned (consciously or subconsciously) to the actual value and effort drivers – i.e. those components that hold particular value for the viability and effectiveness of the system, or those that demand higher effort due to their intrinsic complexity or special requirements. The negligence of the value and effort drivers in favor of boilerplate functionality generates an illusion of project progress that is dangerous because those system aspects that would merit most attention, and should shape the design of the rest of the system, are not addressed until project resources are more scarce, and possibly conflicting design decisions have already been established.

The root of these issues is a **lack of understanding of project aspects that are not explicitly expressed in typical models of software systems,** but crucial to project success. In order to prevent these issues from growing unnoticed until they pose significant risks to a project, we aim to make them more visible and tangible for all

© Springer International Publishing Switzerland 2015
H. Fujita and A. Selamat (Eds.): SoMeT 2014, CCIS 513, pp. 211–222, 2015.
DOI: 10.1007/978-3-319-17530-0_15

stakeholders, and thus bring them into the team's focus before they can develop into problems. In this paper, we introduce the concept of value and effort annotations that are added early in the project to high-level system models in order to achieve this.[1]

2 Value and Effort Annotations

To foster joint understanding of critical aspects of a business domain by technical and domain experts, we encourage the project stakeholders to produce high-level model sketches of key aspects of the business domain and the information system early in the design process, and use these as a basis for identifying particularly valuable, complex, insufficiently understood or otherwise risky aspects of the project [2].

Following the concept of value-based software engineering [3], we are striving to make the value that is inherent in an organization's business processes – and thus the value the information system is expected to provide – explicit in the models of the system used in the engineering process. At the same time, we aim to highlight model elements in whose implementation particular effort must be invested to address issues, requirements or complexity that would otherwise not immediately meet the eye.

Rather than conceiving new types of models to express these value and effort drivers, we make them explicit through graphical annotations of existing models (independently of their notation). This has the advantage that stakeholders can use the same set of annotations in a wide variety of model types (e.g. business process models, architecture models, etc.) to express issues that are often of an overarching nature. We distinguish several classes of annotations that are helpful in different situations:

- **Value annotations** identify aspects directly related to the organization's value creation, i.e. the key features of the system, but also other aspects of the system that have an impact on the ability of the organization to conduct business (e.g. aspects that affect a company's perceived image among clients).
- **Effort annotations** highlight aspects of the business or the system that are particularly complex and thus require more care and effort than initially meets the eye (e.g. allowing for future design changes).
- **Wildcard annotations** express more unspecific warnings about particular business or system aspects that stakeholders want to draw attention on (e.g. to indicate that a particular aspect is still insufficiently understood and needs elaboration).

In the following subsections, we introduce these annotations for a broad spectrum of issues that would otherwise easily remain hidden or implicit in system models.

2.1 Value Annotations

Value annotations identify aspects directly related to the organization's value creation, i.e. the key features of the system, but also other aspects of the system that have an impact on the ability of the organization to conduct business (Fig. 1):

---

[1] This is an extended version of work presented at the 13th International Conference on Intelligent Software Methodologies, Tools and Techniques (SoMeT 2014) [1].

Value driver   Financial responsibility   Image sensitivity   Frequent execution

Fig. 1. Value annotations

- **Value Driver:** The value that an IT system provides to an organization is usually not evenly distributed across the system's components: A few components typically provide the "key" functionality that justifies the existence of the overall system, while other components merely provide secondary or support functionality. Using this annotation, the key components can be highlighted in order to focus appropriate attention on them.
- **Financial Responsibility:** Even if they are quite detailed, models of a business process or software component may not convey the amounts of money or other valuable assets that are processed by them. Some components may perform calculations (e.g. interest adjustments) of such volume that any errors – especially when accumulated over many transactions – can lead to significant financial risks for the organization and its clients, which can be indicated by this annotation.
- **Image Sensitivity:** Any interaction of an organization with outside parties – customers, suppliers, media etc. – affects the organization's image, i.e. its public perception. Even for interactions that are not deemed crucial, quick response times and professional presentation (e.g. of an online customer support interface or a monthly statement layout) can affect the company image positively. This annotation therefore indicates features that may look like candidates for low prioritization, but whose quality can have a significant "soft" impact on a company's image.
- **Frequent Execution:** Awareness of a component's high usage frequency (be it by human users or automated services) is important in order to design it for high performance, as well as to optimize it for the most frequent usage scenarios in order to increase the efficiency of the dependent business processes. A dialog that only a few people work with (e.g. just the Controlling department) does not need to have similarly fine-tuned usability, and must not be suitable for such a diverse audience, as e.g. the point-of-sale interface used by hundreds of cashiers. This annotation indicates that even small improvements made in such a component can yield a significant efficiency gain in a lot of users' work. Like most value and effort drivers, this annotation may be applied not just to process models, but also to data models, where it highlights that a particular data structure should be optimized for efficient access. This annotation may therefore impact developers' choice of implementation technique in significant ways, based on information that they could not have gained from a data model without the additional usage information.

2.2 Effort Annotations

Effort annotations highlight aspects of the business or system that are particularly complex and thus require more effort than one might initially expect (Fig. 2):

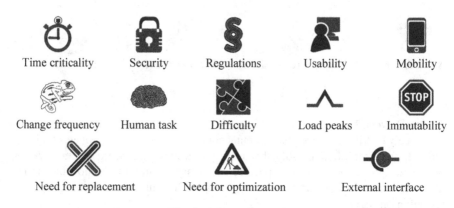

Fig. 2. Effort annotations

- **Time Criticality:** Time constraints in information systems typically refer to pre-scribed processing or response times (e.g. the maximum time it should take to make a decision), the availability of current data records (e.g. stock quotes), or the time of execution of certain operations (e.g. financial transactions). In business processes, time constraints might also indicate certain deadlines or processing times (e.g. the timeframe for filing appeals to legal documents). Thus, this annotation can indicate that developers need to take real-time requirements more strictly into account, or that certain business deadlines need to be observed by the system.
- **Security:** The need for digital signage of certain records to ensure non-repudiation, the need for anonymization of certain records before processing, or the enforcement of confidentiality of certain parts of records (in a bank, e.g., not all staff members that can access a client's checking account may also be allowed to see that client's custody) are special security requirements that the implementation of business process and data structures must respect. This annotation therefore highlights pro-cesses and data structures for which particular security mechanisms need to be implemented that are not part of the organization's overall security standards.
- **Regulations:** For some business processes, there may be legal or procedural prescriptions that govern how the process must be executed. While company pol-icies usually describe preferred best practices, legal policies often do not provide an immediate value for the organization, but are motivated by external interests such as market or consumer protection. This annotation therefore highlights processes or data structures that need to be implemented in particular, non-obvious ways in order to satisfy applicable legislation or organizational policies. It can also indicate areas that are known to become regulated in the future, even if the law's details are still under discussion, and thus serve as a warning that a certain degree of flexibility should be built into that system component.
- **Usability:** While any user-facing system components should of course be designed with good usability in mind (i.e. designed in a way that is intuitive to understand, suitable for the task, easy to use, etc.), some components might pose particular challenges in implementing high usability, e.g. because of the complexity of the

subject matter to be presented to the user, or the use of unusual/customized user interface elements, or non-standard user interface technologies. This annotation should thus mark components whose usability engineering requires particular care.

- **Mobility:** Implementing (part of) a system on a mobile device exposes the mobile components to a number of additional design challenges not found in traditional client/server designs. One of the largest effort drivers is the need for catering to a variety to device platforms, which may either necessitate multiple implementations for all targeted platforms, or considerable optimization, fine-tuning and compromising when cross-platform technologies are used. In addition, applications need to deal with the presence or absence of required hardware features (e.g. cameras), as well as more difficult testing of certain input parameters (e.g. location information). These efforts can be highlighted with the mobility annotation.

- **Change Frequency:** For some model elements, it may be foreseeable that they will change in the future, although it is not clear yet in which way exactly. Especially in domains that are highly regulated (e.g. the financial services sector), it is often known that certain processes will have to be adapted to future legislation. This annotation can therefore be used to highlight system parts where changes will occur predictably, so they should be designed with the flexibility to change in mind.

- **Human Task:** Some tasks that are highly dependent on human cognitive ability cannot be supported by information technology in an efficient manner. Other tasks within a business process may not be completely integrated within the information system (e.g. data aggregation and processing may be performed with separate tools), or the task might not occur frequently enough to warrant the effort of implementing IT support. In such cases, this annotation can be used to indicate that a particular process activity shall not be implemented in the information system, so no effort needs to be expended on developing technical solutions for it.

- **Difficulty:** Some model elements that look quite simple and straightforward in a model might actually involve considerable complexity for a variety of business or technical reasons (e.g. complex interfaces or technologies, difficult algorithms or even a need for research work). While most project stakeholders would usually remain unaware of such complexity unless they actually try to implement the component later in the project, a few domain experts or experienced project members may be able to foresee these issues and highlight them with the difficulty annotation, which indicates particular effort (and possibly outside expert knowledge) will have to be invested in the respective component.

- **Load Peaks:** Parts of a system may experience extraordinarily high load under certain circumstances – be it due to regular batch runs, certain business deadlines, or unforeseen outside events. To be prepared for such cases and ensure reliable system operation even under load peaks, architectural and infrastructural preparations should be put in place. Typically, this calls for a flexible infrastructure that can adapt to varying load levels, instead of providing capacity for peak loads even when it is not needed. Providing such a scalable architecture is not just a hardware issue, but can have far-reaching implications for the design e.g. of replication mechanisms, data and code portability etc. Building and testing the underlying infrastructure for this requires considerable effort, as indicated by this annotation.

- **Immutability:** When maintaining, migrating or extending legacy systems, it is often desirable (or even mandatory) that some system components remain unchanged. This can have several reasons: A component's interface may be defined as stable, because many other systems depend on it, or knowledge about the implementation details of certain legacy system parts may have eroded over time, so it would incur prohibitive effort to re-engineer and adapt the code. Under such circumstances, project stakeholders can be alerted to the fact that a component must not be changed with the immutability annotation.
- **Need for Replacement:** In contrast to immutable components, some legacy components might be explicitly meant for replacement, e.g. because the technology stack is out of date or because the system shall be replaced by a different product. In these cases, this annotation can make it clear to the team that the marked component is to be retired, so the functionality and data it provided will have to be replaced by newly developed or integrated systems.
- **Need for Optimization:** When maintaining, adapting or migrating an existing information system, stakeholders will often identify potential for improvement of the system's functional or non-functional behavior. Such improvement might either be necessary work in order to make a system work in a new context or system landscape, or it might be recommended work that can be performed if the system is undergoing maintenance anyway. In either case, this annotation indicates that work will have to be done on a particular component, which is particularly helpful when stakeholders need to get an overview of which parts of a large system landscape need to change and which ones will remain stable.
- **External Interface:** Interfaces with external components are often effort drivers for two reasons: If the system under construction provides an interface to outside components, particular care must go into the design of the interface, in order to ensure it is suitable for the current uses of the system and extensible in the future. Also, if an existing interface is being extended, special care needs to go into ensuring that existing components using the interface are not broken by any interface revisions. On the other hand, if the system under construction is relying on an external component, the team members need to consider what happens if that component becomes unavailable, if its interface changes, or if the business or technical conditions of using an outside service change (e.g. in terms of pricing models, service levels etc.). Besides awareness of these questions, the external interface annotation may also indicate that a make-or-buy decision for this functionality is required.

2.3 Wildcard Annotations

In addition to the above annotations that highlight specific value or complexity inherent in processes, data structures or components, we use two further annotations to point out issues of a more general nature (Fig. 3):

- **Uncertainty:** In contrast to the previous annotations, which mark effort drivers that some project stakeholders are already aware of, and which shall be communicated

Uncertainty

Project relevance

Fig. 3. Wildcard annotations

to the rest of the team, this annotation highlights parts of a model that all stake-holders feel they do not yet understand sufficiently. This uncertainty may be due to a lack of application domain knowledge or technical expertise, which needs to be remedied through more in-depth research and discussion among the stakeholders, and potentially the consultation of outside experts.

- **Project Relevance:** In some cases, stakeholders may feel they cannot properly express certain value or effort drivers with the previously introduced annotations, but still would like to point out a particularly important piece of information to their team mates. This wildcard annotation can then be used to highlight additional aspects that are crucial for the proper implementation of a particular component.

3   Annotation Elicitation Method

With these annotations, we aim to make knowledge explicit in models that is usually hidden or only known to a few stakeholders who may not even be aware that their knowledge is not shared by all team members. This way, we increase the expressiveness of models – not for the purpose of specification (for which these models are not nearly detailed enough), but to better understand the risks and priorities of a project.

To elicit the knowledge that is expressed in the annotations, we conduct workshops with all stakeholders, following an iterative approach: In the first step, we ask all stakeholders to model the business processes, data structures and IT landscape of a planned or existing system, in order to get a high level overview of the project's problem domain. Often, this high-level modeling step, which we moderate to ensure that models do not get lost in details, but focus on the big-picture dependencies, is already perceived as a helpful exercise in collaboration and communication between stakeholders from business and technical departments who may otherwise find it difficult to find a common language and abstraction level.

Given this set of high-level model sketches, we ask all stakeholders to mark the model elements with annotations as they perceive necessary. This occurs in several rounds of 10–15 min, in which the stakeholders can freely move among the models on the whiteboards and apply small sticky notes with annotation symbols to them. To keep the cognitive load manageable, we limit each annotation round to about five to seven symbols. The types of these annotations will depend on the nature of the project. In a project from the banking domain that we describe in more detail in Sect. 4, for example, we gave the stakeholders the following annotations to work with, as these seemed to cover the expected issues best:

- We always use the "value driver" annotation in the initial annotation round to identify which model elements the stakeholders deem most important. In business process models (which one might superficially consider "all about value creation"), it is especially helpful to focus on those activities that are particularly value-adding.

- We also use the "difficulty" annotation in virtually every initial annotation round, so stakeholders can highlight business and technical aspects that they are particularly apprehensive of. While "difficulty" may seem a rather broad term to highlight risks, stakeholders are encouraged to specify what exactly the difficulty lies in, and thus provide valuable information on steps to mitigate the concrete risks they see.
- In the banking project, we also used the "time criticality" annotation since accounting processes are often subject to various deadlines, and there are timing interdependencies between process steps that the information system needs to heed.
- The "human task" annotation was included in the first annotation round to immediately identify activities that are carried out by humans instead of software components. Discussing the impact of these activities at an early stage is important, since they might on the one hand bear large optimization potential, but on the other hand, they may also be too complex to be suitable for automation.
- The "security" annotation was included in the first annotation round since we expected that business processes would deal with personally identifiable portfolio and tax information, for which we wanted to elicit adequate security requirements from the stakeholders. In the banking domain, it is of course tempting for stakeholders to simply declare "this is all highly security relevant" – and while we were aware that the system would have to implement a higher level of baseline security measures than systems in less critical domains, we wanted to encourage the stakeholders to identify which system aspects required particular care in security matters.
- For similar reasons, we included the "regulation" annotation in the initial annotation round. Banking is a highly regulated domain, so it was important for all stakeholders to realize which activities provided more design leeway, and which had to be implemented according to very precise laws or company policies.

The above set is a typical choice for the initial annotation round of a business process model. Further annotation rounds can then be used to focus on particular aspects of the business domain (e.g. different types of users, expected usage peaks) or the technical environment (e.g. components scheduled for deprecation, available external services, mobile implementation challenges etc.).

After every annotation round, we discuss each annotation. For each annotation, the stakeholder who applied it has to explain their rationale. By discussing the annotations with all stakeholders, we generate a common understanding about possible pitfalls, and can clarify the detailed characteristics of an annotation (e.g. the precise time limit meant by a "time criticality" annotation, or the legal requirement indicated by a "regulations" annotation). Once a common understanding about an annotation has been reached, its characteristics are documented in the workshop notes.

We deliberately exclude the wildcard annotations from the regular annotation rounds because usually, nobody likes to "admit" that they are not sure about a particular aspect of a project. In a final "wildcard round", we instead ask every stakeholder to focus on uncertainty and project relevance, and request that each stakeholder applies at least one uncertainty annotation to some model element. The purpose of this dedicated wildcard round is to provide all stakeholders a "safe" environment in which to reveal which parts they are uncertain about, without feeling embarrassed about their supposed lack of knowledge. With the annotation of project relevance, we aim to motivate stakeholders to reflect on the former annotations and enable them to address project-specific issues that either do not fit the meaning of the other annotations, or that need to be particularly emphasized.

4   Annotations in Practice

We have used the annotation technique described above in a variety of projects with software development companies, insurance companies [4], and banks [14]. Managers and developers have been very open to the idea in every case, and even stakeholders who initially approached "yet another modeling workshop" with considerable hesitation ended up getting very involved in the identification and discussion of annotations, as they realized that they elicited valuable knowledge in themselves and their team members that they had previously been unaware of.

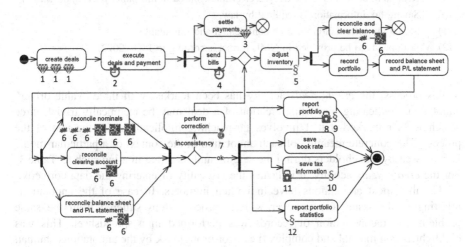

Fig. 4. Example of annotated business process model (original sketch redrawn for readability).

As an example, we show an excerpt of an annotated business process model that was created in a project with a German bank. The project's goal was to optimize accounting processes for all asset classes and migrate them from a legacy system to a commercial off-the-shelf (COTS) product. This involved not just a transition of the data and processes to the new system, but also the standardization of accounting processes across all asset classes. Figure 4 shows the result of one of the modeling and annotation sessions in the project, namely the business process for accounting of shares at the end of a period. The business process was sketched on a relatively high abstraction level, so the involved business and technical experts could come to a joint understanding of the key process steps and the corresponding functionality that would be required of the new COTS system. Duplicate or triplicate annotations on certain model elements indicate that several stakeholders marked the activity with the same annotation, emphasizing the importance of the respective aspect.

In the discussion following the annotation round, the stakeholders voiced the specific issues they associated with each of the annotation symbols they placed on the model. These were cross-referenced with numbers and recorded as shown in Table 1.

Table 1. Specific issues voiced by stakeholders in association with annotations in Fig. 4.

(1)	Correctness of overall process results depends on correctness of entered deal data.
(2)	Execution is time critical since rates change within milliseconds.
(3)	Correctness of algorithm affects general ledger numbers.
(4)	Time-consuming due to large amount of data to be sent.
(5)	Inventory adjustment is required by law.
(6)	Task performed manually in a spreadsheet by staff members.
(7)	Transaction value is usually larger than 1 million EUR.
(8)	Confidentiality of information needs to be ensured.
(9)	Reports to be sent to XXXXX. *[receiver anonymized in this paper for confidentiality]*
(10)	Saving tax information is required by law.
(11)	Stored tax information must be confidential and immutable.
(12)	Data needs to be provided in XML format according to ISO 20022.

In this process, the *create deals* activity has been marked with three "value driver" annotations, indicating that while creation of a deal may be technically trivial, three stakeholders remarked that it involves far-reaching implications for the rest of the process. The concrete meaning of each annotation in the context of a particular model is expressed by stakeholders during the session and recorded in a log such as Table 1. For the *create deals* activity, it indicates the criticality of entering the data correctly.

Usually, most annotations have individual numbers. In case of the annotations referring to the issue (6), however, several process steps suffered from the same problem: the reconciliation of records was performed in a spreadsheet. This was highlighted as a manual and complex (i.e. error-prone) task by the annotations "human task" and "difficulty", leading to the identification of significant optimization potential if the spreadsheet-based reconciliation could be replaced by an automated solution.

The *report portfolio statistics* activity was marked with a "regulations" annotation to indicate that although the process step is simple from a business perspective, particular care needs be taken to ensure that internal regulations for a particular data exchange format are followed, in order to enable the controlling department to analyze all portfolios. The "regulations" annotation on the *report portfolio* step, in contrast, indicates a regulation mandating reporting of information to another unit, which raises security issues – here, that the confidentiality of the report has to be ensured through an encrypted communication channel.

In summary, the annotations provide all stakeholders an intuitive overview not just of the pure process structure (as expressed by the bare model), but also of the constraints, warnings and other background knowledge that the team should be aware of when prioritizing, designing and implementing the components supporting all these steps. This is crucial information for realistic project planning that is usually rarely explicitly expressed in such compressed form – much more likely, it is scattered (incompletely) throughout various bits of project and requirements documentation, or even just exists as tacit knowledge of some stakeholders.

5 Related Work

Joint Application Design [5] and explicit documentation of design rationale [6] were notable earlier approaches to make different project stakeholders more aware of what they are building, and why. Although agile methods such as Scrum [7] encourage interaction between stakeholders, they provide virtually no methods for focusing it on other aspects than progress. In fact, as Petre et al. observed, there are striking differences between how agile vs. traditional teams use their room walls to visualize project progress vs. system aspects [8]. Our research aims to integrate these perspectives on a project and its environment in models that focus on the most critical aspects.

The idea of extending models with extra information is not new – there are several approaches for adding additional information to process models (e.g. [10–12], and [13]). However, our annotations aim to identify critical issues within a process or system, rather than precisely specifying a particular functional or non-functional aspect (e.g. security requirements, as in [11]). The use of collaborative modeling, public representations and physical artifacts has been investigated by many researchers (e.g. [9]). We follow their findings by keeping our models deliberately informal and using low-tech approaches that keep the contribution barrier low. We believe that this is particularly important because team members who are experts in their respective technical or business domain, but have no modeling tool experience, should not be deterred by a steep learning curve from contributing their knowledge to the project.

6 Conclusion

We believe that the main effects of using our annotations are improved communication and clarity about the upcoming challenges in the project. A better understanding of the business domain and its technical implementation, as well as raised awareness of critical system aspects (in terms of value, effort, risks and uncertainties) can benefit business and technical stakeholders in traditional and agile software processes alike. Even if the underlying complexity of a system and its business domain can never be completely overcome, we expect that the annotated models should help all team members to adopt a pragmatic, accessible perspective of their project that enables easier understanding of its details and better control of its risks from very early on.

Our ongoing research and evaluation focuses on how teams work with the different annotations, which subsets of annotations are suitable for which kinds of design challenges, and how the annotation process can be moderated in order to be most effective. We particularly look at how different roles understand the annotations, how prominently a dedicated facilitator should guide the annotation process, and if there are measurable improvements in software quality and project velocity.

References

1. Book, M., Grapenthin, S., Gruhn, V.: Highlighting value and effort drivers early in business and system models. In: Frontiers in Artificial Intelligence and Applications. New Trends in Software Methodologies, Tools and Techniques, vol. 265, pp. 530–544, IOS Press (2014)
2. Book, M., Grapenthin, S., Gruhn, V.: Seeing the forest and the trees: focusing team interaction on value and effort drivers. In: Proceedings of 20th International Symposium on the Foundations of Software Engineering, (ACM SIGSOFT 2012/FSE-20), pp. 11–16. ACM (2012)
3. Boehm, B.W., Sullivan, K.J.: Software economics: a roadmap. In: Proceedings of the Conference on Future of Software Engineering (FOSE 2000), pp. 319–343. ACM (2000)
4. Grapenthin, S., Book, M., Gruhn, V., Schneider C., Völker, K.: Reducing complexity using an interaction room – an experience report. In: Proceedings of the ACM Special Interest Group on the Design of Communication Conference (SIGDOC 2013), pp. 71–76. ACM (2013)
5. Davidson, E.J.: Joint application design (JAD) in practice. J. Syst. Softw. **45**(3), 215–223 (1999). Elsevier
6. Burge, J.E., Carroll, J.M., McCall, R., Mistrík, I.: Rationale-Based Software Engineering. Springer, Heidelberg (2008)
7. Schwaber, K., Beedle, M.: Agile Software Development with Scrum. Prentice Hall, Upper Saddle River (2002)
8. Petre, M., Sharp, H., Freudenberg, S.: The mystery of the writing that isn't on the wall: differences in public representations in traditional and agile software development. In: Proceedings of the 5th International Workshop on Cooperative and Human Aspects of Software Engineering (CHASE 2012), pp. 120–122. IEEE Computer Society (2012)
9. Goldschmidt, G.: The dialectics of sketching. Creativity Res. J. **4**, 123–143 (1991). Taylor & Francis
10. Rodriguez, A., Fernandez-Medina, E., Piattini, M.: Security requirement with a UML 2.0 profile. In: Proceedings of the 1st International Conference on Availability, Reliability and Security (ARES 2006), pp. 670–677. IEEE Computer Society (2006)
11. Rodriguez, A., Fernandez-Medina, E., Piattini, M.: A BPMN extension for the modeling of security requirements in business processes. Trans. Inf. Syst. **E90-D**(4), 745–752 (2007). Oxford University Press
12. Saeedi, K., Zhao, L., Falcone Sampaio, P.R.: Extending BPMN for supporting customer-facing service quality requirements. In: Proceedings of the IEEE International Conference on Web Services (ICWS 2010), pp. 616–623. IEEE Computer Society (2010)
13. Zou, J., Pavlovski, C.: Control case approach to record and model non-functional requirements. Inf. Syst. E-Bus. Manage. **6**(1), 49–67 (2008)
14. Book, M., Grapenthin, S., Gruhn, V.: Value-based migration of legacy data structures. In: Winkler, D., Biffl, S., Bergsmann, J. (eds.) SWQD 2014. LNBIP, vol. 166, pp. 115–134. Springer, Heidelberg (2014)

tReductSA – Test Redundancy Reduction Strategy Based on Simulated Annealing

Kamal Z. Zamli[1(✉)], Mohd Hafiz Mohd Hassin[1],
and Basem Al-Kazemi[2]

[1] Faculty of Computer Systems and Software Engineering,
Universiti Malaysia Pahang, Gambang, Malaysia
kamalz@ump.edu.my
[2] College of Computer and Information Systems,
Umm Al-Qura University, Makkah, Kingdom of Saudi Arabia

Abstract. Software testing relates to the process of accessing the functionality of a program against some defined specifications. To ensure conformance, test engineers often generate a set of test cases to validate against the user requirements. When dealing with large line of codes (LOCs), there are potentially issue of redundancies as new test cases may be added and old test cases may be deleted during the whole testing process. In order to address this issue, we have developed a new strategy, called tReductSA, to systematically minimize test cases for testing consideration. Unlike existing works which rely on the Greedy approaches, our work adopts the random sequence permutation and optimization algorithm based on Simulated Annealing with systematic merging technique. Our benchmark experiments demonstrate that tReductSA scales well with existing works (including that of GE, GRE and HGS) as far as optimality is concerned. On the other note, tReductSA also offers more diversified solutions as compared to existing work.

Keywords: Test suite redundancy reduction · Search based software engineering · Simulated Annealing · Optimization

1 Introduction

The growing complexity of software and its increasing diffusion into various application domains demands highly skilled engineers with appropriate mix of expertise. For this reason, it is no longer unusual for a software project to have teams in more than one location or even distributed over many continents. Owing to the intertwined dependencies of many software development activities and their geographical and temporal issues, coordination of tasks can be problematic. In the case of software testing, there are potentially many overlapping test cases which can cause unwarranted redundancies across the shared modules (i.e. a test for one requirement may be covered by more than one test).

Typically, redundancies increase the size of the test-suite resulting into substantial impact on the overall testing costs. Therefore, the idea of test-suite redundancy reduction (also referred to as test-suite minimization) is highly desirable to find a

© Springer International Publishing Switzerland 2015
H. Fujita and A. Selamat (Eds.): SoMeT 2014, CCIS 513, pp. 223–236, 2015.
DOI: 10.1007/978-3-319-17530-0_16

minimal subset of the test-suite that is sufficient to exercise the given test requirements. As part of our research work, we have developed a new strategy, called tReductSA, to systematically minimize test cases for testing consideration. Unlike existing works which rely on the Greedy approaches, our work adopts sequence permutation and optimization algorithm based on Simulated Annealing with systematic merging technique. Our benchmark experiments demonstrate that tReductSA scales well with existing works (including that of GE, GRE and HGS) as far as optimality is concerned. On the other note, tReductSA also offers more diversified solutions as compared to existing work.

2 Related Work

Often viewed as minimum set covering problem [1], much existing work in the literature has adopted the Greedy Heuristic strategies (e.g. HGS [2], GE [3], GRE [4]) to address the test redundancy reduction problem.

The earliest work on the Greedy Heuristic strategy is highlighted by Chavatal [1]. Chavatal's work forms the basis of most Greedy Heuristic based strategies. Briefly, the strategy greedily picks a test case t_i that covers the most requirements. Then, all the requirements that are covered by t_i are marked. The cycle is repeated until all requirements are marked.

Building from Chavatal's work, Harrold et al. [2] develops a new strategy, called HGS (or Heuristic H). Unlike Chavatal's strategy, HGS greedily selects the test cases associated with the requirements that are hardest to satisfy. A requirement A is harder to satisfy than a requirement B if A is covered by fewer test cases than B. In a nutshell, HGS works as follows. Initially, all covered requirements are considered unmarked. For each requirement that is exercised by one test case (i.e. cardinality of 1), HGS adds the test case into the minimized test suite and marks the covered requirements accordingly. Next, HGS considers the unmarked requirements in increasing order of cardinality of the set of test cases exercising each requirement. Then, HGS chooses the test case that would cover the greatest number of unmarked requirements associated with the current cardinality of interest. When there is a tie amongst cardinality of multiple test cases, HGS breaks the tie in favor of the test case that would mark the greatest number of unmarked requirements with the case sets of successively higher cardinalities. If the highest cardinality is reached, and the tie is not resolved, HGS arbitrarily selects one amongst those tied test case. Then, HGS marks the requirements covered by the selected test case. The whole iteration is repeated until all the requirements are completely marked.

Complementing HGS, Lau and Chen introduce another variant greedy strategy, called GE [3]. In GE, the concept of concept of essential test case is introduced for the greedy selection of test cases. Here, essential test cases represent those test cases that when removed, some test requirements can never be satisfied. Briefly, GE works as follows. Firstly, GE selects the essential test cases $t_{essential}$ that cover the most uncovered requirements. Secondly, GE removes all the requirements covered by the chosen essential test cases $t_{essential}$. The process continues for all other essential test cases until completion. If there are any uncovered requirements, the GE iterative process will continue to greedily select test cases t_i that covers the most uncovered requirements much like Chavatal's approach [1]. Then, all the requirements covered by t_i are removed. The process is repeated until all requirements are covered.

Shengwei et al. [5] adopts similar to GE variants that exploits weighted set covering (for requirements) in order to eliminate test redundancy and rearrange the test suite according to cost priority order. Here, in the case of a tie, lower costs test is selected.

As enhancement of GE, Chen and Lau introduce the GRE strategy [4]. GRE exploits the idea of redundant test case. In this case, if a test case satisfies only a subset of test-case requirements satisfied by another test case, then that particular test case is redundant. GRE starts by first removing redundant test cases from the test suite. In the process, GRE reduces the test suite and may make some test cases essential. Then, GRE applies the same algorithm as GE in order to choose the test cases that cover all the requirements.

In Galeebathullah and Indumathi's work [6], their strategy combines the set theory and greedy algorithm. Initially, the strategy finds the intersection of each requirement with other requirements. If exist any intersection exist, the test cases are greedily combined and added to the final test suite. The process is repeated until all requirements are covered by the test case.

Despite its popularity, the greedy heuristic approach is not without limitations. In some situation, the greedy approach produces poor test reduction [7]. One alternative approach is to address the aforementioned problem based on the Formal Concept Analysis (FCA). FCA is a technique for classifying objects based upon the overlap among their attributes. For reduction, test cases are considered as objects and requirements as attributes. Relationship between objects and attributes corresponds to the coverage information of test case. Using concept analysis, maximum grouping of objects and attributes can be deduced (termed context) in a table. Here, facilitated by graphical concept lattice and based on the object and attribute reduction rules, objects (i.e. test cases) can be systematically reduced. Existing literature that adopts FCA includes the work of Tallam and Gupta [8] and Ng et al. [7].

Although helpful, FCA suffers from the problem of scale – when the formal objects and their attributes grew, it is almost impossible to construct and manipulate the concept lattice graphically. Hence, the applications of FCA for large scale test reduction can be problematic and difficult.

As the test redundancy problem has been regarded as NP complete problem [9], no single strategy can do well in all scenarios considered. As such, new ideas, strategies and algorithms are necessary to improve the current state-of-the-art. Addressing this challenge, this paper proposes a different view on test redundancy reduction. Here, the test suite can be viewed as a sequence of permutation of test cases (i.e. test cases can be represented in any order). Considering exhaustive permutation, it is guaranteed that one of the (concatenated) permutations will minimally cover all the requirements. Nonetheless, exhaustive permutation can be expensive and very hard to handle. Hence, this work also proposes to adopt heuristic search using Optimization Algorithm based on Simulated Annealing. It is the hypothesis that suggests that the adoption of Simulated Annealing with systematic permutation of test cases is useful for test redundancy reduction problem is the main focus of this work.

3 Test Redundancy Reduction with Simulated Annealing Algorithm

Simulated Annealing [10] is an optimization algorithm motivated by the metal annealing process. Here, the given metal is heated and slowly cooled into a uniform structure. In a nut shell, Simulated Annealing starts with an initial configuration (solution) obtained by random or constructive means. Inferior local solutions are always rejected in place of more globally optimal solutions. The annealing algorithm makes a sequence of small random perturbations (i.e. through its neighbourhood search). The perturbation that improves solution is always accepted, whereas a perturbation that worsens the current solution by an amount ΔE, based on predefined cost function, is accepted with:

$$\text{Boltzman's probability} = e^{-\frac{\Delta E}{kT}} \tag{1}$$

where $\underline{T}$ is control parameter analogous to the temperature in the annealing of physical system.

Typically, T is decreased in stepwise manner according to:

$$T_{i+1} = \alpha T_i \tag{2}$$

where T_i is the i-th temperature phase and α determines the gradient of cooling.

The core of simulated annealing algorithm is the Metropolis algorithm, which simulates the annealing process at the given temperature. In case of the high temperature, most uphill perturbations are accepted (i.e. because the Boltzman probability gives ≈ 1). When the annealing process is nearly finished and T is reduced to a small value, any uphill perturbations will only be accepted with a much smaller probability.

The pseudo code for Simulated Annealing can be summarized as follows (Fig. 1):

```
 1:  Select an initial temperature T_initial and final temperature T_final
 2:  Create S_current from S_initial
 3:  T = T_initial
 4:  While (T > T_final) // Temperature Cycle
 5:   While (not Stop Criteria) // Metropolis Cycle
 6:    Create S_new from perturbation of S_current
 7:    Calculate ΔE= F(S_current)- F(S_new)
 8:    If ΔE <=0 then
 9:     Accept S_new
10:    else
11:     Calculate Boltzman's Probability =e^(-ΔE/t)
12:     If Boltzman's Probability >Random[0,1] then
13:      Accept S_new
14:     Endif
15:    Endif
16:   End While
17:   Decrease T=αT
18:  End While
```

Fig. 1. Simulated annealing algorithm

As far as the test redundancy reduction is concerned, any current solution $S_{current}$ is represented as a sequence of test cases making up a test suite. Hence, perturbation of $S_{current}$ involves rearranging the current sequence of test cases. More formally, the test redundancy problem can be expressed as follows:

Given: A test suite T_S, a set of test requirements Req $= \{req_1, req_2, \ldots req_n\}$ that must be covered to provide the desired test coverage of the program, and subset of $T_S = \{T_1, T_2, \ldots T_n\}$, one associated with each of the req_i's such that any one of the test cases t_j belonging to T_i can be used to test req_i.

Problem: Find representative set of test cases, T_M, based on permutation of T_S that satisfies all of the req_i's.

Mathematically, the test redundancy reduction problem can be expressed as set-covering problem.

Let:

$$T_S = \{t_1, t_2, \ldots t_n\}$$

$$\text{Req} = \{req_1, req_2, \ldots req_n\}$$

$$T_M = \{\text{All permutation n! of } T_S\}$$

Hence, the objective function is:

$$f(t) = \min\{T_M \text{ covering Req}\}$$
$$\text{subject to } t = t_1, t_2, \ldots t_j; \ j = 1, 2, \ldots N$$

$$(3)$$

Here, the cost function for the min operator of f(t) adopts the following systematic merger rule:

- Each test case in the sequence, $S_{current}$, will be merged together until all the requirements are covered.
- When all the requirements are covered, the merging process stops. Here, if $S_{current}$ is reduceable, the merging result gives concatenation of $S_{current}$

Upon completion of the cooling temperature cycle, $S_{current}$, represents the global optimum test-suite reduction results in a new test-suite, T_M, where only the relevant subset remains and the other test-cases are discarded.

4   Tuning of Parameters

In order to ensure good performance, a number of parameters within tReductSA need to be properly tuned. Specifically, the parameters of tReductSA that requires tuning include the starting temperature, $T_{initial}$, the final temperature, T_{final}, the temperature decrement,α, and the iterations/stop criteria at each temperature (i.e. also termed the Metropolis cycle).

4.1   Analytical Derivation from Boundary Value Conditions

Using boundary value conditions and the desired Boltzman's probability function, it is possible to perform analytical tuning of parameters. Here, by compromising the diversification (i.e. how diverse of the current solution is) and intensification (i.e. how intensive is the local search of the current solution is) of the Bolztman's probability function can yield different values for all tuning parameters highlighted earlier.

Based on the Boltzman's probability function and using the property of logarithm:

$$T_{initial} = \frac{-\Delta E\text{max}}{\ln(P(\Delta E\text{max}))} \tag{4}$$

$$T_{final} = \frac{-\Delta E\text{min}}{\ln(P(\Delta E\text{min}))} \tag{5}$$

At high temperature, the probability $P(\Delta E_{max}) \approx 1$. Hence, $T_{initial}$ depends on the maximum difference of $\Delta E_{max} = F(S_{current}) - F(S_{new})$. In similar manner, at low temperature, the probability $P(\Delta E_{max}) \approx 0$. Hence, $T_{initial}$ depends on the minimum difference of $\Delta E_{min} = F(S_{current}) - F(S_{new})$. With large ΔE_{max}, the potential solution can be diversified with global search. With small ΔE_{min}, the local search is intensified.

The temperature decrement, α, can be related to $T_{initial}$ and T_{final} with the following relation:

$$T_{final} = \alpha^n T_{initial} \tag{6}$$

where n is the step number from $T_{initial}$ to T_{final}

The iterations/stop criteria at each temperature (or the Metropolis cycle) can be deduced as follows. Here, at high temperatures, the number of iterations can be small as any solution would easily be accepted. However, at low temperatures nearing T_{final}, it is important to have a large number of iterations so that the local optimum can be fully explored and avoided.

Let $L_{initial}$ be the initial iteration value for the overall $T_{initial}$ to T_{final}, L_{max} be the final iteration, and γ be the rate of the increment of the Metropolis cycle (>1), then:

$$L_{max} = \gamma^n L_{initial} \tag{7}$$

where n is the step number from $T_{initial}$ to T_{final}

For Metropolis cycle at each temperature value, the iteration will be iteratively guided by:

$$L_{k+1} = \gamma L_k \tag{8}$$

4.2   Tuning Process

Given the derived equations in earlier section, the tuning of tReductSA can be systematically undertaken. In order to perform the tuning, there is a need for a well-defined test

Table 1. Configuration with Req = $\{req_1, req_2, \ldots req_{24}\}$ and T = $\{t_0, t_1, \ldots, t_{30}\}$

Req_i	T_n
req_1	$\{t_0, t_3, t_7, t_{18}, t_{29}\}$
req_2	$\{t_3, t_{16}, t_{22}\}$
req_3	$\{t_0, t_2, t_{25}, t_{27}\}$
req_4	$\{t_{11}, t_{30}\}$
req_5	$\{t_1, t_4, t_8, t_{14}, t_{25}\}$
req_6	$\{t_9, t_{14}, t_{19}, t_{24}\}$
req_7	$\{t_5, t_{10}, t_{21}\}$
req_8	$\{t_4, t_{20}\}$
req_9	$\{t_7, t_{17}, t_{24}, t_{26}\}$
req_{10}	$\{t_6, t_{15}, t_{29}\}$
req_{11}	$\{t_{10}, t_{15}, t_{23}\}$
req_{12}	$\{t_1, t_6\}$
req_{13}	$\{t_4\}$
req_{14}	$\{t_2, t_8, t_{13}, t_{16}, t_{23}\}$
req_{15}	$\{t_{28}\}$
req_{16}	$\{t_{22}, t_{28}\}$
req_{17}	$\{t_{17}, t_{29}\}$
req_{18}	$\{t_5, t_{20}\}$
req_{19}	$\{t_9, t_{25}\}$
req_{20}	$\{t_{12}\}$
req_{21}	$\{t_9, t_{28}, t_{30}\}$
req_{22}	$\{t_3, t_{24}\}$
req_{23}	$\{t_0, t_{30}\}$
req_{24}	$\{t_5, t_8, t_{11}, t_{26}, t_{27}\}$

and requirements mapping. We have chosen the configuration with Req = $\{req_1, req_2, \ldots req_{24}\}$ and T = $\{t_0, t_1, \ldots, t_{30}\}$ for tuning of tReductSA (refer to Table 1).

The rationale for choosing the aforementioned configuration for tuning purpose stemmed from the fact that it has large number of tests and requirements. Here, the intensification and diversification of the developed strategy can be fully exploited to get the best tuning for the relevant parameters.

In any optimization problem, much of the initial setting of the parameters depends on the problem domain. For tuning purposes, we have set the following as domain specific conditions.

- ΔE_{max} = test suite size − 1
  In the most extreme case, if the most minimum test suite size = 1, it follows that the maximum energy difference of $\Delta E_{max} = f_{max}(t) - f_{min}(t)$ = test suite size − 1.
- ΔE_{min} = 0.01
  Ideally, $\Delta E_{min} \approx 0$. The number 0.01 has been chosen to have a finite and reasonable range of values for T_{final}.
- L_{max} = test suite size

Table 2. Tuning with $\alpha = 0.700$ and varying $P(\Delta E)$

Domain Specific Conditions							
$\Delta E_{max} = $ test suite size-1=30							
$\Delta E_{min} = 0.001$							
$\alpha = 0.7$							
$L_{max} = $ test suite size = 31							
$L_{initial} = 1$							
$P(\Delta E_{max})+P(\Delta E_{min})= 1$							
Predetermined Values		**Calculated Values**					
$P(\Delta E_{max})$	$P(\Delta E_{min})$	$T_{initial}$	T_{final}	n	γ	Average Percentage Reduction	Best Percentage Reduction
0.990	0.010	2984.975	0.000	46.082	1.077	43.412	45
0.900	0.100	284.737	0.000	37.551	1.096	42.390	45
0.800	0.200	134.443	0.001	34.443	1.105	39.433	48
0.700	0.300	84.110	0.001	32.314	1.112	39.635	48
0.600	0.400	58.728	0.001	30.541	1.119	41.810	51
0.500	0.500	43.281	0.001	28.903	1.126	35.633	41
0.400	0.600	32.741	0.002	27.265	1.134	39.812	41
0.300	0.700	24.918	0.003	25.492	1.144	35.607	45
0.200	0.800	18.640	0.004	23.363	1.158	42.212	48
0.100	0.900	13.029	0.009	20.255	1.185	39.633	48
0.010	0.990	6.514	0.099	11.724	1.340	36.813	41

Ideally, L_{max} represents the maximum Metropolis cycle at low temperature. The number of cycles must at least equal to the number of test suite size to get the good exploration at T_{final}.

- $L_{initial} = 1$
  Practically, $L_{initial}$ must be 1 to ensure that the Metropolis cycle is summoned at least once at the start.
- $P(\Delta E_{max}) + P(\Delta E_{min}) = 1$
  In order to balance the intensification and diversification of the potential solution, the sum of both probabilities need to be set to 1.

Having defined the domain specific conditions, the complete tuning process and experimentations are summarized in Tables 2, 3, and 4 respectively. The ranges of α that are used is {0.700, 0.845, 0.990} based on 3 equal divisions of the recommended range between [0.7, 0.99] as suggested in [11]. For Table 2, the value of α is fixed at 0.700, the values for $P(\Delta E_{max})$ and $P(\Delta E_{min})$ are varied in pairs of {0.990, 0.010}, {0.900,0.100}, {0.800, 0.200}, {0.700,0.300}, {0.600, 0.400}, {0.500, 0.500}, {0.400, 0.600}, {0.300, 0.700},{0.200, 0.800}, {0.100, 0.900}, and {0.010, 0.990} with the pair sum of 1. For Table 3, the value of α is fixed at 0.845 with the same pair values for

Table 3. Tuning with $\alpha = 0.845$ and varying $P(\Delta E)$

Domain Specific Conditions							
ΔE_{max} = test suite size-1=30							
ΔE_{min} = 0.001							
α =0.845							
L_{max} = test suite size=31							
$L_{initial}$ = 1							
$P(\Delta E_{max})$+$P(\Delta E_{min})$= 1							

Predetermined Values		Calculated Values					
$P(\Delta E_{max})$	$P(\Delta E_{min})$	$T_{initial}$	T_{final}	n	γ	Average Percentage Reduction	Best Percentage Reduction
0.990	0.010	2984.975	0.000	97.592	1.036	46.621	48
0.900	0.100	284.737	0.000	79.524	1.044	46.633	51
0.800	0.200	134.443	0.001	72.942	1.048	41.012	41
0.700	0.300	84.110	0.001	68.434	1.051	39.411	45
0.600	0.400	58.728	0.001	64.680	1.055	40.212	45
0.500	0.500	43.281	0.001	61.210	1.058	43.223	48
0.400	0.600	32.741	0.002	57.741	1.061	38.333	41
0.300	0.700	24.918	0.003	53.987	1.066	40.091	45
0.200	0.800	18.640	0.004	49.479	1.072	37.612	54
0.100	0.900	13.029	0.009	42.896	1.083	36.215	41
0.010	0.990	6.514	0.099	24.829	1.148	32.413	38

$P(\Delta E_{max})$ and $P(\Delta E_{min})$. Again, for Table 4, the value of α is fixed at 0.990, and using the same pair values for $P(\Delta E_{max})$ and $P(\Delta E_{min})$.

Given the aforementioned parameter values, tReductSA is summoned to minimize redundancies of the given configuration in Table 1. For each row entry (i.e. in Tables 1, 2, and 3), tReductSA is executed and the average percentage reduction from 20 runs is recorded. Here, the best "local" best results from each table are shaded accordingly.

Referring to Tables 2, 3, and 4, the global best from the three shaded rows is when $\alpha = 0.990$, $T_{initial} = 2984.975$, and $T_{final} = 0.000$. These tuned parameters will be used in the next section for benchmarking tReductSA against other existing strategies.

5 Benchmarking Results

In order to benchmark tReductSA against related work, we have divided our comparison into two main parts. In the first part, we have adopted 3 main experiments which are reported in [4]. For the first experiment, we take the tests and requirement mapping involving Req = $\{req_1, req_2, \ldots req_{19}\}$ and T = $\{t_1, t_2, t_3, t_4, t_5, t_6, t_7\}$. In the

Table 4. Tuning with $\alpha = 0.990$ and varying $P(\Delta E)$

Domain Specific Conditions							
$\Delta E_{max} =$ test suite size-1=30 $\Delta E_{min} = 0.001$ $\alpha = 0.990$ $L_{max} =$ test suite size=31 $L_{initial} = 1$ $P(\Delta E_{max}) + P(\Delta E_{min}) = 1$							
Predetermined Values			**Calculated Values**				
$P(\Delta E_{max})$	$P(\Delta E_{min})$	$T_{initial}$	T_{final}	n	γ	Average Percentage Reduction	Best Percentage Reduction
0.990	0.010	2984.975	0.000	1635.396	1.002	55.233	58
0.900	0.100	284.737	0.000	1332.627	1.003	53.133	58
0.800	0.200	134.443	0.001	1222.325	1.003	50.412	54
0.700	0.300	84.110	0.001	1146.779	1.003	48.615	51
0.600	0.400	58.728	0.001	1083.870	1.003	48.201	54
0.500	0.500	43.281	0.001	1025.732	1.003	50.411	54
0.400	0.600	32.741	0.002	967.594	1.004	48.350	54
0.300	0.700	24.918	0.003	904.686	1.004	49.211	54
0.200	0.800	18.640	0.004	829.139	1.004	49.834	54
0.100	0.900	13.029	0.009	718.837	1.005	46.212	48
0.010	0.990	6.514	0.099	416.068	1.008	45.433	51

second experiment, we adopt the tests and requirement mapping with Req = $\{req_1, req_2, \ldots req_{19}\}$ and T = $\{t_1, t_2, t_3, t_4, t_8, t_9\}$. Finally, in the third experiment, we use the tests and requirement mapping with Req = $\{req_1, req_2, \ldots req_{19}\}$ and T = $\{t_1, t_3, t_4, t_5, t_6, t_8, t_{10}, t_{11}, t_{12}\}$. The detailed configurations for the first part are shown in Table 5.

For the second part, we have adopted three new experiments (i.e. with slightly larger configuration than that of the first part) involving Req = $\{req_1, req_2, \ldots req_{24}\}$ and T = $\{t_0, t_2, \ldots, t_{30}\}$. Unlike the first part (where we use the available result from [4]), no results are readily available for comparison in this case. Hence, for all experiments, we compare tReductSA against our own implementation of GE derived from Chen and Lau [3]. The detail configurations for the second part are shown in Table 6.

The complete benchmarking results for both parts of the comparison are tabulated in Table 7 and 8 respectively. Referring to Table 7, tReductSA and GRE outperforms GE and HGS with 62.5 % reduction in the first experiment. In this case, the same set of test suite is generated by tReductSA and GRE. Although not optimal, the same set of test suite is also generated by GE and HGS. For the second experiment, tReductSA and HGS outperforms GRE and GE with 50 % reduction. The same set of test suite is

Table 5. Benchmark case studies for Part 1

Req_i	Experiment 1 T_n	Experiment 2 T_n	Experiment 3 T_n
req_1	$\{t_1,t_2,t_3,t_4,t_5,t_6,t_7\}$	$\{t_1,t_2,t_3,t_4,t_8,t_9\}$	$\{t_1,t_3,t_4,t_5,t_6,t_8,t_{10},t_{11},t_{12}\}$
req_2	$\{t_1,t_2,t_3,t_4,t_5,t_6,t_7\}$	$\{t_1,t_2,t_3,t_4,t_8,t_9\}$	$\{t_1,t_3,t_4,t_5,t_6,t_8,t_{10},t_{11},t_{12}\}$
req_3	$\{t_1,t_2,t_3,t_4,t_5,t_6,t_7\}$	$\{t_1,t_2,t_3,t_4,t_8,t_9\}$	$\{t_1,t_3,t_4,t_5,t_6,t_8,t_{10},t_{11},t_{12}\}$
req_4	$\{t_1,t_2,t_3,t_4,t_5,t_6,t_7\}$	$\{t_1,t_2,t_3,t_4,t_8,t_9\}$	$\{t_1,t_3,t_4,t_5,t_6,t_8,t_{10},t_{11},t_{12}\}$
req_5	$\{t_1,t_2,t_5,t_7\}$	$\{t_1,t_2,t_9\}$	$\{t_1,t_5,t_{10},t_{11},t_{12}\}$
req_6	$\{t_2,t_3,t_4,t_6\}$	$\{t_2,t_3,t_4,t_8,t_9\}$	$\{t_3,t_4,t_6,t_8,t_{10},t_{12}\}$
req_7	$\{t_1,t_7\}$	$\{t_1\}$	$\{t_1,t_{10},t_{12}\}$
req_8	$\{t_2,t_5\}$	$\{t_2,t_9\}$	$\{t_5,t_{11}\}$
req_9	$\{t_1,t_7\}$	$\{t_1\}$	$\{t_1,t_{10},t_{12}\}$
req_{10}	$\{t_1,t_2,t_5,t_7\}$	$\{t_1,t_2,t_9\}$	$\{t_1,t_5,t_{10},t_{11},t_{12}\}$
req_{11}	$\{t_2,t_3\}$	$\{t_2,t_3,t_8\}$	$\{t_3,t_8,t_{10}\}$
req_{12}	$\{t_3,t_4,t_6\}$	$\{t_3,t_4,t_8,t_9\}$	$\{t_3,t_4,t_6,t_8,t_{12}\}$
req_{13}	$\{t_2,t_3\}$	$\{t_2,t_3,t_8\}$	$\{t_3,t_8,t_{10}\}$
req_{14}	$\{t_2,t_3\}$	$\{t_2,t_3,t_8\}$	$\{t_3,t_8,t_{10}\}$
req_{15}	$\{t_3,t_4,t_7\}$	$\{t_3,t_4,t_9\}$	$\{t_3,t_4,t_{12}\}$
req_{16}	$\{t_4,t_6\}$	$\{t_4,t_8\}$	$\{t_4,t_6,t_8\}$
req_{17}	$\{t_3,t_4\}$	$\{t_3,t_4,t_9\}$	$\{t_3,t_4,t_{12}\}$
req_{18}	$\{t_3,t_4\}$	$\{t_3,t_4,t_9\}$	$\{t_3,t_4,t_{12}\}$
req_{19}	$\{t_4,t_6\}$	$\{t_4,t_8\}$	$\{t_4,t_6,t_8\}$

generated by tReductSA and HGS. Similar with earlier case, although not the best, the same set of test suite is also generated by GRE and GE. Finally, in the third experiment, tReductSA and GE gives the same percentage of reduction with 66 %. Nonetheless, GE gives only two sets of possible solution, that is, $\{t_{12},t_8,t_5\}$ and $\{t_{12},t_8,t_{11}\}$. tReductSA, on the other hand, generates four possible set of solutions, that is, $\{t_{12},t_8,t_5\}$, $\{t_{12},t_8,t_{11}\}$, $\{t_4,t_{10},t_5\}$, and $\{t_4,t_{10},t_{11}\}$. In this manner, tReductSA outperforms GE in the sense that it offers a more diversified solution. In fact, for all the experiments in part 1, tReductSA consistently outperforms all the related work.

Concerning the result for part 2 in Table 8, GE outperforms tReductSA for with 64 % reduction as compared to 58 % for experiment 4. On the other hand, tTReductSA outperforms GE with 64 % reduction as compared to 61 % for experiment 5. In experiment 6, both GE and tReductSA achieve the same reduction percentage of 77 %. Here, as with experiment 3, tReductSA offers more diversified solutions as compared to GE in experiment 6. It is worth noting tReductSA require multiple runs in order to produce the best reduction (in our case, we have adopted 20 runs). In any runs, the ordering of test cases is arbitrary owing to its adoption of random permutations for test sequence generation.

Table 6. Benchmark case studies for Part 2

Req_i	Experiment 4 T_n	Experiment 5 T_n	Experiment 6 T_n
req_1	$\{t_0,t_3,t_7,t_{18},t_{29}\}$	$\{t_0,t_3,t_7,t_{18},t_{19},t_{29}\}$	$\{t_0,t_1,t_2,t_3,t_4,t_5,t_6,t_7,t_8,t_9,t_{10},t_{11},t_{12},t_{13},t_{14},t_{15},t_{16},t_{17},t_{18},t_{19},t_{20},t_{21},t_{22},t_{23},t_{24},t_{25},t_{26},t_{27},t_{28},t_{29},t_{30}\}$
req_2	$\{t_3,t_{16},t_{22}\}$	$\{t_1,t_2,t_3,t_6,t_{12},t_{16},t_{22},t_{24}\}$	$\{t_0,t_1,t_2,t_3,t_4,t_5,t_6,t_7,t_8,t_9,t_{10},t_{11},t_{12},t_{13},t_{14},t_{15},t_{16},t_{17},t_{18},t_{19},t_{20},t_{21},t_{22},t_{23},t_{24},t_{25},t_{26},t_{27},t_{28},t_{29},t_{30}\}$
req_3	$\{t_0,t_2,t_{25},t_{27}\}$	$\{t_0,t_2,t_{25},t_{27}\}$	$\{t_0,t_1,t_2,t_3,t_4,t_5,t_6,t_7,t_8,t_9,t_{10},t_{11},t_{12},t_{13},t_{14},t_{15},t_{16},t_{17},t_{18},t_{19},t_{20},t_{21},t_{22},t_{23},t_{24},t_{25},t_{26},t_{27},t_{28},t_{29},t_{30}\}$
req_4	$\{t_{11},t_{30}\}$	$\{t_{11},t_{30}\}$	$\{t_0,t_1,t_2,t_3,t_4,t_5,t_6,t_7,t_8,t_9,t_{10},t_{11},t_{12},t_{13},t_{14},t_{15},t_{16},t_{17},t_{18},t_{19},t_{20},t_{21},t_{22},t_{23},t_{24},t_{25},t_{26},t_{27},t_{28},t_{29},t_{30}\}$
req_5	$\{t_1,t_4,t_8,t_{14},t_{25}\}$	$\{t_1,t_4,t_8,t_{14},t_{25}\}$	$\{t_4,t_8,t_{14},t_{25}\}$
req_6	$\{t_9,t_{14},t_{19},t_{24}\}$	$\{t_9,t_{14},t_{19},t_{24}\}$	$\{t_9,t_{14},t_{19},t_{24}\}$
req_7	$\{t_5,t_{10},t_{21}\}$	$\{t_5,t_{10},t_{21}\}$	$\{t_5,t_{10},t_{21}\}$
req_8	$\{t_4,t_{20}\}$	$\{t_4,t_{20}\}$	$\{t_4,t_{20}\}$
req_9	$\{t_7,t_{17},t_{24},t_{26}\}$	$\{t_7,t_{17},t_{24}\}$	$\{t_2,t_7,t_{14},t_{17},t_{24},t_{26}\}$
req_{10}	$\{t_6,t_{15},t_{29}\}$	$\{t_{15},t_{29}\}$	$\{t_6,t_{15},t_{26},t_{27},t_{28},t_{29},t_{30}\}$
req_{11}	$\{t_{10},t_{15},t_{23}\}$	$\{t_{10},t_{15},t_{23}\}$	$\{t_{10},t_{15},t_{23}\}$
req_{12}	$\{t_1,t_6\}$	$\{t_1,t_6\}$	$\{t_1,t_6,t_{13},t_{14}\}$
req_{13}	$\{t_4\}$	$\{t_6\}$	$\{t_4,t_{17}\}$
req_{14}	$\{t_2,t_8,t_{13},t_{16},t_{23}\}$	$\{t_2,t_8,t_{13},t_{16},t_{23}\}$	$\{t_2,t_8,t_{13},t_{16},t_{23}\}$
req_{15}	$\{t_{28}\}$	$\{t_{20},t_{28}\}$	$\{t_{17},t_{28}\}$
req_{16}	$\{t_{22},t_{28}\}$	$\{t_0,t_{18},t_{22}\}$	$\{t_0,t_1,t_2,t_3,t_4,t_5,t_6,t_7,t_{22},t_{28}\}$
req_{17}	$\{t_{17},t_{29}\}$	$\{t_{17},t_{29}\}$	$\{t_{10},t_{11},t_{13},t_{17},t_{29}\}$
req_{18}	$\{t_5,t_{20}\}$	$\{t_5,t_{20}\}$	$\{t_5,t_{20}\}$
req_{19}	$\{t_9,t_{25}\}$	$\{t_9,t_{25}\}$	$\{t_9,t_{17},t_{18},t_{25}\}$
req_{20}	$\{t_{12}\}$	$\{t_{10},t_{12}\}$	$\{t_{12},t_{16},t_{18}\}$
req_{21}	$\{t_9,t_{28},t_{30}\}$	$\{t_9,t_{28},t_{30}\}$	$\{t_9,t_{28},t_{30}\}$
req_{22}	$\{t_3,t_{24}\}$	$\{t_3,t_{24}\}$	$\{t_0,t_1,t_2,t_3,t_4,t_{10},t_{11},t_{12},t_{13},t_{14},t_{24},t_{25},t_{26},t_{27},t_{28},t_{29},t_{30}\}$
req_{23}	$\{t_0,t_{30}\}$	$\{t_0,t_5,t_{30}\}$	$\{t_0,t_5,t_{30}\}$
req_{24}	$\{t_5,t_8,t_{11},t_{26},t_{27}\}$	$\{t_5,t_8,t_{11},t_{13},t_{26},t_{27}\}$	$\{t_5,t_8,t_{11},t_{26},t_{27}\}$

Table 7. Benchmarking results for Part 1

	Experiment 1	Experiment 2	Experiment 3
GRE	$\{t_2,t_4,t_1(t_7)\}$ *Reduction = 62.5%*	$\{t_1,t_3,t_2(t_9),t_4(t_8)\}$ *Reduction = 33%*	$\{t_5(t_{11}),t_3,t_{10}(t_{12}),t_4(t_8)\}$ *Reduction = 50%*
GE	$\{t_3,t_1(t_7),t_4(t_6),t_2(t_5)\}$ *Reduction = 50%*	$\{t_1,t_3,t_2(t_9),t_4(t_8)\}$ *Reduction = 33%*	$\{t_{12},t_8,t_5(t_{11})\}$ *Reduction = 66%*
HGS	$\{t_3,t_1(t_7),t_4(t_6),t_2(t_5)\}$ *Reduction = 50%*	$\{t_1,t_4,t_2\}$ or $\{t_1,t_8,t_9\}$ *Reduction = 50%*	$\{t_5(t_{11}),t_3,t_1(t_{10},t_{12}),t_4(t_6,t_8)\}$ *Reduction = 50%*
tReductSA	$\{t_1(t_7),t_2,t_4\}$ *Reduction = 62.5%*	$\{t_1,t_2,t_4\}$ or $\{t_1,t_8,t_9\}$ or $\{t_1,t_9,t_8\}$ *Reduction = 50%*	$\{t_5(t_{11}),t_8,t_{12}\}$ or $\{(t_5(t_{11}),t_{10},t_4\}$ *Reduction = 66%*

Table 8. Benchmarking results for Part 2

	Experiment 4	Experiment 5	Experiment 6
GE	$\{t_4,t_{28},t_{12},t_5,t_3,t_2,t_6,t_9,$ $t_{17},t_{10},t_{11}\}$ $Reduction = 64\%$	$\{t_6,t_0,t_5,t_9,t_4,t_{10},t_{17},$ $t_2,t_3,t_{11},t_{15},t_{20}\}$ $Reduction = 61\%$	$\{t_4,t_5,t_{17},t_6,t_9,t_{16},t_{10}\}$ $Reduction = 77\%$
tReductSA	$\{t_7,t_{17},t_{12},t_3,t_{25},t_6,t_{30},t_{28},$ $t_{15},t_4,t_5,t_{24},t_{23}\}$ $Reduction = 58\%$	$\{t_7,t_{29},t_{11},t_3,t_{16},t_{20},t_0,$ $t_{10},t_9,t_6,t_8\}$ or $\{t_{29},t_{27},t_{18},t_{28},t_{20},t_{30},t_{10},$ $t_9,t_6,t_8,t_{24}\}$ $Reduction = 64\%$	$\{t_{16},t_9,t_{20},t_5,t_{15},t_{14},t_{17}\}$ or $\{t_{18},t_{10},t_5,t_8(t_2),$ $t_{14},t_4,t_{28}\}$ or $\{t_{16},t_{10}(t_{23})(t_{15})$ $,t_{20},t_5,t_{30},t_{14},t_{17}\}$ or $\{t_{18},t_9,t_{13},t_5,t_{15},t_4,t_{17}\}$ or $\{t_{18},t_{13},t_5,t_{15},t_4,t_{14},t_{28}\}$ or $\{t_4,t_5,t_{17},t_6,t_9,t_{16},t_{10}\}$ $Reduction = 77\%$

6 Concluding Remark

Summing up, as compared to other strategies, tReductSA is able to match most of the best results from other strategies. Furthermore, tReductSA appears to be superior as compared to other strategies in terms of the potential diversification of solutions. As part of future work, we are looking into integrating multi-objective optimizations as part of tReductSA in order to permit effective test prioritization as well as to cater for other coverage criteria in addition to requirement coverage.

Acknowledgements. This research work involves collaborative efforts between Universiti Malaysia Pahang and Umm Al-Qura University. The work is funded by grant number 11-INF1674-10 from the Long-Term National Plan for Science, Technology and Innovation (LT-NPSTI), the King Abdul-Aziz City for Science and Technology (KACST), Kingdom of Saudi Arabia. We thank the Innovation Office, UMP and the Science and Technology Unit at Umm Al-Qura University for their continued logistics support.

References

1. Chvatal, V.: A greedy heuristic for set covering problem. Math. Oper. Res. **4**, 233–235 (1979)
2. Harrold, M.J., Gupta, N., Soffa, M.L.: A methodology for controlling the size of a test suite. ACM Trans. Softw. Eng. Med. **2**, 270–285 (1993)
3. Chen, T.Y., Lau, M.F.: Heuristics towards the optimization of the size of a test suite. In: 3rd International Conference of Software Quality Management, Seville, pp. 415–424 (1995)

4. Chen, T.Y., Lau, M.F.: A new heuristic for test suite reduction. Inf. Softw. Technol. **40**, 347–354 (1998)
5. Shengwei, X., Huaikou, M., Honghao, G.: Test suite reduction using weighted set covering techniques. In: 13th ACIS International Conference on Software Engineering, Artificial Intelligence, Networking and Parallel & Distributed Computing, Kyoto, pp. 307–312 (2012)
6. Galeebathullah, B., Indumathi, C.P.: A novel approach for controlling a size of a test suite with simple technique. Int. J. Comput. Sci. Eng. **2**, 614–618 (2010)
7. Ng, P., Fung, R.Y.K., Kong, R.W.M.: Incremental model-based test suite reduction with formal concept analysis. J. Inf. Process. Syst. **6**, 197–208 (2010)
8. Tallam, S., Gupta, N.: A concept analysis inspired greedy algorithm for test suite minimization. In: 6th ACM SIGPLAN-SIGSOFT Workshop on Program Analysis for Software Tools and Engineering, Lisbon, Portugal (2005)
9. Yoo, S., Harman, M.: Regression testing minimization, selection and prioritization: a survey. Softw. Test. Verification Reliab. **22**, 67–120 (2012)
10. Kirkpatrick, S., Gelatt, C.D., Vecchi, M.P.: Optimization by simulated annealing. Science **220**, 671–680 (1983)
11. Eaarts, E., Korst, J.: Simulated Annealing and Boltzman Machines: A Stochastic Approach to Combinatorial Optimization and Neural Computing. Wiley, Chichester (1989)

Combining Hidden Markov Model and Case Based Reasoning for Time Series Forecasting

Azunda Zahari[✉] and Jafreezal Jaafar

Computer and Information Sciences, Universiti Teknologi Petronas,
Tronoh, Malaysia
azundaazlina@yahoo.com

Abstract. Hidden Markov Model is one of the most popular and broadly used for representation vastly structured series of data. This paper presents the application of the new approach of Hidden Markov Model and three ensemble nonlinear models to forecasting the foreign exchange rates. The proposed approach and other combination of computational intelligent techniques such as multi layer perceptron, support vector machine are compared with root mean squared error (RMSE) and Mean Absolute Error (MAE) as the performance measures. The results indicate that the new approach of Hidden Markov Model yield the best results consistently over all the currencies. and Case Based Reasoning based ensembles Based on the numerical experiments conducted, it is inferred that using the correct sophisticated ensemble methods in the computational intelligence paradigm can enhance the results obtained by the extent techniques to forecast foreign exchange rates. This suggests that the new approach of HMM is a powerful analytical instrument that is satisfactorily compared to using only the single model and other soft computing techniques for exchange rate predictions.

Keywords: Hidden Markov Model · Case based reasoning · Time series forecasting

1 Introduction

Forecasting time series has been one of the most challenging tasks due to non-linear in nature. Over the past few decades, HMM has been widely applied as a data-driven modeling approach in automatic speech recognition. HMMs applications are now being extended to many fields such as traffic congestion, dynamic system modeling and diagnosis [1], neurosciences [2], stock market [3–9], inflation analysis [10], safety messages [11] and exchange rate [12, 13] and etc.

Hidden Markov Model basically is a statistical model that has been proven useful in wide range applications domain. On the other hand their several limitations and mix results regarding their forecasting rule are creating vagueness about their use in real exchange rate trading environment. This scenario is promoted by the fact that the initialization of model parameters and inputs is difficult because of many factors that

© Springer International Publishing Switzerland 2015
H. Fujita and A. Selamat (Eds.): SoMeT 2014, CCIS 513, pp. 237–247, 2015.
DOI: 10.1007/978-3-319-17530-0_17

leads to diverse conclusions. According to [12, 13], HMM are unstable to be taken in as a trading tool on foreign exchange data with too many factors influencing the results. Time series forecasting has been dominated by linear statistical methods for several decades. Although linear models possess many advantages in application, the serious limitation relies on the inability to capture nonlinear relationships in the data that which are common in real world problems. Soft computing methods have been applied to this area like Artificial Neural Network (ANN), Support Vector Machine (SVM), and Genetic Algorithm (GA). ANN has its complicated structure and over-fitting on training data resulting in poor generalization ability [14]. Whilst SVM has additional hyper parameters (kernel parameter) that need to be adjusted [15] and it has learning methodology [30] GA has no 100 % guarantee that the weight of desired amount will be just as practitioner need [16].

Hybrid model has been proposed in several studies to overcome the limitation perform by a single model. Recently, tremendous studies in hybrid forecasting models have been developed that incorporate statistical model with ANN. A hybrid model of HMM and ANN has been proposed by Rafiul Hassan for forecasting stock market. However, the above-mentioned method showed that the primary weakness with ANNs is the inability to properly explain the models [4]. ANN has some limitations in learning the patterns because foreign exchange rates data has tremendous noise and complex dimensionality [17]. The main aim of this study is to introduce in exchange rate market a hybridization of Hidden Markov Model and Case Base Reasoning for supporting trading decision process.

The objectives of this research are; (1) to investigate the statistical and technical modeling issue in time series forecasting (2) to formulate and introduce a hybrid Hidden Markov Model and Case Based Reasoning in financial time series, (3) to introduce two pillar trading technique based on interpretable intelligent computing models and statistical foundation tool, (4) to introduce nominal trading frequency to improve the accuracy of the propose hybrid HMM-CBR decision trading system. Case-based reasoning works very similarly to the human logic of data handling. A data base of past experiences that may be useful to solve a particular type of query is kept. The difficulty in CBR is the design of a system that is capable of recalling past experiences, which would provide useful information when a new problem is introduced to the system. In CBR terminology, the event in which a solution to a former problem was found is referred to as a "case," and is stored in the system's "case base." For the purpose of CBR, each case should be recorded within the case base systematically and the useful information must be stored consistently through the entire case base, the chosen structure used being referred to as the "case representation" [18]. When a new problem is introduced to the CBR system, it should be represented in the same format as the stored cases, and then the process of deciding which of the past cases may be of use in finding a solution to this problem can begin. The main assumption underlying a CBR methodology is that similar problems will have similar solutions. It follows that the most useful cases in the case base will be those that are similar to the problem case [19].

This paper is to introduce a new approach of Hidden Markov Model which attempt to overcome some of the limitations from the literature. In particular the proposed method is to reduce the numbers of parameters while on the other hand it increases the forecasting ability of the model. The study used the well established technique of HMM in a new way to forecast EUR/USD currency pair. In this paper, the first step is to establish pattern from the past dataset that match with today's currency price behavior to develop forecasts for tomorrow's fluctuation. The proposed methodology is superior in its simplicity in comparison to the applications that have been already presented in the literature [1] and because it make use only on the opening price for entry trigger for each trading decision and forecast. This study benchmark MACD, William Percentage Range, naïve method in a forecasting and trading decision for EUR/USD. The exchange rates are examined from October 2010 to November 2013. Furthermore, this study introduce a two pillar trading strategy based on daily trading position and observe if it is function can enhance the trading efficiency of the proposed method. This study introduces a price range analysis using HMM that not only minimizes the error measurement of forecast techniques but also reduces trading time and increase their profitability. This is essential in forecasting application where statistical accuracy is not always produce consistent profit in the long run.

2 Formulation of the Proposed Model

In spite of the various time series models presented, the accuracy of time series forecasting currently is essential to many decision processes, and for this reason, never research into ways of improving the performance and the effectiveness of forecasting approach been given up. There are many researches in time series forecasting have been argued that predictive performance improves in combined models. In integrated models, the intend is to decrease the risk of using an inappropriate model by combining several models to reduce the risk of failure and achieve results that are more accurate. In general, this is done because the fundamental practice cannot easily be determined. The motivation for combining models comes from the hypothesis that either one cannot identify the true data generating process or that a single model may not be sufficient to identify all the characteristics of time series. In this paper, a novel hybrid model of Hidden Markov Model is proposed in order to yield more accurate results using the Case Based Reasoning approach.

2.1 Hidden Markov Model and Case Based Reasoning

In this section, the basic concepts and modelling approaches of the Hidden Markov Model (HMM) and Case Based Reasoning (CBR) models for time series forecasting are briefly reviewed.

2.2 The HMM Approach to Time Series Modeling

Transitions among the states are governed by a set of probabilities called *transition probabilities*. In a particular state an observation can be generated, according to the associated probability distribution.

HMM contains following elements:

(i) N is Number of hidden states
(ii) Q is Set of states $Q = \{1, 2, ..., N\}$
(iii) M is Number of symbols
(iv) V is Set of observation symbols $V = \{1, 2,...., M\}$
(v) A is State Transition Probability Matrix.

To work with HMM, the following three fundamental questions should be resolved.

1. Given the model $\lambda = (A, B, \pi)$ how do we compute $P(O| \lambda)$, the probability of occurrence of the observation sequence $O = O_1, O_2, ..., O_T$.
2. Given the observation sequence O and a model λ, how to choose a state sequence $q_1, q_2, ..., q_T$ that best explains the observations.
3. Given the observation sequence O and a space of models found by varying the model parameters A, B and π, how do we find the model that best explains the observed data.

Generally exchange rate data is published on daily basis giving exchange rate prices on opening $\{o_i\}$ and projection $\{p_i\}$ price in sliding window. Daily highest $\{h_i\}$ trading price of the exchange rate are also published. With the historical data the objective is to predict the next price range from the projection price from the opening price. Mathematically the problem can be expressed as follows:

$$\{c_{i+1}\} = \prod_{i=1}^{n} f(o_i, h_i, p_i) \tag{1}$$

where i defines the stage in model on daily basis. To get a finite state model let's take the historically published data of last two years. The data is divided into training and testing data. Before applying Hidden Markov Model the main thing is to choose number of states and observation symbols. Given an observation sequence and the set of hidden states, the objective is to learn the Transition probability matrix $\{A\}$ and the Observation probability matrix $\{B\}$, which are determined as follows:

$$\{A\} = \{a_{ij}\} \text{ s.t. } a_{ij} = p[q_{t+1} = s_j / q_t = s_i] \qquad i \leq 1, j \leq N \tag{2}$$

$$\{B\} = \{b_j(K)\} \text{ s.t. } b_j(k) = p[v_k = t / q_t = s_j] \quad 1 \leq j \leq N, 1 \leq k \leq M \tag{3}$$

Where q_t is the state at time t. Baum-Welch algorithm is used as a learning algorithm. The Baum-Welch algorithm is a generalized expectation-maximization algorithm. It can compute maximum likelihood estimates and posterior mode estimates for the parameters (transition and emission probabilities) of an HMM, when given only emissions as training data. Formally Baum-Welch algorithm finds

$$\lambda = \max p(O/\lambda) \tag{4}$$

that is, the HMM λ that maximizes the probability of the observation O.

The algorithm is applied sequentially as follows:

Calculate the forward probability and the backward probability for each HMM state. The forward probability is defined as $\alpha_i(t) = p(O_1 = o_1...O_t = o_t, Q_t = i| \lambda)$, which is the probability of seeing the partial sequence $o_1...o_t$ and ending up in state i at time t. We can efficiently calculate $\alpha_i(t)$ recursively as:

$$\alpha_i(t) = \pi_i b_i(O_1) \tag{5}$$

$$\alpha_j(t+1) = b_j(O_{t+1}) \sum_{i=1}^{N} \alpha_i(t).a_{ij} \tag{6}$$

The backward probability is defined as the probability of the ending partial sequence $O_{t+1}....O_T$ given that started at state i, at time t.

We can efficiently calculate $\beta_i(t)$ as:

$$\beta_i(T) = 1 \tag{7}$$

$$\beta_j(t) = \sum_{i=1}^{N} \beta_j(t+1) a_{ij} b_j(O_{t+1}) \tag{8}$$

Determine the frequency of the transition-emission pair values and dividing it by the probability of the entire string. This amounts to calculating expected count of the particular transition-emission pair. Each time a particular transition is found, the value of the quotient of the transition divided by the probability of the entire string goes up, and this value can then be made the new value of the transition. To predict the next day price range, Baum-Welch algorithm is used to find the similar patterns with the current day from the HMM data pattern. Assume that the likelihood value on day x is lcp_i. Now from the historical data set using the HMM those observation sequences are located which would produce the same or nearly same value of lcp_i. The HMM found the y_{th} day's observation sequences which would produce the same likelihood value lcp_i. Now the price difference of the variable of interest on day 'y' and 'y + 1' is calculated

$$cp_{i+1} = (p_{y+1} - p_y) + cp_i \tag{9}$$

Where p_y = close price of matched data pattern
p_{y+1} = next day close price of matched data pattern
cp_i = close price of today's data.

The HMM is trained to calculate the likelihood values of price range from the open price (Fig. 1) between two data sequences, in which past day price range behaviour is first located which is almost similar to that of the current day. The range calculated produces the likelihood values for the current day, and then observation sequences are located which give nearly equal values which are formed from the past data sets.

Then price difference of that day's price and next to that day's price are taken and hence next day's price range is forecasted by adding the above difference to the current day's opening price.

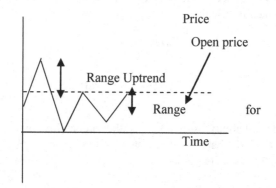

Fig. 1. Pips range of the price projection from the open price

Training Hidden Markov Models
In this section, HMM based tool is developed for time series forecasting, based on historical records of daily opening price utilization. It chooses to use a Hidden Markov Model (HMM) with just two states, P (Profit) and L (Loss).

In this study, 3 input features is considered for exchange rate price range calculation – that is the opening, high and low of the projection price of the day. Projection price that produce range from the daily open price is the new approach of this study compares to previous study that concern more on the closing price of the day. The projection price is important to minimize the risk to be taken in each trading decision. To predict the next day price range, the well known Baum-Welch algorithm is used to find the similar patterns with the current day from the HMM.

The first step in training the parameters of an HMM is to see what states and transitions the model thinks are likely on each trading day. Those likely states and transitions can be used to reestimate the probabilities using the "forward-backward" or Baum-Welch algorithm, increasing the likelihood of the training data.

2.3   Case Based Reasoning

Case based reasoning method defer the decision of how to classify new data, till they actually encounter a new instance. The method deduce the class of the new instance and totally ignoring the instances, which are vastly different from the new instance. While instance based methods represent instances as real valued points in n-dimensional space, case-based reasoning methods use more rich symbolic representations of instances. Correspondingly, the methods used to retrieve similar instances, is more elaborate compared to instance-based learning.

The study adopt Weka stands for Waikato Environment for Knowledge Analysis. It is a software developed by the Univeristy of Waikato in New Zealand. Weka provides implementation of machine learning algorithm. The software is developed in Java, thus enabling porting and compatibility with various platforms.

The IBk Algorithm

Ibk is an implementation of the k-nearest neighbors classifier in Weka. By default, it uses just one nearest neighbor (k = 1), but the number can be specified manually with –K or determined automatically using leave-one-ot cross-validation. The –X option instructs Ibk to use cross-validation to determine the best value of k between 1 and a number given by –K. If more than one neighbor is selected, the predictions of the neighbors can be weighted according to their distance to the test instance, and two different formulas are implemented for deriving the weight from the distance (–D and –F). The time taken to classify a test instance with a nearest-neighbor classifier increases linearly with the number of training instances. Consequently it is sometimes necessary to restrict the number training instances that are kept in the classifier, which is done by setting the window size option.

The MBT Meta Trader sliding window has been used to capture the complete information of price volatility in hourly basis. The output of the Meta Trader sliding window is a file in ARFF format, listing all the instances created, the features chosen and list of values, which each feature can take. The flat file in ARFF format, is provided as input to Weka software. The study apply the weka.classifiers.Ibk, which is an implementation of instance-based learning algorithm, the k-nearest neighbor algorithm, and the output of Weka, the case-based learner, together form the components of the machine learning system.

The proposed CBR-HMM and is a combination of daily opening price range behavior using dynamic time windows, Case based reasoning, and Hidden Markov Model for exchange rate trading prediction. The main purpose of this application is to predict the range of price turning points. A new approach of HMM is applied as a model to search the similar data pattern to assist CBR in validation process to fine tune in the trading decision. The opening price range pattern can easily be found using trading platform sliding window to search the most similar scenario from the previous exchange rate data for particular pair and predict the exchange rate price fluctuation of the next day according to the adaptation of similar patterns.

Nearest-neighbor retrieval is a simple approach that computes the similarity between stored cases and new input case based on weight features. A typical evaluation function is used to compute nearest-neighbor matching [20] as shown in Figure:

Nearest-neighbor evaluation functions as following:

$$similarity(Case_I, Case_R) = \frac{\sum_{i=1}^{n} w_i \times sim\left(f_i^I, f_i^R\right)}{\sum_{i=1}^{n} w_i}$$

Where w_i is the importance weight of a feature, *sim* is the similarity function of features, and f_i^I and f_i^R are the values for feature i in the input and retrieved cases respectively.

To determine the accuracy of the model the root mean square error and Mean Absolute Error (MAE) are calculated. To determine the accuracy of the model the root mean square error is calculated. The Root Mean Square Error (RMSE) (also called the root mean square deviation, RMSD) is a frequently used measure of the difference between values predicted by a model and the values actually observed from the environment that is being modelled. These individual differences are also called residuals, and the RMSE serves to aggregate them into a single measure of predictive power.

$$MAE = \left[\frac{1}{m} \sum_{t=1}^{m} |x_t - \hat{x}_t| \right]$$

The RMSE of a model prediction with respect to the estimated variable X_{model} is defined as the square root of the mean squared error:

$$RMSE = \sqrt{\frac{\sum_{i=1}^{n} \left(X_{obs,i} - X_{model,i} \right)^2}{n}}$$

where X_{obs} is observed values and X_{model} is modelled values at time/place i.

The result indicate the system is more accurate (Table 3) and provide good estimation for short term foreign exchange market.

3 Results

The application of the proposed approach is applied for three major pairs foreign exchange rate currencies – EUR-USD, GBP/USD, and USD/CHF. In order to train the proposed model, the dataset is divided into two sets, one training set (3032 observations) and one test set (2635 observations) begin October 2010 until August 2014. The transitions that best explain of profit gain during trading period are plotted in Fig. 2, which shows positive and negative accumulation respectively. The Single HMM model, HMM combined with neural network, HMM with support vector machine, and the proposed model have been applied to these pairs. Two performance indicators such as Mean Absolute Error (MAE) and Root Mean Squared Error (RMSE) are employed in order to evaluate the performance of the proposed model. Table 1 depicts the performance comparison of the proposed model for overall test set. Table 2, Table 3 and Table 4 show the performance of the proposed model outperform the benchmark models based on 1 month, 6 months, and 12 months trading time period respectively.

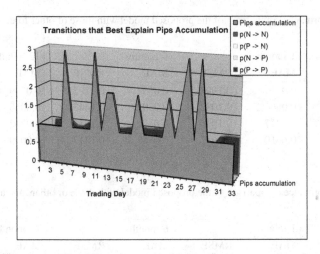

Fig. 2. Positive (P) and Negative (N) transitions of pips accumulation for overall trading period

Table 1. Comparison of the performance of the proposed methodology

Model	MAE	RMSE
HMM	0.1528	0.2764
HMM-ANN	0.0537	0.1261
HMM-SVM	0.4020	0.2596
Proposed model	0.0524	0.0948

Table 2. Performance comparison of the proposed model with those of other forecasting models (EUR/USD)

Model	1 month		6 months		12 months	
	MAE	RMSE	MAE	RMSE	MAE	RMSE
HMM	0.1244	0.2494	0.1107	0.2353	0.1013	0.1638
HMM-ANN	0.1046	0.2682	0.0619	0.1834	0.0220	0.1010
HMM-SVM	0.1239	0.2527	0.1066	0.2296	0.1042	0.2240
HMM-CBR	0.1061	0.2334	0.0616	0.1929	0.0201	0.1009

4 Discussion

The application of quantitative methods for forecasting and assisting investment decision making has become more vital in industry practices than ever before. Time series forecasting is one of the most important quantitative models that has received substantial amount of attention in the literature. Hidden Markov Model have shown to be an effective and powerful for pattern recognition, classification, clustering, and

Table 3. Performance comparison of the proposed model with those of other forecasting models (GBP/USD)

Model	1 month		6 months		12 months	
	MAE	RMSE	MAE	RMSE	MAE	RMSE
HMM	0.0799	0.1998	0.0637	0.1795	0.0539	0.1897
HMM-ANN	0.0661	0.2092	0.0391	0.1443	0.0068	0.0453
HMM-SVM	0.0777	0.1995	0.0772	0.1952	0.0742	0.1902
HMM-CBR	0.6610	0.2082	0.0368	0.1417	0.0029	0.0322

Table 4. Performance comparison of the proposed model with those of other forecasting models (USD/CHF)

Model	1 month		6 months		12 months	
	MAE	RMSE	MAE	RMSE	MAE	RMSE
HMM	0.0713	0.1889	0.0666	0.1825	0.0563	0.1627
HMM-ANN	0.0285	0.1166	0.0206	0.0999	0.0379	0.1398
HMM-SVM	0.0684	0.1833	0.0642	0.1776	0.0646	0.1780
HMM-CBR	0.0248	0.1030	0.0161	0.0917	0.0331	0.1316

especially for dynamic system modeling with a high degree of accuracy. However, the performance of using a single model is not always satisfactory. Theoretical as well practical indication in the literature suggest that by using different models or models that disagree each other strongly, the hybrid model will have minor generalization variance or error. Furthermore, because of the potential unbalanced or changing patterns in the data, using the hybrid method can decrease the model uncertainty, which characteristically occurred is statistical inference and time series forecasting.

In this paper, the Hidden Markov Model and Case Based Reasoning are applied to propose a new hybrid method for improving the performance of the single Hidden Markov Model to time series forecasting. Empirical results with three major pairs exchange rate currencies indicate that the proposed model can be an effective way in order to yield more accurate model than conventional Hidden Markov Model. As a result, it can be used as a proper unconventional for Hidden Markov Model, especially when higher forecasting accuracy is needed.

References

1. Badge, J.: Forecasting of indian stock market by effective macro- economic factors and stochastic model. J. Stat. Econom. Methods 1(2), 39–51 (2012)
2. Rabiner, L.R.: A tutorial on hidden markov models and selected applications in speech recognition. Proc. IEEE **77**, 257–286 (1989). Magazine, p. 4–16 (1986)
3. Qi, Y., Ishak, A.: Hidden Markov Model for short term prediction of traffic conditions on freeways. Transp. Res. Rec. J. **43**(1), 95–111 (2014)

4. Al-ani, T.: Hidden Markov Models in dynamic system modelling and diagnosis. In: Dymarski, P. (ed.) Hidden Markov Models Theory and Applications, pp. 27–50. In Tech, Croatia (2011)
5. Florian, B. et al.: Hidden Markov Models in neurosciences. In: Dymarski, P. (ed.) Hidden Markov Models, Theory and Applications, p. 169. In Tech, Croatia (2011)
6. Hassan, M.R., Nath, B.: Stock market forecasting using hidden markov model: a new approach. In: Proceedings of the 2005 5th International Conference on Intelligent Systems Design and Applications (ISDA 2005)
7. Hassan, M.R.: A combination of hidden markov model and fuzzy model for stock market forecasting. J. Neurocomput. **72**, 3439–3446 (2009)
8. Badge, J.: Future state prediction of stock market using hidden markov model. J. Stat. Syst. **5**(1), 73–80 (2010)
9. Ahani, E., Abbas, O.: A sequential monte carlo approach for online stock market prediction using hidden markov model. J. Mod. Math. Stat. **4**, 73–77 (2010)
10. Gupta, A., Dhingra, B.: Stock market prediction using Hidden Markov Models (2012)
11. Park, S.-H., Lee, J.H., Lee, H.-C.: Trend forecasting of financial time series using PIPs detection and continuos HMM. Intell. Data Anal. **15**, 779–799 (2011)
12. El-Yaniv, R., Pidan, D.: Selective of financial trends with Hidden Markov Models (2011)
13. Hossain, B., Ahmed, M., Rabbi, MdF: A novel approach for inflation analysis using hidden markov model. IJCSI Int. J. Comput. Sci. Issues **9**(2), 619 (2012)
14. Granger, C.W.J., Terasvirta, T.: Modelling Nonlinear Economic Relationships. Oxford University Press, Oxford (1993)
15. Aamodt, A., Plaza, E.: CBR: foundational issues, methodological variations and system approaches. AI Commun. **7**(1), 39–59 (1994)
16. Hastie, T., Tibshirani, R., Fiedman, J.: The Elements of Statistical Learning: Data Mining, Inference, and Prediction, 2nd edn. Springer, New York (2008)
17. Brahmi, I.H., Djahel, S., Ghamri-Doudane, Y.: A Hidden Markov Model based Scheme for Efficient and Fast Dissemination of Safety Messages in VANETs, version 1 (2013)
18. Yaser, S., Atiya, A.: Introduction to financial forecasting. Appl. Intell. **6**, 205–213 (1996)
19. Bekaert, G., Wu, G.: Assymetry volatility and risk in equity market. Rev. Financ. Stud. **13**(1), 1–42 (2000)
20. Hwang, H.B., Ang, H.T.: A simple neural network for ARMA (p,q) time series, OMEGA. Int J. Manag. Sci. **29**, 319–333 (2002)

Software Quality and Assessment for Business Enterprise

High Performance Nanotechnology Software (HPNS) for Parameter Characterization of Nanowire Fabrication and Nanochip System

Norma Alias[1]([⊠]), Noriza Satam[1], Mohd Shahizan Othman[2],
Che Rahim Che Teh[1], Maizatul Nadirah Mustaffa[1],
and Hafizah Farhah Saipol[1]

[1] Ibnu Sina Institute, Faculty of Science, Universiti Teknologi Malaysia,
UTM, 81310 Johor Bahru, Johor, Malaysia
norma@ibnusina.utm.my, crahim@utm.my,
nadirah.mustaffa@yahoo.com, msc.hafizah@gmail.com
[2] Faculty of Computer Science and Information Systems,
Universiti Teknologi Malaysia, UTM, 81310 Johor Bahru, Johor, Malaysia
shahizan@utm.my

Abstract. This paper presents the high performance nanotechnology software (HPNS) to enable scientific researchers for predicting, visualizing and observing the temperature behavior and some parameters characteristics of nanochip system and nanowire fabrication. The analysis of scientific algorithms and high performance computing are searchable through a user friendly web-based system. This software will involve some mathematical modeling, numerical simulations and high performance computing technology to improve the accuracy of prediction, visualization quality and parallel performance indicators. The parameters involve on the thermal control process of nanowire fabrication are focuses on pressure, density, space, time control. The identification of the parameters influences the process of nanowire fabrication. The next focused are parameters characteristics of nanochip system. The parameters that involve are temperature, electromagnetic wave, space, time and other properties impact of the development of multilayer nanochip system. The implementations of parallel algorithms for solving the Partial Differential Equation of heat transfer and wave motion problems are based on large sparse parabolic and elliptic types. The discretization technique to obtain a large sparse linear system of equations is based on Finite Difference Method. The HPNS will support the supercomputing of numerical simulations and its repository using distributed memory architecture. The performance indicators will investigate the parallel programs using Parallel Virtual Machine (PVM) and C language on Linux operating system in terms of run time, accuracy, convergence, errors, speedup, efficiency and effectiveness. As a conclusion, HPNS will be an alternative software system to support huge computational complexity of the multilayer nanochip system and nanowire fabrication model.

Keywords: Nanoscale · Partial differential equation · High performance computing software · Temperature behavior · Electromagnetic wave motion · Visualization

© Springer International Publishing Switzerland 2015
H. Fujita and A. Selamat (Eds.): SoMeT 2014, CCIS 513, pp. 251–268, 2015.
DOI: 10.1007/978-3-319-17530-0_18

1 Introduction

In nanotechnology, the expansion of nanocomponent with new features and functionality involve nanoscale particles, large sparse and complex models, fine granularity computation and high computational computing platform. It is reasonable to explore a new nanomaterial, parameter characterization and identification of the fabrication processes to develop a nanodevice and to grow the nanowire. Based on these limitations, this paper proposes a mathematical modelling and numerical simulation software to predict and visualize some parameter characterization of nanoscale multilayer full chip system and nanowire fabrication.

Two case studies have been selected for investigating the numerical analysis and performance indicators of high performance computing software (HPCS). The first case study is to visualize the temperature behavior for the nanoscale multilayer full chip system and the second is to predict the electromagnetic wave motion of silicon nanowire fabrication using a large scale of partial differential equation models (PDEs) [1–3]. In the length scale of approximately 1–100 nanometer range, modeling and simulation of parabolic and elliptic types are the important solver for the temperature behavior, electromagnetic wave motion and density profile at the molecular scale of nanochip assemble and silicon nanowire (SiNWs) fabrication.

Based on the mathematical simulation and numerical results [2, 3] of non-uniformly heating problem, heat flow, a continuous cross section of the electromagnetic field and changes parameter characterization will be stored via a database library called high performance nanotechnology software (HPNS). HPNS is communication software of parallel programming model, which is supported by PVM as a combination set of software tools and libraries that emulates a flexible, general-purpose, heterogeneous concurrent computing framework in interconnected computers of various architectures. The efficient HPNS is used to understand and control the thermal process of the problems. HPNS will be able to visualize the temperature profile throughout heating process and display an animation of the output obtained in 3-D. Consequently, the researcher will be able to reuse the results and analyze the scientific algorithm [1] for future research.

2 Nanoscale

Nanoscaledenotes a factor of 10^{-9} m and a nanoparticle covers a range between 100 and 2500 nanometers. Meanwhile, an ultra-fine particle size is between 1 and 100 nanometers. Similar to ultra-fine particles, nano-cell size is between 1 and 100 nanometer. The HPNS is a leading to the collection of parallel numerical library for dynamic simulation with high-speed solutions of huge computational cost to support the temperature behavior of multilayer nanochip and chemical vapor decomposition (CVD)-grown nanowire modeling [7, 11].

In order to achieve HPNS implementation in parallel, suitable software and hardware are provided as a platform to support the simultaneous execution on heterogeneous distributed-shared memory cluster systems. All the numerical methods and parallel programming in visualizing and observing the changing parameters of multilayer nanochip assemble and nanowires fabrication models are kept as a web repository in HPNS development. The software is based on open source technology, run on Linux operating system using distributed memory architecture (DMA). The parallel algorithms are programmed in C language while the communication software tools involve the use of PVM, Perl-CGI, HTML, PHP, XML, UML, Java and MySQL database. The parallel performance indicators are analyzed in terms of efficiency, granularity, distributional, robustness, adaptability and stability of the algorithms [4].

2.1 Silicon Nanowire Fabrication

Innanotechnology research, an extremely thin wire with a diameter of nanometer or 10^{-9} m scale is known as nanowire. The diameter of the nanowire is in the nanoscale range from a single atom to a few hundred of nanometers. There are many types of semiconductor nanomaterials for nanowire fabrication such as Si, GaN, GaAs, In2O3, and ZnO. Semiconductor nanowire can be used as electronic elements and semiconductor quantum to assemble the nanodevice product.

The properties of CVD-grown nanowires are highly sensitive to the heat transfer, the diffusion limit of growth and the integrated with molecular dynamics simulation. Higher temperatures are significant to the radial over growth while lower temperatures are significant to electromagnetic field motion. The impact of thermal, energy transport and conversion are presented by Hippalgaonkar, K., et al. [9]. They have suggested the fabrication technique can also be used for thermal transport investigation in a wide-range of low-dimensional structures. Garnett, E.C., et al. [10] has investigated the large-scale chemical synthesis of bottom-up fabrication with the localized nature of low-thermal-budget substrates such as plastics and polymer solar cells. This work opens new avenues to control light, heat and mass transport at the nanoscale.

The challenging issue is to optimize the process control for several parameters identification during nanowire growth at temperature range 363 to 230°C experimentally. As an impact the feature of nanoscale measurement is a gap to retrieve data information of thermal process from the CVD equipment. Based on these limitations, this paper proposes SiNWs nanowire fabrication process model by governing the integration of PDE to predict the independent and dependent parameter characterization such as concentration, pressure, density, temperature and electromagnetic wave. Numerical simulation of PDEs with parabolic and elliptic types will investigate the temperature behavior, steady-state respect to nanowire size. The visualization of the computational molecule to discrete two and three dimensional PDEs equations can be shown in Fig. 1.

2.2 Nanoscale Multilayer Multichip System

The problem of full nanochip production is the integrating of hybrid nanomaterials process and assembling the multilayer fast but yet accurate. Based on these limitations, this paper proposes a mathematical modelling of PDEs with elliptic type to investigate the thermal process control of nanoscale multilayer full chip assembles respect to time

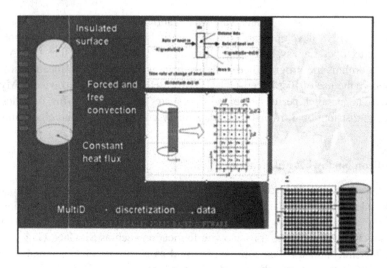

Fig. 1. FDM discretization of 2D and 3D SiNWs nanowire during fabrication processes.

and space. The HPC elliptic PDE solver is the motivation to develop HPNS for high speed computation, accurate prediction and visualization. Figure 2 shows the structure of the multilayer full chip system.

The multilayer full chip structure is based on the 3D integrated circuit [5] involves the layers of devices stacked onto each other. This architecture can potentially enhance the nanochip performance and its functionality, despite of reducing the chip size and distance between devices on a chip [6].

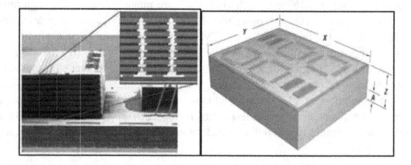

Fig. 2. The structure of multilayer full chip design.

However, the thermal management issues arise with the increasing of packaging densities as well as a rapid increase of power consumed to the circuit. Thermal management issues concern on maintaining very large-scale integration (VLSI) chip performance and reliability [6]. Figure 3 below is a simplified model of the multi-layered chip structure. Each layer have different initial value such as $z_1 = 0$, $z_2 = -d_1$, $z_3 = -d_{N-1}$ and $z_4 = -d_N$. Heat spreader and heat sink are include in the packaging structure.

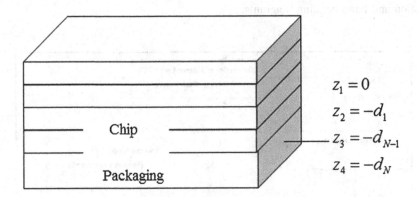

$$z_1 = 0$$
$$z_2 = -d_1$$
$$z_3 = -d_{N-1}$$
$$z_4 = -d_N$$

Fig. 3. Simplified model of multi-layered chip structure

3 PDEs Modelling and Discretization

The heat equation is given as

$$\frac{\partial U}{\partial T} = \kappa \frac{\partial^2 U}{\partial X^2} \tag{1}$$

where κ is a constant. The initial and boundary conditions are given as

$$u(x,t) = g(x,t) \text{ for } x \in \partial\Omega, \ t > 0$$
$$u(x,0) = (x) \text{ for } x \in \Omega, \tag{2}$$

where $u_{xx} = f(u_x, u_y, u, x, y)$ holds in Ω.

The mathematical modeling to present the electromagnetic wave motion of nano-wire fabrication is based on elliptic equation with Poisson type. The elliptic-Poisson equation is given as the following:

$$\alpha^2 u_{xx} = f(x,t), \quad 0 < x < L, \quad t > 0 \tag{3}$$

with initial and boundary conditions are given as

$$u(x,0) = u_0(x), \quad u_t(x,0) = u_1(x), \quad 0 < x < L \tag{4}$$

$$u(0,t) = g_1(t), \quad u(L,t) = g_2(t), \quad t \geq 0 \tag{5}$$

where $u(x,t)$ is displacement at position x and time t; α is wave coefficient and u_0, u_1, g_1, g_2 are initial and boundary functions.

The electromagnetic field of nanowire fabrication has obtained using the integrated among 1D Schrodinger, 2D Poisson and Boltzmann equations as shown in Fig. 4. The sequences of the integrated Schrodinger-Poisson modelling is used to simulate the electronic energy, density behavior, wave and potential functions, wave motion equation and band-bending diagrams.

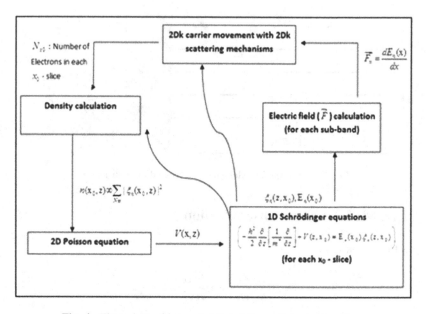

Fig. 4. Flow chart of integrated Schrödinger-Poisson algorithm

4 Numerical Simulation of FDM

Numerical methods are used to solve the large sparse linear systems of FDM discretization. The parallel algorithms of some numerical methods such as Alternating Group Explicit (AGE) and Red Black Gauss Seidel (RBGS) have used to simulate the multidimensional parabolic and elliptic equations [11, 12]. The huge computational complexity and communication cost of numerical simulation of HPNS is supported by HPC platform involving heterogeneous CPUs architectures with the Linux environment, connected with LAN and using message-passing libraries, PVM and MPI.

4.1 Alternating Group Explicit (AGE) Method

AGE is an expansion of Alternating Direction Implicit (ADI) method. It involves a fractional splitting strategy for a tridiagonal linear system of equation [7]. A system linear of equation is given by $Au = f$. Matrix is split into two blocks of matrices, G_1 and G_2 where G_1 and G_2 fulfill the equation $(G_1 + G_2)u = f$.

The formula of AGE is given by

1. At $\left(k + \frac{1}{2}\right)$ time step; $(G_1 + rI)u^{(k+1/2)} = (rI - G_2)u^{(k)} + f$

2. At $(k + 1)$ time step; $(G_2 + rI)u^{(k+1)} = (rI - G_1)u^{(k+1/2)} + f, k \geq 0$.

Four points are needed to compute the new value. AGE method is the most suitable method for parallel distributed computing system as it involves minimum communication and low computational complexity.

4.2 Red Black Gauss Seidel (RBGS) Method

RBGS method contains two subdomains, Ω^R and Ω^B. The loop starts by computing all the odd points (red). Once the calculation finishes the even points (black) computes. The black points are depending on the new value obtained from the red points.

- The grid calculation at Ω^R

$$M_i^{(k+1)} = \left(b_i - \sum_{j>i} a_{ij}M_j^{(k)} - \sum_{j<i} a_{ij}M_j^{(k+1)} \right) \Big/ a_{ii}, \quad i = 1, 3, 5, \ldots, m-1.$$

- The grid calculation at Ω^B

$$M_i^{(k+1)} = \left(b_i - \sum_{j>i} a_{ij}M_j^{(k)} - \sum_{j<i} a_{ij}M_j^{(k+1)} \right) \Big/ a_{ii}, \quad i = 2, 4, 6, \ldots, m.$$

5 Parallel Algorithm

Parallel computing involves teamwork between processors to solve a number of tasks. Thus, the communication and synchronizing the task from separate processes can be done by utilizing the message sending model. The large sparse of solution domain has divided into smaller subdomain for parallelization process. The parallel algorithms are responsible in interfacing with the communication network by linking a number of processors together via message-passing interface. In this paper, SIMD programming model has been implemented on multiple processors in order to achieve high speedup and efficient computational performance of HPNS. Furthermore, connecting a large number of processors into HPC system overcomes the saturation point of higher than the fastest serial computers as long as this power can be translated into high computation rates for actual application. This paper focuses on the PVM to implement the parallel algorithms based on the performance evaluation of PVM compared to the other communication software [11].

5.1   Domain Decomposition Technique

Domain decomposition technique is allowed to divide solution domain of PDEs into a number of subdomain and to minimize the communication as shown in Fig. 5 below. The data structure has to be decomposed where given set of ranges assigned to particular processors must be physically sent to their neighbour. The result must be sent back to whichever processors responsible for coordinating the final result. In this technique, parallel computing executes the same task on multiple processors simultaneously to optimize the ratio of computational complexity and communication cost. The communication structure among subdomain can be visualized as the following:

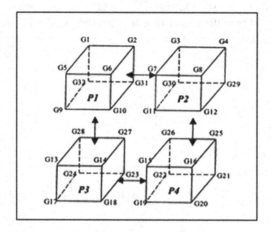

Fig. 5. Domain decomposition techniques within 4 subdomains

5.2   Software Development and Implementation

The repository of HPNS contains the dynamic simulation with a high-speed solution of the nanoscale computing for some parameter characteristics of nanoscale multilayer full chip system and nanowire fabrication. The solution will display the graphic animation in 3D visualization, monitor and observe the temperature profile and electromagnetic wave accurately. This modelling process will improve product quality, product design as well as reduces product development cycle, prototyping and manufacturing costs. There are seven phases for the development of HPNS. The first phase is a data collection from nanotechnology equipment for nanowire fabrication and nanochip assembles. The second phase is converted from analogue to the digital data set. The third phase is obtaining the PDEs model, its discretization and parallel algorithm using the digital data set as initial and boundary conditions. The fourth and fifth phases are the implementation of parallel programming on an HPC platform based on single interaction-multiple data stream (SIMD) model and domain decomposition technique. Figure 6 below is a data structure for parallel programs. The data structure has four steps: (1) partition the problem into smaller independent task, (2) Identify communication requirements between tasks, (3) Agglomerate smaller tasks into larger tasks and (4) Map tasks to actual processors.

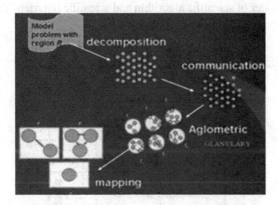

Fig. 6. Data structure for parallel programs

In first phase of HPNS system development, the data mining of temperature profiles is converted from analog to digital data signal by using the Analogue Digital Converter (ADC) to enhance the interpretation of the thermal process control. Next, the PDEs are applied to enhance the monitoring, observing and visualizing the temperature graph base on multidimensional parameter characterization. The last phase is the development of user friendly web based support. The flow chart of the complete embedded system of the nanotechnology characterization is shown in Fig. 7.

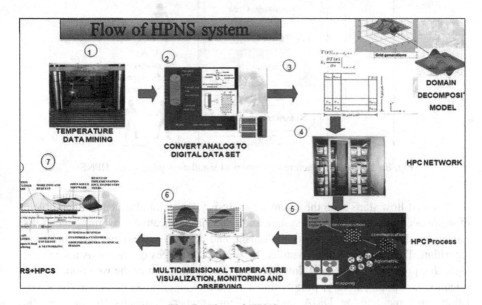

Fig. 7. Flow of HPNS system.

Design Architecture of HPNS. The architecture of the numerical simulation in HPNS consists of two processes; scientific computing analysis and web portal for numerical library. This numerical simulation is handled by the users of the HPNS system consists of consumers, provider of scientific algorithm and scientific librarian. The web portal of the scientific computing library is shown in the Fig. 8.

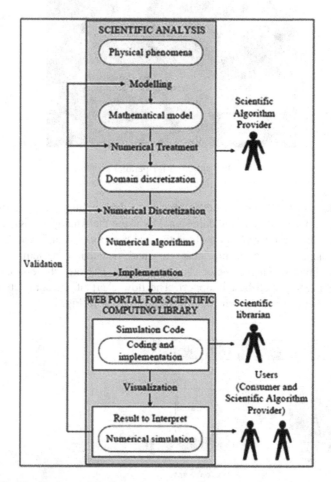

Fig. 8. Design architecture of numerical simulation process for HPNS

The first flow starts with the scientific analysis process for abstracting the problem of nanoscale multilayer full chip system and nanowire fabrication, governing the PDEs modeling, discretizing the solution domain and lastly is obtaining the numerical algorithm. This process will be handled by scientific sciences or known as a scientific algorithm provider. The second flow involves the development of the web portal of the scientific computing library, prototyping the parallel algorithms, obtaining the simulation, implementing on DMA and visualizing numerical results for the specific parameter characterization. The scientific librarian will be in charge as a system administrator to simulate the coding. The scientific algorithm provider also can be one of the HPNS users. The validation of HPNS is based on the comparison between numerical analysis, parallel performance indicators and experimental results of nanoscale case studies.

Architecture of Numerical Simulation in HPNS. The architecture of numerical simulation in HPNS is shown in Fig. 9. The users have private access to access the respiratory of HPNS.

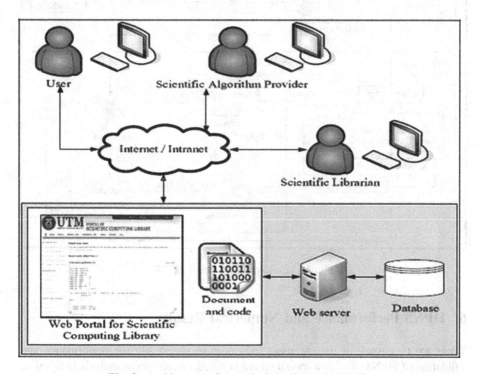

Fig. 9. Architecture of numerical simulation in HPNS.

The conceptual model and use case diagram are drawn to explain more about the HPNS process. The conceptual diagram of HPNS in Fig. 10 explains the process starts with the interaction among the users, scientific algorithm provider and user interface in three different modules. There are 'Authoring, Publishing and Supporting' modules. According to the conceptual diagram, there are several levels to access the HPNS such as dissimilar access to allow the common users browse the code, view tutorials and explore the code. Meanwhile, the approval status for contributing the code and publishing the approved code are done by the scientific librarian.

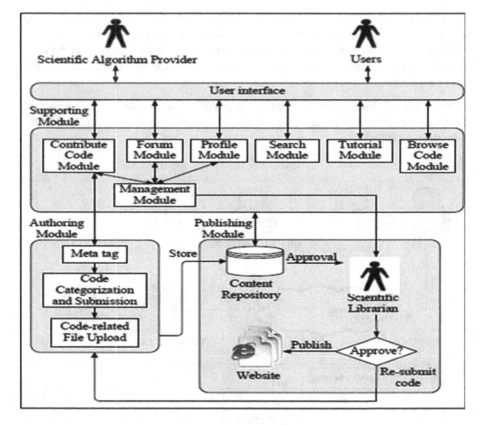

Fig. 10. Conceptual Model of HPNS.

6   HPNS Performance and Numerical Results

There are two types of measurement indicators to investigate the performance and validation of HPNS. The first measurement is based on numerical analysis in terms of run time, accuracy, convergence rate and mean error. The second is based on parallel performance indicators such as speedup, efficiency, effectiveness and temporal performance. HPNS is available to present the grid data set of temperature distribution and electromagnetic motion of nanoscale multilayer nanochip as shown in Tables 1 and 2. The changes parameter characterization of the PDEs model will propose the specific visualization, monitoring and future prediction for large scale of the solution domain. Figure 11 shows the temperature behavior is lower at the corners and higher at the center while in Fig. 12 the temperature is lower at the boundary and higher at the center.

We develop the algorithm introduced by Zhan and Sapatnekar [8] using C language on Linux platform. The development of the algorithm in C language makes it possible for future advancement of the algorithm in DMA environment. HPC will reduce the visualizing process complexity where the task is distributed to several processors and produce results in less time compared to running the code on a single processor. In addition, using Linux as an operating system platform will ensure the low-cost implementation since it is from an open source environment where no licensing procedure required.

Table 1. Electromagnetic wave motion of grid data set respect to x- and y- axis

x/y	0	1	2	3	4	5	6	7	8	9
0	201.95	203.71	205.11	206.00	206.31	206.00	205.11	203.71	201.95	200.00
1	201.76	203.35	204.61	205.42	205.70	205.42	204.61	203.35	201.76	200.00
2	201.40	202.66	203.66	204.30	204.52	204.30	203.66	202.66	201.40	200.00
3	200.90	201.71	202.35	202.76	202.90	202.76	202.35	201.71	200.90	200.00
4	200.31	200.59	200.81	200.95	201.00	200.95	200.81	200.59	200.31	200.00
5	199.69	199.41	199.19	199.05	199.00	199.05	199.19	199.41	199.69	200.00
6	199.10	198.29	197.65	197.24	197.10	197.24	197.65	198.29	199.10	200.00
7	198.60	197.34	196.34	195.70	195.48	195.70	196.34	197.34	198.60	200.00
8	198.24	196.65	195.39	194.58	194.30	194.58	195.39	196.65	198.24	200.00
9	198.05	196.29	194.89	194.00	193.69	194.00	194.89	196.29	198.05	200.00

Table 2. Temperature distribution of grid set respect to x- and y- axis

x/y	0	1	2	3	4	5	6	7	8	9
0	28.00	28.00	28.00	28.00	28.00	28.00	28.00	28.00	28.00	28.00
1	28.00	133.48	181.42	196.61	204.82	203.60	202.44	195.48	179.93	142.96
2	28.00	180.60	248.17	281.48	286.85	290.82	285.59	276.13	250.61	194.51
3	28.00	194.60	279.80	309.06	324.17	322.73	320.49	307.88	279.03	214.80
4	28.00	201.61	283.24	321.92	330.37	334.29	329.42	318.00	287.64	221.29
5	28.00	199.41	285.48	318.24	331.79	332.58	330.04	318.28	288.54	222.04
6	28.00	197.66	279.03	314.17	324.64	327.52	324.51	313.88	284.92	219.70
7	28.00	190.65	269.08	300.50	311.59	313.68	311.56	301.69	274.67	212.19
8	28.00	175.63	244.03	271.69	280.69	282.84	281.02	272.82	249.07	193.42
9	28.00	139.87	189.55	208.99	215.46	216.87	215.71	209.66	192.36	150.17

Based on the computational and communication ratio in Tables 3 and 4, the parallel AGE method is considered as the alternative method for solving elliptic and parabolic problems. AGE method is a superior method and gives significance parallel performance compared to RBGS method. The iterative, explicit and granularity features of AGE and RBGS methods have produced high parallel performance results. The formula of parallel performance indicators is presented in Table 5.

Figure 13 shows the time execution is decreasing with respect to the increasing number of processors. The effectiveness increases as the matrix size increases. Table 6 shows the numerical analysis for 3D semiconductor nanowire for different size of matrices.

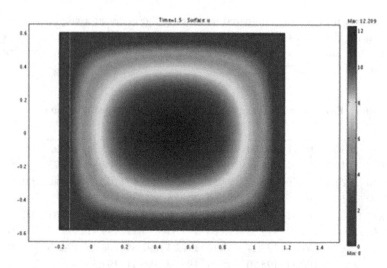

Fig. 11. The 2D visualization of the temperature behavior using PDEs-parabolic equation

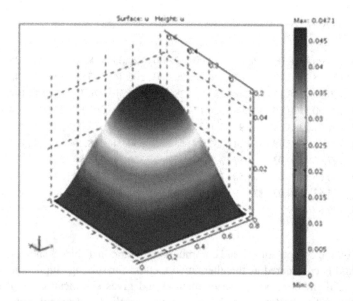

Fig. 12. 2D visualization of 2D electromagnetic wave using PDEs-elliptic equation.

Table 3. Parallel performance indicators versus number of processors for numerical methods comparison in terms of execution time (Exec. time), computation (Comp. time), communication (Comm. time) time and its ratio in solving parabolic equation conduction problem.

| | | | RBGS | | | | AGE | |
p	Exec. Time	Comp. Time	Ratio	Comm. Time	Exec. Time	Comp. Time	Ratio	Comm. Time
5	14.01	8.032	1.3	5.974	9.99710	7.138	2.5	2.859
%		57.4		42.7		71.4		28.6
10	8.201	4.016	1.0	4.185	5.82600	3.569	1.6	2.257
%		49.0		51.0		61.3		38.7
15	6.015	2.677	0.8	3.338	4.4507	2.379	1.2	2.071
%		44.5		55.5		53.5		46.5
20	5.123	2.008	0.6	3.115	3.607	1.785	1.0	1.823
%		39.2		60.8		49.5		50.5

Table 4. Parallel performance indicators versus number of processors for numerical methods comparison in terms of execution time (Exec. time), computation (Comp. time), communication (Comm. time) time and its ratio in solving elliptic equation

| | RBGS | | | | AGE | | | |
p	Exec. time	Comp. time	Ratio	Comm. time	Exec. time	Comp. time	Ratio	Comm. time
2	0.021649	17607	4.4	0.004042	0.042325	0.038203	9.3	0.004122
%		81.3		18.7		90.3		9.7
4	0.014146	10266	2.6	0.00388	0.023918	0.019543	4.5	0.004375
%		72.6		27.4		81.7		18.3
6	0.011692	7515	1.8	0.004177	0.0224602	0.020299	4.7	0.004303
%		64.3		35.7		82.5		17.5
8	0.011603	7498	1.8	0.004105	0.021081	0.014423	2.2	0.006659
%		64.6		35.4		68.4		31.6
10	0.011142	6614	1.5	0.004528	0.014603	0.009606	1.9	0.004997
%		59.4		40.6		65.8		34.2

Table 5. The parallel performance indicators formula.

Parallel Performance Indicators	Formula	Definition
Speedup	$S_p = \frac{T_1}{T_p}$	Time taken for a program to execute in one processor divided by the time taken to execute in many processors.
Efficiency	$C_p = \frac{S_p}{p}$	A measure of processor utilization
Effectiveness	$F_p = \frac{S_p}{p \times T_p}$	The effectiveness increases when then speedup increase.
Temporal performance	$L_p = \frac{1}{T_p}$	Maximum value of L_p shows better performance of parallel algorithm.

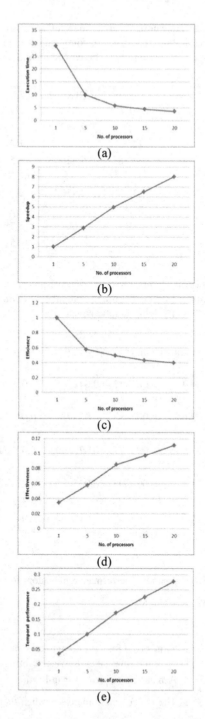

Fig. 13. Parallel performance indicators for semiconductor nanowires fabrication in terms of (a) Execution time (b) Speedup (c) Efficiency (d) Effectiveness (e) Temporal performance

Table 6 shows the numerical analysis for 3D semiconductor nanowire for different size of matrices.

Table 6. Computational and communication cost for different size of matrices

m	$100 \times 100 \times 100$					$140 \times 140 \times 140$				
P	Exec	Comp	Ratio	Comp	Idle	Exec	Comp	Ratio	Comp	Idle
5	99.9	58.59	1.42	41.31	11.87	193	111.8	1.38	81.25	31.11
10	73.01	29.29	0.67	43.71	14.27	136.2	55.89	0.7	80.34	21.21
15	69.11	19.73	0.4	49.27	19.84	121	36.66	0.43	84.29	35.15
20	63.99	15.15	0.31	48.85	19.42	110.7	27.15	0.32	83.55	34.41

7 Conclusion

The originality of our research is the HPNS development for high performance visualization of temperature distribution and electromagnetic field motion inside the nanoscale multilayered full-chip structure and semiconductor nanowire fabrication using PDEs modelling based on parabolic and elliptic-Poisson equations. The parallel performance indicators and numerical analysis have proven the validation of the PDEs modelling for changes parameter characterization of a full-chip system and semiconductor nanowire model associated with the temperature and electromagnetic profile respect to space and time.

The superior of the parallel AGE method is proven to achieve high performance indicators and accurate results for solving FDM of elliptic-Poisson and parabolic modeling. The technology software engineering of HPNS in terms of architecture design, parallel numerical simulation, large sparse visualization and high performance computing platform for solving nanoscale and high complexity problems significantly. HPNS is the alternative tool to enhance the better understanding and knowledge sharing among designer and researcher especially to control the small scale of nonconsistency temperature behaviour and electromagnetic motion toward minimizing a number of rejected nanochips and nanowires in the nanotechnology manufacturing industry.

The transformation phase technology from sequential to parallel algorithm in terms of fine granularity, domain decomposition technique, message passing activities, subdomain partitioning and mapping process can be benefited to improve the speedup for solving larger matrix size that consumed low cost execution time. Enhancement of open source HPNS is well suited as an embedded system to support the nanotechnology instruments such as CVD machine, monitoring machine, visualizing and predicting growth of nanowire as well as to assemble the multilayer nanochip in nanotechnology manufacturing industries. The potential future research is to develop and implement the parallel algorithm of some parameter characterization and its visualization on a next generation of CPU-GPU computer systems.

Acknowledgments. This work was supported in part by Universiti Teknologi Malaysia (UTM) and Research Grant (Tier 2 E) No. (Q.J130000.2626.10J33).

References

1. Hamidinezhad, H., Wahab, Y., Othaman, Z., Ismail, A.K.: Synthesis and analysis of silicon nanowire temperatures using very high frequency plasma enhanced chemical vapor deposition. Appl. Surf. Sci. **257**, 9188–9192 (2011)
2. Hamidinezhad, H., Wahab, Y., Othaman, Z., Ismail, A.K.: Influence of growth time on morphology of nanowires grown by VHF-PECVD. J. Cryst. Growth **332**, 7–11 (2011)
3. Byong, K.K., Ju, J.K., Jeong, O.L.: Temperature-dependent transport properties of an individual GaP nanowire with a Ga2O3 outer shell. J. Korean Phys. Soc. **46**, 1262–1265 (2005)
4. Ahmad, M., Ali, I., Islam, M.U., Rana, M.U.: Investigation of co-substituted nanosized Mn_2Y-hexaferrites synthesized by sol-gel autocombustion method. J. Mater. Eng. Perform. **22**, 3909–3915 (2013)
5. Wang, B., Mazumder, P.: Fast thermal analysis for VLSI circuits via semi-analytical Green's function in multi-layer materials. IEEE Int. Symp. Circ. Syst. **2**, 409–412 (2004)
6. Xia, T., Malasarn, D., Lin, S., Ji, Z., Zhang, H., Miller, R.J., Keller, A.A., Nisbet, R.M., Harthorn, B.H., Godwin, H.A., Lenihan, H.S., Liu, R., Gardea-Torresdey, J., Cohen, Y., Mädler, L., Holden, P.A., Zink, J.I., Nel, A.E.: Implementation of a multidisciplinary approach to solve complex nano EHS problems by the UC center for the environmental implications of nanotechnology. Small **9**, 1428–1443 (2013)
7. Alias, N., Saipol, H.F.S., Asnida, A.G., Mustaffa, M.N.: Parallel performance of group explicit method between parallel virtual machine and Matlab distributed computing for solving large sparse problems. Adv. Sci. Lett. **20**, 477–482 (2013)
8. Zhan, Y., Sapatnekar, S.S.: A high efficiency full-chip thermal simulation algorithm. In: Proceedings of the 2005 IEEE/ACM International conference on Computer-aided design, pp. 635 – 638 (2005)
9. Hippalgaonkar, K., Huang, B., Chen, R., Sawyer, K., Ercius, P., Majumdar, A.: Fabrication of microdevices with integrated nanowires for investigating low-dimensional phonon transport. Nano Lett. **10**(11), 4341–4348 (2010)
10. Garnett, E.C., Cai, W., Cha, J.J., Mahmood, F., Connor, S.T., GreysonChristoforo, M., Cui, Y., McGehee, M.D., Brongersma, M.L.: Self-limited plasmonic welding of silver nanowire junctions. Nat. Mater. **11**(3), 241–249 (2012)
11. Alias, N., Saipol, H.F.S., Ghani, A.C.A., Mustaffa, M.N.: Parallel performance comparison of alternating group explicit method between parallel virtual machine and matlab distributed computing for solving large sparse partial differential equations. Adv. Sci. Lett. **20**(2), 477–482 (2014)
12. Abu Mansor, N., Zulkifle, A.K, Alias, N., Hasan, M.K., Boyce, M.J.N.: The higher accuracy fourth-order IADE algorithm. J. Appl. Math. 2013, 13 pages (2013). Article number 236548

ANFIS Based Intelligent Synchronization Tool on Multi Robot Manipulators System

Parvaneh Esmaili and Habibollah Haron[(⊠)]

Faculty of Computing, Department of Computer Science, Universiti Teknologi
Malaysia, UTM, 81310 Skudai, Johor, Malaysia
p.esmaili1984@gmail.com, habib@utm.my

Abstract. A new intelligent synchronization tool is developed on multi robot
manipulators to handle an object in the desired trajectory. The intelligent synchronization tool is based on the adaptive neuro fuzzy inference systems
(ANFIS) structure which tries to compensate synchronization error between
robot manipulators. To overcome lumped uncertainty of the robot manipulator a
neural network based prediction mode and modified sliding mode control
(SMC) are used. The examples as illustrated can guarantee the robustness,
synchronization and decentralized feature for multi robot manipulator system.

Keywords: Decentralized · Multi robot manipulators · ANFIS · Synchronization

1 Introduction

In the coordination of multi robot manipulators accuracy and robustness which are
important factors in handling and manipulating objects requires more attention in this
field. In conventional coordination methods there are important classifications such as
decentralized, centralized and master slave methods. Conventional decentralized and
centralized methods cannot cover the tasks in which the robots are not physically
connected and several robots are connected to the object to do the same task simultaneously. The master slave methods can cover these kinds of tasks but they already
have a problem with un-calibrated slave robot dynamics. For this reason the synchronization methods are considered as a sufficient solution. The fundamental property
of synchronization methods instead of the conventional methods is to account for the
synchronization error between robots in the controlling signal. The cross coupling
synchronization method in 1980 by Koren was applied for robot manipulators [1]. In
2002 [2] tried to improve the cross coupling method by adding adaptive synchronization scheme in assembly tasks. A leader was used in some works to control the entire
system and the other robots have direct communication with the leader [3]. Other
works only used the neighbor's information to communicate with the others, and not all
robots have direct communication with the virtual leader [4]. All these methods they
used communication graph theory. But in all of these methods, the robots are not
decentralized. Thus, they must have knowledge of others at least neighbors. Therefore,
they need to have a strong communication graph. However, network failure would be
an irreversible problem for the system. In addition, this communication is costly for

© Springer International Publishing Switzerland 2015
H. Fujita and A. Selamat (Eds.): SoMeT 2014, CCIS 513, pp. 269–281, 2015.
DOI: 10.1007/978-3-319-17530-0_19

controlling system. Because of this problem, instead of direct and explicit communi-cation between robot manipulators, the implicit communication has received more attention. Farinelli et al. [5] revealed a classification based on communication between robots as implicit and explicit communication. Direct communication between robots in the form of peer-to-peer or broadcast information exchange is called as explicit communication. Instead of explicit communication, indirect exchange information between robots is called implicit communication that the information is achieved through the environment. In the implicit communication, the forces between manipu-lators are considered as a communication [6]. In practice measurement of internal forces is difficult. To answer these problems in this work is presented a new decen-tralized synchronization approach which is robust and low cost to handle a rigid object in the desired trajectory. This method is combination of ANFIS based synchronization with the modified sliding mode control. The illustrative example can reveal the per-formance of the proposed system.

The rest of the paper is organized in 4 sections. In Sect. 2 the problem definition is mentioned. In Sect. 3 the controlling method is considered. Illustrative examples and simulation results are shown in Sect. 4 and finally in Sect. 5 the conclusion of the work is presented.

2   Problem Definition

The major motivation of this work is using implicit communication between robot manipulators to handle an object in the desired trajectory. The deformation of the end-effectors of each robot with respect to the middle of the object is considered as an implicit communication scheme. The middle of the object is revealed as the object position and is considered as reference. Each robot justifies its trajectory based on the reference position. So, the robots do not need to have information about other robots.

To grasp an object in cooperative multi robot manipulators, the end effectors of each robot are considered as set points. As shown in Fig. 1, the end effectors are fixed on the object. The positions of the set points are related to the reference. Each end-effector tries to compensate for the uncertainty of their trajectory with respect to the reference. The design of a decentralized synchronization approach by using implicit communication is the purpose of this work.

Dynamic equation of PUMA 560 robot based on Lagrange – Euler [7] formula is as follows in Eq. (1).

$$M(\theta)\ddot{\theta} + B\left(\theta, \dot{\theta}\right) + C\left(\theta, \dot{\theta}\right) + G(\theta) = \tau + d(t) \tag{1}$$

where, $\theta = [\theta_1, \theta_2, \ldots, \theta_6]$ is the vector of the angle of the 6-DOF robot manipulator and $\dot{\theta} = \left[\dot{\theta}_1, \dot{\theta}_2, \ldots, \dot{\theta}_6\right]^T$, $\ddot{\theta} = [\ddot{\theta}_1, \ddot{\theta}_2, \ldots, \ddot{\theta}_6]^T$ is the velocity and acceleration of the robot manipulator. M is a $[6 \times 6]$ mass matrix, B is the Carioles- Coefficient which is $[6 \times 15]$, C is Centrifugal- Coefficient which is $[6 \times 6]$ matrix, G is Gravity term $[6 \times 1]$ matrix, τ is Torque $[6 \times 1]$ matrix and d (t) is lumped system uncertainty which may occur by friction, backlash, modeling error and external disturbance, etc.

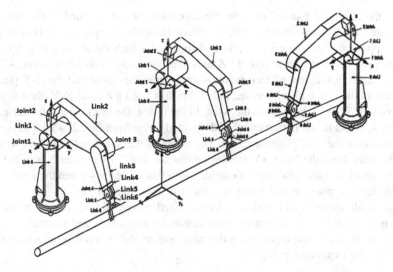

Fig. 1. The scheme of multi robot manipulators to handle an object with coordinated attached to the links

Lemma 1: The inertia matrix $M(\theta)$ is symmetric, positive definite. It satisfies the following inequalities. So, $m_1\|\xi\|^2 \le \xi^T M(\theta)\xi \le m_2\|\xi\|^2, \forall \xi \in R^n$ where, m1, m2 are positive constants, and $\|.\|$ denotes the standard Euclidean norm.

Lemma 2: The inertia and centripetal and coriolis matrices satisfy the following skew-symmetric relationship. $\xi^T\left(\frac{1}{2}\dot{M}(\theta) - \left(B_m\left(\theta,\dot{\theta}\right) + C_m\left(\theta,\dot{\theta}\right)\right)\right)\xi = 0, \forall \xi \in R^n$, where, $\dot{M}(\theta)$ denotes the time derivatives of the inertia matrix. The measured parameters of PUMA 560 are driven using Denavitt-Hartenberg [8]. The coordinate frames which are connected to joints are driven by using the Denavitt-Hartenberg equation [8] in Table 1.

Table 1. The D-H equation table and dynamic parameters for PUMA560 robot manipulator

Link i	θ_i	α_i	α_i	d_i	Movement range	m (kg)	r_x	r_y	r_z
1	θ_1	0	0	0	−160 to 160	0	–	–	–
2	θ_2	−90°	0	0.2435	−225 to 45	17.40	0.068	0.006	−0.016
3	θ_3	0	0.4316	−0.0934	−45 to 225	4.80	0	−0.070	0.014
4	θ_4	90°	−0.0203	0.4331	−110 to 170	0.82	0	0	−0.019
5	θ_5	−90°	0	0	−100 to 100	0.34	0	0	0
6	θ_6	90°	0	0	−266 to 266	0.09	0	0	0.032

The measured parameters of PUMA 560 were set by Armstrong [8]. The mass and the centre of gravity measures are reported in Table 1. The mass of link 1 is not considered because the link is fixed and not removed from the base coordinate. The position of the gravity centres are mentioned in Table 1. For each link, the rx, ry and rz refer to the x, y and z coordinates in the coordinate frame attached to the link. The coordinate frames are assigned by using Denavit-Hartenberg approach (D-H approach). In this approach, the frame i is a attached to link I which the Z_i axis lies along the rotation axis of joint i. For link 1, Z axis lies along the axis of rotation, +Z up; +Y1 ∥ +Z2. In link 2, the +Z in rotation is away from the based and the X-Y plane in the center of the link with +X toward link 3. For link3, Z3 ∥ Z2 and X-Y plane is in the center of link 3; +Y is away from the wrist. In the link 4, the origin is at the intersection of joints 4, 5 and 6; +Z is in rotation and directed away from link 2; +Y4 ∥ +Z3 when the joint 4 is in the base position (zero). The origin of the link 5 is from frame 4; +Z is directed away from the base; +Y is directed toward link 2 when joint 5 is in the base position (zero). In link 6 the origin coincides with that of frame 4 when the joints 5 and 6 are in the zero position and frame 6 is aligned with frame 4.

This work attempts to develop a decentralized robust sliding mode control with neural network for two cooperative manipulators in a synchronized manner.

In general, the dynamic second order nonlinear model of multi input multi output system can be explained in Eq. (2).

$$x_2 = \dot{x}_1 , \ \dot{x}_2 = f(x) + B(x)u(t) \tag{2}$$

where, $x = [x_1, x_2, \ldots, x_n]^T$ is the vector of the generalized coordinates such as position of the n DOF mechanical system and $\dot{x} = [\dot{x}_1, \dot{x}_2, \ldots, \dot{x}_m]^T$, $\ddot{x} = [\ddot{x}_1, \ddot{x}_2, \ldots, \ddot{x}_m]^T$ is the velocity and acceleration of the robot manipulators. In addition, $f(x)$ a bounded nonlinear vector is a function of the state vector to present the nonlinear term of the system and $B(x)$ is a bounded positive definite nonlinear function over the entire state space known as the control gain and $u(t)$ is the control input of the system. Therefore, the proposed dynamic equation for the robot manipulator to handle an object as mentioned above is mapped into Eq. (3) as follows.

$$
\begin{aligned}
M(\theta)\ddot{\theta} + B\left(\theta,\dot{\theta}\right) + C\left(\theta,\dot{\theta}\right) + G(\theta) &= \tau + d(t) \Rightarrow \\
\ddot{\theta} = M(\theta)^{-1}\tau - \left(M(\theta)^{-1} - \left(B\left(\theta,\dot{\theta}\right) + C\left(\theta,\dot{\theta}\right) + G(\theta)\right)\right) &+ d(t) \\
x_1 \equiv \theta, x_2 \equiv \dot{x}_1 \equiv \dot{\theta}, \dot{x}_2 \equiv \ddot{\theta}, B(x) \equiv M(\theta)^{-1}, u(t) \equiv \tau \\
f(x) \equiv \left(M(\theta)^{-1}\left(B\left(\theta,\dot{\theta}\right) + C\left(\theta,\dot{\theta}\right) + G(\theta)\right)\right) &+ d(t)
\end{aligned}
\tag{3}
$$

So, we have $\ddot{\theta} = f(\theta) + B(\theta)u$.

3   The Architecture of the Synchronization Controller

3.1   ANFIS Architecture for Synchronization Multi Robot Manipulators

The synchronization of robot manipulators architecture is shown in Fig. 2. For synchronization the middle of the lightweight beam is considered as a reference. The end- effectors angles of the each robot manipulators are related to a reference. The synchronization function in this work is given by Eq. (4).

$$\theta_i - \theta_o = \theta_{input\,ideal} \tag{4}$$

where θ_o is donated for angle of the middle of beam, θ_i is the end-effectors angle of each robot manipulators $\theta_{input\,deal}$ is the ideal input of the dynamics of the robot manipulators. To enhance the synchronization of two robot manipulators the control law which is mentioned in Eq. (4) is developed by ANFIS for $\theta_{input\,ideal}$. The ANFIS structure has two inputs θ_i , θ_o and $\theta_{input\,ideal}$ is the output. Basically the rule base includes two if-then rules of Takagi and Sugeo's fuzzy with type-3 ANFIS structure [9].

Rule 1: if θ_i is A_1 and θ_o is B_1 then $f_1 = p_1\theta_i + q_1\theta_o + r_1$
Rule 2: if θ_i is A_2 and θ_o is B_2 then $f_2 = p_2\theta_i + q_2\theta_o + r_2$.

The layers of the ANFIS architecture are described as follows.

Layer1: Every node I in this layer is a square node with a node function in which θ_i is input to node i and A_i is linguistic label such as small, large and so on.

$$O_i^1 = \mu_{A_i}(\theta_i) = \frac{1}{1 + [(\frac{\theta_i - c_i}{a_i})^2]b_i} = \exp\{-\left(\frac{\theta_i - c_i}{a_i}\right)^2\} \tag{5}$$

Layer2: Every node which comes from layer1 multiplies and sends the product out.

$$w_i = \mu_{A_i}(\theta_i) \times \mu_{B_i}(\theta_o) \tag{6}$$

Layer3: Every node in this layer with N label accounts the rate of ith rule's firing strength to the sum of the all rule's firing strengths. Layer4: the node function for every node in this layer is as follows.

$$O_i^4 = \bar{w}_i f_i = \bar{w}_i(p_i\theta_i + q_i\theta_o + r_i) \tag{7}$$

where, p_i, q_i and r_i are consequent parameters.

Layer5: In this layer the overall output is calculated as follows.

$$O_i^5 = overal\,output = \theta_{input\,ideal} = \sum \bar{w}_i f_i = \frac{\sum_i w_i f_i}{\sum_i w_i} \tag{8}$$

In Fig. 2, there are two basic controllers to compensate parameter uncertainties. The first one is a neural network based prediction model on dynamic model and the second is modified sliding mode control. Both sections used the prediction model. So, first of all neural network based prediction model is described.

3.2   Neural Network Based Prediction Model.

The model predictive control method is based on the receding horizon technique [10]. This prediction model can acts in two steps such as Identification of the system and Predictive control: the first one is determining the neural network plant model as identification of the system. The second step is using the controller to predict future

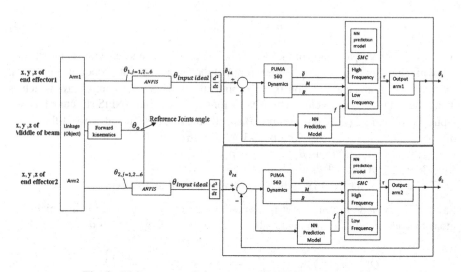

Fig. 2. The structure of the proposed ANFIS synchronization

performance of the system as predictive control. For learning multilayer perception model applies a type of learning algorithm such as back propagation algorithm.

3.2.1 Neural Network Based Prediction Model on Dynamic Model

To compensate for the model uncertainty of the robot manipulator and external disturbance neural network based prediction model $f(x)$ function in Eq. (3) [11] is used and is shown in Fig. 3.

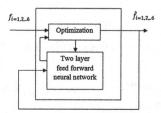

Fig. 3. The prediction model on f function

A two layers feed forward neural network used 10 nodes in hidden layer. The activation function of f function is presented in Eq. (9) as follows.

$$J_1 = \sum_{i=1}^{m} \sum_{j=1}^{k} \left(\hat{f}(t+j) - f_m(t+j)\right)^2 + 0.05 \sum_{j=1}^{2} \left(f'(t+j-1) - f'(t+j-2)\right)^2$$

$$(9)$$

where, m is number of input nodes and k is number of hidden nodes.

3.3   The Modified Sliding Mode Control

The Sliding Mode Control. The sliding mode controller will be designed based on the dynamic equation of the cooperative system. There are two steps needed for the sliding mode controller [12]. In the first step, a sliding surface for the cooperative system is chosen. The second step involves the equivalent controller. In this work, to omit the chattering phenomenon, the sliding mode controller uses the neural network based prediction model. Some researchers used soft computing methods [13, 14]. In the SMC design, tracking control problems can be investigated by holding the system trajectory on the sliding surface. To switch the function design in the first step, the PD type sliding surface is chosen as $s(t) = \dot{e} + \lambda e$, where, $s(t)$ is a 6×1 vector, λ is a constant. So, $e = \theta - \theta_d$, $\dot{e} = \dot{\theta} - \dot{\theta}_d$ are tracking error vector and the rate of tracking error vector. The second step of the controller design is to define the control law with variable parameters. The following control law is considered as:

$$u(t) = u_c + u_{eq} \qquad (10)$$

where, u_c and u_{eq} terms are defined as follows. The u_{eq} term is the equivalent control term which is proposed for the approximately known section of the system in the presence of perturbations. This section makes the derivative of the sliding surface equal to zero in order to remain on the sliding surface that has been previously mentioned as the low frequency control law. The u_c term is the corrective control term which is proposed to compensate the derivatives from the sliding surface known as the high frequency control law. The u_{eq} term helps the system to set on the sliding surface. So, by using $e = \theta - \theta_d$, $\dot{e} = \dot{\theta} - \dot{\theta}_d s = \dot{e} + \lambda e$, $\dot{s} = \ddot{e} + \lambda \dot{e}$, there is $\dot{s} = \ddot{\theta} - \ddot{\theta}_d + \lambda \dot{e}$. To keep the system on the sliding surface requires that $s(t) = 0$ and $\dot{s}(t) = 0$. So, u_{eq} is as follows as expressed in Eq. (11).

$$u_{eq} = B^{-1}\left(\ddot{\theta}_d - \lambda \dot{e} - f\right) \qquad (11)$$

To overcome the dynamic uncertainty in the controlling system caused by system uncertainty, external disturbances, friction and parameter variation, the approximation of f is termed $\hat{f}$ [14]. It should be mentioned that an approximate of an artificial neural network based prediction model has been used [11]. So, the equivalent control is as follows:

$$f = \hat{f} + \Delta f < F, u_{eq} = B^{-1}\left(\ddot{\theta}_d - \lambda \dot{e} - \hat{f}\right) \qquad (12)$$

where, Δf is the difference between real and approximated f function. Thus, the F is a positive function which is bounded by the values of f and $\hat{f}$. The approximation in this work uses a predictive neural network model to find accurate values for dynamic uncertainty in the control input to achieve good trajectory tracking in the presence of uncertainties. Discontinuous control unit (corrector) is used to achieve good trajectory tracking performance in very fast switching.

The u_c term: here is considered a u_c function to compensate for the derivations from the sliding surface and reaching to sliding surface.

$$uc = -\mathbf{B}^{-1} K(s), \; sg(s) = \begin{cases} 1 & s_i > 0 \\ -1 & s_i < 0 \end{cases} \tag{13}$$

To improve the performance of the sliding mode control section of the controller in the high frequency section of the controller a neural network based prediction model was presented which also used the prediction model [10] (Fig. 4).

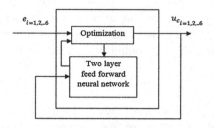

Fig. 4. The prediction model on sliding mode control

The activation function of this model is shown in Eq. (14).

$$J_2 = \sum_{i=1}^{m} \sum_{j=1}^{k} \left(u_c(t+j) - u_{c_m}(t+j) \right)^2 + 0.05 \sum_{j=1}^{2} \left(u'_c(t+j-1) - u'_c(t+j-2) \right)^2 \tag{14}$$

where, m is number of input nodes and k is number of hidden nodes.

Stability Analysis. To stabilize such systems, the differential equation solutions describing dynamic systems can be achieved by Lyapunov stability theory [14] which is concerned with the stability of solutions near the equilibrium point. It also lends qualitative results to the stability equations which may be useful in designing stabilizing controllers of nonlinear dynamic systems. By using the Lyapunov stability method, the parameter boundaries of sliding mode controllers to stabilize the proposed system can be determined. Positive definite Lyapunov function is $V(x) = \frac{1}{2} s(t)^T s(t)$. Thus, for stability the Lyapunov function V(x) should be positive and the derivative of the Lyapunov function should be negative.

$$\dot{V} = S.\dot{S} > 0, \; \dot{V} = s\left(f + \left(\ddot{\theta}_d - \lambda \dot{e} - \hat{f} - K \, sat(s) \right) - \ddot{\theta}_d + \lambda \dot{e} \right) \tag{15}$$

A mentioned before $f - \hat{f} \leq F$ and by considering $= F + \eta$, we have:

$$\dot{V} = s\left(f - \hat{f} - K \, sat(s) \right) < F - K|s|\dot{V} \leq -\eta|s| \tag{16}$$

4 Simulation

As mentioned before, at Fig. 1 in this work, each end-effector of robot manipulators indicates as set points. The synchronization approach is based on difference between each set point with respect to the middle of the grasping rigid object. The trajectory of each set point and the object are on the same frequency. The frequencies of trajectory for every set point are same but trajectory of each set point is different and there is some deviation and uncertainty on the trajectory. The synchronization proposed scheme is performed to solve uncertainty on the trajectory of set point in compare with the trajectory of grasping object. The proposed scheme tries to compensate the difference between trajectories of set point with respect to the trajectory of the grasping object. To analyze the proposed approach, two 6 DOF PUMA560 robot manipulators are modeled by [8]. In this section the simulation cases are mentioned. Case1 is the proposed ANFIS based synchronization controller for two robot manipulators. Case2 is the conventional feedback control of the proposed system. Case 3 is the extension of the proposed scheme for 5 robot manipulators. Case4 is the extension of the proposed scheme for 9 robot manipulators. Case1: At Fig. 5(a) is shown the trajectory of the object and two robot manipulators in the ANFIS synchronization scheme. In this case, two neural network models are used. The first one is neural network based prediction model on f function of model dynamics and the second one is neural network based prediction model on high frequency part of sliding mode control. In both prediction models for each robot manipulator, multi layer feed forward neural network with 10 hidden layers (which is based on the Baum-Haussler rule [15]) is used for approximating. As there are six robot manipulator angles in PUMA 560, neural networks also use six inputs and outputs. To all six neural network prediction boxes is applied 0.05 control weighting (ρ), 0.001 search parameter (α), 2 iteration per sample time, 10 cost horizon (N2), 2 cost Horizon (Nu), 0.2 (s) sampling interval, 2 delayed plant input, 2 delayed plant output and 1000 training epochs. There are two inputs and one output. Because of the 6 DOF robots each input and output has 6 angles. In overall, there are 12 inputs and 6 outputs. As shown in Fig. 5(a) the proposed scheme tried to compensate the lumped uncertainty in the system (Table 2).

Table 2. The regression results for all six angles of PUMA in neural network with training performance and the Neural network training stat (gradient and Mu) with validation check = 6 for prediction model on f function

Angle No.	Training	validation	Test	All regression	Training Performance	Epoch No.	Gradient	Mu
1	0.954662	0.88318	0.71784	0.83915	55.4822	17	483.6533	0.1
2	0.99968	0.98219	0.97627	0.98763	22.5304	54	155.4274	0.001
3	0.99982	0.96905	0.96917	0.95569	9.306	47	1.2332	0.1
4	0.99992	0.88538	0.7119	0.88382	0.47042	40	0.096128	0.0001
5	0.99442	0.94824	0.74094	0.9355	0.32236	21	0.016548	0.001
6	0	0	0	0	0.00018742	497	9.9687e-11	1e-13

The synchronization error in ANFIS for all 6 angles of two PUMA 560 robot manipulators is presented in Fig. 5(b) as follows. Case 2: The trajectory of the object and the two robot manipulators in conventional feedback control is considered. The basic idea of closed feedback controller comes from Eq. (17).

$$\theta_i - \theta_o = \theta_{inputideal}, i = 1, 2 \tag{17}$$

The structure of the feedback control in this work is shown in Fig. 6. The outputs of the feedback controller for two arms with respect to the object are shown in Fig. 7(a). It reveals that the feedback controller has problems compensating for the uncertainty of robot manipulators' trajectory (Table 3).

Table 3. The regression results for all six angles of PUMA in neural network with training performance and the Neural network training stat(gradient and Mu) with validation check = 6 for prediction model on sliding mode control

Angle No.	Training	validation	Test	All regression	Training Performance	Epoch No.	Gradient	Mu
1	0.97957	0.9789	0.97813	0.97899	5.9945	23	0.41704	100
2	0.97615	0.97386	0.97294	0.97493	97.1082	75	199.2144	1000
3	0.98214	0.98475	0.98147	0.98331	16.0793	62	0.72785	100
4	0.0.97572	0.97404	0.9622	0.97022	0.090627	27	2.5985	0.1
5	0.98559	0.98053	0.97018	0.98119	0.030257	31	1.8011	1e-5
6	0.99174	-0.017327	0.15964	0.99061	4.3162e-10	75	9.8117e-06	1e-05

The synchronization error for two robot manipulators in feedback is shown in Fig. 7(b). In Fig. 8, the synchronization error comparison between feedback control and ANFIS control is shown. In the feedback control the synchronization error try to converge to zero but in the ANFIS control the synchronization is converged to the zero.

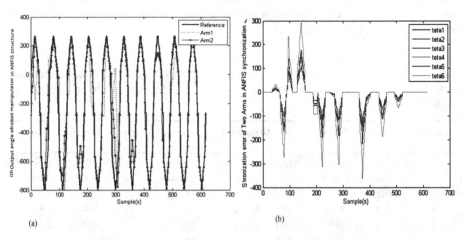

(a)   (b)

Fig. 5. (a) The trajectory of two robot manipulators in ANFIS synchronization, (b) the synchronization error in ANFIS control

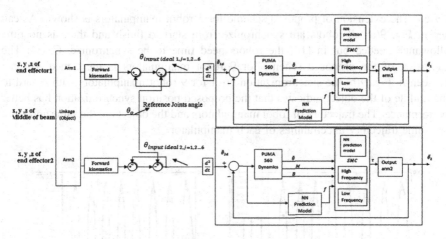

Fig. 6. The feedback method in the proposed system

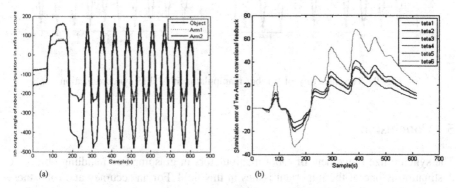

(a)   (b)

Fig. 7. (a) The trajectory of two robot manipulators in ANFIS synchronization, (b) the synchronization error in ANFIS control

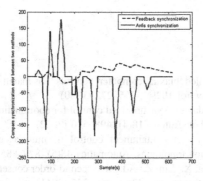

Fig. 8. The trajectory of 9 robot manipulator in ANFIS synchronization

Case3: The extension of proposed scheme for 5 robot manipulators is shown. As can see in Fig. 9(a) all robots are synchronize from start to finish and there is no time allowance needed but in [16] the robots need time to be synchronize. Case4: The extension of the proposed scheme for 9 robot manipulators is mentioned. As can be seen in Fig. 9(b) the synchronization error for 9 robot manipulators with regard to the middle of the object indicates that the proposed position synchronization has better performance. The trajectory of robot manipulators and the object are the same and there are some trajectory uncertainties of each manipulator.

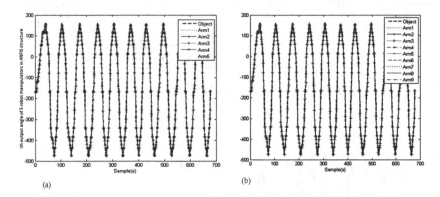

(a)   (b)

Fig. 9. The trajectory of 9 robot manipulator in ANFIS synchronization

5   Conclusion

The synchronize movement of robot manipulators in grasping and handling objects to destination is one of the important issues in this field. For an accuracy and robustness view, in this work an ANFIS based synchronization approach is developed based on sliding mode control. This controller not only tries to move an object accurately but also tries to compensate for lumped uncertainty in the real environment. The simulation results are shown in the performance of the system.

References

1. Koren, Y.: Cross-coupled biaxial computer controls for manufacturing systems. ASME J. Dyn. Syst. Meas. Control **102**(4), 265–272 (1980)
2. Sun, D., Mills, J.K.: Adaptive synchronized control for coordination of multirobot assembly tasks. IEEE Trans. Robot. Autom. **18**(4), 498–510 (2002)
3. Lou, Y., Hong, Y.: Target containment control of multi-agent systems with random switching interconnection topologies. Automatica **48**(5), 879–885 (2012)
4. Su, H., Chen, G., Wang, X., Lin, Z.: Adaptive second-order consensus of networked mobile agents with nonlinear. Automatica **47**(2), 368–375 (2011)

5. Farinelli, A., Iocchi, L., Nardi, D.: Multirobot systems: a classification focused on coordination. IEEE Trans. Syst. Man Cybern. B Cybern. **34**(5), 2015–2028 (2004)
6. Bai, H., Wen, J.T.: Cooperative load transport: a formation-control perspective. IEEE Trans. Robot. **26**(4), 742–750 (2010)
7. Lewis, F.L., Abdallah, C.T., Dawson, D.M.: Control of Robot Manipulators. Macmillan Publishing Co., New York (1993)
8. Armstrong, B., Khatib, O., Burdick, J.: The explicit dynamic model and inertial parameters of the PUMA 560 arm. In: Proceedings of IEEE Conference on Robotics and Automation, pp. 510–518 (1986)
9. Jang, J.: ANFIS: adaptive-network-based fuzzy inference system. IEEE Trans. Syst. Man Cybern. **23**(3), 665–685 (1993)
10. Soloway, D., Haley, P.J.: Neural generalized predictive control. In: IEEE International Symposium on Intelligent Control, pp. 277–282 (1996)
11. Esmaili, P., Haron, H.: Artificial neural network based prediction model of the sliding mode control in coordinating two robot manipulators. In: Nguyen, N.T., Attachoo, B., Trawiński, B., Somboonviwat, K. (eds.) ACIIDS 2014, Part I. LNCS (LNAI), vol. 8397, pp. 474–483. Springer, Heidelberg (2014)
12. Yagiz, N., Hacioglu, Y., Arslan, Y.Z.: Load transportation by dual arm robot using sliding mode control. J. Mech. Sci. Technol. **24**(5), 1177–1184 (2010)
13. Panwar, V., Kumar, N., Sukavanam, N., Borm, J.-H.: Adaptive neural controller for cooperative multiple robot manipulator system manipulating a single rigid object. Appl. Soft Comput. **12**(1), 216–227 (2012)
14. Zeinali, M., Notash, L.: Adaptive sliding mode control with uncertainty estimator for robot manipulators. Mech. Mach. Theor. **45**(1), 80–90 (2010)
15. Baum, E.B., Haussler, D.: What size net gives valid generalization? Neural Comput. **1**, 151–160 (1989)
16. Zhao, D., Zhu, Q., Li, N., Li, S.: Synchronized control with neuro-agents for leader–follower based multiple robotic manipulators. Neurocomputing **124**, 149–161 (2014)

Towards Domain Ontology Interoperability Measurement

Hussein Sseggujja[1] and Ali Selamat[1,2(✉)]

[1] UTM-IRDA Digital Media Centre, UTM and Faculty of Computing,
Universiti Teknologi Malaysia, 81310 Johor Bahru, Johor, Malaysia
segujah@yahoo.com
[2] Software Engineering Research Group (SERG), Faculty of Computing,
Universiti Teknologi Malaysia, 81310 Johor Bahru, Johor, Malaysia
aselamat@utm.my

Abstract. Ontologies are reliable interoperability support components between information systems. However the need to make ontologies themselves interoperable to a measurable degree remains a challenge due to the semantic heteroginity problem. This paper specifically looks at domain ontologies and how to measure the interoperability degree between them to establish the extent to which they can replace each other. Different interoperability operations,semantic distance measures and lexical similarity between ontologies are dicussed. A method based on model management theory with algebraic operations such as match on the ontology models is proposed to measure lexical and structural dimensions of domain ontologies and give a value for their degree of interoperability. An example of how to compute the degree of interoperability between two domain ontologies using the proposed approach is given with an explanation of how the identified gaps can be addressed.

Keywords: Domain · Ontology · Interoperability · Similarity · Measure

1 Introduction

Current development trends in software engineering have created increasing demand for interoperability between the different systems being engineered. Ontologies have been described widely as a representation of common concepts in a given domain and their relationships. This characteristic enables ontologies to be used as an interoperability component for the integration between systems. An ontology is an *"explicit specification of a conceptualization"* [1]. Therefore an ontology is a formal representation of concepts and their relationship within a particular domain. A domain is *"An area of or field of specialization where human expertise is used, and a Knowledge-Based System application is proposed to be used within it."* [2].

Interoperability is referred to as the "capability to communicate, execute programs, or transfer data among various functional units in a manner that requires the user to have little or no knowledge of the unique characteristics of those units" [3]. The EIF (European Interoperability framework) [4] identifies three levels of interoperability: technical, semantic and organizational. This paper aims at semantic interoperability

© Springer International Publishing Switzerland 2015
H. Fujita and A. Selamat (Eds.): SoMeT 2014, CCIS 513, pp. 282–296, 2015.
DOI: 10.1007/978-3-319-17530-0_20

derived from use of ontologies. Among the different types of ontologies, this paper focuses on the domain ontologies which represent the meanings [5] of terminologies as they are perceived in given domain. Domain ontologies therefore offer a platform for interoperability that supports systems engineering benefits such as reusability, reliability, specification and also allow for better communication and cooperation between people and systems. It's also often that ontologies from the same domain are not interoperable due to different perceptions of the domain designers based on cultural background, ideology or because a different representation language was used to build the ontology. Therefore ontology design is subjective and parties may exploit different ontologies related to the same application domain differently thereby causing what is referred to as the semantic heterogeneity [6] problem. To achieve successful communication within heterogeneous environments where ontologies are used, it is necessary to bring them into a mutual agreement by establishing semantically related entities between the two ontologies. It is important to note here that ontology interoperability measurement sits at the intersection of three ontology interoperability areas; the interoperability algorithms or operations, the similarity measures and algebraic model operators.

The objectives of this paper are three. First is to compare and identify gaps in domain ontology interoperability approaches, algorithms and measures. The second is to propose a method for measuring the degree of interoperability between two domain ontologies and thirdly is to explain how the proposed method can be used to compute the interoperability degree. The proposed method utilises an algebraic model that represents the domain ontologies. The approach combines the model and the match operator to produce a measure of the degree of interoperability between two domain ontologies. The benefits of the proposed approach include providing knowledge about the structural and semantic heterogenity degree between two domain ontologies. This information enables system integrators and ontology designers to make better and informed choices between domain ontologies for reuse and other related purposes.

The paper is organized as follows. Section 2 presents a detailed review and analysis of the different domain ontology interoperability approaches. Section 3 covers analysis of different ontological similarity measures and model operators between ontologies. Section 4 presents the proposed improved method to measure the degree of interoperability between one domain ontology and another. An example from the geographical land coverage domain is given using the proposed method. Finally Sect. 5 gives the conclusion.

2 Approaches to Domain Ontology Interoperability

Due to the large variety of information sources, a single universal ontology cannot be built and systems will continue to use different ontologies even if they come from the same domain. Ontologies can interoperate only if correspondences between their elements have been identified through use of methodologies and tools that support the knowledge engineer in discovering semantic correspondences [7]. Therefore if the journey of making ontologies interoperable is still long, the stage of measuring the degree of their interoperability is even longer.

2.1   Operations for Domain Ontology Interoperability

This section covers different operations and approaches or algorithms used in each operation. There exists no clear standard for defining the terms matching, mapping, and alignment [8] hence what is given here includes the definitions adopted for this paper.

Ontology Alignment Operation. Given two ontologies, alignment means that for each entity (concept, relation, or instance) in the first ontology, we get an entity which has the same intended meaning, in the second ontology. The result of matching, called an alignment is a set of pairs of entities e, e' from two ontologies O and O' that are supposed to satisfy [9] a certain relation r with a certain confidence level n. Algorithms which implement the match operator can be generally classified [10] along the following dimensions; schema-based algorithms, instance-based algorithms, element-based and structure-based which compare structures of the ontology to determine the similarity. It is also possible to have combinations of different mechanisms within one algorithm.

Ontology Mapping/Matching Operation. Ontology mapping is a function between the ontologies whereas alignment merely identifies the relation between ontologies. It is a specification of the semantic overlap between two ontologies and consists of three main phases including discovery, representation and execution. Some authors consider ontology mapping as a directed version of an alignment while others like Ehrig and Staab [10] do not distinguish between mapping and alignment.

Ontology Merging/Integrating Operation. Ontology merging is the creation of one ontology from two or more source ontologies [11] and replace the original source ontologies. The outcome may be a new merged ontology that captures the original ontologies or just a 'view' (bridge ontology) that imports the original ontologies and specifies the correspondences using bridge axioms. In integration, one or more ontologies are reused for a new ontology keeping the original concepts unchanged although they can be extended. The most prominent integration approaches are union and intersection where either all entities or only those that have correspondences in both ontologies are taken.

Mediation Operation. Ontology mediation basically reconciles the differences between two or more heterogeneous ontologies. Ontology mediation enables reuse of data across applications on the semantic web and cooperation between different organizations.

Ontology Translation and Transformation Operations. Translation is restricted to data which may also include the syntax for example translating the ontology from RDF (S) to OWL. Transformation involves changing the structure of the ontology without altering its semantics (lossless) or by modifying it slightly for different new purposes.

2.2   Algorithms for Ontology Interoperability

This section outlines different solutions that address the ontology interoperability challenge. Different methods focus on various aspects of the interoperability problem. Some approaches enable interoperability at the language level to unify the specifications and then to compare the elements of the different ontologies. Table 1 gives an analysis of the

Table 1. Key features in Ontology interoperability algorithms

Algorithm	Operation	Basis	Input	Output	Solution
GLUE[12]	Alignment, Mapping	Schema concepts, instances	RDF(s) structures	Alignment proposals	Method and tool
Anchor Prompt[13]	Alignment, Merging	Schema structure	RDF(s) ontologies	Alignment proposals	Tool
QOM[14]	Alignment, Mapping	Schema Concepts	Structure ontology	Match proposals	Method and tool
MAFRA[15]	Mapping	Concepts, instances	Concepts	Alignments	Tool
PROMPT[16]	Mapping, Merging	Concept Schema	Structure	Alignment proposal	Tool
Prompt Diff[16]	Mapping, Merging	Schema concepts	Structure	Proposals for user	Tool
Chimaera[17]	Merging	Schema concepts	Structure	Interactive proposals	Tool
ONION[18]	Merging	Concepts, instances	Structure	Rules	Tool and method
Madhavan[11]	Mapping	concepts	Structures	Rules	Method
MOMIS-OIS[19]	Mapping, Merging	Schema concepts	Queries	Rules	Method, framework
Kiryakov[20]	Mapping	Concepts	Queries	Rules	Method
IFF[21]	Mapping	Instances, concepts	Ontology structures	Agreements, constraints	Method and Tool
HELIOS[22]	Merging, mapping	Schema concepts	Ontology structure	Rules	Method and Tool
ARTEMIS[23]	Mapping	Schema concepts	Schema structure	Class alignments	Tool and Method
HCONE[24]	Merging	Schema concepts	RDF(s) structure	Ontology	Tool
SHOE[12]	Merging	Schema concepts	Ontology	Tag rules	Tool
KRAFT[25]	Merging, Mapping	Schema structures	Ontology structure	Rules	Method and tool
ONTOMerge[11]	Merging, translation	Schema concepts	Ontology structure	Merged ontology	Online Tool
OLA[18]	Alignment	Concept labels	Ontology	alignments	Tool
COMA[26]	Alignment	Schema structures	schemas	Alignment proposals	Method, Tool
FCA-Merge[27]	Merging	Instances	Ontology structure	Merged ontology	Tool and method
FORM[28]	Alignment, mapping	Concepts, instances	Ontology structure	alignments	Method
SAMBO[29]	Alignment, Merging	Instances, concepts	Ontology structure	Merged ontology	Method
S-match[30]	Matching, Mapping	Concepts ,labels	Ontology structure	alignments	Method
RiMOM[31]	Matching	Concepts, instances	Ontology structure	Matches, Alignments	Mainly Framework
DELTA[32]	Mapping	Schema based	Schema	Alignments	Tool
MapOnto[33]	Mapping	Schema based	columns, concepts	rules	Method, tool
iMap[34]	Matching	Instance based	Schema elements	matches	Method
SEMINT[35]	Matching	Schema, instance	Schema structure	Rules	Method
ToMAS[36]	Mapping	Schema based	Schema structure	Mappings	Tool

key features from about 30 commonly used solutions for interoperability among ontologies in literature and the following issues are coming out clearly from the comparison;

- Alignment and merging operations are mainly interactive with the user and produce proposals for the user to adopt or neglect according to his or her experience in the domain concepts.
- Although some algorithms operate on instances in the ontology, the majority base their operations on concepts alone. This allows the operations to keep at the syntax level and metadata level which enables modelling functions for ontology management as mathematical models.
- Some mapping approaches produce mapping rules discovered during the process and these rules can be used for mapping between concepts of different ontologies.
- Although the algorithms cover different aspects of domain ontology interoperability, some of these algorithms are fully automated for their purpose while others are semi-automated or manual.
- Some algorithms take ontology structures as input as opposed to just concepts or instances. Transformations from one representation format to another in order to carry out the processing may affect the semantic level of the original ontologies.
- We have not found clear attempts to measure the degree of domain ontology interoperability, hence a gap that this paper responds to.

3 Measures for Domain Ontological Similarity

3.1 The Nature of Semantic Measures

Defining a measure involves [37] defining information sources, theoretical principles and the semantic class including semantic distance, semantic similarity and semantic relatedness. Mathematical analysis, domain-specific applications, and comparison by human judgments of similarity have been used for measures. The discussion in this section assumes an ontology in Fig. 1 that contains two concepts C1 and C2 for which the distance and corresponding similarity is to be assessed. The concept C3 represents a Least Common Subsumer (LCS) or ancestor of C1 and C2 in the ontology.

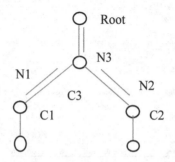

Fig. 1. Basic hierarchical ontology structure

Ontology measuring techniques are mainly classified into structure-based measures, feature-based measures, information content (IC) based measures and hybrid measures. Examples of these measures include; Tversky that looks at a concept in an ontology as an object with a set of features. A concept's similarity is determined by a respective set of ancestors X and Y. The measure is given by the formula below:

$$\frac{f(X \cap Y)}{f(X \cap Y) + \alpha f(X - Y) + \beta f(Y - X)} \tag{1}$$

The determination of α and β is based on the observation that similarity is not necessarily symmetric and gives different measure variations as shown in Table 2.

Table 2. Variations of Tversky similarity measure

α –value	β- value	Measure	Similarity function
1	1	Jaccard index	$\frac{f(X \cap Y)}{f(X \cup Y)}$
1/2	1/2	Dice coefficient	$\frac{2 * f(X \cap Y)}{f(X) + f(Y)}$
1	0	Degree of inclusion of X in Y	$\frac{f(X \cap Y)}{f(X)}$
0	1	Degree of inclusion of Y in X	$\frac{f(Y \cap X)}{f(Y)}$

The Table 3 gives an analytical comparison of the different common measures in literature.

The availability of many measures for semantic similarity raises a fundamental question: How well does a given measure capture the similarity between two concepts, set of concepts or ontology [49]. For information retrieval metrics, it is difficult to determine the evaluation value and measuring process quality independently. Hence need for compliance evaluations such as Precision, Recall, F-measure and performance measures that focus on speed, memory usage and the processing environment.

3.2   Model Management Operators for Ontology Interoperability

The common approach for interoperability computations [50] is to use ontology representation models identified by the root concept, set of reachable concepts through is-a relationships and built-in types of constraints such as the min and max cardinality. The model structure supports algebraic operations to create or delete a concept, read or write a property, and add or remove a relationship. Examples of the operators include;

1. Match – takes two models as input and returns a mapping between them. Figure 2 shows the details.
2. Compose – takes a mapping between models A and B and a mapping between models B and C, and returns a mapping between A and C (Fig. 3).

Table 3. Common similarity measures

Measure	Class / Type	Source	Equation	Description
Rada [38]	Structure-Edge counting	Ontology		Uses shortest distance between two concepts.
Wu and Palmer[39]	Structure –Edge counting	Ontology	$\dfrac{2*N3}{N1+N2+2*N3}$	Path-based distances to measure similarity.
Leacock and Chodorow [40]	Structure- Path - based	Ontology	$Max\left[\ -log\left(\dfrac{Np(c1,c2)}{2D}\right)\right]$	Focuses on node counting
Resnik[41]	IC - Corpus	Corpus and ontology	$-\ log\ p(c)$	Leaves out individual concepts information.
Lin[42]	IC- Corpus	Corpus	$\dfrac{2*IC(c3)}{IC(c1)+IC(c2)}$	Addresses the critism in Resnik
Jiang and Conrath[43]	IC	Ontology	$IC(c1) +IC(c3) - 2 * IC(c3)$	Integrates IC and path based measures.
Tversky [44]	Feature based	Ontology	$\dfrac{f(X\cap Y)}{f(X\cap Y)+\alpha f(X\text{-}Y)+\beta f(Y\text{-}X)}$	Uses ancestors and descendant
Al-Mubaid and Nguyen[45]	Node and path counting	Ontology	$log_2((len(c1,c2)-1)$ $* (D-Depth(LCS(c1,c2)))$ $+2)$	Uses distance and depth of LCS and overall ontology depth
Hirst and St Onge[46]	Edge counting and relations	Ontology relations	C-path length - k * number of changes in direction.	It categorises relations into 4 levels of strength.
Sussna[47]	Path and relations	Ontology relations	$max_r - \dfrac{max_r - min_r}{n_r(c_i)}$	Attaches to each possible link with concept.
Knappe[48]	Hybrid	Ontology	$p*\dfrac{\lvert Ans(c1)\cap Ans(c2)\rvert}{Ans(c1)}+$ $(1-p)*\dfrac{\lvert Ans(c1)\cap Ans(c2)\rvert}{Ans(c2)}$	Considers multiple paths between concept generalisations.
Resnik[48]	IC	Corpus, Ontology	$-\ log\ p(c)$	Focuses on content of shared parents
Shortest path[38]	Structure- Edge counting	ontology	2 * Max(C1,C2) – Shortest_Path	Mainly counts edges

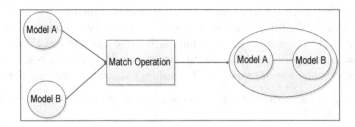

Fig. 2. Basic match operator

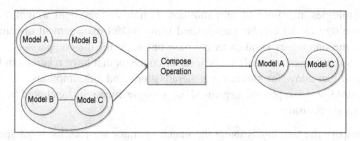

Fig. 3. Compose mapping operator

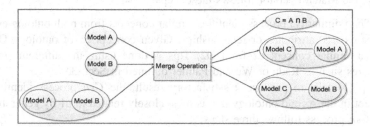

Fig. 4. Merge operator

3. Merge – takes two models A and B and a mapping between them, and returns C as a union of A and B along with mappings between C and A, and C and B (Fig. 4).

Although substantial work on Match has been done, Merge, Compose, and ModelGen are less developed.

4   A Domain Ontology Interoperability Degree Measurement Method

The *Match* operator is widely covered in model management literature. It takes two models and returns two sets of tuples for the similarity and generalization relationships that exist between the concepts of the two ontologies. The operator proposed by Bernstein [50] offers a relatively clearer approach to measure the degree of interoperability between ontologies.

4.1   Proposed Approach Methodology

In order to use the match operator to measure the degree of interoperability between domain ontologies we constrain the proposed approach within the following properties of the ontologies.

1. The ontologies measured share a common domain and are light weight.
2. The ontology model can be manipulated using model management operations.
3. One of the ontologies is taken as the base ontology for the comparison.
4. The two ontologies are made up of a set of concepts that have relations in between them and can allow for similarity, generalisations and subsumptions.
5. The ontology concepts are organised in a single hierarchy anchored at the root down to specialisations.

To compare the ontologies using the match operator we take the most specialized concepts (all leaf-nodes of the ontology tree) from the first or base ontology and attempt to find similar concepts in the second ontology. Given a concept in the base ontology, the Match operator follows these steps:

1. The *Sim* (similarity) process identifies similar concepts from both ontologies based on their parts, attributes or relationships. Given concept c1 of ontology O1, *Sim* finds a similar concept c2 from O2. This is done using the different similarity measures such as Rada or Wu and Palmer outlined in Sect. 3.
2. If step (1) fails to produce a satisfactory result, the *Gen* process identifies the concept in the second ontology that is most closely related to c1 by generalization. The *Gen* process follows three steps;
   (i)   Given a concept c1 of O1 that has no similar match in O2, locate concept d1 that is the generalization of c1.
   (ii) Find a similar concept to d1 in O2, d2. Use *Sim* process to match.
   (iii) If a similar concept (d2) is found, then d2 is a generalization of c1 in O2.
3. The Match function produces two subsets as a result:

   • *Sim* (O1,O2): The similarity subset *Sim* (O1,O2) of O1 in relation to O2 is the set of all tuples <c1, c2> such that the concept c2 in O2 is similar to the concept c1 in O1.
   • *Gen* (O1,O2): The generalization subset *Gen*(O1,O2) of O1 in relation to O2 is the set of all tuples <c1, c2> such that the concept c2 in O2 is a generalization of the concept c1 in O1. Two main forms of the degree of the interoperability between two domain ontologies O1 and O2 are:-

1. **Full interoperability:** If and only if the similarity set *Sim*(O1,O2) contains all concepts in O1.
2. **Partial Interoperability:** Where the generalisation set *Gen*(O1,O2) is not an empty set such that atleast some concepts in O1 have been matched with concepts in O2. The degree of interoperability IntDeg is given formula (2).

$$\text{IntDeg} = \left[f + \frac{\sum_{i=1}^{n} \min\left(t_2^i, t_1^i\right)}{\sum_{i=1}^{n} t_1^i} \right] \Big/ 2 \tag{2}$$

Where

• f is the fraction of concepts of O1 that are contained in *Sim*(O1,O2).
• the second part is the degree of generalisation derived from generalisation.

In formula (2) above l_1^i is the depth of the ith concept of ontology O1 and l_2^i is the depth of the corresponding concept in ontology O2 as given by the tuples in $Gen(O1, O2)$. The degree of generalisation is obtained by comparing the depth of the tree associated with the concepts in the generalization subset $Gen(O1,O2)$. The formula is based on the idea that the greater the difference between the depth levels of the two concepts, the smaller the degree of interoperability between the two domain ontologies. Figure 5 shows an outline of the algorithm for the method.

```
1.  Preprocessing:
2.      Get domain ontology O1 and O2
3.      Compute depth of O1(depth_O1) and depth of O2(depth_O2)
4.      Compute generalisation limit (Gen_limit) { depth_O1/α}
5.      Similarity_Number_found = 0, Initialise L = 0,  Number_of_leafNodesᵢ = 0, Gen_Hopsᵢ = 1
6.  Begin    {Compute Interoperability}:
7.      Read all leaf nodes (Leaf_Nodeᵢ) from O1 into process table (Table _Interoperability).
8.      Update Number_of Nodesᵢ
9.      For each Leaf_Nodeᵢ in Table _Interoperability
10.         Similarity_Number_found  = Similarity(Leaf_Nodeᵢ , Nodeⱼ from O2)
11.         if  Similarity_Number_found = True then
12.             Similarity_Number_found = Similarity_Number_found + 1
13.             Update status in Table _Interoperability
14.         else
15.             While Gen_Hopsᵢ less than Gen_limit
16.                 Get generalisation Gen_d of concept Leaf_Nodeᵢ
17.                 Gen_Number_found  = Similarity(Gen_d, Nodeⱼ from O2)
18.                 Update Table_Interoperability with depth_O1 and depth_O2
19.                 Compute L = min(depth_O1 , depth_O2)
20.                 Update Table _Interoperability with L value
21.                 Gen_Hopsᵢ = Gen_Hopsᵢ + 1
22.             endwhile;
23.         endif
24.     Similarity_Deg(f)   = Similarity_Number_found / Number_of leafNodesᵢ
25.     Generalisation_Deg(m) =  ∑ L  / ∑ depth_O1
26.         Degree_Interoperability = [Similarity_Deg(f)   + Generalisation_Deg(m)] / 2
27. end.
```

Fig. 5. Ontology Interoperability measurement method algorithm

4.2   Method Application Example from the Geographical Domain

To illustrate the method outlined above, we take a look at two domain ontologies from the geographical land coverage domain. The two sample ontologies are LandClimatology (O1) and Landcover (O2). The protégé based structure of the first ontology is given in Fig. 6 and for the second ontology structure in Fig. 7.

From the ontology in Fig. 6, the most specialized classes are descendants of Forest class. The proposed method application uses these 5 leaf nodes for comparison.

Using *Sim* match, only 3 leaf nodes as seen in Table 4 have been matched giving an *f* value of 0.6 from Eq. (2). Therefore we don't have full interoperability hence the

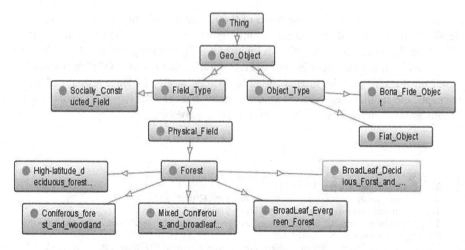

Fig. 6. LandClimatology ontology structure

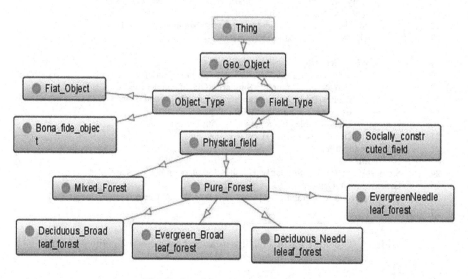

Fig. 7. LandCover ontology structure

method invokes the generalization (*Gen*) process to match the remaining classes as the seen in the Table 5.

Using Eq. (2) the degree of generalisation between the two ontologies is 0.75. Therefore the degree of interoperability between the two sample domain ontologies LandClimatology and Landcover is 0.68. Therefore that 68 % of ontology O1 is replaceable by ontology O2. However the method does not explain how the degree of interoperability computed affects the instance values in dataset likewise the performance reduces as the ontology size increases. We address this challenge by limiting the generalizable number of nodes to a quarter of the length of the base ontology.

Table 4. Similarity table between O1 and O2

#	Concepts from Ontology O1	Concepts from Ontology O2
1	BroadLeaf_Evergreen_Forest	Evergreen_Broadleaf_forest
2	BroadLeaf_Decidious_Forst_and_Woodland	Deciduous_Broadleaf_forest
3	Mixed_Coniferous_and_broadleaf_decidious_fo rest	Evergreen_Broadleaf_forest

Table 5. Generalisation table between ontology O1 and ontology O2

#	Ontology O1 Concepts	Ontology O2 Concepts	Depth l_1^l	Depth l_2^l	$min(l_2^l, l_1^l)$
1	Coniferous_forest_and_woodland	Pure_Forest	4	3	3
2	High_latitude_deciduous_forest_and_woo dland	Pure_Forest	4	3	3
			$\sum = 8$		$\sum = 6$

5   Conclusion

The paper outlined how to measure the degree of interoperability between two domain ontologies and provide a value of the extent to which they can replace each other. The approach is based on a model management operator to define different degrees of interoperability. The method can enable domain ontology designers and system integrators to make quicker and better informed selections between ontologies for adoption but it falls short in explaining the integration impact on the ontology instances. The method performance speed tends to decrease as the depth of the ontology becomes higher

Acknowledgements.   The Universiti Teknologi Malaysia (UTM) and Ministry of Education (MOE) Malaysia under Research University grant Vots 02G31 and 00M19 are hereby acknowledged for some of the facilities utilized during the course of this research work and for supporting the related research.

References

1. Gruber, T.R.: A translation approach to portable ontology specifications. Knowl. Acquis. **5**, 199–220 (1993)
2. Harsu, M.: A survey on domain engineering (2002)
3. Seremeti, L., Kougias, I.: Computation of ontology resemblance coefficients for improving semantic interoperability. Eng. Math. Lett. **2**, 1–19 (2013)
4. Zutshi, A.: Framework for a business interoperability quotient measurement model. Master thesis dissertations, Departamento de Engenharia Mecânica e Industrial, Universidade Nova de Lisboa, Portugal (2010). http://run.unl.pt/bitstream/10362/2646/1/Zutshi_2010.pdf

5. Sanchez Ruenes, D.: Domain Ontology learning from the Web. Ph.D. thesis, Departamento de Lenguajes y Sistemas Informaticos, Universidad Politecnica de Catalufia (2007). http://www.tdx.cat/bitstream/10803/6650/1/01Dsr01de02.pdf
6. Acampora, G., Vitiello, A.: Improving agent interoperability through a memetic ontology alignment: a comparative study. In: Fuzzy-IEEE International Conference on Systems, pp. 1–8 (2012)
7. Interop, N.: State of Art Report Ontology Interoperability, (n.d.)
8. Kalfoglou, Y., Schorlemmer, M.: Ontology mapping: the state of the art. Knowl. Eng. Rev. 18, 1–31 (2003)
9. Euzenat, J.: Semantic precision and recall for ontology alignment evaluation. In: IJCAI, pp. 348–353 (2007)
10. Shvaiko, P., Euzenat, J.: A survey of schema-based matching approaches. In: Spaccapietra, S. (ed.) Journal on Data Semantics IV. LNCS, vol. 3730, pp. 146–171. Springer, Heidelberg (2005)
11. Euzenat, J., Shvaiko, P.: Ontology Matching. Springer, Heidelberg (2007)
12. Bruijn, J., Ehrig, M., Feier, C., Martins-Recuerda, F., Scharffe, F., Weiten, M.: Ontology mediation, merging, and aligning. In: Davies, J., Studer, R., Warren, P. (eds.) Semantic Web Technologies, pp. 95–113. Wiley, Chichester (2006)
13. Noy, N.F., Musen, M.A.: Anchor-PROMPT: using non-local context for semantic matching. Framework 39, 63–70 (2001)
14. Ehrig, M., Staab, S.: QOM – quick ontology mapping. In: McIlraith, S.A., Plexousakis, D., van Harmelen, F. (eds.) ISWC 2004. LNCS, vol. 3298, pp. 683–697. Springer, Heidelberg (2004)
15. Maedche, A., Motik, B., Silva, N., Volz, R.: {MAFRA} - an ontology mapping framework in the semantic web. In: Proceedings of the ECAI Workshop on Transformation, Lyon, France (2002)
16. Noy, N.F., Musen, M.A.: The PROMPT suite: interactive tools for ontology merging and mapping. Int. J. Hum. Comput. Stud. 59, 983–1024 (2003)
17. Amrouch, S., Mostefai, S.: Survey on the literature of ontology mapping, alignment and merging. In: 2012 International Conference on Information Technology and E-Services, ICITeS (2012)
18. Ehrig, M.: Ontology alignment - bridging the semantic gap. In: Management, p. 250 (2005)
19. Beneventano, D., Orsini, M., Po, L., Sorrentino, S.: The MOMIS - STASIS approach for ontology-based data integration. In: Proceedings of the ISDSI (2009)
20. Klein, M., Fensel, D., Kiryakov, A., Ognyanov, D.: Ontology versioning and change detection on the web. In: Gómez-Pérez, A., Benjamins, V. (eds.) EKAW 2002. LNCS (LNAI), vol. 2473, pp. 197–212. Springer, Heidelberg (2002)
21. Kent, R.E.: The IFF foundation for ontological knowledge organization. Cat. Classif. Q. 37, 187–203 (2003)
22. Castano, S., Ferrara, A., Montanelli, S., Zucchelli, D.: HELIOS: a general framework for ontology-based knowledge sharing and evolution in P2P systems. In: Proceedings of the 14th International Workshop on Database and Expert Systems Applications (2003)
23. Choi, N., Song, I.-Y., Han, H.: A survey on ontology mapping. ACM SIGMOD Rec. 35, 34–41 (2006)
24. Kotis, K., Vouros, G.A: The HCONE approach to ontology merging. In: Web. pp. 1–15 (2008)
25. Preece, A., Hui, K., Gray, A., Marti, P., Bench-Capon, T., Jones, D., et al.: KRAFT architecture for knowledge fusion and transformation. Knowl. Based Syst. 13, 113–120 (2000)

26. Do, H.-H., Rahm, E.: COMA: a system for flexible combination of schema matching approaches. In: Proceedings of the 28th International Conference on Very Large Data Bases, pp. 610–621 (2002)
27. Stumme, G.: FCA-merge: bottom-up merging of ontologies. In: International Joint Conference on Artificial Intelligence, pp. 225–230 (2001)
28. Ehrig, M.: Foam - framework for ontology alignment and mapping; results of the ontology alignment initiative. In: Proceedings of the Work Integrated Ontology, vol. 156, pp. 72–76. CEUR-WS.org (2005)
29. Lambrix, P., Tan, H.: SAMBO-A system for aligning and merging biomedical ontologies. Web Semant. **4**, 196–206 (2006)
30. Giunchiglia, F., Shvaiko, P., Yatskevich, M.: S-match: an algorithm and an implementation of semantic matching. In: Bussler, C.J., Davies, J., Fensel, D., Studer, R. (eds.) ESWS 2004. LNCS, vol. 3053, pp. 61–75. Springer, Heidelberg (2004)
31. Li, J., Tang, J., Li, Y., Luo, Q.: RiMOM : a dynamic multistrategy ontology alignment. Framework **21**, 1–15 (2009)
32. Clifton, C.: Experience with a combined approach to attribute-matching across heterogeneous databases. In: Techniques. pp. 1–17 (1997)
33. An, Y., Borgida, A., Mylopoulos, J.: Inferring complex semantic mappings between relational tables and ontologies from simple correspondences. In: Meersman, R. (ed.) OTM 2005. LNCS, vol. 3761, pp. 1152–1169. Springer, Heidelberg (2005)
34. Qian, Y., Li, Y., Song, J., Yue, L.: Discovering complex semantic matches between database schemas. In: International Conference on Web Information Systems and Mining, WISM, pp. 756–760 (2009)
35. Li, W.S., Clifton, C.: SEMINT: a tool for identifying attribute correspondences in heterogeneous databases using neural networks. Data Knowl. Eng. **33**, 49–84 (2000)
36. Velegrakis, Y., Miller, R.J., Popa, L., Mylopoulos, J.: ToMAS: a system for adapting mappings while schemas evolve. In: Proceedings of the International Conference on Data Engineering, p. 862 (2004)
37. Blanchard, E., Harzallah, M.: A typology of ontology-based semantic measures. In: EMOI (2005)
38. Rada, R., Mili, H., Bicknell, E., Blettner, M.: Development and application of a metric on semantic nets. IEEE Trans. Syst. Man. Cybern. **19**, 17–30 (1989)
39. Zhibiao Wu, P.M.: Verb semantics and lexical selection. In: Proceedings of the 32nd Annual Meeting on Association for Computational Linguistics, pp. 133–138 (1994)
40. Leacock, C., Chodorow, M.: Combining local context and WordNet similarity for word sense identification. In: Fellbaum, C. (ed.) WordNet An Electronic Lexical Database, pp. 265–283. MIT Press, Cambridge (1998)
41. Resnik, P.: Using information content to evaluate semantic similarity in a taxonomy. In: Proceedings of the 14th International Joint Conference on Artificial Intelligence (1995)
42. Lin, D.: Principle-based parsing without overgeneralization. In: Meeting of the Association for Computational Linguistics, pp. 112–120 (1993)
43. Gan, M., Dou, X., Jiang, R.: From ontology to semantic similarity: calculation of ontology-based semantic similarity. Sci. World J. **2013**, 793091 (2013)
44. Sánchez, D., Batet, M., Isern, D., Valls, A.: Ontology-based semantic similarity: a new feature-based approach. Expert Syst. Appl. **39**, 7718–7728 (2012)
45. Al-Mubaid, H., Nguyen, H.A.: Measuring semantic similarity between biomedical concepts within multiple ontologies. IEEE Trans. Syst. Man, Cybern. Part C (Appl. Rev.) **39**, 389–398 (2009)

46. Hirst, G., St-Onge, D.: Lexical chains as representations of context for the detection and correction of malapropisms. In: WordNet - An Electronic Lexical Database, pp. 305–332 (1998)

47. Luong, H.P., Gauch, S., Wang, Q.: Ontology learning through focused crawling and information extraction. In: International Conference on Knowledge and Systems Engineering 2009, pp. 106–112. IEEE (2009)

48. Knappe, R.: Measures of Semantic Similarity and Relatedness for Use in Ontology-based Information Retrieval (2005)

49. Pesquita, C., Faria, D., Falcão, A.O., Lord, P., Couto, F.M.: Semantic similarity in biomedical ontologies. PLoS Comput. Biol. **5**, e1000443 (2009)

50. Bernstein, P.: Applying model management to classical meta data problems. In: Proceedings of the CIDR (2003)

Sentence-Based Plagiarism Detection for Japanese Document Based on Common Nouns and Part-of-Speech Structure

Takeru Yokoi[✉]

Computer Science Course, Tokyo Metropolitan College of Industrial Technology,
1-10-40 Higashi-oi, Shinagawa-ward, Tokyo, Japan
takeru@s.metro-cit.ac.jp
https://www.metro-cit.ac.jp/english/

Abstract. Plagiarism by the copy and paste of documents written by other authors has recently become a large problem as electronic documents have increased. In higher educational institutions, it is also of great concern in student reports. In this paper, we have proposed a novel approach to automatically detect plagiarism, especially for student experimental reports in Japanese and focusing on the common nouns and the structure of parts of speech for each sentence. We have also performed experiments to evaluate our approach with actual Japanese experimental reports written by our students with the measures such as precision, recall and F-value. As the experimental results, our proposed approach has succeeded to detect plagiarized pairs of sentences within high accuracy. In addition, we also discuss the parts where our proposed approach miss-detected and couldn't detect.

Keywords: Plagiarism detection · Sentence-based · Part-of-speech

1 Introduction

Plagiarism by the copy and paste of documents written by other authors has recently become a large problem as electronic documents on Web pages and documents written with by word processing have increased [1]. In higher educational institutions, copy/pasting is especially of great concern in student reports. The plagiarism students commit can be classified into two types: one is by copying from public documents that are readily available on the internet; and the other is from texts written by friends or colleagues. The latter is more difficult to automatically detect since the sources are usually not made public. Both should not be permitted, however, it is difficult, time-consuming as well as costly for educators to determine whether each report is an original text or plagiarized from other resources. Moreover, the plagiarism may be committed in such manner that some modifications or additions are made to the original source and it become more difficult to detect.

© Springer International Publishing Switzerland 2015
H. Fujita and A. Selamat (Eds.): SoMeT 2014, CCIS 513, pp. 297–308, 2015.
DOI: 10.1007/978-3-319-17530-0_21

While it has become easy for students to plagiarize using a copy/paste with electronic reports written using word processing, there are also ways for these texts to be analyzed with a computer. Therefore, we can support educators in detecting plagiarized sections in reports by designing a system for automatic plagiarism detection. The research on plagiarism detection is, in fact, of great interest and many techniques have been reported. These have targeted not only natural language documents [2,3] but also the programming source codes [4]. COPS [5] is one of the most well-known traditional plagiarism detection systems for digital documents.

We propose a novel sentence-based approach to detect plagiarism in student reports in Japanese, focusing not only on the surface representation of words, especially nouns, but also the structure of the parts of speech in each sentence. Most of the proposed plagiarism detection approaches target documents in English. In fact, there are some common techniques that are helpful to detect plagiarism for documents in Japanese, however, the grammatical structure of English and Japanese is explicitly different. Moreover, there are some researches that target student reports in Japanese but most of them also focus on surface representation of words such as character-based n-grams and word-based n-grams.

2   Related Works

Various methods and tools have been proposed and developed in the past to detect plagiarism in documents. In this section, we would like to introduce some of them.

"Turnitin"[1] is one of the most famous tools to automatically detect plagiarism in recent. The system compares a document with not only more than 45 billion web pages but also more than 300 million student articles and 130 million publications in order to help educators to find a problem in a student report. This system has been already introduced to 10 thousand organizations and used in 135 countries.

Osman et al. reviewed and categorized various plagiarism detection approaches into four categories: character-based; structural-based; cluster-based; and syntax-based methods [6]. In addition, they proposed a novel plagiarism detection method based on semantic role labeling. The method analyzes and compares the semantic allocation for each word in sentences.

White et al. proposed a sentence-based algorithm to detect plagiarism and implemented software to visualize the plagiarized parts, targeting English documents in higher educational institutes [7]. The approach is categorized as character-based methods by Ahmed etc. and is similar to our approach. Their approach compares sentences to each other and counts their common words, assigning a score to a document based on the number of common words. Gustafson et al. also proposed a method to detect plagiarism in documents with their sentence similarity [2]. They were able to establish a new degree of resemblance between any two documents based on sentence-based similarity.

---

[1] http://turnitin.com.

Most plagiarism detection approaches target only documents in English including the research introduced above. Our approach targets documents in Japanese and focuses not only on the string similarity but also the structure similarity with the edit distance by a unit as a part of speech.

3 Our Plagiarism Detection Approach

We have proposed the sentence-based approach to detect plagiarism with the structure of the parts of speech, focusing on the nouns used in each sentence. The sequence of the parts of speech in each sentence is hereby regarded as the structure of the parts of speech. Our approach compares sentence-to-sentence and detects plagiarism by a sentence as a unit.

3.1 Editing Operations in the Plagiarized Sentence

Our approach especially focuses on three editing operations in Japanese which are often performed because of their easiness.

One is just editing the end of a sentence. This operation corresponds to the slight change in the tense or modality of a sentence in Japanese. More specifically, it adds and removes some words at the end of a sentence which do not have meanings by themselves and also modifies them into a grammatically natural sentence. Both sentences $S1$ and $S2$ are examples that have been translated from Japanese into English meaning "the experiment succeeded" and their contents are almost similar except for the tense.

Example 1
$S1$: "The experiment went well."
$S2$: "The experiment has gone well."

This operation doesn't change the actual content of the sentence by modification and hides a direct copy and paste.

The second operation is the replacement of words so that they are combined with an equivalent conjunction. The following phrases as follow $P1$ and $P2$ are examples that have been translated from Japanese into English.

Example 2
$P1$: "apple and banana"
$P2$: "banana and apple"

Moreover, this operation is applied not only as in this example with an equivalent conjunction but also in more sophisticated phrases due to the characteristic of Japanese. The order of words in Japanese is freer than other languages such as English. For example, the order of a subject can be changed in Japanese so that it is more difficult to detect any plagiarism.

The third operation is rewriting an original word as a synonym or the word with a similar meaning. Examples of this operation are the word *"since"* which can be rewritten as *"because"* as well as the word *"beautiful"* rewritten as *"wonderful"*.

The feature of these editing operations preserves the meaning of the original sentence but just changes the surface structure. Therefore, it is difficult for the educator to see the plagiarism at first glance. The practical plagiarizing sentence is performed with a combination of some of these operations. In addition, direct copy and paste also most certainly exist.

3.2 Processes of the Proposed Approach

The processes of our proposed approach are presented below:

1. Divide a report into sentences based on a period.
2. Select two comparable sentences by the way mentioned in Sect. 3.3.
   (a) Extract the nouns from each sentence with Japanese morphological analysis. Japanese morphological analysis divides a sentence into words and also labels each word with its part-of-speech.
   (b) Select a pair of sentences including the same nouns of which the number is not less than the threshold. The threshold is manually determined.
3. Analyze the sequence of the parts-of-speech for the selected pair of sentences as their structures by the way mentioned in Sect. 3.4. In short words, the edit distance by part-of-speech between the sequences of the selected pair is calculated.
4. Determine if the sentence show plagiarism when the distance is beyond the threshold.

In the following sections, the points in our processes have been detailed.

3.3 Selection of the Comparable Sentences

In order to detect a pair of plagiarized sentences, we first need to select the suspicious candidates. The candidate sentences are selected from the viewpoint of the number of same nouns included in both sentences of the pair. We count the number of the kinds of the same nouns in a pair of sentences and regard the pair as a suspicious candidate if it goes beyond a threshold.

The way to count same nouns in our approach is explained more specifically with the following example sentences $S3$ and $S4$ which have been translated from Japanese into English.

Example 3
$S3$: "I ate strawberries in a strawberry patch yesterday."
$S4$: "I ate fruits in a strawberry patch yesterday"

There are 5 nouns included in the first sentence $S3$, as follows: {*I, strawberry, strawberry, patch, yesterday*}. In addition, the declension of nouns is changed into dictionary form. The second sentence $S4$ includes 5 nouns as well: {*I, fruit, strawberry, patch, yesterday*}. Our approach just counts the kind of nouns so that the number of kinds of nouns in the first sentence and the second sentence are 4 and 5, respectively. Moreover, the number of same nouns in the pair of those sentences is 4, {*I, strawberry, patch, yesterday*} and the pair of sentences is regarded as a suspicious candidate for plagiarism if this number goes beyond a threshold. On the contrary, if the number is less than the threshold, the possibility that the contents of any pair of sentences are similar may be low.

3.4 Analysis of the Parts of Speech

We have defined a novel similarity for the structure of the parts of speech with the edit distance in order to analyze it.

The edit distance, which is also called Levenshtein Distance, is usually to measure the distance between two strings. This distance is defined as the minimum counts of the editing operations so that one string is transformed into the other string. The editing operations here includes insertion, elimination and replacement of a character.

In order to explain the edit distance, there are two example strings $str1$ and $str2$, as follows:

Example 4
$str1$: "AAA_BAAABB_A"
$str2$: "AAA_CAAAC_BB"

In the case of this example, the edit distance is 3 with a character as a unit. The necessary editing operations in order to transform the first string $str1$ into the second string $str2$ are as follows. The 4th character 'B' is first changed to 'C'. This operation corresponds to replacement. Next, a character 'C' is inserted between the 7th character 'A' and the 8th character 'B'. This operation corresponds to insertion. Finally, the character 'A' at the end of string $str1$ is removed and the editing operations are completed. The last operation corresponds to elimination.

Our novel similarity focuses on a sequence of the parts of speech. This similarity is defined as the edit distance by a part of speech as a unit between the sequences of a pair of sentences. An example is shown to calculate this similarity using following pair of sentences $S5$ and $S6$ that have been translated from Japanese into English.

Example 5
$S5$: "I read a book."
$S6$: "I read a weekly magazine."

The calculated edit distance of this pair is 1 by our proposed approach. The sequence of the parts of speech of these sentences are: {*noun, verb, article, noun*} and {*noun, verb, article, adverb, noun*}, respectively. One insertion is, thus, performed when the first sentence is transformed into the second one.

The remarkable feature of this similarity which focuses on parts of speech is to enable us to deal not only with the direct replacement of words but also replacement into their synonyms. For example, our similarity for the pair of phrases, "banana and apple" and "apple and banana" is 0 since the sequence of the parts of speech of these phrases are completely the same: {*noun, conjunction, noun*}. This example corresponds to direct replacement. Moreover, we investigated replacement into synonyms with Example 3 used in Sect. 3.3. The parts of speech of those sentences are {*noun, verb, noun, proposition, article, noun, noun, noun*} and {*noun, verb, noun, proposition, article, noun, noun, noun*}. Therefore, the similarity of those sentences is also 0. In this example, "strawberry" is transformed into the more general "fruit" which is specifically a hypernym of "strawberry". However, they are regarded as the same from the viewpoint of parts of speech.

In this way, the similarity between the structure of the parts of speech enables us to deal not only with the direct replacement of words but also rewriting into synonyms. If we focus only on the surface representation of words, it's difficult to catch the similarities of the structures.

We finally determined that a pair of sentences constitutes plagiarism based on the similarity for each suspicious candidate pair of sentences. If the similarity goes beyond a threshold, the pair can be regarded as plagiarism. On the contrary, if the similarity of a pair of sentences is less than the threshold, the structures of those sentences are supposed to be quit different in which case, the pair may not be regarded as plagiarism but original sentences.

4   Experiments and Results

In this section, the experiments to evaluate the effectiveness of our approach and their results are presented. We carried out two experiments; one is based on text-by-text comparison, and the other is sentence-by-sentence comparison.

4.1   Experimental Conditions and Methods

We used the discussion parts of 10 experimental student reports written in Japanese about the same theme as experimental data. While some differences among these reports should exist even in part since the students need to investigate and consider by themselves in order to write it, it was more difficult to write than the other parts. Therefore, they sometimes tended to copy and paste from other sources such as their friends' reports with some modifications.

At first, we tried to evaluate the similarity among these entire documents with the cosine similarity. In order to calculate the cosine similarity, each document was represented as a document vector. The ith document vector $\mathbf{d}_i$ constructed in this experiment was as follow:

$$\mathbf{d}_i = \begin{bmatrix} d_{i1} \ d_{i2} \cdots d_{iN} \end{bmatrix}$$

where N denotes the total number of specific words included in both original document and compared document. If we calculate the cosine similarity between ith document and jth document, N was defined as follow:

$$N = |W_i \cup W_j|$$

where W_i and W_j denote the word set including words in ith and jth documents, respectively. $| \cdot |$ denotes the number of elements in a set. d_{ik} denotes weight corresponding to a word. In this experiment, the tf-idf weight was used as the weight and it was assigned to each specific word in the documents. The element of document vector d_{ik} assigned by the tf-idf was defined as follow:

$$d_{ik} = tf_{ik} \log(1/df_k)$$

where tf_{ik} denotes the kth word frequency in the ith discussion part of a report and df_k denotes the number of discussion parts in which kth word was included. In addition, if a word $w_k \notin W_i$, i.e., $w_k \in (W_i \cup W_j) \backslash W_i$, the element of document vector d_{ik} was set to be 0. The cosine similarity sim between ith and jth documents was calculated as follows:

$$sim = \frac{\mathbf{d}_i \cdot \mathbf{d}_j}{\|\mathbf{d}_i\|\|\mathbf{d}_j\|} \tag{1}$$

where $\cdot$ denotes the inner product and $\| \cdot \|$ denotes the L_2-norm defined as:

$$\|\mathbf{d}_i\| = \sqrt{\sum_{w_k \in W_i} d_{ik}^2}.$$

In addition, we used a morphological analysis tool named "Mecab" [8] to divide a sentence into words and to extract nouns and the parts of speech of words. In this experiment, we construct two types of document vectors. One consists of only nouns, the other consists of independent words such as a noun, a verb, a adjective and a adverb.

Next, we applied our approach that is a sentence-based approach to 187,730 pairs of sentences included in these documents. In addition, we manually selected the 142 pairs that could be deemed suspicious of plagiarism as the correct data before this experiment was performed. We summarize our experimental data in Table 1. "# of total independent words" and "# of total nouns" denote the total number of independent words and nouns occurred in discussion parts of 10 reports, respectively. Therefore, from the viewpoint of the numbers, we found nouns dominate the discussion parts and each discussion part used in this experiment consists of about 300 nouns in average. In order to determine the optimized parameters of the number of the same nouns included in pairs of sentences and the edit distance, we performed the experiments by changing the parameters. We changed the parameters on the number of the same nouns from 4 to 8 or more, and the edit distance from 3 or less to 8.

We used three measures which were precision P, recall R and the F-value F in order to evaluate the effectiveness of our sentence-based approach. These measures are defined as follows, respectively:

$$P = \frac{\#\ of\ detection\ and\ correctness}{\#\ of\ detection}, \tag{2}$$

$$R = \frac{\#\ of\ detection\ and\ correctness}{\#\ of\ correctness}, \tag{3}$$

$$F = \frac{2PR}{P+R}, \tag{4}$$

Table 1. Experimental data

Item	Condition
# of reports	10
Parts to evaluate	Discussion part
# of total independent words	5,031
# of total nouns	3,390
# of pairs of sentences	187,730
# of ground truth pairs of sentences	142

where "*# of detection*" denotes the number of the pairs which our approach detected as plagiarism, "*# of correctness*" denotes the total number of plagiarized pairs in the test set and "*# of detection and correctness*" denotes the number of correct pairs in which our approach detected plagiarism.

4.2 Results

We first showed the cosine similarity among documents with the document vector consisted of independent words in Table 2. "Doc. #" denotes the No. of document numbered from No.1 to 10 that we used this experiment. Like Table 2, we showed the cosine similarity among documents with the document vector consisted of only nouns in Table 3.

Next, the F-values of our novel approach is shown in Table 4. "# of Nouns" in this table denotes the number of the same nouns included in each pair of sentences. We especially note the value '8' of "# of Nouns" means 8 or more and the value '3' of "Edit Distance" means 3 or less.

We also show their transitions on each number of nouns for the edit distances from Fig. 1 to Fig. 3. 'X' of the "X Nouns" in these figures denotes the number of same nouns in a pair of sentences. Like Table 4, we note "8 Nouns" means 8 or more nouns and the value '3' of horizontal axis means 3 or less.

5   Discussion

We have found that it is difficult to detect plagiarism only by similarity among entire documents from Tables 2 and 3. In fact, we could find high similarities between 2nd and 7th documents, and 4th and 10th documents, respectively, however, almost similarities among these documents are around 0.1, as shown in both tables. Comparing the similarities in Table 2 with Table 3, a lot of similarities with document vectors consisted of independent words in Table 2 were less than the ones consisted of only nouns in Table 3. This indicated that the other words except nouns were rather modified or changed into other words. In addition, we actually glanced over the contents of document numbered 2 and 7 which have high cosine similarity between those documents in both experiments. However, we can't determined whether they were plagiarism report or

Table 2. Cosine similarity with document vectors consisted of independent words

Doc. #	1	2	3	4	5	6	7	8	9	10
1	1	0.047	0.125	0.305	0.054	0.019	0.038	0.024	0.049	0.182
2	-	1	0.102	0.019	0.019	0.106	**0.783**	0.041	0.019	0.018
3	-	-	1	0.059	0.059	0.039	0.100	0.088	0.047	0.076
4	-	-	-	1	0.038	0.014	0.019	0.035	0.026	0.467
5	-	-	-	-	1	0.051	0.023	0.045	0.041	0.042
6	-	-	-	-	-	1	0.064	0.067	0.124	0.009
7	-	-	-	-	-	-	1	0.055	0.018	0.015
8	-	-	-	-	-	-	-	1	0.035	0.050
9	-	-	-	-	-	-	-	-	1	0.046
10	-	-	-	-	-	-	-	-	-	1

Table 3. Cosine similarity with document vectors consisted of only nouns

Doc. #	1	2	3	4	5	6	7	8	9	10
1	1	0.053	0.113	0.311	0.093	0.024	0.041	0.031	0.070	0.212
2	-	1	0.121	0.011	0.020	0.122	**0.844**	0.037	0.018	0.013
3	-	-	1	0.070	0.073	0.031	0.119	0.105	0.040	0.101
4	-	-	-	1	0.041	0.007	0.012	0.070	0.022	**0.557**
5	-	-	-	-	1	0.050	0.022	0.039	0.056	0.047
6	-	-	-	-	-	1	0.067	0.086	0.151	0.006
7	-	-	-	-	-	-	1	0.054	0.020	0.009
8	-	-	-	-	-	-	-	1	0.019	0.057
9	-	-	-	-	-	-	-	-	1	0.046
10	-	-	-	-	-	-	-	-	-	1

not at a glance. We could surely find some suspicious plagiarized sentence pairs by viewing sentence-by-sentence carefully. Therefore, it's not helpful to determine if they were similar and plagiarisms from the other documents with the cosine similarity for entire documents.

While it's difficult to detect plagiarism with the approach based on entire documents, our proposed approach which is sentence-based could detect plagiarism well. The approach showed good results so that the maximum precision and recall are over 0.96 and 0.92, as shown in Figs. 1 and 2, respectively. On the contrary, the minimum precision and recall are about 0.52 and 0.59 at the maximum point of recall and precision, respectively. In fact, several results can depend on the parameters of the number of same nouns and the edit distance, however, we can correctly detect plagiarized sentences when choosing the optimized parameters. The high value of the parameter for the number of

Table 4. F-Values

		Edit Distance					
		8	7	6	5	4	3
# of Nouns	4	0.666	0.833	0.830	0.855	0.841	0.846
	5	0.713	0.845	0.851	0.867	0.856	0.801
	6	0.768	0.849	0.867	0.864	0.850	0.748
	7	0.798	0.836	0.870	0.871	0.841	0.738
	8	0.806	0.848	**0.874**	0.866	0.841	0.711

same nouns decreases suspicious candidates so that a higher precision is obtained as it increases. This property is explicitly found in Fig. 1. In addition, it's also explicit that the farther the edit distance becomes, the lower the precision is overall. On the contrary, the high value of the edit distance increases suspicious candidate pairs constituting plagiarism. In other words, the farther the edit distance, the higher recall is obtained. This is explicitly found in Fig. 2. The trade-off like results is a usual feature of precision and recall.

However, a high F-Value point that is over 0.87 exists, as shown in Table 4, when the parameters of the number of same nouns and the edit distance are 8 and 6, respectively. Therefore, these parameters are supposed to be optimized in this experiment.

Next, we considered the successful detections and failed detections. While our sentence-based approach could detect plagiarism without editing, it also detected plagiarism when the count of the editing operations is less than the parameter of the edit distance. In addition, it could detect plagiarism with the transformation of words into their synonyms such as changes of the kind of characters by focusing on the structure of the parts of speech. In actual, our approach could detect a plagiarized pair despite of following operations; (1) Changing character type; This case changes a word written in Chinese characters into in Hiragana, and vice verse. (2) Changing a word into synonym. (3) Changing modality; This cases changes the end of sentence using a predicate into stopping with indeclinable word. Considering with these results, we suppose our approach can also deal with para-phrase. Para-phrase is one of the great problem for plagiarism from the viewpoint that meaning of those phrases is same but those structure is different. The example of para-phrase is as follows:

Para-phrase Example
*phrase*1: I used this computer.
*phrase*2: This computer was used by me.

It's also a great problem to detect para-phrase plagiarism in English. However, Japanese can almost change the active-voice into the passive-voice such as the above example and vice verse with just modification of the end of sentence. Therefore, it can be also corresponded by changing modality in our approach.

However, some wrong detections that our sentence-based approach detected as plagiarism but wasn't also existed. There was a common feature in the pairs of sentences that our approach detected incorrectly. It almost always includes

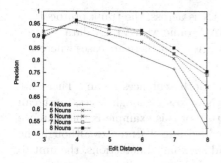
Fig. 1. Precision transitions

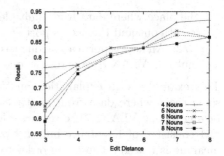
Fig. 2. Recall transitions

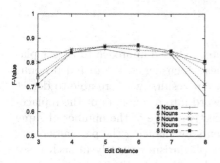
Fig. 3. F-value transitions

a short typical phrase and our approach, thus, judged them as a structure of the parts of speech which is similar. We show an example to miss-detect as a plagiarism.

Miss-detection Example
*str*1: access-list1 permit [network address][mask] This command sets access list.
*str*2: access-list1 permit "network address": Construct and permit access list.

This example is an explanation of a command. As mentioned above, These pairs include a lot of typical short expression and the length of sentence also often short. In order to avoid such wrong detections, we need to add the complete string matching for short typical phrases. Contrarily, there were some pairs of sentences that our approach failed to detect despite constituting plagiarism. We found that the length of sentences was drastically changed in those pairs by dividing a sentence into some sentences and merging some of these sentences into one sentence. Our sentence-based approach failed to detect those pairs as plagiarism since the count of the editing operations, especially insertion, increases. Therefore, the edit distance is high in such cases. We show an example of impossible detection.

Impossible Detection Example
*str*1: An access port can belong to one VLAN but setting a trank port at

the place where data from multiple VLAN is across, the trank protocol carries out and the access port sends MAC frame with VLAN data.

str2: An access port can belong to one VLAN. But there are cases where multiple VLAN data across at one port.

This example is an explanation on VLAN. Both sentences mean "There are some cases where data from multiple VLAN across although access port can belong to one VLAN". The remarkable feature of this example is the sentence *str1* consisted of 1 sentence but *str2* was divided into 2 sentences although the meaning is not so different. In order to avoid such failed detections, the unit to compare should not be one sentence, but divided into smaller parts such as an n-gram model.

6 Conclusion

In this paper, we have proposed a novel-sentence based approach to detect plagiarism in student reports written in Japanese, focusing on the included nouns and the structure of the parts of speech. In our results, we were able to detect plagiarism in sentences by just changing a word into a synonym or the replacement of words. In addition, we found an effective range of the number of same nouns and the edit distance in the experiments by changing the parameters.

However, our approach could not detect plagiarism correctly in such cases where short typical phrases were used or when the length of a sentence was drastically changed such as in the dividing and merging of sentences.

We need evaluate our approach with more actual reports in future work, too.

References

1. Maurer, H., Kappe, F., Zaka, B.: Plagiarism - a survey. J. Univers. Comput. Sci. **12**(8), 1050–1084 (2006)
2. Gustafson, N., Pera, M.S., Ng, Y.K.: Nowhere to hide: finding plagiarized documents based on sentence similarity. In: Proceedings of IEEE/WIC/ACM International Conference on Web Intelligence (WI 2008), pp. 690–696 (2008)
3. See, C.K., Wog, K.S., Woon, W.L.: Text plagiarism detection method based on path patterns. Int. J. Bus. Intell. Data Min. **3**(2), 136–146 (2008)
4. Son, J.W., Noh, T.G., Song, H.J., Park, S.B.: An application for plagiarized source code detection based on a parse tree kernel. Eng. Appl. Artif. Intell. **26**(8), 1911–1918 (2013)
5. Brin, S., Davis, J., Garcia, H.M.: Copy detection mechanisms for digital documents. In: Proceedings of the ACM SIGMOD Annual Conference, pp. 398–409 (1995)
6. Osman, A.H., Salim, N., Binwahlan, M.S., Alteeb, R., Abuobieda, A.: An improved plagiarism detection scheme based on semantic role labeling. J. Appl. Soft Comput. **12**(5), 1493–1502 (2012)
7. White, D.R., Joy, M.S.: Sentence-based natural language plagiarism detection. ACM J. Educ. Resour. Comput. **4**(4), 1–20 (2004)
8. Kudo, T., Yamamoto, K., Matsumoto, Y.: Applying conditional random fields to japanese morphological analysis. In: Proceedings of the 2004 Conference on Empirical Methods in Natural Language Processing (EMNLP-2004), pp. 230–237 (2004)

Software Analysis
and Performance Model

An Evaluation of COCHCOMO Tool
for Change Effort Estimation in Software
Development Phase

Nazri Kama[✉], Sufyan Basri, Mehran Halimi Asl,
and Roslina Ibrahim

Advanced Informatics School, Universiti Teknologi Malaysia,
Johor Bahru, Malaysia
{mdnazri,roslina.kl}@utm.my, msufyan4@live.utm.my,
mehran.netl@gmail.com

Abstract. Software changes are inevitable in any software project. Software project manager is required to make an effective decision when dealing with the software changes. One type of information that helps to make the decision is the estimation of the change effort produced by the changes. Reliable information of estimation on the change effort is significant to decide whether to accept or reject the changes. From software development perspective, the estimation has to take into account the inconsistent states of software artifacts across project lifecycle i.e., fully developed and partially developed. This research introduces a new change effort estimation tool (Constructive Change Cost Model or COCH-COMO) that is able to take into account the inconsistent states of software artifacts in its estimation process. This tool was developed based on our extended version of static and dynamic impact analysis techniques. Based on extensive experiments using several case studies have shown that an acceptable error rates result has been achieved.

Keywords: Change effort estimation · Change impact analysis · Effort estimation · Impact analysis · Software development phase

1 Introduction

Software changes are inevitable in any software project. Software changes may also occur in any stage during the software development life cycle. Thus, it is important to manage the changes in the software to meet the evolving needs of the customer and hence, satisfy them [1–5]. Accepting too many changes causes delay in the completion and it incurs additional cost. Rejecting the changes may cause dissatisfaction to the customers. Thus, it is important for the software project manager to make effective decisions when managing the changes during software development. One type of information that helps to make the decision is the estimation of the change effort produced by the changes. This prediction can be done by combining two most related concepts which are impact analysis and effort estimation.

On one hand, impact analysis is a process of identifying potential consequences of change, or estimating what needs to be modified to accomplish a change [6–8].

H. Fujita and A. Selamat (Eds.): SoMeT 2014, CCIS 513, pp. 311–328, 2015.
DOI: 10.1007/978-3-319-17530-0_22

The motivation behind the impact analysis activity is to identify software artifacts (i.e., requirement, design, class and test artifacts) that are potentially to be affected by a change. On the other hand, change effort estimation is the process of predicting how much work and how many hours of work are needed for a particular change request. In recent project management processes, the effort invested in a project has become one of the most significant and most studied subjects.

Challenge with the current change effort estimation approaches [9] that uses impact analysis technique as the source of input is that there is no consideration on the inconsistency states of software artifacts across the project. This consideration is crucial since in the software development phase: (1) some artifacts are partially developed and; (2) some of them have been developed conceptually but not technically (or have yet been implemented). Failure on this consideration will lead to inaccuracy of estimation that eventually contributes to project delay or customer dissatisfaction.

We have extended our previous works on change impact analysis approach [9, 10] to support the development of change effort estimation model for the software development phase [11]. This paper focusing on the demonstration of the change effort estimation tool that has been built based on the previously developed change effort estimation model [11]. Also, we demonstrate the accuracy of the developed tool to support change effort estimation in the software development phase.

This paper is laid out as follow. Section 2 presents related work whereas Sect. 3 demonstrates our new change effort estimation tool. Section 4 evaluates the accuracy of the tool and followed by Sect. 5 discusses the results. Finally, Sect. 6 describes conclusion and future works.

2 Related Work

There are several categories of effort estimation which are: (1) Expert Judgment [12]; (2) Estimation by Analogy [13]; (3) Function Point Analysis [14]; (4) Regression Analysis [15, 16]; and (5) Model Based [17].

Study by Jorgensen [12] shows that, expert judgment in effort estimation is one of the most common approaches today. Now more project managers prefer to use this method instead of formal estimation models, while the other techniques are simply more complex and less flexible than expert judgment methods. There is currently no method in effort estimation, which can prove its result to be hundred percent accurate. So, project managers just prefer to accept the risks of estimation and perform the expert judgment method for their effort estimation.

Effort estimation by analogy uses information from the similar projects which has been developed formerly, to estimate the effort needed for the new project. The idea of analogy-based estimation is to estimate the effort of a specific project as a function of the known efforts from historical data on similar projects. This technique could be combined with machine learning approaches for automation and to become more effective [13].

Traditionally, software size and effort measured using LOC (Lines of Code) measure. However, earlier studies [14] show that when the scale of the development grows, estimating using LOC fails to achieve accurate software effort estimation.

Also using different languages could be a problem; different languages could create different values of LOC. The addressed problems could be solved by using Function Point in software measurement and estimation. Function Point Analysis uses Function Point (FP) as its measure; therefore, it is suggested for improving the software measurement and estimation methods.

Another way to estimate software development effort is to use regression analysis; also known as algorithmic estimation. It uses variables for software size such as LOC and FP as independent variables for regression-based estimation and mathematical methods for effort estimation [18, 19]. Some multiple regression models also use other parameters such as development programming language or operating system as extra independent variables. The advantage of regression models is their mathematical basis as well as accuracy measurements.

3   A New Change Effort Estimation Tool

Our previously developed change effort estimation model [11, 20] has five main steps which are: (1) Developing class interactions prediction (CIP) model; (2) Acquiring change request attributes; (3) Performing static change impact analysis; (4) Performing dynamic change impact analysis; and (5) Estimating required change effort using change impact analysis results

Our new change effort estimation tool (which we called as COCHCOMO- Constructive Change Cost Model) has five main steps which are:

Step 1: Importing Class Interactions Prediction (CIP)
Step 2: Acquiring Change Request (CR)
Step 3: Performing Impact Analysis
Step 4: Estimating Change Effort
Step 5: Analyze Results.

Figure 1 shows the Main form of the tool that reflects to the five main steps of the model. We will describe in details each steps in the subsequent sections.

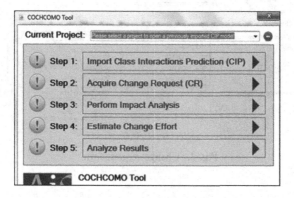

Fig. 1. Main form user interface

3.1 Step 1: Importing Class Interactions Prediction (CIP)

In the first step, this tool requires the Class Interaction Prediction (CIP) [21] file to be imported in the database. There are two sub-steps in the import process which are extracting information from the CIP file, and saving the CIP information into the database. Later, the tool will allow the user to print the CIP report accordingly. The screen shot of the Import CIP form is shown in Fig. 2:

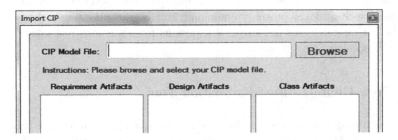

Fig. 2. Import CIP form

3.2 Step 2: Acquiring Change Request (CR)

Next, this step will get change request details from the user. We have designed a specific form based on the important change request attributes. The tool will automatically assign a unique identification number for each change request. Figure 3 shows the change request form.

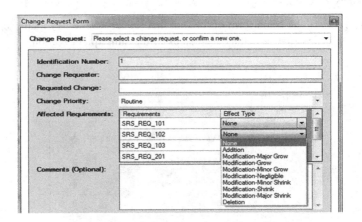

Fig. 3. Change request form

3.3   Step 3: Performing Impact Analysis

There are three sub-steps to perform impact analysis: (1) perform static change impact analysis; (2) filter static impact analysis results using class dependency filtration and (3) perform dynamic change impact analysis. In performing static change impact analysis, we employ two levels of search. First, an optimized breadth-first search (BFS) algorithm [22] to be performed on the directed graph created from the CIP model without any vertical interactions to find the directly impacted classes. Next, a complete BFS search will be performed on the overall CIP model to find all the indirectly impacted classes.

The next sub-process is filtering the static change impact analysis results using class dependency filtration (CDF). In CDF, each indirectly impacted class that has been identified by the static change impact analysis will be suspected. In this suspicion, a BFS search will be performed to dependent class artifacts tree. The goal of this search is to find a path from the indirectly identified impacted classes to the directly impacted classes; if such a path do not exists, this indirectly impacted class is considered as a false detection and it will be removed or filtered in the CDF results. Figure 4 explains the CDF concept.

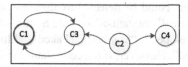

Fig. 4. Sample of dependent directed graph

In Fig. 4, C1 is a direct impacted class. C4 is considered as a false detection artifact because there is no path from C4 to C1. CDF will remove the C4. Figure 5 shows the sample of CDF results.

Perform Impact Analysis				
Source Code Address: us\Documents\Visual Studio 2010\Projects\MyCPPSampleProject	Browse			
Programming Language: C++: Win32 Console Application (Accepted code extensions are: [*.h] and [*.cpp])				
Instructions: Class dependency Filteration process is finished, press continue to begin the dynamic impact analysis process.				

No	Impacted Class	Code Status	Class Size	Impact Size (%)	Impact State
1	Class_101	Unkown	Unkown	18%	Indirect Impact
2	Class_102	Unkown	Unkown	45%	Direct Impact
3	Class_104	Unkown	Unkown	35%	Filtered by CDF
4	Class_201	Unkown	Unkown	18%	Indirect Impact

Legends

Code Status: The status of the class code which could be Unkown, Not Developed, Partly Developed, or Fully Developed.
Class Size: Class size in logical source lines of code (SLOC).
Impact Size: Size of the impact on the class in percentage.
Impact State: The state of impact which could be: Direct Impact, Indirect Impact, Dynamic Analysis, Filtered by CDF and Filtered by MDF.

Fig. 5. Sample of class dependency filtration results

The last sub-step is performing dynamic change impact analysis. This sub-step is a complex process. For simplicity, there are five sub-steps under this sub-step which are: (1) detect code status; (2) create actual method execution paths; (3) perform method dependency filtration (MDF); (4) perform method dependency addition (MDA); (5) perform dynamic change impact analysis.

The first sub-step, source codes will be inspected to find all the developed classes. Since our implementation scope is only C++ Win32 console applications, all the CPP (.cpp) and header (.h) files will be identified. Content of all files will be inspected to find if there exist any declarations of class from CIP model. Typical practice of C++ Win32 console application development, the programmer will declare all class names in header file and define them in the CPP file. However, it is also common that both declaration and definition of the class are written in the header file. Our code inspector will identify both types of class definition and declaration; categorize their development status; and save code information into the database. If the code file for a class is not found in the development directory, it will be considered as not developed class; but if it was found, another process will inspect the code to determine if the code is partially developed or fully developed.

Technically, we describe partially developed class as a class that contains stubs, fake methods, or incomplete methods in its current states of implementation. These partially developed methods could be detected by the code status tag; code status tag structure in C++ is as follow: ["///<status>" + Code Status + "</status>"]; where code status could be "Not Developed", "Stubbed", "Faked", "Mocked", "Partially Developed", or "Fully Developed". However, if the code status tag is not clearly defined, the code inspector will automatically detect as a partially developed method. At the same time, as the process is looking for the fully developed classes, it also detects fully or partially developed methods in all classes. The methods will be saved as method artifacts in the CIP artifacts database.

Furthermore, the tool also will calculate class size of fully developed classes in logical source lines of codes (SLOC) using pre-defined language specific rules. In C/C++, logical SLOC is calculated by counting the not-auto-generated codes containing preprocessor directives, terminal semicolons and terminal close-braces. A method is implemented in the code inspector of the tool, to first remove all comments from the codes and the calculate SLOC exactly based on the defined C/C++ language rules.

For each code inspection, a regular expression has been created to identify the match pattern for that inspection. The regular expressions used in the tool are shown in Table 1.

The next sub-step is to create method execution paths for all detected methods in fully developed classes. This sub-step reads the content of all methods and finds the methods executed by each identified method. The relation between methods and their executed methods will be saved to the CIP artifacts database to create the method execution paths. Based on the method executions paths that are created, two other sub-steps will be performed to improve the CIP model.

First, Method Dependency Filtration (MDF) will be performed to filter over-estimated interactions between the classes; a BFS search is used to find if there is any relation method between two interacting classes in CIP model. If there is no relation, the current relationship between two classes will be removed. Later, MDA will be

Table 1. Regular expression table

Regular Expression	Purpose
//\s*<status>\s*([\w\s]*)\s*</status>	To get the code status
::@MethodName\s*\((?:[\s\w]*)\)\)\s*{\s*return\s*(null|\d|".*"|'.'|)	To detect faked methods which returns null, a number, a string, or a character in the first life of method
::@MethodName\s*\((?:[\s\w]*)\)\)\s*{\s*throw	To detect stubs that throws an exception in their first line
(?:\.|->|::)([A-Za-z_][\w]*)\s*\(	To identify executed methods
class\s+([A-Za-z_][\w]*)	To identify class declarations
::([A-Za-z_][\w]*)\s*\((?:[\w\s]*)\)\s*{	To identify class definitions
@ClassName\s*::\s*([A-Za-_][\w]*)\s*\((?:[\w\s]*)\)\)\s*{	To identify methods definition of a declared class
@ClassName\s*::\s*([A-Za-z_][\w]*)\s*\((?:[\w\s]*)\)	To identify methods definition in class declaration
\#include\s+(?:<|")([\w/.]+)(?:>|")	To find the include files

performed to inspect whether if there exist actual interactions between two classes or not. If the MDA results show a relationship is exist, the new detected relationship will be added to the CIP model to become the new improved CIP model.

Lastly, the dynamic impact analysis sub-step will be performed on the improved CIP model. The dynamic change impact analysis will be performed by BFS search algorithm and new impact sizes will be determined as in static impact analysis. Figure 6 shows an example of dynamic analyses results in the tool.

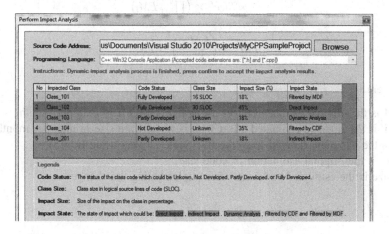

Fig. 6. Sample of dynamic analysis results

3.4   Step 4: Estimating Change Effort

The final step of our model is to estimate the required change effort based on the change impact analysis results. To estimate the change effort, we use COCOMO II [23] effort estimation model as a basic reference. In our calculation, we propose a mathematical equation to calculate change effort (CPM) according to the original estimated effort (PM) and updated effort estimation (PM′). CPM is the total effort need to implement the change; it is equal to priority multiplier multiplied by the deviation of estimated effort with new software size (PM′) and original estimated effort (PM) plus the extra effort needed for change the developed code as in Eq. (1):

$$CPM = ((PM' - PM) + abs[(PM' - PM) \times DSF]) \times PR \qquad (1)$$

Where,

- DSF is the development status factor based on Eq. (8),
- PM is the original estimated effort using COCOMO II in man per month,
- PM′ is the updated estimated effort after change using new software size in man per month and it is calculated using Eq. (2),
- PR is the priority multiplier which is determined by the effect of the change request priority and how much it will affect the change effort; this value should be selected according to the development methodology of the development group.

Equations (2)–(4) show how PM′ is calculated. This equation will be justified with the assumption that the cost factors and the scale factors will not change with the change request. Accordingly, the mathematical justification for producing this equation is as follow:

$$PM' = \frac{PM'}{PM} \times PM \qquad (2)$$

$$PM' = \frac{A \times CSize^E \times \left(\prod_{i=1}^{n} EM_i\right)}{A \times Size^E \times \left(\prod_{i=1}^{n} EM_i\right)} \times PM \qquad (3)$$

$$PM' = \left(\frac{CSize}{Size}\right)^E \times PM \qquad (4)$$

Where,

- PM is the original estimated effort using COCOMO II in man per month,
- PM′ is the updated estimated effort with new software size in man per month,
- E is the exponent derived from the five Scale Drivers using Eq. (5),
- Size is the original estimation of code size,
- CSize is the estimated code size after implementing the change.

$$E = B + 0.01 \times \sum\nolimits_{i=1}^{5} SF_i \tag{5}$$

Where,

- B are constant variables;
- SF_i stands for scale factor, which will be derived from the five scale factors.

Assuming that the initial effort estimation was done before the change request, the only unknown variable in Eq. (4) is CSize. Exponent E, PM, and Size are the known variables which can be easily obtained from the initial effort estimation. CSize is equal to the original estimated size plus additional size from impacted classes. The size of fully developed impacted classes can be calculated in dynamic change impact analysis process, but the size of other impacted classes should be provided according to the initial effort estimation. CSize is calculated by the following Eq. (6):

$$CSize = Size + \sum\nolimits_{IC} (Size_{IC} \times ISF_{IC}) \tag{6}$$

Where,

- Size is equal to initial estimation of software size,
- $_{IC}$ stands for impacted class,
- Size $_{IC}$ is the size of the impacted class $_{IC}$,
- ISF_{IC} is the impact size factor for the impacted class $_{IC}$ which is calculated using Eq. (7).

$$ISF_{IC} = \sum\nolimits_r P_{AT} \frac{CTF_r}{NR} \tag{7}$$

Where,

- ISF_{IC}: Impact size factor for impacted class (IC),
- r: Relation from requirement to the impacted class,
- NR: Number of requirement artifacts that have relation to the impacted class,
- P_{AT}: A constant value for probability of change for affect type (AT) – where AT could be direct or indirect affection type),
- CTF_r: Change type factor based on the affected requirement change type which leads to the relation r. Due to space limitation, please refer our previous works in [11].

DSF in Eq. (1) is the development status factor. This value indicates how much extra effort is needed to change the impacted developed classes. This value will specify that, if the impacted class is a fully developed class, it will need more effort to change it than a partly developed class, and moreover changing a partly developed class needs more effort than a not developed class. By using DSF in our calculation we are generalizing the fact that the change effort will intensively increase as more classes are being fully developed, and implement changes in early stages of development is less costly. DSF will be calculated using the following Eq. (8):

$$DSF = \left(\frac{ND \times NND + PD \times NPD + FD \times NFD - NIC}{NIC} \right) \qquad (8)$$

Where,

- DSF stands for development status factor (DSF $\geq$ 0),
- ND is equal to affect multiplier for not developed classes (see Table 3),
- NND is the number of not developed impacted classes,
- PD is equal to affect multiplier for partly developed classes (see Table 3),
- NPD is the number of partly developed impacted classes,
- FD is equal to affect multiplier for fully developed classes (see Table 3),
- NFD is the number of fully developed impacted classes,
- NIC is the total number of impacted classes.

The multipliers ND, PD and FD multipliers should be selected according to the phase distribution of the software development methodology used for the project. They can have different values for each project or development team. Moreover, there has been a research on the phase distribution of the development effort which could be used to estimate multiplier values. Here is a sample of phase distribution weight of schedule and effort for a typical project using Rational Unified Process (RUP) [24]:

Table 2. Phase distribution weight in RUP

Phase	Schedule	Effort
Inception	10 %	5 %
Elaboration	30 %	20 %
Construction	50 %	65 %
Transition	10 %	10 %

Table 2 shows how much effort is needed in each phase of a typical project which is using RUP methodology. Accordingly, a sample of ND, PD and FD multiplier values are created as in Table 3:

Table 3. Estimated values for the multipliers

Multipliers	Related Phases	Value
ND	Inception, Elaboration	0.25
PD	Inception, Elaboration and a quarter of Construction	0.4125
FD	Inception, Elaboration and Construction	0.9

The last process of the model is to prepare its change effort estimation results, which will be used to analyze the costs and impacts of change on the software. The results of the model are a set of prioritized impacted classes by their impact size, and the total effort required to implement the change. Figure 7 shows the implementation of change effort estimation in our tool and its sample results.

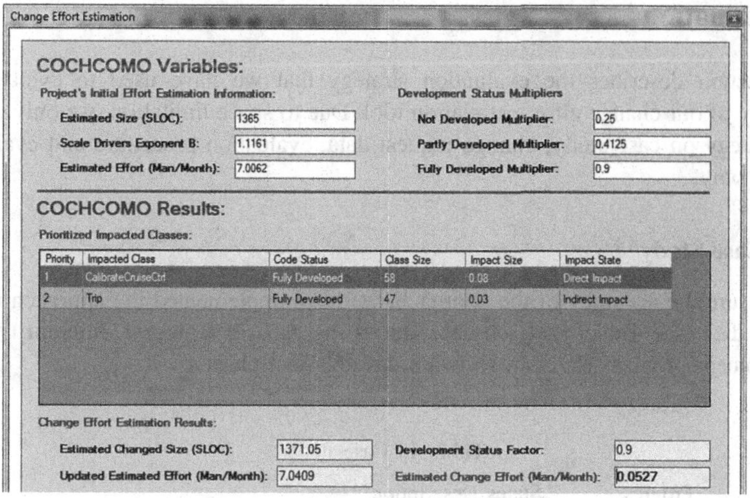

Fig. 7. Sample of change effort estimation results

3.5 Step 5: Analyze Results

The final step of COCHCOMO tool is to automatically analyze the results of change impact analysis and change effort estimation. This analysis results will be used to evaluate the COCHCOMO model. The metrics used for analyzing change impact analysis results are Completeness, Correctness, and Kappa Value. Moreover, the metrics used for analyzing change effort estimation results are Relative Error (RE), Magnitude of Relative Error (MRE), and Mean Magnitude of Relative Error (MMRE). MMRE shows the overall accuracy of the COCHCOMO model for T number of change requests as tests. Figure 8 shows the implemented graphical user interface for analyzing the results with sample data. Also it is possible to print or save a report from this analysis results which could be used in evaluation.

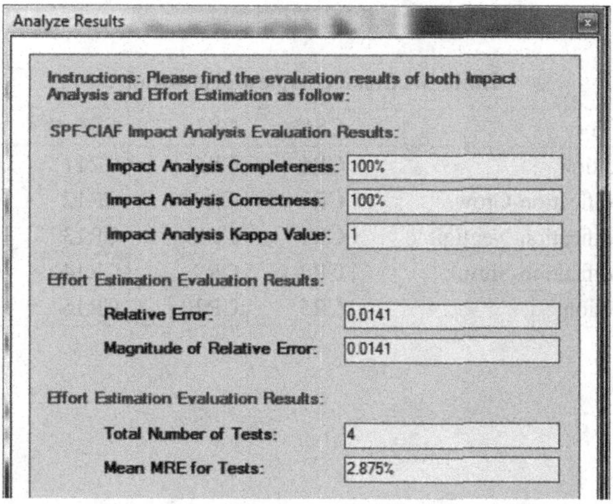

Fig. 8. Sample of change effort estimation analysis results

4   Evaluation

This section describes the evaluation strategy that we have used to evaluate the accuracy of our change effort estimation tool. Due to space limitation, we only present our strategy on case study, change request data, evaluation procedure and evaluation metrics only.

4.1   Case Study

To measure the accuracy of the approach, we have implemented the approach in four case studies (see Table 4). Each case study was used to represent different types of development progress states in software development phase.

Table 4. Case studies

Case Study	Progress	States Description
CS1	Analysis	Software design is finished, but none of the classes are developed yet
CS2	Coding	Software design is finished, and some partially developed classes exist
CS3	Testing	All the classes are developed, and some of them are fully developed
CS4	Deployment	All the classes are fully developed, and the development phase is finished

4.2   Change Request

Considering four case studies (CS) with different development progress states, twenty change requests with different change types have been issued. Table 5 shows the distribution of the change requests.

Table 5. Change request distribution

Change Type	CS1	CS2	CS3	CS4
CT1- Addition	CR1	CR6	CR11	CR16
CT2- Modification-Grow	CR2	CR7	CR12	CR17
CT3- Modification-Negligible	CR3	CR8	CR13	CR18
CT4- Modification-Shrink	CR4	CR9	CR14	CR19
CT5- Deletion	CR5	CR10	CR15	CR20

4.3   Evaluation Procedure

The evaluation procedures are: (1) estimating change effort using tool; (2) performing actual change implementation to get the actual results; (3) measuring the accuracy of the estimated change effort results using evaluation metrics.

4.4   Evaluation Metrics

Three effort estimation metrics were employed to measure the accuracy of the change estimation results. The metrics are Relative Error (RE) [25], Magnitude of Relative Error (MRE) [25], and Mean Magnitude of Relative Error (MMRE) [26].

RE: The RE shows the rate of relative errors and the direction of the estimation deviation [19]. A positive RE value matches to an under-estimate and a negative RE value to an over-estimate. The RE value is calculated as in Eq. (9):

$$RE = \frac{ActualResults - EstimatedResults}{ActualResults} \tag{9}$$

MRE: The MRE is similar to RE, but it is a metric for the absolute estimation accuracy only [25]. It calculates the rate of the relative errors in both cases of over-estimation or under-estimation as shown in Eq. (10):

$$MRE = abs\left[\frac{ActualResults - EstimatedResults}{ActualResults}\right] \tag{10}$$

MMRE: The MMRE or the Mean Magnitude of Relative Error is the percentage of average of the MREs over an entire data set [26]. It is used for calculating the accuracy of an estimation technique using t number of tests as it is shown in Eq. (11):

$$MMRE = \frac{100}{t}\sum_i^t MRE_i \tag{11}$$

The RE and MRE metrics will be calculated for each predicted impacted class from the change request experience to measure the accuracy of the change impact size estimation in our approach. But the MMRE will be calculated for the whole case study, which contains ten change requests and several impacted classes.

The results of our approach are more accurate when the MMRE values are smaller. Study by [27] stated that in estimation models, if MMRE value is less than 25 % then the estimation results is considered as an accurate estimation model. Therefore, if the MMRE values calculated from results of estimation in the approach are less than 25 %, the proposed approach will be proved to be acceptably accurate.

5   Results and Discussion

In this section the change effort estimation and error analysis results for all case studies (CS1 to CS4) are demonstrated (Table 6).

Table 6. Evaluation results of RE and MRE for all case studies

Case Study	CR No	Change effort		Tool evaluation	
		Actual	Estimated	RE	MRE
CS1	CR1	0.17619	0.1439	0.18327	0.18327
	CR2	0.1924	0.1696	0.11850	0.11850
	CR3	0.0078	0.0055	0.29487	0.29487
	CR4	-0.0478	-0.0401	0.16109	0.16109
	CR5	-0.9108	-0.9034	0.00812	0.00812
	MMRE				**15.32 %**
CS2	CR6	0.1600	0.1626	-0.01625	0.01625
	CR7	0.24107	0.2003	0.16912	0.16912
	CR8	0.00378	0.0059	-0.56085	0.56085
	CR9	-0.03986	-0.0481	-0.20672	0.20672
	CR10	-0.69118	-0.6876	0.00518	0.00518
	MMRE				**19.16 %**
CS3	CR11	0.2248	0.2187	0.02714	0.02714
	CR12	0.1924	0.1851	0.03794	0.03794
	CR13	0.0253	0.0109	0.56917	0.56917
	CR14	-0.0319	-0.0251	0.21317	0.21317
	CR15	-0.3901	-0.394	-0.01000	0.01000
	MMRE				**17.15 %**
CS4	CR16	0.2900	0.3281	-0.07117	0.07117
	CR17	0.3227	0.2578	0.20112	0.20112
	CR18	0.0125	0.0084	0.32800	0.32800
	CR19	-0.0065	-0.0064	0.01538	0.01538
	CR20	-0.1109	-0.1205	-0.08656	0.08656
	MMRE				**14.04 %**

To recap, the evaluation has been focusing on comparing results between the estimated change effort with the actual change effort. We have used the MMRE as the comparison metric.

According to [28] most effort estimation techniques having difficulty to produce accurate effort estimation results as they produced more than 30 % MMRE value compared to the actual results. In other study [29], proposed an acceptable MMRE value (or error rate) for software effort estimation is 25 %. This value shows that on average, the accuracy of the estimation is more than 75 %. For our evaluation, we have used this guideline to assess the accuracy of our proposed approach by targeting the MMRE value (or acceptable error rate) should be less than 25 %.

Since our proposed model is a change effort estimation model and not general effort estimation model, we assume that the change effort is slightly smaller than the overall effort needed for developing a software package. Therefore, a small miscalculation or an error will cause a large relative error in the estimations, so it has been expected to have moderate accuracy in the proposed change effort estimation model. Table 7 shows the MRE and MMRE of change requests in each case study.

Table 7. MRE and MMRE based on change types (CT) across case study (CS)

CT	CS1	CS2	CS3	CS4	Average
CT1	0.1832	0.0162	0.0271	0.0711	0.074458
CT2	0.1185	0.1691	0.0379	0.2011	0.131670
CT3	0.2948	0.5608	0.5691	0.3280	0.438223
CT4	0.1610	0.2067	0.2131	0.0153	0.149090
CT5	0.0081	0.0051	0.0100	0.0865	0.027465
MMRE	15.3 %	19.2 %	17.2 %	14.0 %	16 %

A quick look on the average MMRE value revealed that: (1) our proposed tool has 16 % relative error on average which is better than our expectation; and (2) all MMRE values for the case studies is less than 20 %. This analysis indicated that the proposed tool is acceptably accurate.

The result of MRE and MMRE above have been further analyzed using scatter chart and stacked. Figures 9 and 10 shows further analysis of the sums of magnitude relative errors in each case study using scatter chart and stacked chart respectively. Analyzing the charts exposed that the results of the proposed tool are more accurate for the changes with larger impacts. For instance in change type 3 (CT3) where the change is minimal or small (change type negligible modification), the sum of magnitude relative errors is at peak. However since the change efforts for the negligible modification changes are so small that even this larger amount of errors are completely insignificant and does not affect the overall results of this case study.

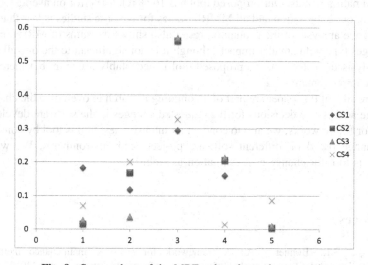

Fig. 9. Scatter chart of the MRE values for each case study

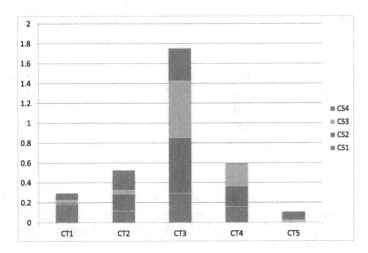

Fig. 10. Stacked chart of the MRE values for each case study

6 Conclusion

We have developed a change effort estimation tool that utilizes our previous work on change impact analysis. This tool is meant to support the implementation of our previous change effort estimation model. Basically, the tool automates both change impact analysis and change effort estimation processes that exist in the model.

The tool was evaluated by four different case studies over twenty change requests. The presented evaluation results demonstrate that the tool produces a reliable change effort estimation results. Our proposed tool has 16 % relative error on average which is better than our expectation and all MMRE values for the case studies is less than 20 %. Subsequence analysis of the evaluation result also shows the sums of MRE are higher for changes type with smaller impacts, though it is not significant to the overall results. This analysis indicated that the proposed tool is acceptably accurate, but there is still room for improvement.

The results of this paper are part of an ongoing research to overcome the challenges of change acceptance decisions for the requested changes in the software development phase. For future works, we aim to conduct an intensive test to this tool by considering more change based on different software projects and environments. We will also extend this tool for change cost estimation as well.

References

1. Pfleeger, S.L., Bohner, S.A.: A framework for software maintenance metrics. In: Proceedings of the International Conference on Software Maintenance, pp. 320–327 (1990)
2. Bennet, K.H., Rajlich, V.T.: Software maintenance and evolution: a roadmap. In: Proceedings of the International Conference on the Future of Sofware Engineering, pp. 75–87 (2000)

3. Finkelstein, A., Kramer, J.: Software engineering: a roadmap. In: Proceedings of the Conference on the Future of Software Engineering, pp. 3–22 (2000)
4. Brooks, F.P.: No silver bullet. IEEE Comput. 25(1), 91–94 (1987)
5. Kotonya, G., Somerville, I.: Requirements Engineering: Processes and Techniques. Wiley, Chichester (1998)
6. Arnold, R.S., Bohner, S.A.: Impact analysis-towards a framework for comparison. In: 1993 Proceedings., Conference on Software Maintenance, CSM 1993, 27–30 September 1993, pp. 292–301 (1993)
7. Antoniol, G., Canfora, G., Casazza, G.: Information retrieval models for recovering traceability links between source code and documentation. In: Proceedings of the International Conference on Software Maintenance, pp. 40–44 (2000)
8. Bianchi, A., Fasolino, A.R., Visaggio, G.: An exploratory case study of maintenance effectiveness of traceability models. In: Proceedings of the 8th International Workshop on Program Comprehension, pp. 149–158 (2000)
9. Kama, N.: Integrated change impact analysis approach for the software development phase. Int. J. Softw. Eng. Appl. 7(2), 293–304 (2013)
10. Kama, N., Azli, F.: A change impact analysis approach for the software development phase. In: Proceedings - Asia-Pacific Software Engineering Conference, APSEC, vol. 1, pp. 583–592 (2012)
11. Asl, M.H., Kama, N.: A change impact size estimation approach during the software development. In: Proceedings of the Australian Software Engineering Conference, ASWEC, pp. 68–77 (2013)
12. Jørgensen, M.: Practical guidelines for expert-judgment-based software effort estimation. IEEE Softw. 22(3), 57–63 (2005)
13. Li, J., Ruhe, G., Al-Emran, A., Richter, M.M.: A flexible method for software effort estimation by analogy. Empirical Softw. Engg. 12(1), 65–106 (2007)
14. Yinhuan, Z., Beizhan, W., Yilong, Z., Liang, S.: Estimation of software projects effort based on function point. In: 2009 4th International Conference on Computer Science & Education, ICCSE 2009, 25–28 July 2009, pp. 941–943 (2009)
15. Garcia, C.A.L., Hirata, C.M.: Integrating functional metrics, COCOMO II and earned value analysis for software projects using PMBoK. In: Proceedings of the 2008 ACM Symposium on Applied Computing, Fortaleza, Ceara, Brazil, pp. 820–825 (2008)
16. Nguyen, V., Huang, L., Boehm, B.: An analysis of trends in productivity and cost drivers over years. In: Proceedings of the 7th International Conference on Predictive Models in Software Engineering, Banff, Alberta, Canada: pp. 1–10 (2011)
17. Attarzadeh, I., Mehranzadeh, A., Barati, A.: Proposing an enhanced artificial neural network prediction model to improve the accuracy in software effort estimation. In: 2012 Fourth International Conference on Computational Intelligence, Communication Systems and Networks (CICSyN), 24–26 July 2012, pp. 167–172 (2012)
18. Finnie, G.R., Wittig, G.E., Desharnais, J.M.: A comparison of software effort estimation techniques: Using function points with neural networks, case-based reasoning and regression models. J. Syst. Softw. 39(3), 281–289 (1997)
19. Grimstad, S., Jørgensen, M.: A framework for the analysis of software cost estimation accuracy. In: Proceedings of the 2006 ACM/IEEE International Symposium on Empirical Software Engineering, Rio de Janeiro, Brazil, pp. 58–65 (2006)
20. Kama, N., Basri, S.: Extending change impact analysis approach to support change impact size estimation for software development phase. In: 2014 6th International Conference on Computer Research and Development (ICCRD 2014), Hanoi, Vietnam (2014)

21. Kama, N., Ridzab, F.A.A.: Requirement level impact analysis with impact prediction filter. In: 4th International Conference on Software Technology and Engineering (Icste 2012), pp. 459–464 (2012)
22. Zhou, R., Hansen, E.A.: Breadth-first heuristic search. Artif. Intell. **170**(45), 385–408 (2006)
23. Sharif, B., Khan, S.A., Bhatti, M.W.: Measuring the impact of changing requirements on software project cost: an empirical investigation. IJCSI Int. J. Comput. Sci. Issues **9**(3), 170–174 (2012)
24. Kruchten, P.: The Rational Unified Process: an Introduction. Addison-Wesley, Reading (2004)
25. Jøgensen, M., Molokken-Ostvold, K.: Reasons for software effort estimation error: impact of respondent role, information collection approach, and data analysis method. IEEE Trans. Softw. Eng. **30**(12), 993–1007 (2004)
26. Nguyen, V., Steece, B., Boehm, B.: A constrained regression technique for cocomo calibration. In: Proceedings of the Second ACM-IEEE International Symposium on Empirical Software Engineering and Measurement (ESEM 2008), pp. 213–222. ACM, New York (2008)
27. Huang, L., Song, Y.-T.: Precise dynamic impact analysis with dependency analysis for object-oriented programs. In: 2007 5th ACIS International Conference on Software Engineering Research, Management Applications, SERA 2007, August 2007, pp. 374–384 (2007)
28. Basha, S., Ponnurangam, D.: Analysis of empirical software effort estimation models. Int. J. Comput. Sci. Inf. Secur. (IJCSIS) **7**(3), 68–77 (2010)
29. Huang, S.-J., Chiu, N.-H., Chen, L.-W.: Integration of the grey relational analysis with genetic algorithm for software effort estimation. Eur. J. Oper. Res. **188**(3), 898–909 (2008)

Type-2 Fuzzy Logic Based Prediction Model of Object Oriented Software Maintainability

Sunday Olusanya Olatunji[1(✉)] and Ali Selamat[2]

[1] College of Computer Science and IT, University of Dammam,
Dammam 31441, Kingdom of Saudi Arabia
osunday@ud.edu.sa, oluolatunji.aadam@gmail.com
[2] Faculty of Computing, Universiti Teknologi Malaysia,
81310 Johor Bahru, Johor, Malaysia

Abstract. In this work, a maintainability prediction model for an object-oriented software system based on type-2 fuzzy logic system is presented. With the proliferation of object-oriented software systems, it has become very essential for concerned organizations to maintain those systems appropriately and effectively. However, it is pathetic to note that just very few number of maintainability prediction models are currently available for object oriented software systems. In this work, maintainability prediction model based on type-2 fuzzy logic systems is developed for an object-oriented software system. Earlier published object-oriented metric dataset was used in building the proposed model. Comparative studies involving the prediction accuracy of the proposed model was carried out in relation to the earlier used models on the same datasets. Empirical results from experiments carried out indicates that the proposed type-2 fuzzy logic system produced better and interesting results in terms of prediction accuracy measures authorized in object oriented software maintainability literatures. In fact, the proposed method satisfies the three major conditions stated in the literatures as basis to determining a good maintainability prediction model.

Keywords: Software maintainability · Type-2 fuzzy logic system · Prediction models · Object-oriented software systems · Software metrics

1 Introduction

The maintainability of Software is the process of modifying a software product to improve performance or other attributes, correct faults, or to adapt the product to an altered environment. On the face value, majority usually assume that the maintenance of software starts when the product is completed and handed over to the client. While this could be formally true, but the fact is that decisions that affect the maintenance of the software product are usually made starting from the earliest stage of the system design.

Software maintenance could be: adaptive, corrective, preventive, and perfective. Adaptive maintenance involves modifications that will make the software adapt to changes in the data environment, such as new product codes or new file organization or changes in the hardware or software environments. Corrective maintenance is the

© Springer International Publishing Switzerland 2015
H. Fujita and A. Selamat (Eds.): SoMeT 2014, CCIS 513, pp. 329–342, 2015.
DOI: 10.1007/978-3-319-17530-0_23

process of fixing any error detected in the software. The preventive maintenance refers to the maintenance that is carried out in order to try to prevent malfunctions or improve maintainability of the software while perfective maintenance include making enhancements that could lead to making the software product become better, faster, smaller, better documented, better structured, or coming up with additional functions or reports.

A situation where a software system is not designed to be maintenance-friendly, will definitely create a software that ii characterized by lack of stability under any needed modification. In such case, any change effected in a section of the system will have side effects that ripple throughout the entire system. Therefore, one of the major challenges in the area of software maintenance centers on how to understand an existing system in order to make it possible to effect changes without introducing new bugs.

It is an established fact that several object-oriented (OO) software systems are presently and actively being used all over the world. It is also a fact that the growing popularity of OO programming languages, such as Java, as well as the increasing number of software development tools built upon and supporting the Unified Modelling Language (UML), cannot be over emphasized. These realities will definitely encourage more OO systems to be designed and developed at very rapid rate now and in the future. Hence there is a great need to come up with ideas and models that could facilitate the ease of maintaining those systems effectively and efficiently. A software maintainability prediction model will assists organizations to predict the maintainability of a software system thereby facilitating effective and efficient management of maintenance resources. Aggarwal et al. [1], studied the application of artificial neural networks (ANN) using object-oriented (OO) metrics for predicting software maintainability. Zhou and Leung [2] used a novel exploratory multivariate analysis technique called Multivariate Adaptive Regression Splines (MARS) for the prediction of maintainability of object oriented software systems. Olatunji et al. [3] developed a maintainability prediction model for object-oriented software systems using extreme learning machine (ELM). Their model was based on extreme learning machine algorithm for single-hidden layer feed-forward neural networks (SLFNs) which randomly chooses hidden nodes and analytically determines the output weights of SLFNs [4]. Object-Oriented (OO) software datasets published by Li and Henry [5] were used in the study.

Furthermore, the availability of an accurate maintainability prediction model for a software system will facilitate the adoption of an appropriate defensive design mechanism. This would definitely lead to a drastic reduction, or at least minimize the needed effort to carry out future maintenance of the system. There are different ways through which maintainability of a software system could be measured. It could be estimated as the number of changes made to the code during a maintenance period or it could be estimated as effort expended in making those changes. When the maintainability is measured in terms of efforts expended, the resultant predictive model is called a maintenance effort prediction model. It is rather unfortunate, that there are currently very few software maintainability prediction models available in literature including those that centred on maintenance effort prediction.

In this paper, a new maintainability prediction model for an object-oriented software system using type-2 fuzzy logic system (T2FLS) is proposed and implemented. T2FLS has proved itself to be one of the most sought after regression techniques in recent time due to its accurate and reliable performance, especially in face of uncertainties that characterize our day to day activities and datasets and it has been used in several published works often with promising results [6–12].

The rest of this paper is organized into sections as follows. Section 2 contains the description of the proposed type-2 fuzzy logic systems. Section 3 discussed empirical studies and discussions that include comparison with other models. It also contains the description of the dataset together with the metrics used in the studies conducted and also the descriptions of the metrics were included in this section. Section 4 concludes the paper and also offered future research directions.

2 Proposed Type-2 Fuzzy Logic Systems

An adaptive network that learns the fuzzy rules and functions from dataset based on type-2 fuzzy set is called type-2 adaptive fuzzy inference systems, details of which can be found in [13–15]. Dubois and Prade [16] stated that "type-2 fuzzy sets are fuzzy sets whose grades of membership are, them-selves, fuzzy. They are intuitively appealing because grades of membership can never be obtained precisely in practical situations". In scenario where there exist uncertainties about the grades of membership, type-2 fuzzy logic readily comes to essential use because classical fuzzy logic (type-1 fuzzy logic) cannot handle such situation. Generally, it has been stated that "a fuzzy set is of type n, $n = 2, 3, \ldots N$ if its membership function ranges over fuzzy sets of type $n - 1$" [17].

Interval type-2 fuzzy sets are the most widely used type-2 fuzzy sets because they are easy to use and implement. When the type-2 fuzzy sets are interval type-2 fuzzy sets, all secondary grades (flags) are equal to 1 [18]. In general, a type-2 fuzzy logic system contains five components that are: fuzzifier, rules, inference engine, type-reducer and defuzzifier which are inter-connected as shown in Fig. 1. The fuzzifier takes in the values of the OOP metric input parameters and then produce the fuzzified values that will be fed into the inference engine. Thereafter, the inference engine will produce its output as a type-2 fuzzy set. This will in turn be subjected to a type-reduction process by the type-reducer in order to produce type-reduced fuzzy set. The type reduced fuzzy set is an interval set that represents the possible range of target output. Finally, the output value from the defuzzification process will be calculated from the generated interval set using the defuzzifier. In developing the proposed model, the unique steps that include initializing the system, training the system, and testing or validating the system have been considered.

The interval type-2 fuzzy set has been used in this work because it is the form of type-2 fuzzy logic system that is presently computationally feasible and realistic to use [14, 19].

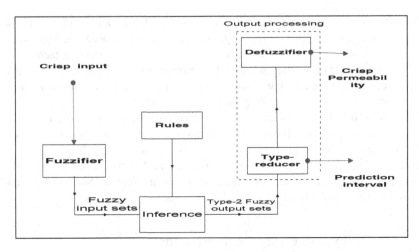

Fig. 1. Schematic diagram of a type-2 fuzzy logic system

2.1 Initializing the Interval Type-2 Fuzzy Logic System

When initializing the proposed system, it involves the process of defining the components of a typical interval type-2 fuzzy logic system from the perspective of the target variable to be estimated [6, 12]. In this work, the system was initialized using part of the available numerical dataset. In the proposed model, internal attributes (antecedents) include the independent variables; while target output or dependent variable (consequent) is the external attribute to be predicted. In this model, type-2 Gaussian with uncertain mean (m) have been considered, as indicated in Eq. (1) and Fig. 2, to be the membership function for the antecedent and consequent variables. The type-2 Gaussian with uncertain standard deviation (σ) have been considered, as indicated in Eq. (2) and Fig. 3, to be the membership functions for the input (antecedent).

$$\mu_A(x) = \exp\left[-\frac{1}{2}\left(\frac{x-m}{\sigma}\right)^2\right] m \in [m_1, m_2] \tag{1}$$

In this case (Eq. (1)), the membership function has a fixed standard deviation, σ, and an uncertain mean, m, that takes values in the range $[m_1, m_2]$ as depicted in Fig. 2. Thus, corresponding to each value of m, there will be a different membership curve as shown in Fig. 2.

$$\mu_A(x) = \exp\left[-\frac{1}{2}\left(\frac{x-m}{\sigma}\right)^2\right] \sigma \in [\sigma_1, \sigma_2] \tag{2}$$

In case of using Eq. (2), the membership function has a fixed mean, m, and an uncertain standard deviation, σ, that takes values in the range $[\sigma_1, \sigma_2]$ as depicted in Fig. 3. Thus, corresponding to each value of σ, there will be a different membership curve as shown in Fig. 3 [6, 12].

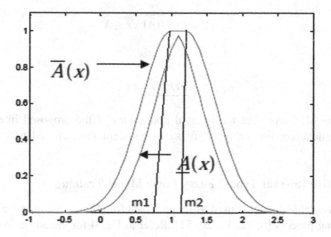

Fig. 2. Gaussian MFs with uncertain mean.

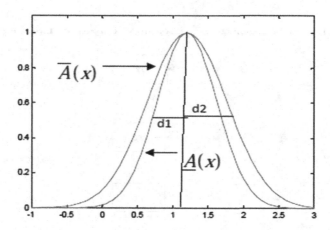

Fig. 3. Gaussian membership functions (MF) with uncertain standard deviation.

As for the $\bar{A}(x)$ and $\underline{A}(x)$, indicated in Figs. 2 and 3, they stand for the upper membership function and lower membership function (MF), respectively. Referring to Fig. 3, the uncertain standard deviation of Gaussian membership functions are $d1 = \sigma_1$ and $d2 = \sigma_2$. These two MFs are two type-1 membership functions that are bounds for the foot print of uncertainty (FOU) of a type-2 fuzzy set $\tilde{A}$ [6, 12, 19]. The foot print of uncertainty (FOU) is the space between the lower and the upper membership functions. The upper MF is associated with the upper bound of $FOU(\tilde{A})$ and it is usually denoted as $\bar{\mu}_{\tilde{A}}(x)\ \forall x \in X$. On the other hand, the lower membership function is associated with the lower bound of the $FOU(\tilde{A})$ and it is usually denoted as $\underline{\mu}_{\tilde{A}}(x)$ for any $x \in X$, that is, the upper and lower MFs can be represented as follows:

$$\bar{\mu}_{\tilde{A}}(x) = \overline{FOU(\tilde{A})} \; \forall x \in X \tag{3}$$

and

$$\bar{\mu}_{\tilde{A}}(x) = \underline{FOU(\tilde{A})} \; \forall x \in X \tag{4}$$

Thus, the MFs represent the interval boundaries of the proposed interval based model. More details on interval type-2 fuzzy logic systems can be found in [6, 12, 14, 18].

2.2 Adaptive Interval Type-2 Fuzzy Logic Model Training

Part of the available dataset is used as training data for training the model using type-2 fuzzy learning process [6, 12, 14, 20, 21]. Refer to Fig. 4 for the adaptive network of the interval type-2 fuzzy based system. Since the output of the network is numeric, then this can be compared with the expected output from a teacher (i.e. supervised learning) and back propagation used to feed the error back to adjust the parameters in the nodes.

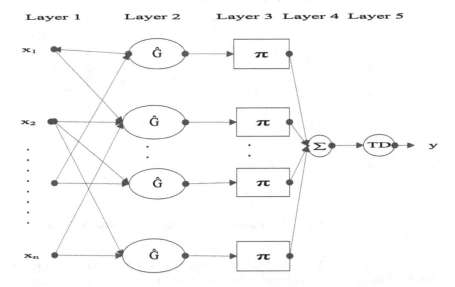

Fig. 4. General adaptive network of the proposed interval type-2 fuzzy inference systems; (TD = type reduction and Defuzzification, $\hat{G}$ = type-2 MF handler, π = PRODUCT (meet) operator, $\sum$ = Join(union) operator).

The procedure in the adaptive type-2 fuzzy logic system is made up of forward and backward passes while using a combined gradient descent and least square error method for the learning process required to determining the parameters' values for the adaptive nodes [6, 12, 14, 21, 22]. The descriptions on the parameters of the modified forward pass with brief emphasis on operations in each layer as shown in Fig. 4 are as follows:

In the symbols that follow shortly, the subscript ij indicates the j-th term of the i-th input $O_{ij}^{(k)}$, where $j = 1, \ldots \ldots, l$, and the superscript (k) means the k-th layer.

1st layer: This is the input layer for the network. The net input and the net output for the i-th node of this layer are indicated as:

$$O_i^{(1)} = w_i^{(1)} x_i^{(1)} \tag{5}$$

where, the weights $w_i^{(1)}, i = 1, \ldots, n$ are set to be unity and $x_i^{(1)}$ is the input to the i-th node in this first layer.

2nd layer: Every node here is an adaptive node. This layer handles the type-2 membership functions (MF). The nodes here consist of linguistic membership grades to be matched with the input variables used in the training process. Two types of MF earlier described (as in Eqs. (1), (2) and Figs. 2 and 3) are adopted here. Based on these two MFs, the two kinds of output from this layer are presented in cases 1 and 2 as follows [6, 12, 21]:

The σ_{ij} and m_{ij} represent the standard deviation (or width) and mean of the MFs, respectively. Also it must be noted that interval type-2 fuzzy is being use here and therefore these type-2 MFs can be represented as interval bound by the upper MF and the lower MF, which are denoted as $\bar{\mu}_{\tilde{F}_i}$ and $\underline{\mu}_{\tilde{F}_i}$ respectively.

Case 1: This is the case involving the antecedent and consequent membership functions that has been defined to be Gaussian MF, having uncertain mean (m), for type-2 fuzzy logic as in Eq. (1) and Fig. 2. The output for this case is follows:

$$O_{ij}^{(2)} = \exp\left[-\frac{1}{2}\left(\frac{O_{ij}^{(1)} - m_{ij}}{\sigma_{ij}}\right)^2\right] = \begin{cases} \bar{O}_{ij}^{(2)} \text{ as } m_{ij} = \bar{m}_{ij} \\ \underline{O}_{ij}^{(2)} \text{ as } m_{ij} = \underline{m}_{ij} \end{cases} \tag{6}$$

Case 2: This is the case involving the input membership functions that has been defined to be Gaussian MF having uncertain standard deviation (σ) as in Eq. (2) and Fig. 3. The output from this case is as follows:

$$O_{ij}^{(2)} = \exp\left[-\frac{1}{2}\left(\frac{O_i^{(1)} - m_{ij}}{\sigma_{ij}}\right)^2\right] = \begin{cases} \bar{O}_{ij}^{(2)} \text{ as } \sigma_{ij} = \bar{\sigma}_{ij} \\ \underline{O}_{ij}^{(2)} \text{ as } \sigma_{ij} = \underline{\sigma}_{ij} \end{cases} \tag{7}$$

Based on the fact already stated earlier in this Sect. 2, the type-2 MFs can be represented as interval bound by the upper MF and the lower MF, which is denoted as $\bar{\mu}_{\tilde{F}_i}$ and $\underline{\mu}_{\tilde{F}_i}$ respectively, therefore the output from the 2nd layer is represented as an interval $\left[\underline{O}_{ij}^{(2)}, \bar{O}_{ij}^{(2)}\right]$ where $\underline{O}_{ij}^{(2)}$ represents the output from the lower MF and $\bar{O}_{ij}^{(2)}$ is the output from the upper MF.

3rd layer: This is the layer where the operations involving fuzzy rules are carried out. The antecedent matching takes place in this layer following the type-2 fuzzy rules. The operation in this layer is implemented as PRODUCT (meet) operation. Thus, the output from this layer for the j-th rule node is as follows [6, 12]:

$$O_j^{(3)} = \prod_{i=1}^{n} (w_{ij}^{(3)} O_{ij}^{(2)}) = \begin{cases} \bar{O}_{ij}^{(3)} = \prod_{i=1}^{n} \left(w_j^{(3)} \bar{O}_{ij}^{(2)} \right) \\ \underline{O}_{ij}^{(3)} = \prod_{i=1}^{n} \left(w_j^{(3)} \underline{O}_{ij}^{(2)} \right) \end{cases} \tag{8}$$

where the weights $w_{ij}^{(3)}$ are set to be unity. Therefore, similar to the previous layer 2, the output $O_{ij}^{(3)}$ from this layer is represented as an interval $\left[\underline{O}_{ij}^{(3)}, \bar{O}_{ij}^{(3)} \right]$.

4th layer: The node here is responsible for the generation of the rules' output by carrying out consequent matching. The "join" operation (UNION) regarding the grades of membership also takes place in this layer).

$$O^{(4)} = \prod_{i=1}^{n} (w_j^{(4)} O_j^{(3)}) = \begin{cases} \bar{O}_j^{(4)} = \prod_{i=1}^{n} \left(w_j^{(4)} \bar{O}_j^{(3)} \right) \\ \underline{O}_j^{(4)} = \prod_{i=1}^{n} \left(w_j^{(4)} \underline{O}_j^{(3)} \right) \end{cases} \tag{9}$$

The details of the operations involved in this layer particularly the rule firing strength composition and matching is presented in Sect. 2.3 below.

5th layer: This is the layer where the type reduction and final defuzzification takes place. The only node here is a fixed node. It is in this layer that the final output is generated as crisp value, being the final result from the defuzzification process that takes place. By comparing the produced crisp output with the target value, an error, which can be used in back-propagation for tuning the parameters, can easily be determined. Details of the operations involved in the procedures used for computing the crisp final output is presented in Sect. 2.4 below, including the type-reduction and final defuzzification processes.

2.3   Type-2 Fuzzy Rule Consequent Matching in the 4th Layer

Let us assume a type-2 Mamdani fuzzy logic system [6, 12, 14] supplied with n inputs $x_1 \in X_1, \ldots \ldots x_n \in X_n$ and an output $y \in Y$. The number of type-2 fuzzy rules will be L and they are represented as follows:

$$R^l : \text{IF } X_1 \text{ is } F_1^l \text{ and } X_2 \text{ is } F_2^l \text{ and} \ldots \ldots \ldots \text{and } X_n \text{ is } F_p^l \text{ THEN } y \text{ is } G^l$$

Where $l = 1, 2, \ldots \ldots .L$, F_i^l and G^l are fuzzy sets of type-2, and p is the number of antecedents. The stated rule is the relationship between the input space $X \in X_1 \times X_2 \times \ldots \ldots .X_n$ and the output space Y of the interval type-2 fuzzy system, and its MFs that is represented as follows:

$$\mu_{F_1^l} \times \ldots\ldots\ldots \times F_p^l \to G^l(x, y) \tag{10}$$

where $F_1^l \times \ldots\ldots \times F_n^l$ represents the Cartesian product of $F_1^1, F_2^1, \ldots\ldots F_p^1$ and $x = \{x_1, x_2 \ldots\ldots x_p\}$.

The meet (intersection) operation is used to connect the antecedents in the fuzzy rules, the extended sup-star composition is used to combine the output fuzzy sets and firing strength of the input fuzzy sets (as illustrated below in this same Sect. 2.3), while the join (Union) operation is used to combine multiple rules [14]. The membership grades of the proposed system is usually represented by the upper and lower membership grades of the footprint of uncertainty (FOU) [6, 12, 14, 23]. To illustrate the extended sup-star composition using the above stated type-2 fuzzy rules, as a hypothetical case, let $\mu_{F_i^l}(x) = \left[\underline{\mu}_{F_i^l}(x), \overline{\mu}_{F_i^l}(x)\right]$ and $\mu_{G^l}(y) = \left[\underline{\mu}_{G^l}(y), \overline{\mu}_{G^l}(y)\right]$ for each of the samples (x, y). The T2FLS' firing strength given as $\mu_{F^i}(x) = \bigcap_{i=1}^{n} \mu_{F_i^l}(x)$ is an interval [14] i.e. $\mu_{F^i}(X) = \left[\underline{f}^i(X), \overline{f}^i(X)\right]$. Given that the proposed interval T2FLS made use of meet operation under product t-norm, therefore the firing strength, as presented below in Eq. (11) will be an interval type-1 fuzzy set [6, 12, 14, 23].

$$f^i(X) = \left[\underline{f}^i(X), \overline{f}^i(X)\right] = \left[\underline{f}^i, \overline{f}^i\right] \tag{11}$$

Since * represents the t-norm product operation, then $\underline{f}^i(X)$ and $\overline{f}^i(X)$ will now be the following form as shown in Eqs. (12) and (13) as follows:

$$\underline{f}^i(X) = \underline{\mu}_{\overline{F}_1^j}(x_1) * \ldots\ldots * \underline{\mu}_{\overline{F}_n^j}(x_n) \tag{12}$$

$$\overline{f}^i(X) = \overline{\mu}_{\overline{F}_1^j}(x_1) * \ldots\ldots * \overline{\mu}_{\overline{F}_n^j}(x_n) \tag{13}$$

Therefore, Eq. (11) shows that the firing level of rule R^l can be determined by computing the lower and upper membership grades. Type-reduction and defuzzification are then performed to calculate the crisp output.

2.4 The Type Reduction Process

This is the process that handles the conversion of the generated type-2 fuzzy output into a type-reduced fuzzy format. It is after this reduction has been carried out that a defuzzification process can then be used to generate the actual final crisp output. In this work, a type reducer algorithm proposed by Mendel and Karnik [14, 19] known as Centre-of-sets (COS) is used, being the most preferable in literatures. The type-reducer consists of two steps that include: (i) computing the interval type-2 fuzzy rule consequences' centroids and (ii) computing the reduced fuzzy sets. Details of these steps are well explained in [6, 12, 14, 18, 20, 24, 25].

3   Empirical Studies and Discussions

In this work, we made use of one of the OO software datasets published by Li and Henry (1993) [4].

3.1   Dataset and the Metrics Studied

This study makes use of one of the two object oriented software data sets published by Li and Henry (1993) [5]. These metric data were collected from a total of 110 classes in two OO software systems The data set is called user interface management system (UIMS) dataset, which contains the metric data of 39 classes collected from a UIMS.

The dataset used consist attributes that includes: WMC (Weighted methods per class), DIT (Depth of inheritance tree), RFC (Response for a class), NOC (Number of children), LCOM (Lack of cohesion in methods), MPC (Message-passing coupling), DAC (Data abstraction coupling), NOM (Number of methods), SIZE1 (Lines of code), SIZE2 (Number of properties), and CHANGE (Number of lines changed in the class) which is the attributed to be predicted in this work [5]. Maintainability was measured in CHANGE metric by counting the number of lines in the code, which were changed during a three-year maintenance period.

3.2   Methodology, Model Building and Evaluation

The available data set was partitioned into two parts. The larger part was considered as training set used for the building of a maintainability prediction model. The second part was then used as testing set in order to determine the prediction accuracy of the proposed model. Even though dataset could be divided into training and testing sets in different ways, the stratify sampling approach in breaking datasets have been used in this work due to its ability to break data randomly with a resultant balanced division based on the supplied percentage. The splitting could be made in the ratio 70 %:30 % for training and testing sets respectively. In the studies being reported here, 70 % of the data has been used in building the model (training set) while the remaining 30 % was used for testing/validation.

It must be noted that the proposed fuzzy logic system made use of the "let the data speak concept", which is a fuzzy approach that automatically learn the rules and membership functions from the data [14, 19, 20]. During the implementation process for the proposed T2FLS model, the implementation process progresses by supplying the system with the available input data sets, one sample at a time, while the rules and membership functions are automatically leaned from the available input data. Gaussian membership function was considered and used based on two different learning criteria that include least squares and back-propagation. The same parameter combination was utilized in training FLS membership function parameters. Further details on initializing, training and validating type T2FLS could be found in [14, 19, 20]. The outputs from the proposed T2FLS model are reduced type-2 fuzzy sets, from where the prediction intervals for the predicted output are generated. The type-reduced fuzzy sets are finally defuzzified to produce the final crisp output representing the predicted crisp value.

The proposed model was evaluated and compared with other earlier published OO software maintainability prediction models referred to earlier. Quantitatively, the comparison was made using the following prediction accuracy measures recommended in the literatures: absolute residual (Ab. Res.), the magnitude of relative error (MRE) and the proportion of the predicted values that have MRE less than or equal to a specified value suggested in the literature (Pred measures). Further details on these measures of performance will be provided shortly.

3.3 Prediction Accuracy Measures Used

In this work, the comparative studies done were carried out on the software maintainability prediction models using the following prediction accuracy measures, based on recommendation found in literatures [5, 26]: absolute residual (Abs Res), the magnitude of relative error (MRE) and Pred measures (which is a measure of what proportion of the predicted values that have MRE less than or equal to a specified value).

The absolute value of residual (Ab.Res.) is computed using the formula: Ab. Res. = abs (actual value − predicted value). Other quality measures used include the sum of the absolute residuals (Sum.Ab.Res.), the median of the absolute residuals (Med.Ab.Res.) and the standard deviation of the absolute residuals (SD.Ab.Res.).

The sum of the absolute residuals (Sum.Ab.Res.) measures the total residuals over the dataset. The median of the absolute residuals (Med.Ab.Res.) measures the central tendency of the residual distribution. It is chosen to be a measure of the central tendency due to the special fact that the residual distribution is usually skewed in software datasets. The standard deviation of the absolute residuals (SD.Ab.Res.) measures the dispersion of the residual distribution.

The magnitude of relative error (MRE) is a normalized measure of the discrepancy between actual values and predicted values given by MRE = abs (actual value − predicted value)/actual value.

The Max.MRE measures the maximum relative discrepancy, which is equivalent to the maximum error relative to the actual effort in the prediction. The mean of MRE, the mean magnitude of relative error (MMRE) is computed as follows:

$$MMRE = \frac{1}{n} \sum_{i=1}^{n} MRE_i \qquad (14)$$

According to Fenton and Pfleeger [28], Pred is a measure of what proportion of the predicted values that have MRE less than or equal to a specified value, given by:

$$Pred(q) = k/n \qquad (15)$$

where q is the specified value, k is the number of cases whose MRE is less than or equal to q and n is the total number of cases in the dataset.

According to Conte and Dunsmore [29], and Gray & Macdonell [26], in order for an effort prediction model to be considered accurate, it must achieved MMRE ≤ 0.25

and/or either pred (0.25) $\geq$ 0.75 or pred (0.30) $\geq$ 0.70. These are the suggested criteria to be met in literature as far as effort prediction is concerned before a model could be adjudged to be good.

3.4   Results' Discussion and Comparative Studies

Below is the table showing the results of the proposed T2FLS model in comparison to the other earlier used models on the same dataset.

3.5   Results from UIMS Dataset

Table 1 contains the values of the prediction accuracy measures achieved by each of the maintainability prediction models for the UIMS dataset. From the results presented, the proposed T2 model has achieved the MMRE value of 0.000014, the pred (0.25) value of 0.862 and the pred (0.30) value of 0.921. These values are all better than those of the other models considered. Specifically, the quality measures of the other models are far lesser than those of the proposed T2FLS model. It is clear from these, that the T2FLS model has met all the conditions stipulated and it is the only model that has achieved better than all the required values for all the three essential prediction measures [23, 24], hence it is the best among all the presented models. Thus, the proposed T2FLS outperforms all the other models in terms of all the predictive measures used.

In comparison with the UIMS dataset, the performance of the models generally on QUES dataset is far better than that on UIMS. It is only the proposed T2FLS that achieve better result in both dataset considered.

Table 1. Prediction accuracy for the UIMS dataset (ELM = extreme learning machines, T2FLS = Type-2 fuzzy logic systems)

Model	Max. MRE	MMRE	Pred (0.25)	Pred (0.30)	Sum Ab.Res.	SD Ab.Res.
Bayesian network	7.039	0.972	0.446	0.469	362.300	46.652
Regression tree	9.056	1.538	0.200	0.208	532.191	63.472
Backward elimination	11.890	2.586	0.215	0.223	538.702	53.298
Stepwise selection	12.631	2.473	0.177	0.215	500.762	54.114
ELM	4.918	0.968	0.392	0.450	39.625	16.066
T2FLS	0.000014	0.00007	0.862	0.921	22.0	8.418

With the exception of T2FLS that has values satisfying the earlier stated criteria on the used dataset, none of the other prediction models presented get closer to satisfying any of the criteria of an accurate prediction model cited earlier. However, it is reported that prediction accuracy of software maintenance effort prediction models are often low and thus, it is very difficult to satisfy the criteria [20]. This acclaimed difficult task has been successfully fulfilled by the proposed T2FLS with results satisfying the established criteria on the datasets investigated. Thus, it can be concluded that the proposed T2FLS model is able to predict the maintainability of the OO software systems reasonably with very high level of accuracy.

4 Conclusion

T2FLS based object-oriented software maintainability prediction model has been constructed using the OO software metric dataset earlier published [5, 26, 27]. The prediction accuracy of the model is evaluated and compared with the Bayesian network model, regression tree model, back ward elimination model, stepwise elimination model and extreme learning machines models using the popular prediction accuracy measures that include: the absolute residuals, MRE and pred measures. The results indicated that T2FLS model is able to reliably model and predict maintainability of the OO software systems. The proposed T2FLS model has achieved significantly better prediction accuracy than the other models on the same dataset used. In fact, the proposed model satisfies all the three accuracy conditions stipulated in the literatures [5, 26, 27] as earlier presented in Sect. 3. Finally, it could be concluded here that the proposed T2FLS model is able to predict maintainability of the OO software systems with very high accuracy while achieving the minimal errors possible. Based on the interesting performance of the proposed method on this lonely dataset, we hope to extend this work further in our future work by considering additional dataset and also comparing with more prediction models. It is recommended that T2FLS should also be investigated in the area of fault prediction and other interesting software engineering predictions tasks based on the encouraging performance displayed by the proposed type-2 fuzzy based systems.

References

1. Aggarwal, K.K., et al.: Application of artificial neural network for predicting maintainability using object-oriented metrics. In: World Academy of Science, Engineering and Technology, vol. 22 (2006)
2. Zhou, Y., Leung, H.: Predicting object-oriented software maintainability using multivariate adaptive regression splines. J. Syst. Softw. **80**(8), 1349–1361 (2007)
3. Olatunji, S.O., et al.: Extreme learning machine as maintainability prediction model for object-oriented software systems. J. Comput. **2**(8), 42–56 (2010)
4. Huang, G.B., Zhu, Q.Y., Siew, C.K.: Extreme learning machine: theory and applications. Neurocomputing **70**(1–3), 489–501 (2006). Elsevier
5. Li, W., Henry, S.: Object-oriented metrics that predict maintainability. J. Syst. Softw. **23**(2), 111–122 (1993)
6. Olatunji, S.O., Selamat, A., Raheem, A.A.A.: A hybrid model through the fusion of type-2 fuzzy logic systems, and extreme learning machines for modelling permeability prediction. Inf. Fusion **2014**(16), 29–45 (2014)
7. Olatunji, S.O., Selamat, A., Raheem, A.A.A.: Predicting correlations properties of crude oil systems using type-2 fuzzy logic systems. Expert Syst. Appl. **38**(9), 10911–10922 (2011)

8. Olatunji, S.O., Selamat, A., Raheem, A.A.: Modeling the permeability of carbonate reservoir using type-2 fuzzy logic systems. Comput. Ind. **62**(2), 147–163 (2011)

9. Zarandi, M.H.F., et al.: A type-2 fuzzy rule-based expert system model for stock price analysis. Expert Syst. Appl. **36**(1), 139 (2009)

10. Liang, Q., Mendel, J.M.: Equalization of non-linear time-varying channels using type-2 fuzzy adaptive filters. IEEE Trans. Fuzzy Syst. **8**, 551–563 (2000)

11. Karnik, N.N., Mendel, J.M.: Applications of type-2 fuzzy logic systems to forecasting of time-series. Inf. Sci. **120**(1–4), 89–111 (1999)

12. Olatunji, S.O., Selamat, A., Raheem, A.A.A.: Improved sensitivity based linear learning method for permeability prediction of carbonate reservoir using interval type-2 fuzzy logic system. Appl. Soft Comput. **14**, 144–155 (2014)

13. Liu, F.: An efficient centroid type-reduction strategy for general type-2 fuzzy logic system. Inf. Sci. **178**(9), 2224–2236 (2008)

14. Mendel, J.M.: Uncertain Rule-Based Fuzzy Logic Systems: Introduction and New Directions, 1st edn, p. 555. Prentice-Hall, Upper-Saddle River (2001)

15. Greenfield, S., et al.: The collapsing method of defuzzification for discretised interval type-2 fuzzy sets. Inf. Sci. **179**(13), 2055–2069 (2009)

16. Dubois, D., Prade, H.: Fuzzy Sets and Systems: Theory and Applications. Academic Press, New York (1982)

17. Zadeh, L.A.: The concept of a linguistic variable and its application to approximate reasoning - I. Inf. Sci. **8**, 199–249 (1975)

18. Liang, Q., Mendel, J.M.: Interval type-2 fuzzy logic systems: theory and design. IEEE Trans. Fuzzy Syst. **8**, 535–550 (2000)

19. Karnik, N.N., Mendel, J.M., Liang, Q.: Type-2 fuzzy logic systems. IEEE Trans. Fuzzy Syst. **7**, 643–658 (1999)

20. Mendel, J.M., John, R.I.B.: Type-2 fuzzy sets made simple. IEEE Trans. Fuzzy Syst. **10**(2), 117–127 (2002)

21. Olatunji, S.O.: Data mining in identifying carbonate lithofacies and permeability from well logs based on type-1 and type-2 fuzzy logic inference systems: methodology and comparative studies (MS thesis). In: Information and Computer Science. King Fahd University of Petroleum and Minerals, Dhahran, Saudi Arabia, p. 179 (2008)

22. Yu-ching, L., Ching-hung, L.: System identification and adaptive filter using a novel fuzzy neuro system. Int. J. Comput. Cogn. **5**(1), 1–12 (2007)

23. Chen, X., et al.: Type-2 fuzzy logic-based classifier fusion for support vector machines. Appl. Soft Comput. **8**(3), 1222–1231 (2008)

24. Mendel, J.M.: Fuzzy sets for words: a new beginning. In: The 12th IEEE International Conference on Fuzzy Systems, Los Angeles (2003)

25. Mendel, J.M.: Type-2 fuzzy sets: some questions and answers. IEEE Connections Newsl. IEEE Neural Netw. Soc. **1**, 10–13 (2003)

26. Gray, A.R., MacDonell, S.G.: A comparison of techniques for developing predictive models of software metrics. Inf. Softw. Technol. **39**, 425–437 (1997)

27. van Koten, C., Gray, A.R.: An application of Bayesian network for predicting object-oriented software maintainability. Inf. Softw. Technol. **48**(1), 59–67 (2006)

28. Fenton, N.E., Pfleeger, S.L.: Software Metrics: A Rigorous and Practical Approach. PWS Publishing Co., Boston (1998)

29. Conte, S.D., Dunsmore, A.H.E., Shen, A.V.Y.: Software Engineering Metrics and Models. Benjamin-Cummings Publishing Co. Inc., Boston (1986)

Adaptive Learning for Lemmatization in Morphology Analysis

Mary Ting[1]([✉]), Rabiah Abdul Kadir[2],
Tengku Mohd Tengku Sembok[3], Fatimah Ahmad[3],
and Azreen Azman[1]

[1] Faculty of Computer Science and Information Technology,
Universiti Putra Malaysia, 43400 Serdang, Selangor, Malaysia
`maryting.research@gmail.com`
[2] Institute of Visual Informatic, Universiti Kebangsaan Malaysia,
43600 Bangi, Selangor, Malaysia
`rabiah.akadir@gmail.com`
[3] Department of Computer Science, Faculty of Defence Science
and Technology, National Defence University of Malaysia,
Kem Sungai Besi, 57000 Kuala Lumpur, Malaysia

Abstract. Morphological analysis is used to study the internal structure words by reducing the number of vocabularies used while retaining the semantic meaning of the knowledge in NLP system. Most of the existing algorithms are focusing on stemmatization instead of lemmatization process. Even with technology advancement, yet none of the available lemmatization algorithms able to produce 100 % accurate result. The base words produced by the current algorithm might be unusable as it alters the overall meaning it tried to represent, which will directly affect the outcome of NLP systems. This paper proposed a new method to handle lemmatization process during the morphological analysis. The method consists three layers of lemmatization process, which incorporate the used of Stanford parser API, WordNet database and adaptive learning technique. The lemmatized words yields from the proposed method are more accurate, thus it will improve the semantic knowledge represented and stored in the knowledge base.

Keywords: Lemmatization · Morphology analysis · Natural language processing · Adaptive learning · Semi-supervised learning

1 Introduction

Morphological analysis is one of the earlier stages of natural processing technique that is used to study the internal structure of inflected words or formation, which later can be used for semantic analysis in NLP systems. The purpose of the technique is to improve the retrieval result by limiting the number of vocabularies used in the knowledge base. Some will look at it as a simple process, where each individual word from the context is transformed into its smallest unit form that is known as the root or base word. Converting each word without considering the meaning of an entire sentence or paragraph might change the overall meaning it tried to convey to the user.

© Springer International Publishing Switzerland 2015
H. Fujita and A. Selamat (Eds.): SoMeT 2014, CCIS 513, pp. 343–357, 2015.
DOI: 10.1007/978-3-319-17530-0_24

Among the existing techniques, most of them focus on stemmatization, where the stem words generated might be unusable as they might change the original meaning of the knowledge, they not appear in English language or have no meaning. These words need to be reprocessed again via the lemmatization process in order to transform it into a meaningful English morphemes [1]. Even then, none of the existing lemmatization algorithm can yield 100 % accurate result. These inappropriate base words generated will affect accuracy of dependency parsing [2], which will directly affect the identification of the relation between the concepts to provide a meaningful knowledge [3–5]. As a result it will eventually affect the overall accuracy of semantic knowledge the knowledge base trying to represent [6].

The proposed method consists of three layers of lemmatization process, which incorporate Stanford parser API for lemmatization, WordNet database for lexicon item extraction and adaptive learning framework. Since inflected words are being passed through different process in each layer, thus generated base words are more accurate when comparing to the other algorithms, at the same time it will improve the retrieval process.

2 Natural Language Processing

Natural language processing (NLP) can be used to interpret and store the meaning embedded in the paragraph by means of knowledge representation. In order to understand the natural language texts, inputted texts or queries are processed through several levels of natural language processing methods depending on the purpose of NLP systems. Each level is implemented to handle different analysis on the natural language, starting with internal word structure on the lowest level, moving upward towards the context knowledge, which requires the world knowledge at the highest level. Thus, the number of analysis required are dependent on the nature of the NLP systems.

Among the existing NLP applications, majority of them have implemented the lower levels of natural language processing techniques, which have the abilities to analyse the morphology of the words, syntactic analysis of the sentence and also a basic semantic analysis [7]. Natural language texts entered into these systems will need to be processed before it can be used. Since the outcome of each process become the input of the next process, hence any error occurred from one process will directly affect the result of the subsequence processes.

3 Morphological Analysis

Morphological analysis is the first of the major processes that will change the meaning of the entire sentence if it was not done properly. The technique segments the word into morphemes, where the interaction between morphemes is analysed to determine the syntactic class of the word form as a whole. In order to perform word segmentation, there is a need to study the internal structure of word formation within the language. Due to grammatical reasons, each word must appear in different formation structure by adding suffix and prefix to the root word. Only then, it can be categorised into different lexical classes accordingly. Normally inflected or derived words appear when the base word evolves from the evolution of suffix and prefix.

A word such as "develop" can appear in many different formations; develops, developed, developable, development, developer, redevelop, undeveloped and developing. When forming a sentence, each of these words will serve different purposes. The morpheme word for develops, developing and developed provides the same meaning after stemming process, whereas other formations such as developer, development, redevelop contributes to different meaning even though they have the same morpheme word. Table 1 shows the different formation of word "develop" used in sentences for different grammatical reason. Through the stemming process, these words will be transformed back to its morphemes word.

Table 1. Different formation of "develop" word used in sentence

Item	Sentence	After stemming process	Remarks
1	Ahmad develops the system	Ahmad develop the system	–
2	Ahmad developing the system	Ahmad develop the system	–
3	Ahmad redevelops the system	Ahmad develop the system	Missing the real meaning "improvement" of the previous system
4	Ahmad monitors the development of the system	Ahmad monitor the develop of the system	It should emphasis on the progress of the system implementation. Changing of lexical classes of the word from noun to verb.
5	Ahmad, the developer of the system.	Ahmad, the develop of the system.	The word "develop" here should be a person not the process.

The first 2 sentences from the Table 1 show provide the same meaning after stemming process, where it represents Ahmad "make" the system. In the third sentence, the morpheme word "develop" here should represent the meaning of re-create the system or improvement of the existing system. As for the fourth sentence, "development of the system" represents the system progress where Ahmed monitors the system progress. Users are able to understand the phrase "develop of the system" as the system progress through deduction of their knowledge, but a machine will not be able to do so. Same issue goes to the fifth sentence, where the original word "developer" transforms to "develop" after stemming process. The word "developer": should be devised as a person instead of an action after stemming process. As the result, inappropriate base word "develop" generated from stemming process from sentence 3 to 5 will change the meaning it tries the convey.

Generating a base word from different tenses is more complicated, especially when the inflected word does not follow the formula of adding a prefix or suffix. The process of reverting the inflected word for irregular verbs will become more complicated when the word appears in other tense than the present tense. This is because the simple past and past participle of irregular verbs can end in a variety ways without any consistent pattern [8]. For example an irregular verb present tense for "throw"; the inflected words for "throw" can appear as "threw", "thrown", "throws" and "throwing". The process of retracting the base word from simple past and past participle tenses like "threw" and "thrown" will not be as simple and straight forward as removing suffix such as "ing", "ness", "tion", "s" and etc. Given that there are no specific patterns on how to inflect irregular verb, thus there are no specific ways on how to extract base word out of the inflected word.

3.1   Stemmatization

Stemmatization is a linguistic normalisation technique that converts variant forms of a word back to its original form. The process will remove the affixes from words by producing the smallest unit of word known as stem or root word [1]. This technique groups a group of inflected words, which have the same common form together so that it is able to improve the performance of information retrieval or extraction. The stemming process can be done in two different ways; one is through iteration and another is through the longest-match [9].

Iteration is usually based on the fact that suffixes are attached to root word in a certain order. The technique is simply a recursive procedure, which removes strings in each order-class one at a time starting with the last character then moving backward towards the earlier character. As for the longest-match technique, it will remove the longest ending of inflected words in the situation, where more than one result produced from ending class matching.

Sometime the output of the stemming process may be ambiguous and does not appear in English word. Stemming algorithm implemented in the [10] does not consider the validity of the stem word created. Stem words produced from stemming algorithm can either be the invalid, inappropriate or modified the original meaning it is trying to represent. Some experimental data generated from research done by [9], shows that base word "met" generated from "metal" has changed the meaning of the original word. Base words such as "induc" and "angl" generated from "induced" and "angle" does not carry any meaning and do not appear in English. This happens when the suffix of the inflected word is identical.

Base words generated in the research carried out by [9] and [10] might not be usable since the methods do not take into the consideration of their validity from the dictionary.

3.2   Lemmatization

Lemmatization process provides a productive way to generate generic keyword (base word), which can be used in search engines or labels for concept mapping. The process uses dictionaries and morphological analysis to generate base or dictionary form of an inflected word. Lemmatizing is similar to stemming, where it is used to identify the base form of words that are known to the users and to normalise the word. Even though both processes are similar, only different inflectional forms of the word are being lemmatized. Lemma words generated from lemmatization process does not need to be a root/morpheme and executes on the different inflectional forms of the word, whereas the stem word generated from the stemmatization process must be a root/morpheme.

Adding a suffix to the end of a base word will change its internal structure and sometime the word class. For instance, the suffixes for word "fit" are "er", "est","ed", "ing", "ness" and "ly". As a result, Table 2 shows the inflected word for "fit" after adding different suffixes. These inflected words might change its original meaning or word class.

Table 2. Inflected words generated by adding suffix to "fit"

Suffix	Inflected word	Word class
er	fitter	Adjective
est	fittest	Adjective
ed	fitted	Verb
ing	fitting	Verb
ness	fitness	Noun
ly	fitly	adverb

Lemmatization technique will group a group of inflected or derived words, which have the similar meaning together through a limited number of vocabularies [11]. For example, those inflected words that have similar meaning in the Table 2 are grouped together through a common word, "fit". By reducing the number of vocabularies used, the ability to retrieve relevant information will improve significantly as different word formations are used for matching in the searching process.

Inappropriate base (stem) words that are generated from the stemming process might not be usable or meaningful. These words need to be lemmatized before it can be used for mapping process. Using the example from research carried out by [9], base word for "metal", "absorb" and "angle" should remain as it is. As for the base word for "induced", instead of removing "ed" for past tense, the proper lemmatize word should be "induce" with a removal of "d".

In the [23] research, they introduced a lemmatizer technique that focuses on unknown words. They introduced lemmatization rules from full form lemma training dictionary that consist of full form - lemma word pairs. The rules are based on searching the longest common substring of the full form-lemma pair via dynamic programming.

Since both stemming and lemmatization techniques are aimed to normalise words by stripping down its' suffix in a situation, where the inflected words are irregular verbs, the lemma words generated from lemmatization process might be different because the relationship is not always predictable.

With the advancement of the technologies that promote information sharing among users, the knowledge base will increase the size when new knowledge is added into it. Thus, it is important to decrease the amount of vocabularies used by saving the space required and reducing the processing time when searching the stored knowledge. Moreover, grammatical normalisation of the word also plays an important role in retrieving relevant data. Application of these techniques will reduce the number of vocabularies used and stored in the knowledge base without losing the meaning it tried to represent. It will also improve the query matching regardless of its grammatical forms in documents or queries. This is because it will be easier to perform matching during the retrieval process by using a single base word for variant formation of the same meaning of the word.

4 Related Works

4.1 Existing Morphological Analysis Tools

Some of the famous morphological analysis tools that have been used in researches are Natural Language Toolkit (NLTK) [12] and Stanford parser [13]. NLTK consist of a bundle of collection of morphological algorithms like Porter, Lancaster, Snowball and WordNet [14]. The bundles of algorithms in the NLTK are stemmers except WordNet, which is the lemmatizer. As for the Stanford parser, it has the capability of performing lemmatization. Base words produced from WordNet and Stanford parser are more accurate comparing to the others as shown in Table 3.

Table 3. Base word generated from existing algorithm.

Inflected Word	Lemmatizer		Stemmer		
	Stanford	WordNet	Snowball	Porter	Lancaster
Induced	Induce	Induced	Induc	Induc	Induc
Angle	Angle	Angle	Angl	Angl	Angl

One of the most famous and applied stemmer is Porter stemmer, which is based on the idea that English suffixes are made up of a combination of smaller and simpler suffixes. The algorithm removes the commoner morphological and inflexional endings from words for the term normalisation process [15]. The algorithm consists of a set of condition/action rules that categorise the conditions into 3 different classes; stem, suffix and rules. The stem is measured based on its alternative vowel-consonant sequences and its ending letter. As for the rules condition, it is divided into six steps to get rid of suffixes such as plurals, tenses and final 'e' and also convert the terminal 'y' to 'i' when there is another vowel in the stem [16]. In order to map the suffix, these rules are examined in sequence with the condition of only applying one rule at each step. Execution of these six steps might cause over-stemming errors where the stem words produced became meaningless if the suffix removed is too long [17].

Other than Porter stemmer, he also has developed a series of stemmer in other languages than English. These stemmers are included in stemmer framework known as Snowball in 2001 to overcome the lack of available stemming algorithm for other language than English [10] and improve his previous work by eliminating the inaccurate stem words produced in Porter stemmer [1, 18].

Paice and Husk first introduced the Lancaster stemmer in 1990, which able to address the context awareness issue. The algorithm is based on rule execution mechanism and able to act as a finite state automaton. It utilises a single table of rules, which specifies the removal or replacement of inflected word suffix. It is a conflation based iterative stemmer that removes the endings of a word in an indefinite number of steps [19, 20]. The stemmer has been implemented to enhance the knowledge comprehension for English and Swahili [21].

In the situation where the stemming process does not provide the desired result, the stemmer outputs are required to go through another process known as lemmatizing. Lemmatizer itself can be used in place of stemmer because this technique can incorporate the same stemmer processes at the same time without losing its meaning.

Among the algorithms in the NLTK bundle, WordNet algorithm can be categorised as the lemmatizer because the base word produced from inflect word still retain its original meaning. There are two types of processes used in WordNet to convert inflected word to its base form. It starts with checking the exception list for each syntactic category followed by executing the detachment rule based on the list of inflectional ending on each syntactic category [22]. The exception lists contain a list of strings in alphabetical order, which are not able to be processed by morphological transformation algorithm. Each line of the exception list contains an inflected word with its base form(s). If the inflected word is not found in exception list, it will be passed to the morphological transformation process, which is based on detachment rules to find the base word by suffix matching.

The morphological analysis incorporated in the Stanford parser works on the inflected words like noun plurals, pronoun case and verb endings [13]. The algorithm is based on finite-state transducer implemented by John Carroll. The root words generated from the parser are even more accurate than the WordNet lemmatizer as it takes the meaning and the lexical class of the word into consideration. Stanford parser can handle most of the type of the tense, whereas WordNet lemmatizer not able to do so such as past tense and present progressive tense; "archived", "induced", "presented", "swimming" and "playing".

Both stemming and lemmatization techniques process the inflect words from the natural language context to produce the base word. The lemmatization technique produces a more accurate outcome when compared to the stemming process because it will transform the inflect word back to its base form without losing its meaning. The outcome of the sentence "What make Argia different from other cities is that it has earth instead of air" from research [24] has shown that word "different" become "diff", "other" become "oth" and "earth" become "ear". These stem words are not usable as it does not carry any meaning.

4.2   Machine Learning

In computational linguistics, machine learning can be applied into 3 parts; feature extraction, training and testing. Once the features are extracted, it will be train by examining these features with an associated individual document that makeup of corpus and learn how to classify them. New testing data will be passed into the existing training model to predict the classification with machine learning approaches. There are two training models, where one of them is designed to find the morpheme boundaries and another one for assigning grammatical classes to each morpheme [24, 25].

Supervised learning is the most common approach applied in natural language processing. The approach has been applied in morphological analysis to transform the inflected word back to its base form, which requires extensive use of annotate data. This can be seen in the work carried out by [26] to acquire the orthographic transformation rules of morphological paradigms from labeled given. In [27] research, a minimal supervised morphology induction algorithm is introduced to deal with highly irregular inflected forms. The algorithm refines alignment between inflected and root word through training a supervised morphological analysis learner on a weighted subset of alignment between inflected and root word.

Memory base learning is also known as instance-based or example-based learning. It is a class of inductive, supervised machine learning, which learns by storing example of a task in memory. When new instances are presented with a memory-based learner, it will search for the best- matching instances in memory. The computational effort is on the "call-by-need" basis for solving a new instance of the same task. This technique has been successfully applied to morphological analysis and part-of- speech tagging [28]. Other than that, [29] also implemented this technique using k-nearest neighbor (KNN) classifier. Lexicons created from training and testing material are converted to instances. Instances from frequent tokens are more likely to occur in KNN set which improve the prediction accuracy and increasing the performance of recalling words.

Even though unsupervised learning is not commonly used in natural language processing, it has been applied in word segmentation [30] or [31] to handle morphological segmentation using minimum description length analysis. Through the adoption of an approach proposed by [30, 31] implements an unsupervised learning morphological rule learning algorithm to learn affix rules from wordlist and tested it using wordlist of different scales. However the system performances obtained are different due to the different coverage and correctness of rules obtained previously.

Semi-supervised learning combines both label and unlabeled data in a model for training. The approach has been applied in segmenting the inflected word, which can be seen in [34, 35] researches. Reference [34] utilized the heuristic model to learn morpheme segmentation on training data of a statistical machine translation. The model consists of Stem, Affix, Seed and Word tables, where segmentations learned previously are recorded in the Seed and Word tables. These tables are used as a reference to segment new words, according to rule-based segmentation.

As for an online application, usually the new training data provided to the system will depend on the system performance of the previous training data [35]. The research carried out by [36] to study the effect of user interaction on the performance of the matching system through an adaptive machine learning framework. The framework uses both supervised and semi-supervised learning. User participation through the relevance feedback process with semi supervised learning has improved the system performance. There is another research by [37] where user input into the machine learning for feature ranking. The previously ranked feature in the research, shown the user preferences, thus is interpreted as being preferred and more important.

5 A-Lemmatizer

Currently, lemmatization techniques are focusing on the base/root word by taking the semantics of the words into consideration when removing the suffix or prefix of the word. In the new approach, the same process will be retained when stemming the word. The lemmatizer consist of three different layers of lemming process by incorporating Stanford API in the first layer, follow by the WordNet lexical dictionary in the second layer and finally an another layer of lemmatization by the system if not result returned from both incorporated APIs in the first two layers during the stemming process. Figure 1 in the below, shows the lemmatization technique implemented in each layer.

The process starts with document processing to extract the contents follows by string retrieval and sentence tokenization. Once the extracted strings are tokenized, each of the token will pass through a list of special words to check on against words such as "is" and "are", where it will be changed to "be" in the other lemmatizers previously. These words play an important role in semantic analysis, especially in showing the relationship among the classes. Thus, A-Lemmatizer will retain the entire list of stop words before performing lemmatization.

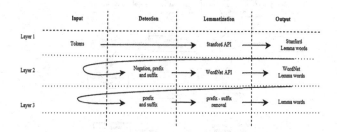

Fig. 1. Three layers of lemmatization process.

After stop word removal process, the each token will be passed into the Stanford lemmatization algorithm, which is incorporated in Stanford Corenlp parser to perform lemmatization on top of the inflected words. The outcome from the Stanford parser will be passed to another layer to check against inflection of the word on prefix and suffix as well as the negation detection. If no inflection and negation are detected, the process will terminate with Stanford lemma words as the output.

Any detected negation in the token will be passed to a chunking process. The process will chunk the inflect word into two parts; the first part consists of the negation prefix, where it will be removed and replace by adding the "not" word into the sentence. The second part will be remained and pass to the next layer to check against any further inflection.

If the system again detects the word as an inflected word, it will be passed into an adaptive learning framework. This happens in the second layer of lemmatization process. The WordNet lexical database is incorporated in the adaptive learning to enhance the lexical richness. Inflected words will pre-aligned with a learning model to get the lemma words. If the inflected is categories as unknown, the system will then retrieve a new set of synsets generated from the WordNet lexical database for user to choose from. If none of the listed words are appropriate, users have an option not to select any of the synsets provided and the system will move the next layer of lemmatization. The outcome of the process will be known as WordNet lemma word, if the base word is chosen and the process will terminate at this layer.

In the situation where no output is generated from the second layer, the word will be passed into the third or final layer to perform suffix removal. The suffix will be removed using the longest-match technique. The algorithm will check on the number of suffix matches between the suffix list and the ending of the inflected word. The longest suffix of the inflected word ending will be removed, when the word ending matches more than one of the listed suffixes.

The overall flow of the A-Lemmatizer processes is shown in Fig. 2. The lemma words generated from the Stanford lemmatizer, WordNet dictionary and final lemmatization processes are stored in a lemma file for further NLP processing such as syntactic and semantic processing.

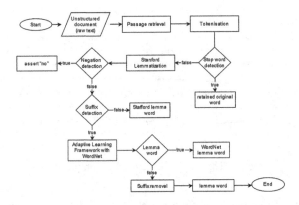

Fig. 2. A-Lemmatizer flowchart

6 Adaptive Learning Framework

The adaptive learning framework comprised of both supervised and semi-supervised learning. Since supervised learning has been commonly applied in machine learning, it will be implemented at the entrance of adaptive learning framework, where the inflected word will be entered. If the inflect word is pre-aligned with the list of user previous choices of the same domain, it will perform supervised training against the set of existing training set on the inflected - base word pair.

In a situation the inflect word are not pre-aligned with the list of user previous choices; the system will execute a semi-supervised learning, where users will participate in selecting an appropriate base word from a list of possible base words generated from the available synsets of the WordNet lexical database. User selection of the choice will be updated into the model for training purpose. The result of user selection and pre-alignment are used to train the learning model. Then, the model will be used to generate the base word for inflected word. Figure 3 shows the adaptive learning framework implemented in the second layer of the lemmatization technique.

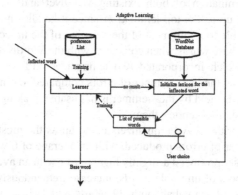

Fig. 3. Adaptive learning framework for lemmatization process.

7 Results and Discussion

Random selections of 10 English news documents from different fields are selected from online Cable News Network (CNN), The New York Times (NYT) and International Business Times. Each document consists of 100 to 550 words from various fields such as tourism, economy, politics, sport and etc. These documents are fed into the A-lemmatizer to perform lemmatization as seen in Fig. 4. The generated results are then compared with the word – lemma pairs in the lexical data provided by PanLex.

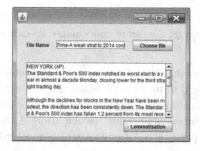

Fig. 4. News document feed into A-lemmatizer to perform lemmatization process.

Among these six different algorithms, three of them are stemmers and another three are lemmatizers. Base/root words produced are checked against its meaning to ensure its usefulness for further processing. The result has shown that lemmatizer algorithms are more efficient compared to stemmer algorithm because lemma root words generated are more accurate and usable whereas stem words generated contains lots of ambiguous base words and none English word.

Among the existing stemmer in the NLTK, Snowball comes out as the top stemmer by producing less errors (9.5 %) when compare with Porter (10.3 %) and Lancaster (15.2 %) because these two algorithms do not handle past tense. Lancaster stemmer came up with the highest number of unusable base words due to inability to handle entity name.

Through the examination of both existing WordNet and Stanford lemmatizers, Stanford parser came up as the top lemmatizer since it handles most of the past tense correctly and is still able to retain most of the meaning of the inflect words by yielding only 3 % of unusable base words when compared with the WordNet lemmatizer. As for the A-Lemmatizer, which incorporated two lemmatizer APIs and machine learning technique had produced the least number of errors compared to other algorithms. Only 1.9 % of the base words yield by the stemmer is not usable, making it the most efficient morphological analysis tool among them.

Among these algorithms, A-Lemmatizers come up as the most efficient algorithm with the lowest number of errors produced, with an average of 6 words per document, whereas Stanford parser produced a slightly higher error with an average of 9 words per document. The numbers of unusable words, increase tremendously for WordNet with 22 words, follow by the Snowball with 29 words and Porter, 31 words and lastly Lancaster with 46 words. Figure 5 in the below shows the average number of errors occur in each document for six different algorithms.

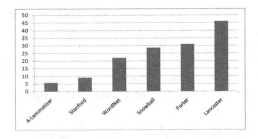

Fig. 5. Average number of errors occurs for each algorithm

Following Fig. 6 shows that most of the unusable base words are produced from the document that is in the field of investment, nature and science. Inflected word such as climate that appear in the nature document will return a base word "climat" when using Porter or Snowball stemmers and "clim" when using Lancaster stemmer. Word-Net algorithms, Stanford parser and A-Lemmatizer have yielded an accurate base word, which is "climate".

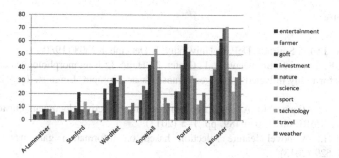

Fig. 6. The number of unusable base word occurs from each document for each morphological algorithm

The results of Morphological analysis are being further processed for higher levels of natural language processing such semantic or discourse analysis. Therefore, it is important that the results produced are usable and accurate as it will affect the overall results of the subsequent levels. Since A-lemmatizer had produced better results than others, it will also increase the precision level of any natural language systems that require higher level of natural language processing.

8 Conclusion

In the experiment, various fields of documents are chosen to ensure there are varieties of words being analysed and at the same time reduce the number of repeating words. Based on the experiment carried out in the previous section, it has been clearly shown that lemmatization algorithms yield a better result than the stemming algorithms. The base words produced from the stemmer algorithms will not be usable if it is ambiguous or not in English form. In order to use these words, it needs to go through another process known as lemmatization in order to make it usable.

Most of the current lemmatizer able to generate base words for inflected word that appear in the form of past tense and at the same time still retains the same lexical class. Even though most of the lemmatizer has taken the lexical class categorisation into the consideration, but none of them able to produce 100 % usable base words. By incorporating the two existing lemmatizer APIs into A-Lemmatizer, it has either maintain or reduce number unusable base words. User participation in selecting base words in the adaptive learning framework also has significantly improved the accuracy of the base word generated from the A-Lemmatizer.

Since A-Lemmatizer has yielded better results than other algorithms, it should be incorporated into any system that requires the lemmatization process as it will improve the precision level of that system.

Acknowledgments. The work presented in this paper has been supported by the Long Term Research Grant Scheme (LRGS) project funded by the Ministry of Higher Education (MoHE), Malaysia under Grants No. LRGS/TD/2011/UiTM/ICT/03.

References

1. Smirnov, I.: Ilia Smirnov DePaul University, 3 December 2008 (1980)
2. Bohnet, B., Nivre, J., Boguslavsky, I., Ginter, F., Hajič, J.: Joint morphological and syntactic analysis for richly inflected languages. Trans. Assoc. Comput. Linguist. **1**(2012), 415–428 (2013)
3. Patil, L.H., Atique, M.: A Semantic approach for effective document clustering using WordNet. CoRR abs/1303.0489, pp. 1–5 (2013)
4. Patil, L.H.: A novel feature selection based on information gain using WordNet, pp. 625–629 (2013)
5. Ferreira, R., Freitas, F., Cabral, L.D.S., Lins, R.D., Lima, R., Franca, G., Simskez, S.J., Favaro, L.: A four dimension graph model for automatic text summarization. In: 2013 IEEE/WIC/ACM International Joint Conferences on Web Intelligence (WI) and Intelligent Agent Technologies (IAT), pp. 389–396 (2013)
6. Corro, L.D., Gemulla, R.: ClausIE: clause-based open information extraction. In: 22nd International Conference on World Wide Web, WWW 2013, pp. 355–365 (2013)
7. NLP Meets the Jabberwocky: Natural Language Processing in Information Retrieval. http://www.scism.lsbu.ac.uk/inmandw/ir/jaberwocky.htm. Accessed 22 April 2014
8. Irregular Verbs — Rules! http://www.chompchomp.com/rules/irregularrules01.htm. Accessed 23 April 2014
9. Lovins, B.: Development of a stemming algorithm. Mech. Transl. Comput. Linguist. **11**, 22–31 (1968)
10. Emerging Issues in the Natural and (2013)
11. Frakes, W.B., Tech, V., Fox, C.J.: Strength and similarity of affix removal stemming algorithms stemmer strength metrics stemmer similarity metrics the wordlist descriptive stemmer data. ACM SIGIR Forum **37**(1), 26–30 (2003)
12. Natural Language Toolkit — NLTK 3.0 documentation. http://www.nltk.org/. Accessed 13 April 2014
13. The Stanford NLP (Natural Language Processing) Group. http://nlp.stanford.edu/software/lex-parser.shtml. Accessed 13 April 2014
14. Augat, M., Ladlow, M.: CS65: An NLTK Package for Lexical-Chain Based Word Sense Disambiguation (2004)
15. Chintala, D.R., Reddy, E.M.: An approach to enhance the CPI using Porter stemming algorithm. Int. J. Adv. Res. Comput. Sci. Softw. Eng. **3**(7), 1148–1156 (2013)
16. Porter Stemmer. http://www.comp.lancs.ac.uk/computing/research/stemming/Links/porter.htm. Accessed 03 June 2014
17. Ali, N.H.: Porter stemming algorithm for semantic checking, pp. 253–258 (2012)
18. Snowball: A language for stemming algorithms. http://snowball.tartarus.org/texts/introduction.html. Accessed 19 March 2014
19. Paice/Husk Stemmer. http://www.comp.lancs.ac.uk/computing/research/stemming/Links/paice.html. Accessed 14 April 2014
20. What is Paice/Husk Stemming? http://www.comp.lancs.ac.uk/computing/research/stemming/general/paice.htm. Accessed 28 April 2014
21. Muchemi, L., Popowich, F.: An Ontology-based Architecture for Natural Language Access to Relational Databases, pp. 1–11. Springer, Heidelberg (2011)
22. MORPHY(7WN) manual page. http://wordnet.princeton.edu/wordnet/man/morphy.7WN.html. Accessed 18 April 2014

23. Kanis, J., Müller, L.: Automatic lemmatizer construction with focus on OOV words lemmatization. In: Matoušek, V., Mautner, P., Pavelka, T. (eds.) TSD 2005. LNCS (LNAI), vol. 3658, pp. 132–139. Springer, Heidelberg (2005)
24. Hart, L.: The linguistics of sentiment analysis (2013)
25. Dhanalakshmi, V., Anandkumar, M., Rekha, R.U., Arunkumar, C., Soman, K.P.: Morphological analyzer for agglutinative languages using machine learning approaches (2009)
26. Durrett, G., Denero, J.: Supervised learning of complete morphological paradigms. In: Proceedings of NAACL-HLT, pp. 1185–1195 (2013)
27. Kirschenbaum, A., Wittenburg, P., Heyer, G.: Unsupervised morphological analysis of small corpora: First experiments with Kilivila. vol. 3, no. 3 (2012)
28. Mugdan, J., Booij, G., Lehmann, Ch.: Morphology. A Handbook on Inflection and Word Formatio, pp. 1893–1900. Walter De Gruyter, New York (2004)
29. Van Den Bosch, A., Marsi, E., Soudi, A.: Memory-based morphological analysis and part-of-speech tagging of Arabic, Sect. 4, pp. 1–15 (1999)
30. Kohonen, O., Virpioja, S., Lagus, K.: Semi-supervised learning of concatenative morphology (2005)
31. Goldsmith, J.: Unsupervised learning of the morphology of a natural language. Comput. Linguist. 27(2), 153–198 (2001)
32. Keshava, S., Haven, N., Pitler, E.: A Simpler, intuitive approach to morpheme induction. In: Proceedings of 2nd Pascal Challenges Workshop, pp. 31–35 (2006)
33. Tang, X.: English Morphological Analysis with Machine-learned Rules, pp. 35–41 (2005)
34. Yang, M., Zheng, J., Kathol, A.: A semisupervised learning approach for morpheme segmentation for an Arabic dialect (2007)
35. Van Leeuwen, J.: Algorithms that Learn. Algorithms in Ambient Intelligence Philips Research, Chap. 1, vol. 2, pp. 151–166. Springer (2004)
36. To, H., Ichise, R., Le, H.: An Adaptive machine learning framework with user interaction for ontology matching. In: Proceedings of the International Joint Conferences on Artifical Intelligence, Workshop on Information Integration on the Web, pp. 35–40 (2009)
37. Comput. J. 50(4) (2007)

Software Applications Systems

Inducing a Semantically Rich Nested Event Model

Nyuk Hiong Siaw[⊠], Bali Ranaivo-Malançon,
Narayanan Kulathuramaiyer, and Jane Labadin

Faculty of Computer Science and Information Technology,
University Malaysia Sarawak, Kuching, Malaysia
ftsm2006@yahoo.com,
{mbranaivo,nara,ljane}@fit.unimas.my

Abstract. Research has revealed that getting data with named entities (NEs) labels are laboured intensive and costly. This paper is proposing two approaches to enable NE classes to be added to the semantic role label (SRL) predicate-argument structure of Nested Event Model. The first approach associates SRL to Named Entity Recognition (NER), which is named as SRL-NER, to tag the appropriate entity class to the simple argument of the model. The second approach associates SRL to NER by fine-tuning entities in complex argument structures with Automatic Content Extraction (ACE) structure. This approach is called SRL-ACE-NER. Stanford NER tool is used as the benchmark for evaluation. The result shows that the proposed approaches are able to recognize more PERSON entities. However, the approaches are not able to recognize LOCATION/PLACE as efficiently as the benchmark. It is also observed that the benchmark tool is sometimes not able to tag as comprehensively as the proposed approaches. This paper has successfully demonstrated the potential of using a semantically enriched Nested Event Model as an alternative for NER technique. SRL-ACE-NER has achieved an average precision of 92 % in recognising PERSON, LOCATION/PLACE, TIME, and ORGANIZATION.

Keywords: Named entity recognition · Nested event model · Semantic · Semantic role label · Predicate argument structure

1 Introduction

Named Entity Recognition (NER) is the task of identifying the names of entities from unstructured text and grouped them into predefined semantic categories [1]. Semantic categories provide same types of entities into classes such as PEOPLE, PLACE, ORGANIZATION, TEMPORAL and NUMERICAL EXPRESSIONS. NER is a very important part of an Information Extraction (IE) system. Handcrafted rules and learning based methods are the two main approaches for NER [2]. However, these two approaches have some drawbacks. The handcrafted rules method relies fully on rules created manually. As for the learning based methods, training labelled data is needed which can be created manually or semi-automatically. The manual process of creating extraction rules and training data is claimed to be costly and time consuming. Another issue related to

© Springer International Publishing Switzerland 2015
H. Fujita and A. Selamat (Eds.): SoMeT 2014, CCIS 513, pp. 361–375, 2015.
DOI: 10.1007/978-3-319-17530-0_25

NER is its inability to recognize ambiguous names. Polysemous words create ambiguity, which can be solved by a word sense disambiguation system but cannot be recognized by NER. Word sense disambiguation can be carried out as a post NER task as in research carried out by TAC KBP Track [3]. Zhang [4] has identified three goals for NER as: (a) identifying named entities (NEs) in text, (b) assigning semantic categories to these NEs, and (c) assigning referent entities to them (disambiguation).

It has been revealed by research that it is laboured intensive and costly to get data with NEs label. The main objective of this paper is to propose two approaches to enable name entity (NE) classes to be added to the semantic role label (SRL) predicate-argument structure (PAS) of Nested Event Model. Nested Event Model is defined in Sect. 3 of this paper. The first approach, SRL-NER, associates SRL to NER to tag the appropriate entity class to the simple argument of the model. The second approach, SRL-ACE-NER, associates SRL to NER by fine-tuning entities in complex argument structures with Automatic Content Extraction (ACE) structure. The approaches use Stanford NER as the benchmarking tool for evaluation.

2   Existing NER Techniques

Mutual Understanding Conference (MUC6 [1], MUC7 [5]) and Automatic Content Extraction (ACE) are two important platforms through which many NER related researches have been carried out. Events have been defined in a more fine-grained structure by ACE. For example, ACE has used different entity sub-types to differentiate government, educational and commercial organisations. According to Doddington et al. [6], these can be grouped under one entity type ORGANIZATION. The NER tasks incur labour intensive template definition in MUC and event annotation in ACE. Thus, both platforms faced the similar problem of being costly and time consuming. Two main techniques for NER are handcrafted rules and learning based methods [2]. Related research using handcrafted rules for NER has been carried out by [7, 8]. As for learning based techniques, it has been carried out by [9–11]. However, these methods are costly and time consuming as has been described earlier.

Automation of NER can be carried out using NER tools. A few NER tools have been developed and they are free for use in research. These tools are Stanford NER [12], Illinois NET [13], OpenCalais NER WS [14] and Alias-i LingPipe [15]. Stanford NER is found to be the best among the four [16]. This tool is implemented in Java. Conditional Random Field (CRF) classifier is used in the tool that classifies entities into different classes such as PERSON, ORGANIZATION and LOCATION. Illinois NET uses a few supervised learning methods such as hidden Markov models, multi-layered neural networks and other statistical methods. n-gram character language models that applied hidden Markov models and conditional random field methods for data training are used in Alias-i LingPipe. OpenCalais NER WS is a web based NER tool.

The development of natural language processing (NLP) tools has enabled some researches to employ SRL approach to identify entities in unstructured text. Exner and Nugues [17] have successfully extract event properties (NEs) from the arguments of PAS labelled by a SRL tool. The tool has enabled entities to be collected automatically from the unstructured text in Wikipedia and used for the Linking Open Descriptions

Events (LODE) event model. SRL PAS related researches have been carried out by [18, 19] for unstructured text. In the research carried out by [18], knowledge was extracted based on SRL PAS and stored in a database. Surdeanu et al. [19] has used SRL PAS to identify entities to fill in slots specify for event. Siaw et al. [21] has proposed a Nested Event Model with PAS. The model's application has been illustrated through semantic parsing which output semantic PAS. It is observed that the semantic PAS has features that can be exploited to obtain entities from unstructured text. It is the interest of this research to explore the exploitation of SRL PAS to semantically induced Nested Event Model with entities information.

3   Nested Event Model

The dependency graph with projectivity property defined by Johansson [20] has been used by [21] as the foundation to define the tasks in Nested Event Model.

> A dependency edge g $\rightarrow$ d in a dependency graph G for a sentence x is called projective if all tokens in x between g and d are dominated by g. The graph G is called projective if all its edges are projective. Johansson [20].

3.1   Definition 1: Relation Mention

Relation mention will determine the extent of association between a predicate and the arguments. The numbers of argument obtained are depended on the output of the dependency parsing. Based on dependency PAS, the predicate-argument has a parent-child relation with the arguments depended on the predicate. The possible parent-child relation can be a direct dependency or indirect dependency. The argument can be a predicate for indirect dependency. This "argument as predicate" can define a relation mention for an event thus resulted in nested event.

- Definition 1(a): Direct Dependency
  Direct dependency indicates that the argument(s) is(are) directly depended on the predicate. Only one level of parent-child relation exists in this type of dependency.
- Definition 1(b): Indirect Dependency
  Indirect dependency indicates that argument(s) exists in more than one level of PAS frame. The 'frame' refers to the predicate and their arguments. Nested events exist only in cases where there is argument as non-root predicate.

Figure 1 shows a direct dependency between predicate and arguments. The arity of the predicate can range from 1 to n depending on the output of the dependency parsing. Figure 2 shows indirect dependency between predicate and arguments. Nested event only exist in Fig. 2(b) and (c) since there exist non-root predicate(s) as argument(s) in the structure.

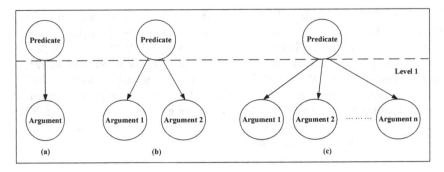

Fig. 1. Direct parent-child dependency of PAS

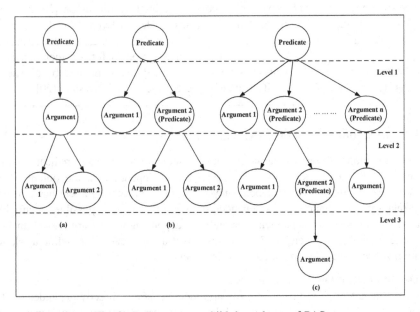

Fig. 2. Indirect parent-child dependency of PAS

3.2   Definition 2: PAS Predicate

In this model, a predicate is defined as the trigger of event. For a predicate to function as a trigger, it must exist in PAS frame. Dependency parsing usually output verb, noun or adjective as the predicate. Based on this property, trigger of this model is constrained to verb, noun or adjective that exists in PAS frame of dependency parsing.

3.3   Definition 3: PAS Argument

In this model, the arguments of a predicate that exist in PAS frame are defined as the arguments of event. These arguments can correspond either to a single entity or a combination of several entities. The later may contain entities that are the arguments of another event. Entity type can be identified through NER or argument roles.

Based on the proposed nested event model, the direct and indirect dependency of PAS can output many different possibilities for event extraction. Constraints can be imposed on the type of predicate to extract, for example verbal or nominal predicate. Part of speech (POS) can impose constraints on the type of entities to be extracted for the arguments, for example nouns or adjectives. Besides, the type of dependency relation between predicate-argument can be constrained based on the needs of the research. These constraints can contribute towards a more objective-oriented application of the model in research.

4 Semantically Induced Nested Event Model

Based on semantic dependency PAS, semantic event identified based on the model inherited the following properties:

(a) Continuous embedded projective dependency-syntactic structure for capturing nested event.
(b) Relative prominence relations among arguments via thematic hierarchy determined by the thematic properties of the predicate.

The application of property (a) for the model has been illustrated by [21]. The model has a few characteristics as shown in Table 1. It is observed that some characteristics of the model can be employed to overcome some of the problems that have been identified for NER as described in the earlier part of this paper. For example, "data economy" characteristic can address the problem of "labour intensive and time consuming training data preparation". Besides, semantic dependency PAS using SRL tool can overcome word sense disambiguation problem since different diathesis alternations of a verb is addressed by SRL.

Table 1. Characteristics of Nested Event Model

Characteristics	Nested Event Model	Evaluated Against 27 ACE Events (8 Types, 25 Subtypes)
Portable	✓	Nested Event Model is performing well when evaluated against 8 types and 25 subtypes of ACE specified event by obtaining high precision and recall
Data economy	✓	Nested Event Model obtains a precision of 94.44 % and a recall of 62.86 % without using any training data.

(Continued)

Table 1. (*Continued*)

Characteristics	Nested Event Model	Evaluated Against 27 ACE Events (8 Types, 25 Subtypes)
Single event extraction	✓	Evaluation data has 16 simple sentences
Complex event extraction	✓	Evaluation data has 11 complex sentences
Consider underlying structure of event	✓	PAS of Nested Event Model inherited the property of relative prominence relations among arguments via thematic hierarchy determined by the thematic properties of the predicate
Event extraction based on annotated list	✓	Nested Event Model does not have an annotated list of events as ACE

4.1   SRL-NER

Exner and Nugues [17] have associated SRL PAS to the relevant thematic roles of VerbNet to identify the appropriate NE class for LODE event model (Table 2). Employing similar approach, it is possible to associate to a simple SRL argument the relevant NER class (SRL-NER association). For instance, [The minister]$_{AGENT}$ (Fig. 3) is associated to the class PERSON. However, some of SRL PAS arguments may consist of different entities. For example, the expression [their tourists from the outskirts of the cities]$_{THEME}$ consists of the entities (tourists$_{entity1}$, tourists$_{entity2}$, tourists$_{entity3}$. Thus, associating one single NER class to an argument with multiple entities will decrease the accuracy. A fine-grain analysis of arguments with multiple entities will be more appropriate. Another example to illustrate the difference between SRL-NER and SRL-ACE-NER association using an ACE sentence is shown in Table 3. The example shows that SRL-NER will not associate [including the senseless slaying of Bob Cole and the assassination of Joe Westbrook]$_{C-A1}$ to any entity class. However, when ACE data is used as an intermediate step to fine-tuned entity association, two entities [Bob Cole]$_{VICTIM}$ and [Joe Westbrook]$_{VICTIM}$ associated with PERSON can be identified.

Table 2. Associating semantic role label to NE class

Thematic Roles		NE Class
PropBank	VerbNet	
Agent	Actor, agent, beneficiary, Experiencer, Recipient, Theme	PERSON
AM-LOC	Location, source	PLACE
AM-TMP	Time	TIME

Table 3. An example to show the difference between SRL-NER and SRL-ACE-NER

Sentence:	Three murders occurred in France today, including the senseless slaying of Bob Cole and the assassination of Joe Westbrook.
SRL	Three murders$_{\text{AGENT}}$ in France$_{\text{AM-LOC}}$ today$_{\text{AM-TMP}}$ including the senseless slaying of Bob Cole and the assassination of Joe Westbrook $_{\text{C-A1}}$
SRL-NER Association (refer Table 2)	Threemurders$_{\text{PERSON}}$ in France$_{\text{PLACE}}$ today$_{\text{TIME}}$ including the senseless slaying of Bob Cole and the assassination of Joe Westbrook$_{\text{NIL}}$
ACE Role	France$_{\text{PLACE}}$ Today$_{\text{TIME}}$ Bob Cole$_{\text{VICTIM}}$ Joe Westbrook$_{\text{VICTIM}}$
SRL-ACE-NER	Three murders$_{\text{PERSON}}$France$_{\text{PLACE}}$ in today$_{\text{TIME}}$ Bob Cole$_{\text{PERSON}}$ Joe Westbrook$_{\text{PERSON}}$

4.2 SRL-ACE-NER

SRL-NER association could be enhanced to identify entities in complex argument. This is addressed by a different research which has been carried out by [22]. Weighted graphs that take into consideration the frequency and relative prominence of collocate words based on Semantic Window of Collocate Word have been constructed. The tasks of Semantic Window of Collocate Word are defined based on Nested Event model. The weight for relative prominence is defined based on property (b) of the model. The graphs are defined as below:

Definition 1. A relation that exists between w and w_i constitutes the edge of the graph. Frequency of co-occurrence constitutes the weight. The adjacency matrixA = $[a_{ij}] \in R_{n \times n}$ of the weighted collocate word graph G of order n is given by:

$$a_{ij} = \begin{cases} 1, & if (v_i, v_j) \in E \\ 0, & otherwise \end{cases}$$

where,

w = word
Vertices: $v_i \in V$
Edges: $a_{ij} = (v_i, v_j) \in E$

Definition 2. The structural information of PAS can be characterized by assigning different weight to the thematic relation for collocate words. The weight indicates the order of ranking in the thematic relation. The adjacency matrix A = $[a_{ij}] \in R_{n \times n}$ of the thematic relation weighted graph G of order n is given by:

$$a_{ij} = \begin{cases} 0.9, & if (v_i, v_j) \in E, E \in A0 \\ 0.6, & f(v_i, v_j) \in E, E \in A1 \\ 0.3, & f(v_i, v_j) \in E, E \subset A0 \text{ or } \subset A1 \end{cases}$$

where,

Vertices: $v_i \in V$
Edges: $a_{ij} = (v_i, v_j) \in E$
A0 = AGENT
A1 = THEME

Definition 3. Weight for graph from definition 1 and 2 are compounded to represent collocate word and their thematic relations into a single graph. The adjacency matrix of the graph $A = [e_{ij}] \in R_{n \times n}$ for weighted graph G of order n is given by:

$$
w_{ij} =
\begin{cases}
w_i\,(v_i, v_j) * w_i\,(v_i, v_j) &
\begin{aligned}
& v_i, v_j \in E \\
& w_1 = \varphi_1(e_{ij}) \\
& \varphi_1 : E \to R \\
& w_2 = \varphi_2(e_{ij}) \\
& \varphi_2 : E \to R
\end{aligned} \\
0 & otherwise
\end{cases}
$$

where,

Vertices: $v_i \in V$

Edges: $e_{ij} = (v_i, v_j) \in E$

$w_{ij} = \varphi(e_{ij})$ is called a weight to an edge $e_{ij} = (v_i, v_j) \in E$, $\varphi : E \to R$ ($R =$ real number)

The relative importance of nodes in a graph can be computed using graph centrality measures. Kappa coefficient (κ) is used for evaluation and the results showed that thematic relation can improve the score of κ. The prominence of the relation that exist between entities in PAS can be shown through graph to represent augmented Nested Event Model to index multiple events for event-based knowledge representation. The knowledge base has key event information which could be part of a framework to support event level semantic applications.

A research has been carried out by [23] which used a different approach to extract key events for the news domain. Ontology based event knowledge is constructed and it is applied to support the Semantic Understanding of Chinese News Story. The Chinese event extraction system has combined NER lexical analysis of NLP, machine learning (SVM, CRF) and semantic web technology (ontology, OWL, rules). In this paper, the event knowledge base can be associated to the structural ACE event model for NER identification. The fine-grained event definition in ACE can be grouped together into more general event type [6]. For example, different government, educational and commercial organisations have been classed under one entity type ORGANIZATION. Based on SRL-ACE-NER association, NEs can be tagged to the complex arguments of SRL PAS. Attaching NE class to PAS has directly enriched the semantic information contain in Nested Event Model. The model now contains not only thematic relation between predicate and arguments but also the semantic information with weight for the entities in the arguments. An example of knowledge induction for a sentence: *The minister warned that drivers must remove their tourists from the outskirts of the cities*, is illustrated in Fig. 3. The figure shows the output for induction of semantic entities for SRL PAS arguments of the sentence in Nested Event Model through SRL-NER and SRL-ACE-NER association.

5   Implementation, Evaluation and Discussion

5.1   Implementation

Recent years' researches have shown an increasing interest in employing parsers based on dependency structure to induce predicate argument structure for semantic dependency parsing. It is claimed that the dependency structure can provide a simple and transparent encoding of PAS [24–28]. The semantic relation between a predicate and the different semantic categories assigned to the arguments based on the roles they

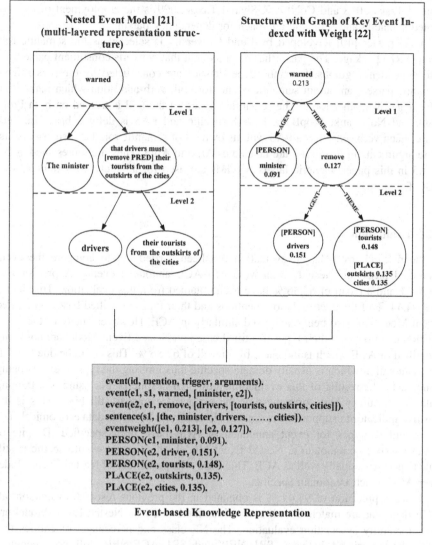

Fig. 3. Event-based knowledge representation

played with respect to the predicate can be represented as PAS [29, 30]. A core task that has almost become a surrogate for semantic dependency parsing in recent year is semantic role labelling [30]. SRL assigned semantic roles to a group of sequence words with respect to the chosen predicate. The availability of PAS scheme corpus for semantic roles like FrameNet [31], PropBank [32], VerbNet [33] and NomBank [34] have enabled accurate and efficient semantic dependency parsers to be developed based on the annotated corpora. The recent semantic dependency parsing researches have been fostered through CoNLL Shared Tasks 2006, 2007, 2008 [35–37] and CoNLL-X Shared Tasks 2009 [38]. Malt parser [39] and MST parser [36] have obtained state of the art performance in CoNLL Shared Tasks 2006 and 2007 while LTH parser [40] has the best performance in CoNLL Shared Tasks 2008. The characteristic of CoNLL Shared Tasks 2008 and CoNLL-X Shared Tasks 2009 is the employment of an integrated syntactic and semantic approach for dependency parsing.

LTH parser [40] developed by Lund University is selected as the semantic role label (SRL) package. The parser has a component that converts constituent parse trees into dependency graphs. Semantic dependencies are constructed by the parser. This semantic parser can output semantic events for both verb and noun which make it an advantage over other tools. The semantic parsing of the tool is trained on both Prop-Bank and NomBank. PropBank is verb-specific and PAS is defined based on verb sense. Each verb sense has a PAS with its own set of semantic role labelled arguments. Core arguments in PropBank are labeled as Arg0 to Arg5. They are represented as A0 to A5 in this paper. Generic labels ARGMs are used for adjuncts, for example AM-LOC for place.

5.2   Evaluation

In the research by [21], an evaluation has been carried out to compare the event identified based on Nested Event Model to ACE annotated events. A precision of 94.44 % and a recall of 62.86 % have been obtained from this evaluation. This shows that 94.44 % of the event relation mentions and their types identified based on Nested Event Model are also being annotated similarly in ACE. However, many of the event relation mentions and their types identified based on Nested Event Model are not being identified in ACE which is indicated by a recall of 62.86 %. This could be due to ACE data annotation which is usually domain specific thus limiting the type of events being annotated. The results of this evaluation show that despite of not using any training data, the accuracy and correctness of the extracted events is still high. This is the positive indicator to support the claim that Nested Event Model is data economical. The types and subtypes for event annotated in ACE have been specified. Despite of the event specific annotation, Nested Event Model which is not event specific is still able to perform equally well as ACE. This shows the portability of Nested Event Model over ACE which is domain specific.

Since a precision of 94.44 % is obtained in the previous research evaluation, all ACE data that are matched with events identified based on Nested Event Model are used for entity association evaluation. The NE class and percentage of entities that could be associated between SRL-NER and SRL-ACE-NER will be computed.

Three NE classes are used for SRL-NER association (PERSON, PLACE, TIME) and four NE classes are used for SRL-ACE-NER association (PERSON, PLACE, TIME, ORGANIZATION). The Stanford NER tool, using *english.muc.7class.distsim.crf.ser.gz* classifier, is used for benchmarking. This classifier is able to output seven NER classes (LOCATION, TIME, PERSON, ORGANIZATION, MONEY, PERCENT, DATE). The tool's output is compared with those entities obtained through SRL-NER and SRL-ACE-NER association. The two proposed approaches, SRL-NER and SRL-ACE-NER have also been evaluated using two standard performance metrics, precision and recall, to assessing their performance. The equations are as below:

$$Precision = \frac{Sysentity \cap Refentity}{Sysentity}$$

$$Recall = \frac{Sysentity \cap Refentity}{Refentity}$$

These equations have been used by [41] in TempEval-3 evaluation to compare their systems to a reference system, TIPSem [42]. The variable Sysentity represents entities associated with SRL-NER and SRL-ACE-NER. Refentity are entities identified by Stanford NER tool. The precision and recall of recognised entities are shown in Table 4.

Table 4. Precision and recall of recognised entities

	SRL-NER		SRL-ACE-NER	
	Recall	Precision	Recall	Precision
PERSON	100 %	64.29 %	100 %	**69.23** %
PLACE/LOCATION	26.32 %	100 %	42.11 %	100 %
TIME	**76.47** %	100 %	58.82 %	100 %
ORGANIZATION	–	–	50.00 %	100 %
Average	**67.59** %	88 %	62.73	**92.31** %

5.3 Discussion

This section will first describe the results by comparing the number of recognised entities by SRL-NER and SRL-ACE-NER against Stanford NER results as the benchmark. The results of the comparison showed that both SRL-NER and SRL-ACE-NER have high percentage for PERSON entity with 60.87 % and 55.32 % respectively. Both SRL-NER and SRL-ACE-NER associations are able to tag TIME entity with average percentage of 28.26 % and 21.28 % respectively. The LOCATION entity has a lower percentage for both associations at 10.87 % and 17.02 % respectively. On the other hand, Stanford NER tools is able to tag PERSON, LOCATION and TIME entity classes with almost equal percentage of 33.33 %, 35.19 % and 31.48 % when compared to the output from SRL-NER association. A percentage of 30 %, 31.67 %, 28.33 % and 10 % respectively is

Table 5. Percentage of recognised entities

Named Entity	Stanford NER (Benchmark)	SRL-NER	Stanford NER (Benchmark)	SRL-ACE-NER
PERSON	33.33 %	**60.87 %**	30 %	55.32 %
PLACE/ LOCATION	35.19 %	10.87 %	31.67 %	17.02 %
TIME	31.48 %	28.26 %	28.33 %	21.28 %
ORGANIZATION	–	–	10 %	6.38 %

obtained when the entity PERSON, PLACE, TIME and ORGANIZATION is compared to SRL-ACE-NER association. The results of the evaluation are shown in Table 5.

Based on the evaluation results, it is observed that the proposed SRL-NER and SRL-ACE-NER association is able to tag more PERSON entity than Stanford NER tool. This could be due to the fact that SRL-NER and SRL-ACE-NER association has grouped different fine-grained entities into a general entity class. For example, Agent and Theme SRL have been associated to the class PERSON. However, both SRL-NER and SRL-ACE-NER association has a lower percentage in tagging LOCATION/PLACE and ORGANIZATION entity. This could be due to the reason that AM-LOC label for location in SRL is not the core argument but only as a generic label. Thus, it is not the main focus for LOCATION tagging as in Stanford NER tool. On the other hand, it is observed that Stanford NER tool is sometimes weak in giving comprehensive tagging as in SRL or ACE, especially for PERSON entity. An example is given in Table 6 which shows that only DATE is tagged whereas both SRL and ACE are able to output more comprehensive tagging which include PERSON. This is proven by the results obtained in Table 5 which indicated that SRL and ACE has the highest percentage for PERSON entity compared to Stanford NER. Overall, it can be concluded that the potential of enriching Nested Event Model with semantic entities through NER is promising and more study could be carried out to improve the efficiency of the model.

Table 6. An example of Stanford NER vs. SRL-NER, SRL-ACE-NER

Sentence: David Goran was executed by lethal injection in March 1987			
Stanford NER Tool	March 1987 $_{Date}$		
SRL	David Goran $_{A1}$ in March 1987 $_{TIME}$	**SRL-NER Association**	David Goran $_{PERSON}$ in March 1987 $_{TIME}$
ACE Annotation	David Goran $_{PERSON}$ March 1987 $_{TIME}$	**SRL-ACE-NER Association**	David Goran $_{PERSON}$ March 1987 $_{TIME}$

The precision and recall results (Table 4) show that a recall of 100 % is obtained by both SRL-NER and SRL-ACE-NER in recoginising PERSON entity. However, SRL-NER has the second highest recall of 76.47 % in recognising TIME entity. The overall highest average recall is obtained by SRL-NER at 67.59 %. As for precision, both SRL-NER and SRL-ACE-NER obtained 100 % in recognising LOCATION and TIME entity. The second highest precision at 69.23 % is obtained by SRL-ACE-NER in recognising PERSON entity. Overall, the highest average precision is obtained by SRL-ACE-NER at 92.31 %. These results indicate that SRL-NER has a better performance in recognising TIME entity whereas SRL-ACE-NER performed better in recognising PERSON entity. Fine-tuning SRL with ACE for NER has improved the precision of SRL-ACE-NER over SRL-NER.

6 Conclusion

This paper has successfully demonstrated the enrichment of Nested Event Model with semantic information induced through two approaches proposed in this research: SRL-NER and SRL-ACE-NER. The evaluation results show that both approaches are able to recognise more PERSON entity compared to Stanford NER as the benchmark. Similarly, both approaches also obtained the highest recall of 100 % in recognising PERSON entity. On the average, SRL-NER obtained the highest average recall of 67.59 % in recognising PERSON, LOCATION and TIME whereas SRL-ACE-NER obtained the highest average precision of 92.31 % in recognising PERSON, LOCATION, TIME and ORGANIZATION. It is not the intention of this paper to claim that the two approaches are better that the free NER tools but rather to demonstrate the potential of using a semantically enriched Nested Event Model as an alternative for NER technique. The core task of Nested Event Model is event identification. NER could be a subsidiary task on top of the core task.

Acknowledegement. The sponsorship of this research is by the Education Sponsorship Division, Ministry of Education Malaysia.

References

1. Grishman, R., Sundheim, B.: Message understanding conference - 6: a brief history. In: Proceedings of the 16th International Conference on Computational Linguistics (COLING), pp. 466–471 (1996)
2. Sarawagi, S.: Information extraction. Found. Trends Databases. **1**(3), 261–377 (2007)
3. TAC KBP Track: TAC 2009 Knowledge Base Population Track. http://apl.jhu.edu/ ~ paulmac/kbp.html
4. Zhang, Z.: Named entity recognition-challenges in document annotation, Gazetteer construction and disambiguation. Doctor of Philosophy, The University of Sheffield (2013)
5. Chinchor, N.: Overview of MUC-7/MET-2. In: Proceedings of the 7th Message Understanding Conference. (1998)
6. Doddington, G., Mitchell, A., Przybocki, M., Ramshaw, L., Strassel, S., Weischedel, R.: The automatic content extraction (ACE) program – tasks, data, and evaluation. In: Proceedings of the Conference on Language Resources and Evaluation (LREC), pp. 837–840 (2004)

7. Nadeau, D.: A survey on named entity recognition and classification. Linguisticae Investigationes. **30**(1), 1–26 (2007)
8. Roberts, A., Gaizasukas, R., Hepple, M., Guo, Y.: Combining terminology resources and statistical methods for entity recognition. In: Proceedings of the 6th Language Resources and Evaluation Conference (LREC), pp. 2974–2980 (2008)
9. Ponomareva, N., Pla, F., Molina, A., Rosso, P.: Biomedical named entity recognition: a poor knowledge HMM-based approach. In: Kedad, Z., Lammari, N., Métais, E., Meziane, F., Rezgui, Y. (eds.) NLDB 2007. LNCS, vol. 4592, pp. 382–387. Springer, Heidelberg (2007)
10. Kazama, J., Torisawa, K.: Exploiting wikipedia as external knowledge for named entity recognition. In: Proceedings of the Joint Conference on Empirical Methods in Natural Language Processing and Computational Natural Language Learning, pp. 698–707 (2007)
11. Arnold, A., Nallapati, R., Cohen, W.: Exploiting feature hierarchy for transfer learning in named entity. In: Proceedings of ACL-08: HLT 245–253 (2008)
12. Finkel, J., Grenager, T., Manning, C.: Incorporating non-local information into information extraction systems by Gibbs sampling. In: 43rd Annual Meeting on ACL, pp. 363–370 (2005)
13. Ratinov, L., Roth, R.: Design challenges and misconceptions in named entity recognition. In: 13th Conference on Computational Natural Language Learning, pp. 147–155 (2009)
14. Thomson Reuters. Calais Web Service. http://www.opencalais.com/
15. Alias-i. LingPipe 4.1.0. http://alias-i.com/lingpipe
16. Atdag, S., Labatut, V.: A comparison of named entity recognition tools applied to biographical texts. In: 2nd International Conference on Systems and Computer Science, pp. 228–233 (2013)
17. Exner, P., Nugues, P.: Using semantic role labeling to extract events from wikipedia. In: Proceedings of the Workshop on Detection, Representation, and Exploitation of Events in the Semantic Web (DeRiVE 2011). Workshop in Conjunction with the 10th International Semantic Web (DeRiVE 2011) (2011)
18. Hung, S., Lin, C., Hong, J.: Web mining for event-based commonsense knowledge using lexico-syntactic pattern matching and semantic role labeling. Expert Syst. Appl. **37**(1), 341–347 (2010)
19. Surdeanu, M., Harabagiu, S., Williams, J., Aarseth, P.: Using predicate argument structures for information extraction. In: Proceedings of the 41st Annual Meeting on Association for Computational Linguistics, ACL 2003, pp. 8–15. Association for Computational Linguistics, Morristown, NJ, USA (2003)
20. Johansson, R.: Dependency-based semantic analysis of natural-language text. Doctor of Philosophy, thesis, Lund University (2008)
21. Siaw, N.H., Narayanan, K., Bali, R.-M., Jane, L.: Nested event model. In: SoMET: The 13th International Conference on Intelligent Software Methodologies Tools and Techniques (2014)
22. Hiong, S.N., Ranaivo-Malançon, B., Kulathuramaiyer, N., Labadin, J.: Linguistically enhanced collocate words model. In: Jaafar, A., Mohamad Ali, N., Mohd Noah, S.A., Smeaton, A.F., Bruza, P., Bakar, Z.A., Jamil, N., Sembok, T.M.T. (eds.) AIRS 2014. LNCS, vol. 8870, pp. 230–243. Springer, Heidelberg (2014)
23. Wang, W., Zhao, D.: Ontology-based event modeling for semantic understanding of Chinese news story. In: Zhou, M., Zhou, G., Zhao, D., Liu, Q., Zou, L. (eds.) NLPCC 2012. CCIS, vol. 333, pp. 58–68. Springer, Heidelberg (2012)
24. Culotta, A., Sorensen, J.: Dependency tree kernels for relation extraction. In: Proceedings of the 42nd Annual Meeting of the Association for Computational Linguistics (ACL2004), pp. 423–429 (2004)

25. Ding, Y., Palmer, M.: Synchronous dependency insertion grammars: a grammar formalism for syntax based statistical MT. In: Proceedings of the Workshop on Recent Advances in Dependency Grammar, pp. 90–97 (2004)
26. Quirk, C., Menezes, A., Cherry, C.: Dependency treelet translation: syntactically informed phrasal SMT. In: Proceedings of the 43rd Annual Meeting of the Association for Computational Linguistics (ACL2005), pp. 271–279 (2005)
27. Johansson, R., Nugues, P.: Dependency-based semantic role labeling of PropBank. In: Proceedings of the 2008 Conference on Empirical Methods in Natural Language Processing, pp. 69–78 (2008)
28. Nivre, J.: Dependency parsing. Lang. Linguist. Compass 4(3), 138–152 (2010)
29. Hacioglu, K:. Semantic role labeling using dependency trees. In: Proceedings of COLING (2004)
30. Zhao, H., Zhang, X., Kit, C.: Integrative semantic dependency parsing via efficient large-scale feature selection. J. Artif. Intell. Res. 46, 203–233 (2013)
31. Fillmore, C.J.: Frame semantics and the nature of language. In: Annals of the New York Academy of Sciences: Conference on the Origin and Development of Language and Speech, pp. 20–32 (1976)
32. Palmer, M., Gildea, D., Kingsbury, P.: The proposition bank: an annotated corpus of semantic roles. Comput. Linguist. 31, 71–105 (2005)
33. Kipper-Schuler, K.: Verbnet: a broad-coverage, comprehensive verb Lexicon. Doctor of Philosophy, thesis, University of Pennsylvania (2005)
34. Meyers, A., Reeves, R., Macleod, C., Szekely, R., Zielinska, V., Young, B. et al.: The NomBank Project: An interim report. In: Meyers, A. (ed.) HLT-NAACL 2004 Workshop: Frontiers in Corpus Annotation, pp. 24–31 (2004)
35. Buchholz, S., Marsi, E., Dubey, A., Krymolowski, Y.: CoNLL-X shared task on multilingual dependency parsing. In: Proceedings of the 10th Conference on Computational Natural Language Learning (CoNLL-2006) (2006)
36. Nivre, J., Hall, J., Nilsson, J., Chanev, A., Eryigit, G., Kübler, S., et al.: MaltParser: a language-independent system for data-driven dependency parsing. Nat. Lang. Eng. 13(2), 95–135 (2007)
37. Surdeanu, M., Johansson, R., Meyers, A., Màrquez, L., Nivre, J.: The CoNLL-2008 shared task on joint parsing of syntactic and semantic dependencies. In: Proceedings of the 12th Conference on Computational Natural Language Learning (CoNLL-2008), pp. 159–177 (2008)
38. Hajic, J., Ciaramita, M., Johansson, R., Kawahara, D., Marti, M.A., M`arquez, L. et al.: The CoNLL 2009 shared task: syntactic and semantic dependencies in multiple languages. In: Proceedings of the 13th CoNLL-2009, pp. 1–18 (2009)
39. McDonald, R., Crammer, K., Pereira, F.: Online large-margin training of dependency parsers. In: Proceedings of ACL-2005 (2005)
40. Johansson, R., Nugues, P.: The effect of syntactic representation on semantic role labeling. In: Proceedings of the 22nd International Conference on Computational Linguistics (COLING 2008), pp. 393–400 (2008)
41. UzZaman, N., Llorens, H., Derczynski, L., Verhagen, M., Allen, J., Pustejovsky, J.: SemEval-2013 Task 1: TempEval-3: evaluating time expressions, events and temporal relations. In: Proceedings of the 7th International Workshop on Semantic Evaluation (SemEval 2013), pp. 1–9 (2013)
42. Llorens, H., Saquete, E., Navarro, B.: TipSem (English and Spanish): evaluating CRFS and semantic roles in Tempeval-2. In: Proceedings of the 5th International Workshop on Semantic Evaluation, pp. 284–291 (2010)

Service-Oriented Tsunami Modeling: VMVC-Based Functional Engines

Kensaku Hayashi[1]([✉]), Alexander Vazhenin[1], and Andrey Marchuk[2]

[1] University of Aizu, Aizuwakamatsu, Japan
{d8161103,vazhenin}@u-aizu.ac.jp
[2] Institute of Computational Mathematics and Mathematical Geophysics SD RAS,
Novosibirsk, Russia
mag@omzg.sscc.ru

Abstract. Lessons learned from the Great Japanese Earthquake and Tsunami provide direction to research and emergency management communities on how to develop tools, models, and methods for mitigating impact for such devastating event both locally and globally. The solution of this problem is that it is more effective to integrate the applications and services rather than rebuilding because redevelopment is a costly affaire. The presented paper demonstrates an approach for developing the service-oriented Tsunami Modeling Environment as a framework of the original Virtual Model-View-Controller (VMVC) design pattern. It is based on decoupling of the view from the mode. The Model-View link is redirected within an enhanced controller as a virtual layer for distributed and service-oriented applications. This allows the programmers to concentrate on building new functionalities and services without bothering on how the services will be exposed, consumed, and maintained. To simplify the structure of services, the Model is represented as a set of application-oriented components named Engines. We are describing the main Tsunami Modeling Functional engines allowing to model each stage of a tsunami process including tsunami wave propagation over the deep ocean water, inundation of these waves on the coast area, and impaction on the coast object. We are also describing in detail the Tsunami Visualizing Engine (TVE) showing the modeling results in a convenient multimedia form. For each engine, we are showing its functionality and corresponding services that are provided by it.

1 Introduction

Re-usability and interoperability of applications and data are of vital importance with the increasing adoption of Cloud Computing, Mobile technologies, and Big data. An enabler to these technologies is Service-Oriented Architecture (SOA) introducing principles, strategies, and patterns to develop loosely coupled, standard based software components where services are the main building blocks. Design patterns are a strategy to reutilize the knowledge of software artifacts. A pattern encodes the strategic knowledge to resolve a particular problem, and provides a standard language to share this knowledge among developers [1].

© Springer International Publishing Switzerland 2015
H. Fujita and A. Selamat (Eds.): SoMeT 2014, CCIS 513, pp. 376–390, 2015.
DOI: 10.1007/978-3-319-17530-0_26

One of the main benefits of SOA is to reduce the complexity of enterprise applications once is fully adopted. The architecture is composed in several layers to conceptually organize all the elements involved has to deal with basic services functionality such as capability, interface, quality of services, publication, discovery, and selection. However, implementing a SOA solution is currently a complex and costly endeavor because of necessity in scalable technologies oriented to an arbitrary number of users and requirement of a personalized and customizable working environment. Modern applications are rather diverse and disparate with respect to the various development platforms and architectures [2].

Reflections brought about by the Great Japanese Earthquake and Tsunami raise questions how to mitigate the impact of such events at different time scales, resolutions, real-time tsunami warning and long-term hazard assessment. Accordingly, the SOA seems to be very attractive for creating the Tsunami Modeling Environment because of complexity and versatility of tsunami modeling methods and tools described for example in [3–6]. As shown in [7], SOA is an interesting approach to designing and managing large system landscapes. When ignoring the marketing hype, well established ideas like modularity and loose coupling build the foundation of the concept which is then enriched with business oriented concepts that make SOA more tangible and facilitate transfer to real systems. Moreover, SOA should not only be implemented for big size enterprises but also for next generations of applications of any company of any size.

The presented paper demonstrates an approach for developing the service-oriented Tsunami Modeling Environment as a framework of the original Virtual Model-View-Controller (VMVC) design pattern. It is based on decoupling of the View from the Model. The Model-View link is redirected within an enhanced controller as a virtual layer for distributed and service-oriented applications. This allows the programmers to concentrate on building new functionalities and services without bothering on how the services will be exposed, consumed, and maintained [8,9]. To simplify the structure of services, the Model is represented as a set of application-oriented components named Engines. We are describing the main Tsunami Modeling Functional engines allowing to model each stage of a tsunami process including tsunami wave propagation over the deep ocean water, inundation of these waves on the coast area, and impaction on the coast object. We are also describing in detail the Tsunami Visualizing Engine (TVE) showing the modeling results in a convenient multimedia form. For each engine, we are showing its functionality and corresponding services that are provided by it.

This article is structured as follows. In Sect. 2 we discuss principles and main elements of VMVC-based Tsunami Modeling Architecture as well as modeling scenario. Section 3 shows features and components of Tsunami Functional Engines. In Sect. 4, we present the system interface features and typical examples of modeling process. Finally, Sect. 5 presents the conclusions of the research work.

2   VMVC-Based Tsunami Modeling Architecture

Our research is based on an original programming approach named Virtual Model-View-Controller (VMVC) that is motivated from the traditional Model-View-Controller (MVC) design pattern that decomposes applications in three components: Model, View and Controller. However, the standard MVC pattern is based on Object Oriented concepts, and it does not address SOA key elements (services, compositions, and service management). To adopt the MVC to SOA-requirements, the Controller was extended comprising the integration logic, and performing functions for data and protocol transformation, message exchange, and intelligent routing that is necessary for service composition. As shown in Fig. 1a, this makes possible to remove the link between View and Model, and reorganize it within the enhanced Controller as a virtual link [8,9]. This reorganization was implemented in the framework of the Enterprise Service Bus (ESB) that fosters interconnectivity between services, and reduces the size and complexity of interfaces. Service virtualization and workflow composition is implemented following the Dependency Injection (DI) pattern. It allows the decoupling services from hard-coded dependencies on its collaborators, including expensive initialization logic facilitating the test of individual services.

The Model is partitioned into two types: a Service Model (Inventory) as a Business Object Pool, and Data Model. This allows storing the endpoint services definitions under a service schema including information about user profiles, tasks rules, session control, verification templates, etc. To process a request, the Model makes the use of the Data Model, and the business logic organized under a Service Inventory, which is a design pattern standardizing a collection of services. The concept of Engine was introduced in the service inventory to define a set of services that belong to a sub-domain. The view handles the user requests, interaction, and view logic. Examples of applications designed using the VMVC concept can be found in [8,9].

Figure 1b shows the main elements of the VMVC-based Tsunami Modeling Infrastructure presented as an Usecase diagram. It supports the typical working scenario including the following steps:

- Specifying information on the modeling scenario including bottom topography or bathymetry data, initial and boundary conditions, information about earthquake data, modeling parameters such as time-steps and resolution of computational grid, etc.
- Defining a computational resource (engine) taking into account the scenario parameters.
- Launching a modeling engine, and monitoring modeling process with on-line storing of intermediate and final results.
- Viewing/analyzing/visualizing results in human-centered representation.

To simplify the structure of services, we decompose the Model so that every scenario step is supported by a corresponding functional Engine. The first step supported by the Propagation Engine is to calculate tsunami wave propagation

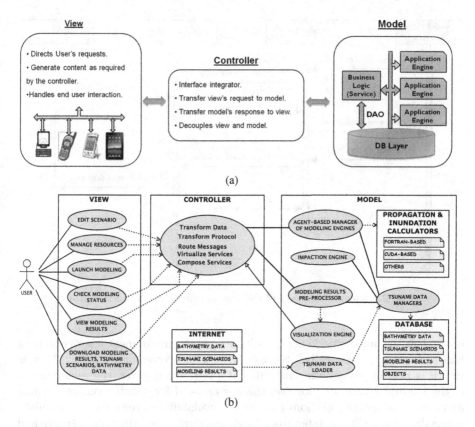

Fig. 1. VMVC-based tsunami modeling architecture

over the deep ocean provided that initial displacement of earthquake is known. The results of a tsunami inundation modeling include information about the tsunami parameters such as wave height and current speed as a function of location, maximum inundation line as well as time series of wave height at different locations indicating wave arrival time, etc. The Impaction Engine is to model impaction taking into account the tsunami wave parameters and physical characteristics of objects (artificial or natural) such as houses, bridges, etc. Tsunami Visualizing Engine (TVE) is a converter of digital results of modeling to the human-centered data representation. Tsunami Data Loader downloads the bathymetry data, tsunami scenario and modeling results from the Internet and stores them in the database.

Agent-based Manager of Modeling Engines analyzes the request, selects a corresponding calculator (computer) of Tsunami Modeling Calculation, and monitors a modeling process. This scheme is realizing by means of the agent-semantic system, designed for resource management and adopting to the tsunami modeling research [10]. Putting the agent system to work for tsunami modeling we have made a few observations. First, computers made available to the tsunami

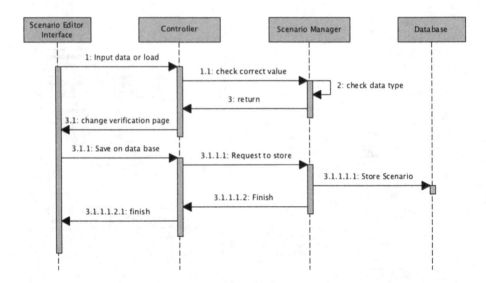

Fig. 2. Sequence diagram of the tsunami-modeling scenario editor

research at the university do not constitute an open environment where resources join and leave "dynamically." Second, there is no "economic aspect." That is why it is possible to assume safely that if a resource matches the requirements of the job and is available for use, there is no need for negotiations concerning its price. However, negotiations concerning availability of resources are required especially when a given laboratory is in use during certain class periods and machines cannot be used for other purposes then instruction.

The tsunami-modeling scenario can be created/edited at the View part by filling special forms. Example of this interface is presented in Sect. 3. Figure 2 illustrates the sequence diagram for this process reflecting synchronization over all MVC-parts.

3   Functional Engines

As was pointed above, the Tsunami Modeling components should be embedded in the system in the form of Engines. This adaptation is mainly focused on designing the service endpoints. The application functionality is divided into atomic operations [8,9]. Each service should be designed as agnostic as possible, avoid direct calls between other endpoints, and represent one specific and autonomous function. Accordingly, we are distinguishing the following main application engines: Tsunami Wave Propagation/Inundation, Impaction and Visualization Engines each of which reflects a corresponding stage of modeling process. In this section we are showing mechanism of each engine as well as services that they are providing.

3.1   Propagation/Inundation Modeling Engines

These engines implement calculations based, usually, on approximations of the shallow-water theory (both linear and non-linear) used as the basic models for describing wave propagation throughout the ocean. These models rather accurately reflect basic wave parameters such as propagation time period from the source to the recording device, wave height and velocity for a rough or accurate numerical bathymetry of the bottom relief. There are several software packages for modeling wave propagation throughout the ocean and estimation of the run-up heights [11–13].

The method described in [11] is oriented to create a parallel hybrid tsunami simulator that can mix different models, methods and meshes, maybe even incorporate "alien software". This goal is achieved by combining overlapping domain decomposition and object-oriented programming. In paper [12], eight different parallel implementations were used to simulate tsunami propagation with the help of the shallow water equations. Each of these implementations has used a mixed-mode programming model from thread based shared memory to distributed memory and, finally, to a virtual shared memory. TUNAMI-N2 software [13] is a tsunami numerical simulation program with the linear theory in deep sea and with the shallow water theory in coastal areas and on dry land with constant grid size in the entire calculation domain. All of these examples can be considered as candidates to be adopted to the VMVC environment.

Currently we are working with the MOST (Method Of Splitting Tsunamis) software package that uses numerical model of calculating wave propagation applying decomposition method for spatial variables [14]. This method was initially developed in the Tsunami Laboratory (Computer Center of the Siberian Division of the USSR Academy of Sciences, Novosibirsk). Then the method was updated in the Pacific Marine Environmental Laboratory (NOAA, Seattle, USA), and was adapted to the models and standards of data accepted by tsunami watch services in the United States as well as widely used in tsunami research works in many countries. MOST simulates numerically three processes of tsunami evolution: the estimation of residual displacement area resulting from an earthquake and tsunami production, transoceanic propagation through deep-water zones, and contact with land (run-up and inundation). In [15], we are demonstrating a set of engines developed for different programming platforms. The detailed analysis of the MOST package was implemented taking into account the workload of the main program components. Taking into account this analysis, it was ported on the Tesla K20c and GeForce GTX Titan architectures allowing decreasing the solution time significantly and reaching high level of performance. Figure 3 shows chronometry of the high-performance tsunami wave propagation modeling with the two types of bathymetry and initial sources.

Figure 4 shows a sequence diagram illustrated how the modeling process is executed. After editing parameters of the modeling scenario, the user should define a computational resource (engine) taking into account the scenario parameters. Then the modeling engine can be launched. The resources manager copies all data into selected resource and starts calculations. The modeling engine

Processor	Pacific Ocean (test source)	Tohoku (great earthquake)
Core i7 3770X (single-core)	6672 sec (111.2 min)	4974 sec (82.9 min)
Tesla C2050 *	208 sec (3.38 min)	167 sec (2.12 min)
Tesla K20c	110 sec	87 sec
GeForce GTX Titan	84 sec	69 sec

Fig. 3. High-performance tsunami modeling

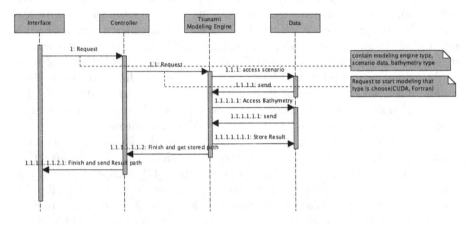

Fig. 4. Sequence diagram of the tsunami modeling process

implements calculations. It stores results as a series of frames with a time interval defined in the scenario. Calculations can be paused and resumed later on the same or different computational resource. The user can check the modeling status during modeling time.

3.2 Visualization Engine

As was mentioned above, the tsunami modeling engines store results as a series of frames (time steps) with specified time interval. There are a lot of formats to store the geographical data. Similarly to the original MOST package, we use the NetCDF format that is a set of software libraries and self-describing data formats supporting creating, accessing, and sharing array-oriented scientific data [16]. The access and activation of the TVE from the View layer is realized via a set of services each of which implements a corresponding stage of the data transformation (Fig. 5).

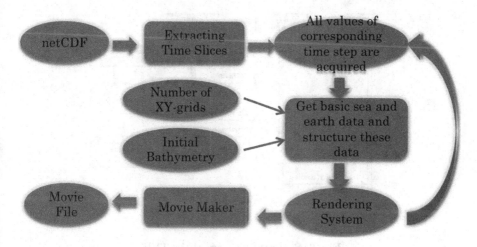

Fig. 5. Stages of data transformation in TVE

There are five stages/services of this transformation. First stage is to extract the tsunami wave parameters such as time step, horizontal flow velocity components and wave height from the NetCDF storage data. Second service allows collecting all data of specified time step. Third service is to integrate the wave heights with bathymetry in order to reach shallow water or coast areas. Fourth service sets color validation those areas and implements rendering of the whole image/picture. The final service allows converting these images collecting for all time steps to a movie file. The second, third and fourth services should be implemented in a loop in order to obtain all frames. Each image frame corresponds to a modeling time step. Importantly, these stages can be pipelined with the calculations provided by Modeling Engines. Movie Maker joins all frames in a movie with rendering for frame transitions. Figure 6 shows process of the one image generation over all TVE components and over all MVC parts. The process starts from a request generated by the visualization interface at the MODEL. The conversion is implemented into five steps. Next four steps correspond to the stages described above. Fifth step is to update information at the VIEW and display a result picture.

The bathymetry and tsunami waves can be represented as a wireframe model or shaded 3D-surface. Accordingly, it is convenient to use the so-called view from the top on the investigated surface showing all smallest details of the bottom relief or ocean surface. In order to create such an image it is necessary to divide every grid cell of the surface by 2 or more triangles and then to calculate the illumination of each one. Finally, the program creates a bitmap image according to the specified color legend. The image can be as large as grid dimensions of digital array being visualized. This allows easily integrating graphics with earthquake epicenter locations, tsunami source data, geo-coordinates, etc. As shown in Fig. 10 (Subsect. 3.1), we are also using the illumination source placed

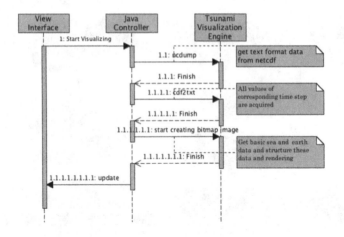

Fig. 6. Sequence diagram of the TVE

in the top left corner that seems to be attractive for visual perception. This method of visualization of surfaces adopted in TVE was developed in late 90-s and was used for asteroid impacts traces on the Earth surface [17].

The information about tsunami height maxima at each grid-point of the computational area is of great importance for tsunami warning and research purposes. Visualization of such a data makes it easy to analyze the directivity of the tsunami wave energy radiation and define most dangerous places on a coast for case that was concerned.

Wave height maxima all around computational grid are saved in netCDF file that accumulates results of numerical computations by MOST software. After finishing work of Propagation Modeling Engine it is possible to visualize distribution of tsunami height maxima. Before drawing image it is necessary to specify a color legend which is corresponding colors to small intervals of wave height. Figure 7 presents distribution of tsunami height maxima all around Pacific Ocean as a result of numerical modeling of tsunami generated by model (ellipsoidal) source located near Aleutian Islands. The visualization color of the grid point is as deeper, as higher the wave amplitude maximum at the location. Color legend is shown in the right part of figure. Such kind of visualizing helps to make decision about tsunami danger reality for Hawaii.

3.3 Impact Engine

The Impact Engine is to model an impaction on the objects taking into account the tsunami wave parameters evaluated during propagation/inundation modeling and physical characteristics of objects (artificial or natural) such as houses, bridges, etc. These objects can be broken depending on the tsunami wave power. Actually, the wave propagation modeling is often based on finite-difference or fine-elements methods for solving systems of differential equations. The impaction modeling is implementing using particle-based approaches in which any object is represented

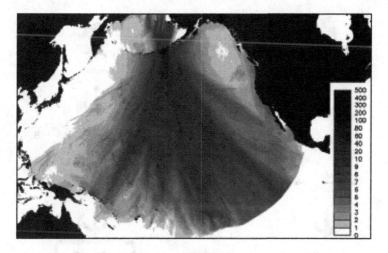

Fig. 7. Visualization of wave height maxima for tsunami generated by a model source located near Aleutians

as a set of particles with physical characteristics. These particles interact each with other and can change their features according to results of these interactions. This leads to switching models by passing/converting wave parameters from, for example, NetCDF format to a format of Impact Engines.

Currently, the Impact Engine is under development. So, here we are focusing only on describing of some preliminary steps of this development. RealFlow modeling tool was chosen as a basic for this design [18]. It is a fluid and dynamics simulator for the 3D industry, created by Madrid-based Next Limit Technologies. Currently at version 2013, the stand-alone application can be used to simulate fluids, water surfaces, fluid-solid interactions, rigid bodies, soft bodies and meshes. The technology uses particle based simulations. These particles can be influenced in various ways by point-based nodes, known as daemons, which can do tasks such as simulating gravity or recreating the vortex-like motion of a tornado. RealFlow can also simulate soft and rigid body collisions and interactions. The inclusion of Python scripting and C++ plug-ins allows users to program their own tools to improve RealFlow capabilities, adding control to most aspects of the RealFlow workflow including batch runs, events, daemons, waves and fluids. It has two modifications. The GUI stand-alone version allows to prepare and model processes in interactive mode. RealFlow Nodes are non-GUI modifications, which contain all the power of RealFlow and can be included into the customer workflow that seems to be very convenient to the engine requirements.

The one of the key problem is in necessity to prepare a library of 3D-models combining physical features of geographical objects, coast and bathymetry. Google Earth Map has a library of 3D-visual models stored in the COLLADA file format [18]. COLLADA defines an open standard XML schema for exchanging digital assets among various graphics software applications that might otherwise store their assets in incompatible file formats. The data transformation scheme

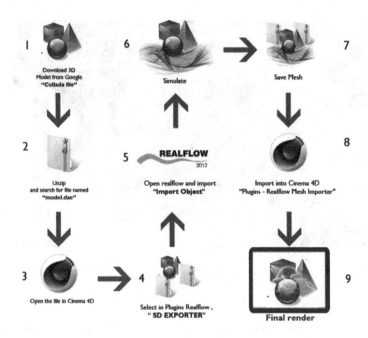

Fig. 8. Impaction model design stages

was designed allowing to integrate the Google Map objects and the RealFlow modeling package. Figure 8 illustrate stages of the impaction model design as well as an execution of RealFlow Modeling process. Accordingly, the Cinema 4D software is used for intermediate conversion. In this picture, steps 5 and 6 include editing procedures needed to assign physical features of natural materials to the 3D-visual objects (homes, buildings, etc.). These features can be classified as stone, wood, water with physical parameters like density, weight, etc. An example of Impaction Modeling via RealFlow is shown in Fig. 9.

4   System Interface

4.1   Scenario Editor

The application can be started from any browser after inputting the URL. Figure 10 demonstrates elements of the Scenario Editor Interface. The user should input attributes of source parameters including link to the bottom topography or bathymetry data, initial and boundary conditions, information about earthquake data, modeling parameters such as time-steps and resolution of spatial grids, etc. The experiment parameters can be edited in a special window using a form-filled interface. The scenario data can be used immediately or stored in the database. Then, it is necessary to define/choose a computational resource (engine) taking into account the scenario parameters. Current version of the system includes three computational nodes with two types of Modeling Engines. The first type of engine is made from the sequential FORTRAN program, can be

Fig. 9. Example of impaction modeling via realflow

implemented on any computer, and has relatively low performance. The second engine is developed based on the GPU CUDA hardware, and allows implementing modeling significantly faster than sequential one (Fig. 3). In principle, both programs can work simultaneously in the same computational node. The user can watch the calculation process in a special window that refreshes data according to experiment parameters specified.

4.2 TVE Interface

Figure 11 demonstrates elements of the interface that allows working with the TVE in interactive mode. The application can be started via browser after inputting the URL. To define visualization parameters, the user should fill the corresponding fields in the form provided including links to the numerical experiments data (NetCDF), links to the output data, number of frames (modeling time steps), the image size and rendering parameters.

After launching, TVE implements conversion procedures, and results can be shown on special window or downloaded to the client computer. Figure 12 shows an example of visualization the results of tsunami propagation modeling. We developed the original bathymetry covering the area of the Pacific Ocean adjacent to the northwest of the Honshu island (Japan). The gridded digital bathymetry was created using bathymetry with resolution of approximately 300 m around Japan [20], and 1 arc sec ASTER Global digital elevation model [21]. A computational rectangular grid of 2413 x 2405 points includes knots

Area Information	Values
Grid Name	Pacific
Grid Axes Version	20060823
Grid Filename	pacific.corr

Computational Parameters	Values
Input minimum depth for offshore (m)	10
Input time step (sec)	10
Input amount of steps	500
Input number of steps between snapshots	4
...Starting from time step	6
Save output every n-th grid point	1
Input global b.c.s (1=global, 0=nonreentrant)	0

Naming Rules	Values
Output filename (prefix_ha.nc, or "auto")	auto
Source Zone Name	Aleutian-Cascadia2

Fig. 10. Interface of scenario editor

Convert netCDF File To Bitmap Image

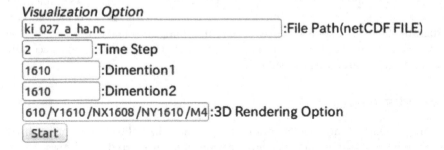

Visualization Option

| ki_027_a_ha.nc | :File Path(netCDF FILE) |

| 2 | :Time Step |

| 1610 | :Dimention1 |

| 1610 | :Dimention2 |

| 610 /Y1610 /NX1608 /NY1610 /M4 | :3D Rendering Option |

[Start]

Fig. 11. TVE-conversion start page

of presetup values of depth. Length of a spatial step in both directions made 0.0024844 geographical degrees that is about 277 m in a North-South direction and about 221 m in the West-East direction. The bottom relief of this computational domain A1 is stretching from 34 to 40 degrees of North Latitude and from 140 to 146 degrees of East Longitude. We have also provided modeling according the tsunami data generated from the Great Japanese Earthquake $(38.322N, 142.369E, Mw = 8.9 at 5 : 46 : 23UTC)$ on March 11, 2011 [22]. The fault length and width are estimated as 400 Km x 150 km.

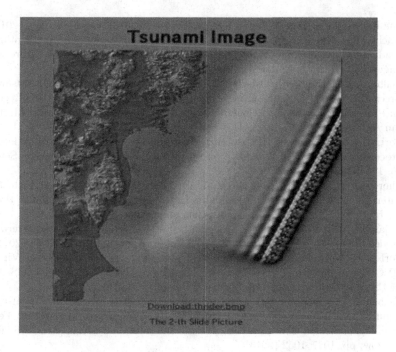

Fig. 12. Example of visualization of a frame

5   Conclusion

In the presented paper, we demonstrated the way of decomposing of the Tsunami Modeling Environment in the framework of the VMVC paradigm. Focusing of the model layer, a set of modeling engines were presented to cover all stages of tsunami process: tsunami wave propagation over the deep ocean water, inundation of these waves on the coast area, and impaction on the coast object. Each engine simulates a corresponding stage of modeling process. We also described in detail the Tsunami Visualizing Engine (TVE) to show the modeling results in convenient multimedia form. For each engine, we showed its functionality and services provided by them. The numerical experiments and validation procedures confirm the reliability of proposed technique. The VMVC-design patterns allow also designing a variety of applications based on component-wise design approach. For example, we are now extending the current Tsunami Modeling software by the special editor allowing the user to change the bathymetry data by including and manipulating artificial objects of variable placement, shape and sizes.

References

1. Erl, T.: SOA Design Patterns. Prentice Hall, Upper Saddle River (2009)
2. Kuniavsky, M.: Smart Things: Ubiquitous Computing User Experience Design. Elsevier, Amsterdam (2009)

3. The International 26th Tsunami Symposioum (ITS2013), Gosek, Turkey (2013)
4. Wachter, J., Babeyko, A., Fleischer, J., Haner, R., Hammitzsch, M., Kloth, A., Lendholt, M.: Development of tsunami early warning systems and future challenges. Nat. Hazards Earth Syst. Sci. **12**, 1923–2012 (2012)
5. Denbo, D., McHugh, K., Osborne, J., Sorvik, P., Venturato, A.: NOAA tsunami forecasting system: design and implementation using service oriented architecture. In: Proceedings of the 23rd Conference on IIPS, The 87th AMS Annual Meeting, San Antonio, TX (2007)
6. Hori, M.: Application of HPC to earthquake hazard and disaster estimation. In: Proceedings of the 19th Workshop on Sustained Simulation Performance, Sendai, pp. 11–40. 27–28 March 2014
7. Thorsten, H., Ebert, N., Hochstein, A., Brenner, W.: Where to start with SOA: criteria for selecting SOA projects. In: Proceedings of the 41st Annual Hawaii International Conference on System Sciences, pp. 314–314 (2008)
8. Rajam, S., Cortez, R., Vazhenin, A., Bhalla, S.: Modified MVC-design patterns for service oriented applications. Front. Artif. Intell. Appl. **231**(2), 977–988 (2011)
9. Cortez, R., Vazhenin, A.: Developing re-usable components based on the Virtual-MVC design pattern. In: Madaan, A., Kikuchi, S., Bhalla, S. (eds.) DNIS 2013. LNCS, vol. 7813, pp. 132–149. Springer, Heidelberg (2013)
10. Vazhenin, A., Watanobe, Y., Hayashi, K., Paprzycki, M., et al.: Agent-based resource management in tsunami modeling. In: Proceedings of the 2013 Federated Conference on Com-puter Science and Information Systems (FedCSIS 2013), Krakow, pp. 1047–1052 (2013)
11. Cai, X., Langtangen, H.P.: Making hybrid tsunami simulators in a parallel software framework. In: Kågström, B., Elmroth, E., Dongarra, J., Waśniewski, J. (eds.) PARA 2006. LNCS, vol. 4699, pp. 686–693. Springer, Heidelberg (2007)
12. Ganeshamoorthy, K., Ranasinghe, D., Silva, K., Wait, R.: Performance of shallow water equations model on the computational grid with overlay memory architectures. In: Proceedings of the Second International Conference on Industrial and Information Systems (ICIIS 2007), pp. 415–420. IEEE Press, Sri Lanka (2007)
13. Shuto, N., Imamura, F., Yalciner, A., Ozyurt, G.: TUNAMI2: Tsunami Modeling Manual. http://tunamin2.ce.metu.edu.tr/
14. Titov, V., Gonzalez, F.: Implementation and testing of the method of splitting tsunami (MOST), Technical Memorandum ERL PMEL-112. NOAA, Washington DC (1997)
15. Vazhenin, A., Lavrentiev, M., Romanenko, A., Marchuk, An: Acceleration of tsunami wave propagation modeling based on re-engineering of computational components. Int. J. Comput. Sci. Netw. Secur. **13**(3), 24–31 (2013)
16. NetCDF (Network Common Data Form). http://www.unidata.ucar.edu/software/netcdf/
17. Petrenko, V., Marchuk, An.: Estimation of the big cosmic bodies impact frequency and possibility of cosmogenic tsunamis. In: Proceedings of the International Emergency Management Society Conference on Disaster and Emergency Management: International Challenges for the Next Decade, pp. 435–443. The George Washington University, Washington DC (1998)
18. RealFlow. Fluids & dynamics simulation tool. http://www.realflow.com
19. Google Data. http://googledata.org
20. http://jdoss1.jodc.go.jp/cgi-bin/1997/depth500_file
21. http://www.gdem.aster.ersdac.or.jp/search.jsp
22. http://iisee.kenken.go.jp/staff/fujii/OffTohokuPacific2011/tsunami.html

Effect of Web Advertisement for Finding Target Users Interested in Rural Areas

Jun Sasaki[✉], Issei Komatsu, Masanori Takagi, and Keizo Yamada

Faculty of Software and Information Science of Iwate
Prefectural University, Iwate, Japan
jsasaki@iwate-pu.ac.jp

Abstract. In Japan, the population flow into urban areas has seen the economic power of rural areas decrease. This has made it difficult for rural areas to maintain their historical and cultural heritage. Strategies combining information technology with tourism have been applied in many local areas, but the effects have not been remarkable. In this study, we aim to grow local charms buried within rural areas, and publicize them on a nationwide or worldwide scale using information systems. We develop systems for growing local charms, and discuss on issues for the systems to be used. We then propose a model to fine local charms in rural areas and to spread them by using web advertising and social network services. The effect of web advertising and the possibility of targeting users are further examined based on the experimental results.

Keywords: Information systems · Information strategy · Web advertising · Social network services · Information distribution · System modeling

1 Introduction

In Japan, the population is generally flowing toward urban areas [1], reducing the population in rural areas. This has reduced the economic power of rural areas, making it difficult for them to maintain their historical and cultural heritage. Additionally, the number of visitors to less well-known rural areas is decreasing. Local revitalization is needed to solve these problems and re-establish some economic power. The strategy for local revitalization can be classified into three categories [2]:

(1) The region becomes economically activating,
(2) The population increases,
(3) It improves amenity to live in the area comfortably.

In this research, we focus on item (1), the enforcement of economic power in rural areas. We study the tourism industry, which is expected to have direct and earlier economic benefits. Tourism is an important force not only for the economically effect but also for retaining historical and cultural values, and we believe there are many cases in which information technology can be effectively applied.

In this study, we aim to grow local features of interest that are hidden within rural areas, and publicize them across the nation and the world. This will contribute to the tourism industry and local revitalization. In this paper, we define implicit and explicit

H. Fujita and A. Selamat (Eds.): SoMeT 2014, CCIS 513, pp. 391–403, 2015.
DOI: 10.1007/978-3-319-17530-0_27

local features of interest, and determine a strategy whereby local features can go from being implicit to explicit. Then, our developed systems are introduced to grow the implicit features in a local area. We present experimental results from the developed systems and, based on these, propose a model to find local charms in rural areas using information technology to increase tourist numbers. In the proposed model, web advertising and social network services (SNS) are used to find target users. We produce a web advertisement for a sales project in a local farm within a residential area of Shizukuishi, Iwate Prefecture, and carry out experiments to evaluate the effect of this advertisement and the possibility of defining target users.

2   Research Approaches

We define "local charms" in rural areas as attractive or interesting things for tourists, and divide them into the two categories shown in Fig. 1. Explicit local charms are famous features that are recognized by tourists as well as local residents. Implicit local charms are not recognized by tourists. They may not be well known, but they have historical or cultural value, and thus the potential to provide economic benefits to the area. Most rural areas do not have explicit charms, but they may have a number of implicit charms. The aim is to grow these implicit charms into explicit charms. We therefore examine methods of growing implicit charms in rural areas, and enabling them to become explicit charms.

The explicit charms are already publicized widely in terms of commercial tours and famous products. A previous system is shown in Fig. 2. In this case, travel agents are sending mainly explicit charms to people by Websites. Tourists look at the explicit charms and make their travel plans. The implicit charms are not recognized in the previous system. The aim of our research is to establish an effective method to find and grow the implicit charms into be explicit charms. In order to realize the aim, we have

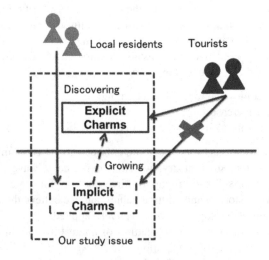

Fig. 1. Categories of local charms.

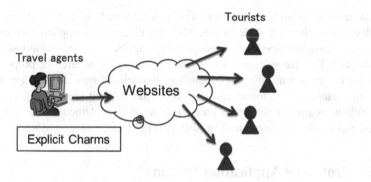

Fig. 2. Previous system.

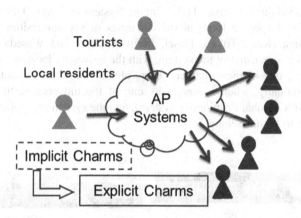

Fig. 3. Approach 1; development application systems and making many users.

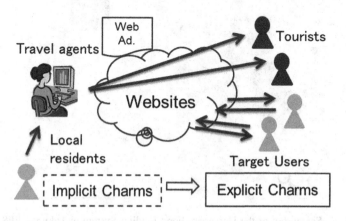

Fig. 4. Approach 2; using Web advertisement and finding target users.

taken two research approaches. The first approach is shown in Fig. 2, where we develop application systems like SNS for distributing implicit charms and to make many users. We developed some prototype application systems introduced in the next chapter. The second approach is shown in Fig. 3, where we propose to use Web advertisement with Websites including implicit charms. In this approach, we think target users can be found and we expect the implicit charms will be changed to be explicit charms by the target users. The detail is explained in the Sect. 5 and experimental results are introduced in Sect. 6 (Fig. 4).

3 Prototype Application Systems

3.1 University Food Finding System in Tokyo (UFFST)

We first developed the University Food Finding System in Tokyo (UFFST) [3]. Users are invited to find specific foods at the cafeterias of six universities in the Tokyo metropolitan area (Keio, Tokyo, Hosei, Meiji, Rikkyo, and Waseda Universities). Figure 5 shows a screenshot of the system, with the university locations marked on the map. By tapping one of these markers, users obtain information about that school's cafeteria. Additionally, when a user visits one of the universities, their location is identified by GPS (Global Positioning System), and the system recognizes that the user has checked-in to the university.

Fig. 5. Screenshot of the University Food Finding System in Tokyo (UFFST).

3.2   Iwate Food Finding System (IFFS)

We also developed the Iwate Food Finding System (IFFS) [4]. This system is similar to the UFFST, but its target users are in a rural area, rather than a large city. Figure 6 shows a screenshot of the system, where the locations of good restaurants are given on the map. The system incorporates the check-in and information sharing functions. The recommended restaurants were selected by conducting a questionnaire on the favorite restaurants of students at Iwate Prefectural University.

Like UFFST, IFFS encourages the discovery of local charms, and provides a sense of achievement and element of competition.

Fig. 6. Screenshot of the Iwate Food Finding System (IFFS).

3.3   Recovering Quiz System (RQS)

Finally, we developed the Recovering Quiz System (RQS) [5], which is a smartphone-based quiz. This was developed with the aim of remembering the Great Earthquake, which struck the Tohoku area of Japan in 2011, and to continue the recovery process in the area. The system includes information on the recovery process and issues to be resolved. Figure 7 shows a screenshot of the system, where the white map is of the Tohoku area. The system provides a question about each area (city, town, or village) damaged by the Great Earthquake. Questions are selected at random from a database. If a user gives the correct answer, the color of the corresponding area changes from white to green. The system also grades the user according to the number of correct answers.

Fig. 7. Screenshot of Recovering Quiz System (RQS).

4   Experimental Results from the Prototype Systems

Figure 8 shows the number of downloads for each application. Although the number of downloads and actual users was large just after the application was released, the number of users for each system was not so remarkable. Though we have developed prototype systems to grow local charms by providing a sense of achievement and element of competition, we noticed that simply distributing the applications was not enough. Therefore, we researched a more effective mechanism of discovering local implicit charms and growing them into explicit local charms.

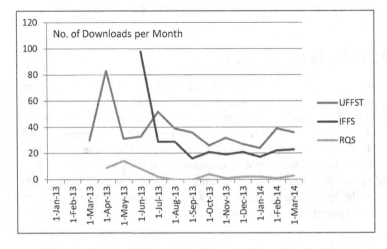

Fig. 8. Number of downloads per month for each application.

5   Proposed Model to Find Local Charms in Rural Areas and to Spread Them

We considered why the number of users did not increase, and believe that it is because the applications are only recognized by a limited number of users. Namely, the applications are passive services, known only to interested users, and the information does not expand to encourage other users. We think the services should be more active, and the target users should be clarified. Active services include push-type applications and recommendation services focused on target users. There are several studies on destination recommendation systems for tourists [6–9]. We believe our systems must identify target users and employ a recommendation service.

First, we encourage the discovery of implicit local charms that are unknown even to people living in the area. We call this the "Local Charm Finding Cycle". Then, we propose a "Targeted Advertisement" [10, 11], which is a web advertisement distribution method designed to arouse the interest of users without requiring them to visit the area.

An overview of the proposed model is shown in Fig. 9. We consider the following seven steps.

(1) Finding of local implicit charms by residents of the area. The newly found local charms are stored in a database (DB) of "Local Charm Contents".
(2) New information found by non-residents who experienced a particular place is accumulated in the same DB.
(3) Delivery of web advertisement by linking to Website, blogs, or SNS, thus connecting the DB of "Local Charm Contents" to metropolitan areas.
(4) Users interested in the web advertisement (target users) will access the "Local Charm Contents".

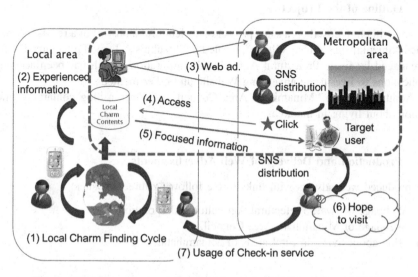

Fig. 9. Model to activate rural areas using web advertisements and SNS.

(5) The profiles and access logs of target users are analyzed, and their interests are used to produce focused web adverts, which are delivered to the target user.
(6) Target users plan to visit the area after seeing the focused web adverts.
(7) If the target user visits the local area, their experience information will be accumulated using SNS check-in services.

Repeating the above steps will accumulate a rich body of content in the Local Charm Contents DB, and the delivered information will be more attractive to other target users. As a result, we expect the number of people visiting local areas to increase, and it is possible that some will live in the area in the future.

In this paper, we present experimental results on the effect of these web adverts and the possibility of finding target users, which is related to processes (3), (4), and (5) indicated by a red dashed line in Fig. 9.

6 Experiment on the Effect of Web Advertising

6.1 Aim of the Experiment

The aim of this experiment was to clarify the effect of web advertising and the possibility of finding target users. The experiment included the following steps.

(1) Select a project to activate a local area.
(2) Produce web adverts linked to the project's purpose.
(3) Distribute the adverts to major websites without targeting.
(4) Analyze the access logs to the web adverts.
(5) Estimate the profile of target users based on the analyzed results.

6.2 Outline of the Project

The experiment focused on a sales project of agricultural land within a residential area, called "Shizukuishi Cottage Village", located in Shizukuishi, Iwate Prefecture. The sale is managed by Iwate Prefectural Agricultural Corporation, which has been accepting applications to live in the area using Website and other methods.

Additionally, the "Minamihata Area Council" produces a blog containing information about living in the area.

6.3 Production and Delivery of Web Advertisements

We produced web adverts with links to the following three websites:

(1) Webpage of Iwate Prefectural Agricultural Corporation.
(2) Webpage of Minamihata Area Council.
(3) Blog about living in rural areas of Minamihata.

Regarding the destination of the web adverts, we selected the following three mediums:

(i) Facebook Advertising.
(ii) Yahoo! JAPAN Promotion Ad.
    (ii-1) Sponsored Search (Listing Ad); related with Keywords,
    (ii-2) Display Ad. (Interest Match Ad); not related with Keywords.

Three adverts with links to (1)–(3) were displayed on (i), (ii-1) and (ii-2) according to the service conditions of each medium. For example, the Facebook advertisement linking to (1) is shown in Fig. 10.

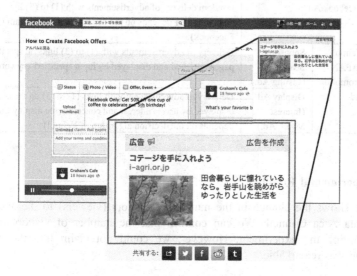

Fig. 10. Example web advertisement.

Table 1 lists the delivery method of the web advertisements in this experiment. There is no charge for displaying the advertisements, but they contain a charging mechanism when the links are followed (pay-per-click). The fee per click (unit price) differs depending on the medium and conditions of display.

The effect of the Web advertisements is evaluated according to the following criteria:

– Number of impressions (NI): number of times the Web advertisement appeared on users' Web browsers.
– Number of clicks (NC): number of clicks on an advertisement.
– Click-through rate (CTR): percentage of clicks per impression:

$$CTR = NC/NI \times 100\% \tag{1}$$

The CTR is usually used to measure the effect of Internet advertisement. It is said that the CTR has higher value, the effect of the Internet advertisement is higher.

In this experiment, we delivered a total of ten advertisements via three mediums, as shown in Table 1. However, considering our limited research budget, we set the following constraints:

- Experimental period: 1–28 February, 2014 (28 days).
- Budget: 300 yen/day per Website (6-10 clicked).

Table 1. Delivery Method of Web Advertisements.

No.	Mediums		Delivering method
(i)	Facebook Ad.		Random delivery of advertisements with (1) to (3) links (the display timing depends on the determination algorithm of Facebook)
(ii-1)	Yahoo! JAPAN Promotion Ad.	Sponsored Search (Listing Ad.)	Delivery of advertisements with (1) to (3) links on specific pages retrieved and displayed by input specified keyword [12]
(ii-2)		Display Ad. (Interest Match Ad.)	Delivery of advertisement with links (1) to (3) on the pages displayed by user's interest and concerns (the display timing depends on the decision algorithm of Yahoo!)

6.4   Experimental Results

Figure 11 shows the change in the number of visitors (viewers) to the Website of Minamihata Area Council. We can confirm that the number of visitors increased slightly during the experiment. However, we could not claim that the effect of advertising was remarkable.

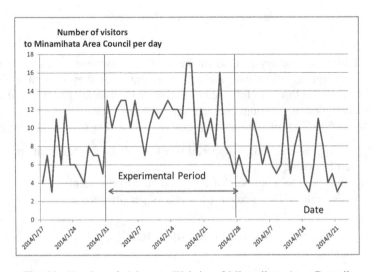

Fig. 11. Number of visitors to Website of Minamihata Area Council.

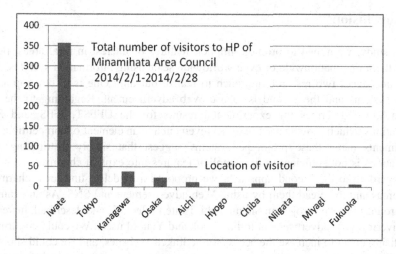

Fig. 12. Total number of visitors to Website of Minamihata Area Council from 1 to 28 February, 2014.

Figure 12 shows the relationship between the total number of visitors to the Minamihata Area Council Website and their living areas. The results in Figs. 11 and 12 were obtained using the Google Analytics tool. It can be seen that most viewers lived in Iwate Prefecture, followed by Tokyo and Kanagawa. From this result, we inferred that the web advert should be delivered to people living in Iwate Prefecture, rather than those living in other areas.

Figure 13 shows that the CTR was highest in the over-45 age groups, and the most popular links for this group were to Websites (1) and (3).

From these results, we can identify the target users in this project as women aged above 45 living in Iwate Prefecture.

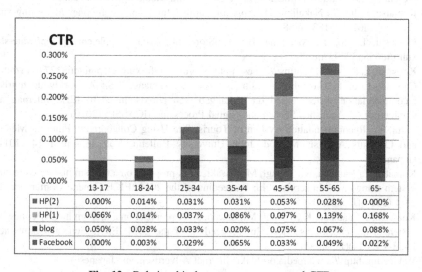

Fig. 13. Relationship between age group and CTR.

7 Conclusions

In this study, we aimed to promote implicit features of interest in rural areas, publicizing them on a nationwide or even worldwide scale using information systems. This paper introduces two research approach to realize our aim. One is to develop application systems and the second is to use Web advertisement. Regarding to the first approach, we describes the experimental results for the UFFST, IFFS, and RQS applications, which provide a sense of achievement and an element of competition. The experiments using these prototype systems suggest that simply distributing such applications is not sufficient to turn implicit features into explicit charms.

Regarding to the second approach, we proposed a model to find local charms in rural areas and to spread them by using Web advertisement and SNS. As an example, we introduced a sales project in Shizukuishi, Iwate Prefecture, and described the results of delivering Web advertisement to Facebook and Yahoo! users. We could confirm the advertising effect to increase the access to the linked Websites, and we could show the possibility to find the target user groups interested in rural areas by analyzing the CTR.

Acknowledgement. We would like to thank the Morioka-wide area Promotion Bureau of Iwate Prefecture, Minamihata Area Council, and Shizukuishi town office for their cooperation with our research and experiments. We would also like to thank Minamihata Project members Mr. Takuya Sakuyama and Ms. Shizune Takahashi, and Yuki Tetsuka in Iwate Prefectural University, for their cooperation in the experiments.

References

1. Census of Japanese government
2. Tsukuwa, M.: Considering new "community development" of the Tokachi region: presenting case studies of the Tokachi region. J. Int. Media **8**, 89–170 (2009)
3. Komatsu, I., Ito, T., Nakajima, H.: AppStore. https://itunes.apple.com/jp/app/dong-jing-xue-shi-xunri/id624075183?mt=8
4. Komatsu, I., Ito, T., Nkaajima, H.: AppStore. https://itunes.apple.com/jp/app/iwate-shi-xunri/id655530793?mt=8
5. Komatsu, I., Ryosuke, S. https://itunes.apple.com/uy/app/fu-xingsuteppu/id633274686?mt=8
6. Cao, L., Luo, J., Gallagher A., Jin, X., Han, J., Hauang, T.S.: A worldwide tourism recommendation system based on geotagged web photos. In: 2010 IEEE International Conference on Acoustics Speech and Signal Processing (ICASSP) (2010)
7. Tarui, Y.: Recommendation System of Tourist Site Using Collaborative Filtering Method and Contents Analysis Method. Jobu University Bulletin, Vol. 36, pp. 1–14 (2011). (Japanese)
8. Komatsu, I., Yamada, K., Takagi, M., Sasaki, J.: A proposal on a tourism history collecting system using check-in services. In: Proceeding of the 2014 IEICE General Conference, D-23-4 (2014)(Japanese)
8. Komatsu, I., Yamada, K., Takagi, M., Sasaki, J.: A proposal on a tourism history collecting system using check-in services. In: Proceeding of the 2014 IEICE General Conference, D-23-4 (2014)(Japanese)
9. Wikipedia. http://ja.wikipedia.org/wiki/ Internet Advertisement (Japanese)

10. Kurata, Y.: Day tour plans only for you: development of an interactive tour planner. Inst. Syst. Control Inf. Eng. **57**(8), 348–353 (2013)
11. Sasaki, J., Sakuyama, T., Takahashi, S., Komatsu, I., Yamada, K., Takagi, M.: Local-charm-content delivering model by using web advertisement and SNS. In: The 8th International Conference on Advanced Information Technologies (AIT), No. 221 (2014)
12. Fujita, A., Ikushima, K., Sato, S.: Automatic generation of listing ads and assessment of their performance on attracting customers: a case study on restaurant domain. Inf. Process. Soci. Jpn (IPSJ) J. **56**(6), 2031–2044 (2011). (Japanese)

Author Index

Printed in the United States
By Bookmasters